NATIVE TREASURES

NATIVE TREASURES

GARDENING WITH
THE PLANTS
OF CALIFORNIA

M. NEVIN SMITH

A PHYLLIS M. FABER BOOK

UNIVERSITY OF CALIFORNIA PRESS

Berkeley   Los Angeles   London

FOR WAYNE RODERICK

who shared his time, his knowledge, and

all that he brought back from the wild,

and brightened the lives of all who knew him.

University of California Press, one of the most distinguished university presses in the United States, enriches lives around the world by advancing scholarship in the humanities, social sciences, and natural sciences. Its activities are supported by the UC Press Foundation and by philanthropic contributions from individuals and institutions. For more information, visit www.ucpress.edu.

University of California Press
Berkeley and Los Angeles, California

University of California Press, Ltd.
London, England

Library of Congress Cataloging-in-Publication Data

Smith, M. Nevin, 1944–.
    Native Treasures : gardening with the plants of California / by M. Nevin Smith.
        p.   cm.
    Includes bibliographical references and index.
    ISBN 0-520-24425-7 (alk. paper).—ISBN 0-520-24426-5 (pbk. : alk. paper)
    1. Native plants for cultivation—California.   2. Native plant gardening—
California.   I. Title.

SB439.24.C2S65   2006
635.9'51794—dc22   2005052888

Book design and typesetting by Beth Hansen-Winter
Cover design by Nicole Hayward
Cover photographs by M. Nevin Smith
All photographs by M. Nevin Smith unless otherwise noted

Manufactured in Hong Kong by Global Interprint, Santa Rosa, CA

15   14   13   12   11   10   09   08   07   06
10   9   8   7   6   5   4   3   2   1

The paper used in this publication meets the minimum requirements of ANSI/NISO z39.48-1992 (R 1997) (*Permanence of Paper*).

CONTENTS

ACKNOWLEDGMENTS   VII

PREFACE   IX

INTRODUCTION: CALIFORNIA AND ITS PLANTS   1

GARDENING WITH CALIFORNIA NATIVES   9
    DESIGNS GREAT AND SMALL   9
    NUTS AND BOLTS   19
    FILLING YOUR GARDEN: PROPAGATION OF NATIVE PLANTS   41

A FEW OF MY FAVORITE THINGS: NATIVE PLANTS
    FOR THE GARDEN   55

  THE TREES   55
    ODE TO AN OAK   57
    MADROÑO   73

  THE SHRUBS   77
    IN PRAISE OF THE WILD LILAC   79
    SO MANY MANZANITAS   95
    CURRANTS AND GOOSEBERRIES   111
    HOLLY GRAPES, OREGON GRAPES   121
    THE FLANNEL BUSHES   127
    WESTERN REDBUD   133
    MOCK-ORANGES AND THEIR KIN   137
    DISCOVERING THE GLOBE MALLOWS   143
    THE GIANT POPPIES   147
    SNOWDROP BUSH   151
    FRAGRANT CLOUDS OF LUPINE   153
    BLUE CURLS   161
    TOYON ON MY MIND   165

  SOUP TO NUTS: TWO BROADER GENERA   169
    SAGES FOR THE SENSES   171
    BUCKWHEATS I HAVE KNOWN   179

SUBSHRUBS AND HERBACEOUS PERENNIALS   189

    DAZZLED BY PENSTEMONS   191
    IRIS ALL AROUND US   201
    ALUM ROOTS AND CORAL BELLS   209
    CALIFORNIA FUCHSIAS   215
    LIVING WITH LEWISIAS   221
    BLUE EYES, GOLDEN EYES   225
    COYOTE MINTS   229

BULBS AND CORMS   235

    THE MAGIC OF LILIES   237
    BRODIAEAS AND FRIENDS   245

SMALL MATTERS   255

    THE TROUBLE WITH ANNUALS   255

RESOURCES   272

INDEX   275

ACKNOWLEDGMENTS

This is not a research work in the usual sense, yet it owes a great debt to many different people, some of whom may be unaware of having offered their assistance. When I reach the limits of my own knowledge or want to hear another person's views and experience with a plant, a place, or something more general, I call freely on a group of obliging friends, who are also distinguished botanists, tenders of arboreta and botanic gardens, nursery and landscaping professionals, and enthusiastic private gardeners. Jeff Bohn, Carol Bornstein, Barbara Coe, Dr. Ray Collett, Dr. Steve Edwards, Mike Evans, Jenny Fleming, David Fross, Brett Hall, Phil Johnson, Ron Lutsko, Bart O'Brien, Roger Raiche, Warren Roberts, the late Marjorie Schmidt, and Phil van Soelen have all been immensely helpful at times when I had burning questions. Each of them sent me away with more than I asked for, including new questions to pursue, new plants to grow, and new places to see.

I owe a more general debt, personal and professional, to several individuals who have shared their knowledge and wisdom and have given focus to my often scattered pursuits. Marshall Olbrich and Lester Hawkins sent me off on many fruitful expeditions between arguments on politics and philosophy. John Dourley, while he was Superintendent of Horticulture at Rancho Santa Ana, provided both inspiration and a wonderful palette of under-appreciated native cultivars to bring to the gardening public. The late Dara Emery, during his years at the Santa Barbara Botanic Garden, did much the same. Throughout these years, the late Wayne Roderick was a superb teacher, great friend, and provider of a constant stream of new plants and seeds to try.

Finally, and most pertinent to the book at hand, I offer my thanks for years of effort by Phyllis Faber. First as editor of *Fremontia*, more recently as a producer of books for the University of California Press, she has kept me moving forward with just the right combination of friendly encouragement and unyielding pressure. Though I must have seemed at times like a wayward child, she lost neither faith nor direction. What you hold in your hands is both her inspiration and the product of her inspiration, enhanced by the beautiful design work of Beth Hansen-Winter.

Initial editing and helpful comments were graciously provided by Lenore Luscher. Anne Canright brought a relentless quest for logic and clarity to the final edits. Any errors and omissions are, of course, my own.

PREFACE

. . . .

W*hen I was a small boy, my family moved to a scenic stretch of countryside in the Valley of the Moon, not far from Santa Rosa. I was immediately drawn to explore the mountains and canyons around us, with their rugged terrain and wonderful variety of plant and animal life. Within perhaps a year, I was trying to grow my favorite* wildflowers, mostly dug from the surrounding woods. I had scant success, for I understood very little about the basic needs of plants. And yet I kept trying, for reasons I am helpless to explain.

Years later, after some strange twists of fate had brought me back to manage my parents' nursery, I began to travel widely in northern California and to collect seeds and cuttings nearly everywhere I went. This time most of my subjects thrived. Soon I had a sizeable menagerie of bulbs and annuals, flowering perennials, and shrubs from my favorite haunts. These formed the foundation for about three decades' work with native plants, in the wild and in my own and others' nurseries.

My life with natives has involved an odd combination of joyful forays to the most beautiful and interesting places in California, stunning discoveries among their inhabitants, and a good deal of hard and sometimes frustrating effort solving the puzzles of their propagation and culture. I have never felt a moment's regret.

Writing about native plants came almost naturally, for I enjoyed sharing my experience with anyone who would listen. In 1974 I was invited by Lester Hawkins, one of California's outstanding plantsmen of the time, to join a group whose optimistic purpose was to write a definitive horticultural encyclopedia of California native plants. In this group I met people like Wayne Roderick and Marjorie Schmidt, people with seemingly endless first-hand knowledge and an almost missionary desire to share it.

Several years later, after that encyclopedia dissolved into an impossible dream, I was asked by Marjorie to take over her column on growing native plants for *Fremontia*, the journal of the California Native Plant Society. Though I had a certain dread of seeing my words in print, I accepted the challenge. At least, I decided, I could share what I had learned over the years.

Marjorie was sensible and methodical, each month coming up with a succinct piece for *Fremontia*. I tended to take on recklessly large groups of plants, then to spend months waiting for sufficient time to write about them (the nursery life being all-consuming). Yet somehow these essays managed find their way to paper, and eventually a substantial and diverse collection was at hand. That collection formed the foundation for the present book.

This is not a "how-to" gardening book, though practical subjects are addressed here in detail, and it is certainly not the comprehensive encyclopedia of which Lester's group of bright enthusiasts once dreamed. Rather, it combines my own personal thoughts, sometimes maverick opinions, and experience with a goodly measure of plainer facts on selected

---

FLOWERY SWALE AT RANCHO SANTA ANA BOTANIC GARDEN.

groups of native plants and their culture. The plant genera described here include most of the major ones in cultivation, but also some more obscure but garden-worthy groups, thrown in as whim and personal interests dictate. I hope, above all, that as you read each piece, you will find in your heart a little more appreciation of California's rich store of native plants. And I hope that you will be encouraged to see them in their native haunts, and to invite them into your garden.

INTRODUCTION

. . . .

CALIFORNIA AND ITS PLANTS

F *or as long as I can remember, California has held me in its spell. Living in any other state,* I would probably have found something wonderful in its natural landscape, and certainly in its natural flora. But I think I would have been drawn far beyond its borders searching for more. Not so with California, for it is a vast domain in every way, holding endless surprises for anyone willing to go out and experience them.

Begin with simple dimensions. Measured near the coast from the Oregon border to Baja California, Mexico, the state is around 800 miles in length, while average east–west width is about 250 miles. More obvious to the casual traveler is topography. The western edge of the state, facing the Pacific Ocean, varies from the high, steep wall of the spectacular Big Sur region to the plains and shallow terraces common in parts of southern California. Just inland lie the peaks and ridges of the Coast Ranges, some of them quite substantial, with many beautiful valleys in their midst. These give way, in the central portion of the state, to the Great Valley, a vast, flat to gently undulating plain. Then comes a broad staircase of foothills and mountains leading ultimately to the high, jagged crest of the Sierra Nevada. A steep plunge to the east marks the beginning of the Basin and Range province, a series of alternating plains and narrow, often islandlike mountain ranges that extends to the Rocky

LOOKING EAST AT THE WHITE MOUNTAINS.

Mountains. Southern California is a variation on this theme, with similar Basin and Range topography lying to the east of the Transverse and Peninsular Ranges.

This diverse terrain would on its own nearly guarantee a wealth of plant species, but its effects are greatly augmented by smaller-scale features. Steep northern slopes and the deep clefts between mountains can provide shady, water-conserving sites suitable for forest trees and their understories, while the exposed portions of southern slopes create warmer and drier sites, which are often home to the distinctive shrub-forest known as chaparral. Smaller features, like the convoluted rock outcrops one often sees projecting from a mountain slope, can provide a remarkable variety of exposures along with moisture-trapping crevices and other features.

Interacting with these land forms is climate. Moisture-laden storms sweep in from the Pacific from roughly November through March, their actual timing varying radically from year to year. Precipitation is hastened by uplift and cooling over each new mountain spine, leaving lands to the east successively drier. A final, great wringing-out is performed by the Sierra Nevada and southern Cascades to the north, and the Transverse and Peninsular Ranges to the south. Some of the driest deserts in North America lie in the deeper valleys beyond these ranges. A similar though more gradual harvesting of cloud water proceeds from north to south. Storms from the Gulf of Alaska carve great southeasterly arcs, often veering inland somewhere between Monterey Bay and the southern Santa Lucia Mountains. Only the largest and most vigorous northern systems

thrust all the way to far southern California, though this pattern is mitigated somewhat by storms of subtropical origin that sweep up from the southwest. Both east-west and north-south gradients are mirrored in a transition, at the gross level, from dark and lush to more parklike forests, then through oak woodland to chaparral, and finally to the hard, open scrub of the true desert.

Climate consists of more than wet and dry, of course. Average temperatures increase from north to south, accelerating the rate of water loss by plants, and

TOP TO BOTTOM: THE BIG SUR COAST NEAR GORDA; SUMMER IN THE HILLS OF SONOMA COUNTY; THE OPEN DESERT, DEATH VALLEY.

they fall with increasing elevation. At a variable middle altitude that generally rises from north to south—5,000 feet is a rough average—the dominant precipitation shifts from rainfall to snowfall. Much of the moisture that arrives as snow is withheld until spring or summer thaws. This shortens the growing season and shifts its onset from winter and spring to summer and early fall.

At any given elevation, as one moves away from the coast, both winter cold and summer heat tend to be more severe, and humidity declines. Coastal and interior regions continually interact: Higher heat in the interior leads to air pressure differentials that create afternoon breezes from the west and draw moisture-laden air over cold ocean currents, spawning coastal fog. The fog, in turn, further moderates coastal temperatures and supplements normal rainfall through condensation on leaves and other surfaces. The lush redwood belt of our northern and central coasts owes its existence to this process.

Then there is the matter of geology. California has large areas of each of the major rock types, including magma-based granites and basalts, sedimentary shales and sandstones, and both familiar and bizarre examples of metamorphic rocks—those altered by heat, pressure, and chemical solutions. One of the most common and interesting of the metamorphic types is serpentine, often visible in broad greenish or grayish bands along our highways.

Each rock type breaks down over time into a chemically distinctive soil that tends to support a distinctive flora. Granitic soils, for example, tend to be acidic, porous, and low to moderate in nutrients. They support an amazing variety of plant life. Serpentine-based soils are low in many nutrients but particularly in calcium, which is essential to many plants; however, they are quite high in magnesium. Purer forms of serpentine support only plants with very unusual physiological adaptations.

A final element of critical importance, unseen except in rare, sometimes terrifying moments, is fire. The current vegetation of large ar-

TOP: WATER, WATER EVERYWHERE: CANYON CREEK LAKES, THE TRINITY ALPS. **BOTTOM:** DEEP RELIEF: THE TUOLUMNE RIVER CANYON.

eas of California evolved with recurrent fire, which became even more frequent after the arrival of the first humans. Survival of periodic conflagration has required the development of unusual coping features. Examples are underground root crowns and aboveground burls that generate new shoots following destruction of the main plant body, and hard-walled seeds that resist incineration or even require it for germination. Some chaparral vegetation is laden with flammable oils and resins to encourage burning and its gift of renewal.

The combined variety of landform, climate, rock and soil type, and fire (or lack thereof) in California is truly staggering, as are its effects on plant diversity. Coastal fogs can promote rich carpets of soft vegetation on coastal dunes and bluffs, while exposed sites in the interior favor hard, drought-adapted shrubs. Shade, protection from wind, and downslope movement of water all make canyon bottoms conducive to the growth of deep forests with delicate understories. The rocky, windswept tops of adjacent mountains are often home to unique assemblages of low shrubs and perennials that have much in common with those of alpine regions, like the matting buckwheats (*Eriogonum* spp.). Even on one meadowy hillside, a large band of serpentine or other unusual rock and soil type may support a plant community completely different from that of nearby shales or granites. And the frequency of fire will affect the composition of plants adapted well or poorly to it.

All of this helps to explain the sheer number of different plants in California: 6,000-plus species and many more subspecies and varieties are documented in the recent Jepson Manual. It also gives basis to the tremendous variety of plant features encountered, some of them quite striking, others merely curious or too obscure to be noticed by the nonbotanist. We humans often take great delight in features evolved to meet specific environmental challenges. For example, the matting habit of many high mountain plants, which are treasured aesthetically by mountaineers and amateur naturalists alike, has a very practical advantage,

TOP: NEW LIFE AFTER A BURN. HILLS WEST OF CARRIZO PLAIN. **BOTTOM, LEFT TO RIGHT:** CALIFORNIA'S FLORAL DIVERSITY: *ERIOPHYLLUM LANATUM* VAR. *LANCEOLATUM, RUBUS PARVIFLORUS, ARNICA CORDIFOLIA.*

placing them beneath the path of high, desiccating winds. The contorted forms of oaks are fashioned in part by decidedly unromantic forces, like insect attack and drought, yet they rival sculptures drawn from our own imagination. And the leathery crowns of yuccas and fantastic forms of certain cacti, though concerned with the mundane business of water storage and protection from predators in a harsh competitive setting, intrigue nearly every human who views them.

WHY GROW CALIFORNIA NATIVES?

This is a fair question. It is one thing to admire a plant in the wild, where it exists in a certain context, and quite another to want to make it part of your own surroundings at home.

At its simplest, a desire to grow certain California native plants reflects the same forces that draw us to garden plants from many exotic places. You might encounter a particular species, perhaps in pictures or text or, better yet, in the wild, and be intrigued—by its shape or flower color, its stature, its aroma, or any of a host of other endearing features. Your focus is on the plant itself, as it would be if you were viewing a painting or other work of art. For my part, I find it impossible to travel in any part of the California outback without stumbling upon plants that surprise and enchant me. A summer visit to favorite haunts in the Sierra, for example, may bring an encounter with a new, dazzling form of one of the many penstemons or of the dozens of showy daisies. I find it nearly impossible to admire one of these treasures without wanting to grow it, or at least to try.

The fact that California's native plants are here all around us, and that there are many from which to choose, is surely significant. But California gardeners, like their counterparts the world over, can be woefully ignorant of the flora close at hand. They are influenced by a long and hallowed tradition of importing horticultural treasures from Europe, Asia, and other far-flung regions. Although certain natives like the wild lilacs (*Ceanothus*) and manzanitas (*Arctostaphylos*) have been cultivated sparingly for over a century, widespread public interest in them is a relatively recent phenomenon. Typically, instead, the question a gardener asks is how a particular plant will contribute to the larger landscape, without special thought to its native origins. Perhaps there is a vacant spot to fill, requiring a tall, colorful shrub. You might see or read about a particular wild currant (*Ribes*), for example, that sounds like just the plant for the space. A fair number of native plants are now used interchangeably with exotics of similar features even by gardeners whose notion of geographic origin is the local nursery.

A critical push toward an increased use of California natives came with the severe drought of the middle 1970s. Growing fears of chronic water shortage, combined with appreciation of some highly visible landscapes planted during this period, led proponents of new approaches to horticulture to focus on native plants as "more appropriate" for California gardens, usually implying that as a group they are tolerant of summer drought.

Clearly, a fair number of native plants fit this description. Yet given the variety of habitats found in California, the matter is far more complex than it might at first appear. Transport a coastal ceanothus or manzanita from its native haunts, where it is perfectly at home with a benign version of summer drought, to Sacramento, and cultural rules have to be rewritten. Summer days in the Central Valley are frequently hot, warm nights offer little relief, and there are no evening fogs to replenish water transpired during the day. More

frequent and heavier irrigation will be required here for a plant considered "drought tolerant" by coastal gardeners. However, additional irrigation can introduce new problems, like high-temperature fungus root rots, that may be rare on the coast. Similar considerations apply to plants brought down from the high mountains, or to those transferred from the shores of streams and lakes to more arid zones. Thus, if water conservation is your goal, it is wise to be skeptical and to learn a bit in advance about the origins and tolerances of your garden candidates. (Or course, all the same considerations apply to the better-known exotics.)

A concept that guides many native plant gardeners, at least at a subconscious level, involves capturing an impression or ambience in the garden related to the features we treasure in the natural landscape. Members of some of the most extensive and visible plant communities in California, like chaparral and oak woodland, often share certain traits that make them beautiful and distinctive to our eyes. Slow growth and a certain amount of torture by weather and predators give many of our native trees odd, contorted forms. Many native shrubs respond to similar stress with dense, billowy, but never quite perfectly regular growth.

In place of the huge glossy, sometimes dramatically colored leaves and ropy stems of plants from monsoonal climates, natives of drier haunts in California have smaller, water-conserving leaves with muted colors and often hairy surfaces, lining intricately branched trunks. Plants from moister sites offer their own bevy of attractive features, while still generally of quieter impression than popular exotics. Many, like the coffeeberries (*Rhamnus*), wax myrtles (*Myrica*), and huckleberries (*Vaccinium*) have graceful, willowy branches and dark, lustrous leaves set off by colorful fruits. Many of our herbaceous perennials, bulbs, and annuals from all environments are quite delicate in appearance—deceptively so, since they must endure essentially the same regimes as their shrubby neighbors.

Whatever the permanent features of our showier natives, many are utterly transformed in late winter and spring. Leafy trees and shrubs become great puffs of blue or gold or pink or white, while smaller plants—particularly the bulbs and annuals—burst forth with riotous displays of color. This is perhaps the appearance for which the California landscape is most acclaimed. Yet whereas easterners often scoff at our supposedly drab autumns, an October trip into the hills tells quite a different story, with lovely pastel yellows, oranges, and pinks among the oaks, gold in streamside maples, and still more vivid shades adorning the wild grapes, redbuds, and much-maligned poison oak (*Toxicodendron*).

TOP: *Calochortus uniflorus*, Bear Valley. BOTTOM: *Mimulus aurantiacus* (former *M. bifidus*), Cone Peak.

Another important aspect of the wild, not always fully grasped on a conscious level, is its sheer diversity. The garden, in contrast, given constraints of space and cultural possibilities, is necessarily a much more impoverished environment. Yet it can at least suggest the natural diversity, in the same way that a fine painting can represent an impossibly detailed scene with but a few of its most salient elements. The trick is to select a palette of native plants that covers a variety of different forms, textures, colors, and seasons. Although conveying the full essence of a favorite wild haunt is not always possible—something like describing the emotional resonance of a memorable concert or play—with a little effort and planning, plus perhaps a few well placed rocks and stumps, it is possible to create at least a hint of the original scene.

An argument heard increasingly as the human tide rolls over the California landscape is that the garden can provide a refuge for plants that are waning in the wild. This argument is valid in a narrow sense: already, for example, far more individuals of Vine Hill manzanita (*Arctostaphylos densiflora*) exist in cultivation than in the wild. However, this so-called benefit must be looked at with some skepticism. The cultivated material generally belongs to a very limited subset of the natural entity—in many cases just a single clone. Thus, it seldom captures anything approaching the full genetic diversity found in the wild. More important, this line of thought begs the question of habitat integrity: the fate of all the other plants and animals that consort with the species being "saved." If you care about this larger issue, I encourage you to work energetically for habitat preservation rather than to concentrate on growing a few token representatives in a private garden (though you can certainly do that too).

Finally—actually, there is much more, but you may have had quite enough of theory—growing native plants can relate the act of gardening to a much broader and richer experience, if you have an inquiring mind. It is only natural that the enjoyment of some new plant acquaintance should lead you to want to know more about it. Where did it come from? What was the terrain, the climate? What were this plant's neighbors, both plant and animal? What ate it, or lived on or beneath it? What visited its flowers? These questions may have direct, practical applications in the garden. Knowing a plant's habitat (for example, streamside) rather than simply the geographic region (say, interior foothills) lets us make much better guesses about how to meet its needs. And often, the desire to see these relationships first-hand leads us onto new paths and expands our lives. I have gone out many times to a site in the wild just to see a particular plant or population, but found myself visiting it again for quite different reasons: the solitude perhaps, or a beautiful crag, or the warm glow of autumn.

SPRING EXTRAVAGANZA AT SANTA BARBARA BOTANIC GARDEN.

GARDENING WITH CALIFORNIA
NATIVES

DESIGNS GREAT AND SMALL

· ·

Permit me to rant a little. As nearly as I can tell, both private and commercial landscapes of nouveau California, as represented by huge swaths of tract houses bearing the names of their former natural inhabitants ("Willow Glen," "Oak Knolls," and so forth), are almost devoid of philosophical underpinning. There is an unwritten social mandate that one must cover bare ground—or at least a substantial part of it—with something green and living. But exactly what, or for what other purpose, seems not to matter much, as long as it is well behaved. The common result is what we might call the Green Desert, with great expanses of neatly trimmed grass or shrubby ground covers, punctuated by a few token trees and shrubs as one would never find them in nature: stranded and unpro-tected by others of their kind, and inca-pable of offering haven to other creatures, plant or animal. Or perhaps even worse: the same sprinkling of trees and shrubs, often in garish shades of gold and scarlet, floating instead in a barren sea of bark or volcanic cinders. A more benign and re-cent variant, usually planted by individual, color-loving gardeners, dispenses with the trees and shrubs altogether and fills the space with an assortment of flowering perennials and annuals, possibly accented by a bit of rockery, a wrought-iron bench, or statuary.

The result is colorful and usually friendly in its impression but has no particular structure. When flowers fade, so too does any sense of the garden as a coherent entity.

It is no more difficult to lose one's way with California native plants than it is with exotics; in fact, it seems to be the norm. Acres of ground may be covered by a single clone of coyote brush (*Baccharis pilularis*) or bearberry manzanita (*Arctostaphylos uva-ursi*). In their midst will be a few large ceanothus, like the durable 'Ray Hartman', and perhaps a flannel bush (*Fremontodendron*) or two, for a bold dash of spring flower color. All of this may be quite defensible on economic grounds, or as an alternative to truly barren ground in a large commercial plot. But it has been imitated by admiring home gardeners throughout the state, becoming a sort of archetypal Native Garden.

This book being an ode to beauty and diversity, perhaps you will bear with me as I ask you to consider the basics. What purposes does a garden serve (or we could simply ask, why have a garden at all)? Besides simply giving the gardener something to do, I believe a garden has some unique and important roles. These might be grouped in the broad categories of

---

LEFT: Garden steps, Regional Parks Botanic Garden at Tilden. **ABOVE:** Landscaping in the "green desert" style.

creating an environment, display or ornament, and a broad catch-all of practical functions, or utility, with the three of these blended in various proportions. As the gardener, you are entitled to choose the proportions that suit your fancy. However, failure to think about them may yield results that are not satisfying in any respect.

CREATING AN ENVIRONMENT

Let us begin with the concept of the garden as creating an environment. Above all, it can—and I would insist, should—be a comfortable place to wander and work, or just to sit and ponder the universe. In all cases it can be a place to enjoy being in. If this is important to you, then there are certain steps to take from the start. One is to provide a basic and substantial structure. Take a walk in the wild, and try to notice the features of particular spaces that feel comfortable and pleasant. Then think how you might fashion something similar at home. If you are among the fortunate few, with acres rather than feet

of space and the financial means to do it, you might think in terms of a small woods and meadow. If these are already present in their more or less natural state, let them be. If your yard is a small city lot, even one substantial tree can create at least a suggestion of woods and provide some of their basic services: an overhanging canopy of branches, some summer shade, and the evaporative cooling effect of large, transpiring foliage masses. Further structure is lent by shrubs of various sizes—shade-loving shrubs beneath the trees, more sun-tolerant shrubs in exposed locations. Their arrangement may be used to frame a path or to define a perimeter in much the same way as a fence, but with more friendly and interesting textures. Once the shrubs have filled in a bit, they will also offer a little privacy, allowing you to relax without the feeling of being on stage. Even where a physical wood or wire fence is already in place, as it is in the typical tract home, you can use the same shrubby congregation to soften its impact and shape your surroundings to suit your fancy.

Having this basic structure in place, you might embellish it with stepping-stone walkways to create paths. Or you might mold the remaining space with contoured plantings of smaller shrubs, foliage, and flowering perennials and annuals, or all of these elements. Often you will want to reshape this space a little as time goes on. Or the growth of certain plants and the new physical or visual dominance of certain ones over others may change the feeling of a given area for you, offering inspiration for further steps you might take.

COASTAL PLANTING, REGIONAL PARKS BOTANIC GARDEN AT TILDEN.

Before you ride off into the sunset with these pleasant notions, of course, there are some legal and social constraints to consider. In the typical tract setting, only the walled-off back yard is available as a truly personal environment. For the front, a well kept lawn or its equivalent may be de rigueur, with only a few token shrubs of controlled size being considered generally acceptable. Testing the limits with something more imaginative can bring admiration from more timid neighbors, or it can invite the wrath of an all-powerful homeowners' association. This alone may be sufficient reason to look for housing in the older parts of town, where standards are more relaxed and an overstory may be well established.

THE GARDEN AS HABITAT

There is another, related sense in which the garden can be an environment: in offering shelter and sustenance to creatures besides yourself. Well branched trees, like the oaks and maples, offer nesting sites for birds. Many shrubs offer protected places for small animals like lizards to scrabble around. Leaves provide sustenance to both insects and larger animals—sometimes distressingly so in the case of smaller, more delicate plants, though often without visible effect on larger ones. The litter from all types of plants supports earthworms, a host of soil insects, and mycorrhizal fungi, all of which improve the tilth and nutrient levels of the soil itself. Some of the more floriferous natives, like the sages (*Salvia*), are wonderful attractors of butterflies and other nectar-sipping insects. Still oth-

ers, like the California fuchsias (*Epilobium*), are beacons for hummingbirds. The edible fruits of plants like the holly grapes (*Berberis*) and currants (*Ribes*) support many birds and other animals, as do the dry seeds of everything from mighty oaks to delicate grasses. As one who lives in the midst of an undeclared nature preserve, I can vouch that life is far more enjoyable with animal neighbors in the garden.

DISPLAY

The element of display is nearly always present in a personal garden, but for some gardeners it may be the primary element. In this role, the garden is analogous to a painting or sculpture, to be viewed and admired. The ornamental features of its plants, from trees to the smallest perennials and annuals, are strongly emphasized, as is their arrangement. As in shaping one's surroundings, structure is an es-

TOP: WOODLAND HABITAT IN THE GARDEN, TILDEN. BOTTOM: SPRING DISPLAY AT RANCHO SANTA ANA BOTANIC GARDEN.

sential element of a pleasing display. Some ancient rules, like creating a backdrop of larger, more erect plant forms and descending to a foreground of smaller features, work as well with native plants as with exotics. In this case, everything is visible, both collectively and individually, and there is a vertical sweep of view that seems to have universal appeal. Arcs and alcoves can mark off individual scenes, something like the stage of a theater. For most of us, curves and sinuous lines along the edges of plantings have a far more pleasant and relaxed feel than military rows and ranks.

At the level of individual plants and smaller groupings, structure—including the sort of microstructure we call "texture"—has a different significance. Regardless of how showy a plant may be in flower, there will be a point when you are left with foliage and form alone. If the form is stiff and awkward, it may be something to be suffered for several months, until the next wave of flowers arrives. On the other hand, a really distinctive and beautiful framework of branches can be a major feature of the garden. The arching, zigzag branches of our native redbud (*Cercis occidentalis*), for example, can be appreciated even more when the plant is leafless than in its summer growth.

Texture is a special feature of trees, like the oaks, and of larger shrubs, though they by no means have sole title to it. Bark may be fissured or platy, rough or smooth, even silky. Leaves often present interesting shapes, as in the classic silhouettes of bigleaf maple, *Acer macrophyllum*. Or they may present fabriclike swatches en masse, with billows containing thousands of tiny individuals. Some natives possess distinctive textures at a nearly microscopic level, like the

silky hairs of lupines and sagebrushes (*Artemisia*), that give whole plants a special sheen or soften their impression.

Many of these features are available not only in woody plants, but also in the generally smaller herbaceous perennials and even the annuals. Some examples are the lacy patterns of the columbines (*Aquilegia*) and meadow rues (*Thalictrum*), and the myriad silken threads of the needle grasses (*Nassella*).

Colors are, of course, indispensable to a garden display. Hearing the word, one automatically thinks of flowers, but leaf and bark colors can be equally

TOP: THE BROADER VIEW: MIXED PLANTING AT RANCHO SANTA ANA BOTANIC GARDEN. BOTTOM: A FINELY TEXTURED SEDGE, *CAREX SUBFUSCA*.

important. Here California's native plants offer an almost unlimited array of possibilities. Some of the more popular shrubs and trees—the ceanothus, coffeeberries, oaks, and many others—present foliar masses of deep, rich green and form beautiful backdrops or counterpoints for plants with lighter color schemes. Others, like the manzanitas, add exquisite soft blue-greens and grays. When all of these are combined in swatches—particularly on the grander scale, if space permits—one can weave tapestries that are nearly as beautiful without flowers as with them.

Seasonal changes in color are also important features. Easterners' impressions notwithstanding, there are many trees and shrubs here—and even a few herbaceous perennials—with beautiful fall leaf colors. These are generally more muted than those of the eastern seaboard, but not always. Oaks and maples, aspens and ashes, dogwoods and redbuds can all give a colorful last performance before retiring for the winter. Even then, some show off colorful bark, from the ghostly white trunks of our native sycamore to the glowing reds of creek dogwoods. Foliage comes again to the fore in spring, with brilliant green, bronze, pink, and red in new growth. Choosing at least a few representatives from this group will greatly extend the variety and seasonal interest of your garden.

It would be unfair, however, to slight the role of flowers in making a garden display. They are the most dazzling features of a California spring and summer, and one that is easy to capture at home. Even our largest trees, which few people think of as "flowering," are often beautiful in bloom. There are the orange to yellow tassels of tiny male flowers on our oaks, the bright chartreuse panicles of bigleaf maple, and narrow cream to rosy spikes of the buckeye (*Aesculus californica*). The floral bounty of popular shrubs like the wild lilacs are, of course, legendary. But many lesser-known shrubs, like snowdrop bush (*Styrax*), are equally lovely. Some of the currants and gooseberries push the start of the floral season back to midwinter, while others like mock-orange (*Philadelphus*) and bush anemone (*Carpenteria*) extend it to midsummer. While fall is a quiet time for flowering  trees and shrubs, it brings forth a grand array of decorative fruits. There are blue, purple, and occasionally red berries among both the currants and the holly grapes; acorns with interesting shapes and rich brown hues among the oaks; and the tan to mahogany winged samaras of maples.

Many herbaceous perennials and annuals are planted almost exclusively for their floral displays, though they may offer beautiful foliage textures and colors as a bonus. Here the variety becomes so great as to be nearly overwhelming. You can reduce the confusion by focusing more strategically on sizes and forms, to permit a good variety. The ranks of the penstemons, for example, include towering giants that naturally assume background roles

FALL COLOR IN QUAKING ASPEN, *POPULUS TREMULOIDES*.

in a border; many of more moderate stature; and some matting plants, like *P. procerus,* that are beautiful subjects for the rock garden. There is a somewhat smaller range among the annuals, with a few of the clarkias hovering close to three feet, goldfields (*Lasthenia*) and baby blue eyes (*Nemophila menziesii*) often sitting just above the ground, and many others in between.

One should think also of pleasing color combinations, taking inspiration from the wild. The blues and violets of lupines, for example, contrast beautifully with the oranges and golds of native poppies (*Eschscholzia*). There are colors, too, like the blazing scarlet of *Penstemon rostriflorus,* for brightening up any drab corner of the garden. As with the woody natives, flowering season is important far beyond the familiar months of spring. One can say farewell to winter with the lovely white milkmaids (*Cardamine*) and trilliums, enjoy dazzling penstemons and buckwheats (*Eriogonum*) through the summer months, and savor an autumn finale with the wildly showy California fuchsias.

As if all this were not enough, other senses than sight are easily pleased by natives in the garden. Most striking is the wonderful variety of smells they present. Floral fragrances come first to mind, of course, of which there are many. The fruity fragrances of a mock-orange can cover an entire garden for weeks in early summer. Several lupines broadcast their sweet perfume throughout the garden. Then there are the many delightful smells one discovers only by coming close to a flower for a better look. The rich perfumes of the shooting stars (*Dodecatheon*) and some of the mariposa lilies (*Calochortus*) belong to this group. Each year I am surprised to discover an unexpected fragrance in the flowers of some plant I have known for years, simply by getting a little closer.

Less obvious, except to those of us who have pushed our way through the chaparral, are the many sweet, spicy, or otherwise interesting scents of leaves and stems. Perhaps my favorite of all is the piercingly sweet, complex fragrance of the leaves of woolly blue curls, *Trichostema lanatum,* but there are many others. Even the bark of some natives is pleasantly fragrant: that of Jeffrey pine (*Pinus jeffreyi*), for example, with its vanilla-like scent, and the unusual spicy fragrance of incense cedar (*Calocedrus decurrens*).

The element of sound might never occur to you, but this can be yet another treat in the native garden, particularly when the wind blows. Examples are the soft whoosh of pines and the musical fluttering of the leaves of quaking aspen (*Populus tremuloides*).

All of these sensory features can add immeasurably to the enjoyment of a native garden.

TOP: The winter tassels of *Garrya congdonii.* **BOTTOM:** Colorful fruits: Snowberry (*Symphoricarpos albus*).

All that is required is a little reading or first-hand experience to permit you to choose the plants that possess them.

UTILITY

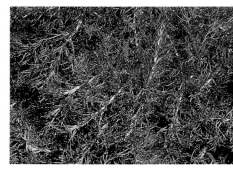

The element of utility lurks just beneath the surface of many garden decisions. A tree may be planted mainly for the shade and cooling it will provide. Larger shrubs help to hide unwelcome views. But sometimes specific, practical uses are of primary concern. Of these, the one that generates the overwhelming majority of native plant sales in California is the covering of bare ground. Most of the plants assigned this use are low though often widely spreading shrubs.

Certain ground-covering natives find favor simply because they are tough, reliable, and at least inoffensive to the eye. The several named cultivars of coyote brush (*Baccharis pilularis*) fall into this realm. Others are used because they are both beautiful and reasonably forgiving of the "purple thumb." Virtually all the popular low manzanitas fit this description. Sometimes the additional element of huge spread (as much as twenty to thirty feet) is a valued trait, as it is for low forms of Carmel ceanothus, *C. griseus.* It is here that you will run headlong into an unfortunate truth: The most commercially important—and thus the most available—of native ground covers were chosen with little, if any, reference to the private garden. Some, like the smaller forms of *Arctostaphylos edmundsii, A. uva-ursi,* and the hybrid *A.* 'Emerald Carpet', happen to be of sufficiently moderate or controllable growth for use at home. Beyond these, you will need to search among more obscure—though at least equally beautiful—candidates, including both woody plants and herbaceous perennials. A few examples are the sulphur-flowered buckwheat, *Eriogonum umbellatum;* a low yellow-flowered daisy, *Heterotheca villosa;* and some of the smaller carpeting sedges (*Carex*). It is also possible to fashion a beautiful ground cover from colonies of narrower plants; in fact, this is part of the essence of a natural meadow. Here the more decorative bunchgrasses, such as the fescues (*Festuca*) and needle grasses, truly shine.

Then there is the matter of soil stabilization and erosion control, the two going hand in hand. Ground-covering shrubs shed some rain and break its force, reducing the loss of soil beneath them. The ability of these same plants to actually slow the process of slumping and sliding of larger soil masses depends partly on the extent and strength of their root systems, partly on features of the site itself, like drainage patterns and the shape and strength of soil layers beneath the surface. Some thicketing grasses—several *Leymus* species, for example—bunchgrasses, and sedges may be even more useful than shrubs in this regard. For the home gardener with a relatively small plot to worry about, almost any sturdy vegetation is a great improvement over bare—especially disturbed—ground.

An unlikely but common use for some of the harder shrubs is that of a living barrier, placed across the path of any unwelcome travel or to protect a particular area from invasion. The wicked spines of a wild rose or of a gooseberry like *Ribes speciosum* are a valuable

---

ARTEMISIA CALIFORNICA 'CANYON GREY', AN UNUSUAL GROUND COVER.

feature for this task, producing a little pain but no lasting damage on contact. The stouter spines of chollas and prickly pears (*Opuntia* spp.) or the leaf tips of yuccas present a more serious hazard, especially to children, and can raise issues of legal liability.

MAKING ARRANGEMENTS

There are many possible approaches to arranging native plants in the garden. One of these relies on a traditional set of roles that imply a sort of order of dominance.

I have already argued that, assuming space permits, any garden should have at least one honest tree, both for its structure and for the benefits of shade, cooling, and the creation of a protected understory where more delicate species can be planted. Given an interesting form, such as that of many oaks, the tree can also be a visual focal point of the entire garden. Although few of us will be able to make a place for more than one individual, a whole grove is a pleasant thought.

The role of "specimen shrub" is also important. This implies a plant sufficiently impressive that it provides a natural focus of attention in one visual field of the garden. Some shrubs will fade in and out of this role with their flowering season; others, like toyon (*Heteromeles arbutifolia*), with its combination of large size, beautiful form, and bold, large leaves, will capture it throughout the year. While a large garden may support several individuals in this role, you may want to use them cautiously, to avoid the impression of competition and clutter.

Less striking shrubs and small trees can be grouped in various ways. The smaller ones can flank the more dominant shrubs, creating a field from which they stand out. They may be planted to provide visual screens, either to block out an undesirable view or to afford privacy. The ultimate development of this style of planting, of course, is the formal hedge. While a few dense native shrubs lend themselves to this use (or perhaps abuse)—wax myrtle (*Myrica californica*) and spice bush (*Calycanthus occidentalis*), for example—it clashes loudly with an otherwise naturalistic setting. Something friendlier is the shrubby border. Here not military rows but more informal clusters of shrubs can define the perimeter of a portion of the garden, the entire plot, or a larger piece of land.

Farther down the scale, and very much in vogue at the moment, are plants that can be

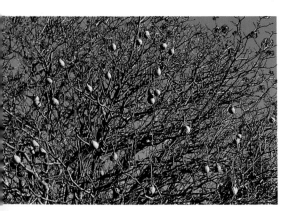

combined in an arrangement known as the perennial border. As sometimes seen, this structure can be quite formal, with well defined ranks of flowering and leafy perennials (and even smaller shrubs) of ascending size as one moves away from the foreground. As it is practiced by some of my best friends, it is a far more whimsical and informal assemblage, tied together more by shared space and similar plant types than by actual lines. This also presents the greatest opportunity for placing a great variety of your favorite native perennials and—why not?—annuals.

CALIFORNIA BUCKEYE (*AESCULUS CALIFORNICA*) IN FRUIT.

Another, broader way of looking at plant gatherings is that of visual settings or scenes. Here nature provides by far the best inspiration. Even one oak, preferably multitrunked, can form the foundation for a suggestion of natural woods. A few shade-tolerant shrubs, like the beautiful pink flowering currant (*Ribes sanguineum* var. *glutinosum*), may be planted beneath it to further the impression. Groups of native iris, heucheras, and perhaps one of the more drought-tolerant ferns, like *Dryopteris arguta,* supply the finishing touches.

A naturalistic miniature meadow can be constructed using a variety of native bunch grasses, like the fescues, needle grasses, and melics (*Melica*), perhaps augmented by some of the less aggressive sedges. All of these provide permanent structural features as well as the seasonal decoration of flowering and seeding heads. Between them— at least until they have filled in their allotted space—can go the smaller spring annuals and sun-loving bulbs, like the brodiaeas, often found in similar settings in the wild. These give a welcome burst of spring and sometimes summer color, then quietly disappear until the rains come once again. Larger and more durable accents can be provided by perennials like the coyote mint (*Monardella villosa*), the brilliant blue-flowered *Penstemon heterophyllus*, and yellow false lupine (*Thermopsis macrophylla*).

Some of the essence of an alpine setting can be captured in a small rock garden. In its most basic form, this is simply a modest mound of reasonably well drained soil or planting mix, dressed with gravel and accented by a few well placed, preferably angular boulders. The rest is limited only by your imagination—or the severity of your climate. Some matting penstemons and buckwheats, the wonderful lewisias, and many other smaller perennials will graciously share a limited space. Those of us who live in places too searingly hot for the true alpines can create a similar impression with certain smaller lowland perennials, like the Oregon sunshine (*Eriophyllum lanatum*), and a variety of small bulbs, though the extended drought-dormancy some of these require may leave the spot looking a bit vacant in summer.

It is unlikely that you will want to fully replicate a swatch of chaparral, since it can be an impenetrable tangle of hard vegetation. However, given a generous space—even better, space on a bank or slope—its best visual elements can be simulated by informal mixtures of some of its inhabitants. Various manzanitas, ceanothus, the silktassels (*Garrya*), shrubby oaks, and many others make pleasing combinations of forms, textures, and colors. Many annuals, herbaceous perennials, and bulbs can be planted at the edges of these assemblages, receiving a little protection from them and livening up the overall impression.

TOP: SEASIDE DAISY (*ERIGERON GLAUCUS*) AND ROCKERY, TILDEN. BOTTOM: *SILENE CALIFORNICA*, A PERENNIAL FOR LOW-ELEVATION ROCK GARDENS.

Even a streamside setting can be had, though with a few more limitations than others—assuming that you have an interest in conserving water. Rockwork can suggest the streambed, riparian shrubs like spice bush and western azalea (*Rhododendron occidentale*) can provide the main body, and herbaceous perennials like the sedges and scarlet monkey flower (*Mimulus cardinalis*) can complete the impression, all without requiring vast quantities of water to maintain them.

Ponds are more challenging. There is no denying that they can add a bold, refreshing touch to an otherwise ordinary landscape. Further, there is an abundance of beautiful native plants on which to draw for them, ranging from our native water lily (*Nuphar luteum*) to aquatic veronicas. However, little matters like the breeding of mosquitoes and the inevitable springing of leaks sometimes make them troublesome out of all proportion to their rewards. You must consider your own level of commitment before you start such a project. It should be noted, in any case, that many plants found at the edges of ponds and lakes thrive with generous watering in other parts of the garden.

MIXING CALIFORNIA NATIVES AND EXOTICS

I have never been a purist about native plants, and my own garden (or perhaps more accurately, plant menagerie) is full testimony to cosmopolitan tendencies run amok. However, I would be loath to force my tastes on another gardener. The matter of plant mix, from purely local to international, is for you to decide, according to your own concerns. What can be said, without fear of contradiction, is that many plants from other Mediterranean-climate areas of the world (those with cool, rainy winters and warm, dry summers) are visually and culturally compatible with our own natives. Particularly among plants of

more exposed places, similar strategies for coping with summer drought result in some uncanny similarities. Common examples are the various Australian mint-bushes, like *Prostanthera* and *Westringia,* and some of the Mediterranean rockroses (*Cistus* and *Halimium*). These examples combine moderate size, billowy forms, and soft gray leaves, though the flowers of certain species may look a bit garish beside those of a typical manzanita. Many are also useful for food or shelter to wildlife, and some, like *Berberis darwinii,* a Chilean barberry, are strikingly so. On the other hand, the introduction of one of the large-leaved, huge-flowered proteas into a garden populated by visually "quieter" natives would be the rough equivalent of a trumpet blast in a library. You can avoid many pitfalls simply by asking yourself what overall impression you would like to create in each part of the garden, asking questions, and doing a little reading about your prospective guests.

OUR NATIVE *LAYIA* WITH EXOTIC SAGES AND *PHLOMIS.*

NUTS AND BOLTS

. . . .

W*ith California natives, as with any group of plants, anticipation of new planting* is a pleasant thing. You read books and find intriguing descriptions, browse catalogs—or their latter-day equivalent, Web sites—and dream. But dreams alone do not put plants in the ground, nor do they guarantee their survival. There are still several steps to take before you find yourself sitting in a flowery garden, watching the birds and butterflies. These involve some diligent effort. The process begins with a little self-education and strategic thought.

THE LARGER SETTING

Try to think about where you garden from the perspective of a plant. Beyond gases ever-present in the air, a plant needs both light and water for basic life processes, and especially to grow. Light levels are affected by orientation and slope of the site and by shade-casting features like buildings and larger leafy neighbors. A plant is also constantly losing water by transpiration from its leaves. That loss may be reduced by adaptive features of the plant itself, like small or hairy leaves, while resupply may be assisted by an extensive root system or high efficiency in absorption. But the process never stops.

Extremes of heat and cold can damage or kill plant tissues. While plants from more severe climates have coping mechanisms, like thick cell walls and chemical brews serving the functions of antifreeze, there are always limits of endurance. Whatever form environmental stress may take, a plant cannot pull up stakes and flee. The best substitute it can normally manage is some form of dormancy.

With this in mind, think about the basic features of your local climate. What are your extremes of cold in winter, and of heat in summer? If either of these is severe, it can have a devastating impact on plants from mild climates, as I found by bitter experience in the "hundred-year freezes" of 1972 and 1990 and in many sudden bouts of intense heat.

Are strong winds a regular feature, as they are in the high desert, or is the air fairly calm except in storms? High winds can dehydrate plants at an appalling rate, and they magnify the effects of severe heat and cold. Relative humidity is an additional factor. Low relative humidity accelerates water loss even under calm conditions, but its effects are far more dramatic during high winds.

Rainfall or snowfall totals are critical for established, deeply rooted trees and shrubs, because they affect the ability of plants to supply themselves with water through the summer months. The greater the available moisture at root level, the less you need to intervene with the hose. Recently installed plants will have shallow roots and be unable to reap the benefits of groundwater, though frequent winter rains can hasten the rooting process and at least make cool-season irrigation unnecessary.

You can make spot checks on all of these features for your area by consulting weather reports in print, on NOAA weather radio, or on the Internet (some sites are listed in the

Appendix). Better yet, install your own rain gauge and recording thermometer, and make notes of what you see and feel.

THE GARDEN SETTING

Each broad geographical region of California has distinctive climatic features that can vitally affect gardening. However, the many variations within each region—for example, between hilltop and valley floor—make direct observations indispensable.

The coastal strand and a variable strip within several miles of it are home to mild weather from the northern border of California to the southern. Severe bouts of heat and cold are rare. Humidity is relatively high (though it descends gradually from north to south). Winds can be strong at times, especially on coastal bluffs, bending and breaking branches and giving trees and large shrubs a characteristic lean. In more protected locations, how-

ever—or behind a fence or wall—a huge range of plants from around the world can be grown. Keep in mind, though, that plants from severe-climate areas may not receive enough heat or cold to flower well, and they may also be subject to mildew and other foliar diseases.

As the garden moves inland, humidity drops and the extremes of summer heat and winter cold broaden progressively, reducing the palette of garden candidates with sufficiently broad tolerances. A corresponding decline in rainfall is reflected in less available soil moisture in summer and thus a need for more supplemental irrigation.

The Central Valley presents its own special set of challenges. While winters are generally mild, summers are almost incessantly hot, with "normal" daytime highs hovering between the middle 80s and low 100s Fahrenheit. Warm summer nights offer no real recovery period for stressed cool-climate plants and can be quite debilitating. Humidity is variable but highest near crop lands and other densely vegetated areas. Rainfall is moderate in the north but declines sharply in the south. This imposes a need for high to very high levels of summer irrigation, sometimes leading to toxic accumulations of sodium salts and other minerals present in local water.

The Sierra Nevada and other mountain regions vary in climate largely according to elevation. The lower foothills are hot and dry in summer, with low humidity, creating high water stress. They are cool and moist in winter. Both summer and winter temperatures descend as one proceeds to higher elevations, until one reaches the zone of regular winter snowfall. Forests appear at middle elevations and become increasingly luxuriant, providing

GARDEN BY THE SEA, SANTA CRUZ.

both natural shade and wind protection for the homes and gardens tucked within them. Although summer humidity is lower here than on the coast, a wide range of natives can be grown with moderate levels of irrigation.

The once-shunned but now increasingly populated desert areas, both low and high, present by far the greatest challenges to the would-be gardener. Here nearly all climatic factors are hostile to life for many plants. Rainfall is very low, as is daytime relative humidity. Wind is common—in some areas nearly ever-present. In the low desert, searing summer heat adds to water stress and can kill the tissues of more delicate plants. However, winters are often quite mild. The higher Mojave Desert region, covering vast areas of southeastern California, may have slightly lower average summer temperatures (still frequently over 100°F), but these are coupled with winter lows that on occasion reach 0°F. Although a wonderful array of desert natives, from cacti to desert asters, are growable in this region (and in many cases, only in this region), they lie beyond the scope of this book.

Growing plants from less arid regions requires, at the least, high levels of summer irrigation, but this may be complicated by the toxic effects of highly mineralized water.

ROCKS AND SOILS

Rock types and the soils they produce comprise another vital feature of any gardening site in California. Some of these, like the deep alluvial soils of the Central Valley and the granites of the Sierra, cover large and coherent regions. Others occur in widely scattered pockets and bands that reflect a more specific, small-scale geologic history. Signs of past volcanism linger in many parts of California, sometimes as visible cinder cones and other features, sometimes only in basaltic or other volcanic soils. Serpentine, slates, and other metamorphic rocks are the remnants of intense compression and heating of preexisting rock types. The soils they yield are quite distinctive—at times distressingly so for the gardener.

Both physical and chemical features of the various rocks and soils are important for the gardener to understand. Alluvial soils are often quite fertile, but some are high in surface clays or have shallow "hardpans" of the same, impeding both circulation of air and drainage of water away from plant crowns and root bases. The granites of many mountain regions decompose into mostly sandy or gravelly soils, wonderful for aeration and drainage but some-

TOP: WIDE-OPEN SPACES OF THE GREAT VALLEY. BOTTOM: GRANITE BECOMING SOIL IN THE HIGH SIERRA.

what wanting in retention of water. Gardens in these soils may require more supplemental irrigation. Granite-based soils are also benign chemically—moderately acid, low to moderate in essential nutrients (something that is easy to remedy), and low in toxic salts. Volcanic rocks vary from a fine-grained version of granite (rhyolite), similar chemically but producing finer-grained soils, to basalt and other "basic" rocks, low in silica and producing mostly neutral to moderately alkaline soils of variable texture. Sandstones and the finer-grained mudstones are also highly variable, as are the soils they produce. Some of these are coarse-grained and fairly neutral, some are fine and alkaline. Their fertility also varies considerably.

Relatively few gardeners occupy one of the many bands of more exotic rock and soil, like serpentine, but those who do know that it can pose quite a challenge. Exposed serpentine decomposes rather quickly, often forming what can best be described as "heavy goo" in winter and becoming close to concrete in summer. Its nutrient deficits are fairly easy to redress, but dealing with the poor texture and high density requires patient effort (some techniques are discussed below).

Most unfortunate, in my mind, is the would-be gardener who inhabits one of the "salt sink" portions of the San Joaquin Valley or a similar setting in the desert. There are attractive inhabitants of these and similar settings, like the salt bushes (*Atriplex*), growable in gardens. Fashioning a more diverse landscape, however, may require importing quantities of decent soil from more benign regions and building mounds as large as one can afford on top of the existing surface.

PLANT HABITAT AND ADAPTABILITY

Plants from each of California's major geographic regions have their own special adaptations, but these vary according to more specific habitats. The environment of a deep canyon—particularly one with a running stream—is far more protected and benign than that of a nearby windswept mountaintop. However (and fortunately for gardeners), some plants in any given setting will be far more tolerant than others of alien conditions. Familiar examples are the coffeeberries (*Rhamnus*) and California poppies (*Eschscholzia*).

This is a good place to reassert one of the most widespread features of California: its pattern of winter precipitation, summer drought. What follows from this is that many natives from exposed habitats offer fair to excellent drought tolerance in the garden. However, some of these same plants have little resistance to root pathogens that proliferate where heat and moisture are combined. Thus if irrigation is required, either for plant health or simply for better appearance, one risks rotting of roots and crowns. I will discuss some methods for reducing this risk shortly. For some herbaceous perennials and bulbs, though, like the mariposa lilies (*Calochortus*), an enforced summer drought is sometimes a nonnegotiable requirement.

A related matter is that native soils in many areas are rocky or sandy, and thus naturally well drained. Enhancing their effect is sloping terrain, where surface water naturally runs away from plant crowns. Sites where people live and garden, in contrast, tend to be on level ground, where rainfall or irrigation water can linger around plant bases unless the ground itself is raised. Worse, the soil in these sites is often dense and clayey. The disparity between natural adaptation and cultivated conditions is simply beyond the limits of tolerance for some plants. Again, however, there are often simple remedies, discussed below.

The coastal and near-coastal band is of special importance because it has been the source of many—perhaps a preponderance—of our commonly cultivated natives. Generally speaking, plants from this region live with mild temperatures and fairly abundant moisture, from both soil and air. Some of them tolerate more severe conditions than we might expect, but this is an individual matter, even within a given species. *Ceanothus thyrsiflorus,* the classic blueblossom, is a good example, with both more rugged and more delicate forms. Even the tougher individuals will require higher levels of irrigation as they are carried into the hotter interior, increasing the risk of attack by root pathogens. Plants from coastal and near-coastal streamside and forest sites are generally easy to grow but require still more irrigation when planted inland, with the addition of shading and wind protection for the forest dwellers. Some, like the more delicate ferns and redwood sorrels (*Oxalis oregana*), are simply not suitable for the summer stresses of the Central Valley.

Plants from a range or two inland are adapted to higher summer heat and drought, colder winters, and lower humidity. Many are easy to grow, in the strict sense, but cosmetic matters may intrude for those from exposed sites, like hillside chaparral. One of the standard drought responses for shrubby sages (*Salvia*), sagebrushes (*Artemisia*), and others is the shriveling of shoot tips and peripheral leaves. This is not much appreciated by the typical gardener, who will usually choose continued good appearance through moderate watering over a distressed look in the cause of water conservation.

Understory plants of oak and other light woodlands of the inner Coast Ranges often require either light shading or extra irrigation to look their best. Streamside plants can usually be grown with ordinary garden care alongside thirstier imports from Europe and Asia.

Not much of the Central Valley still exists as wildlands, and few of our cultivated plants originate there, with the dramatic exception of some beautiful trees and large shrubs of river banks and benches. Trees like the cottonwoods (*Populus fremontii* and *P. trichocarpa*), box-elder (*Acer negundo*), and Oregon ash (*Fraxinus latifolia*) are adaptable to ordinary garden conditions,

---

TOP: DEEP FOREST IN THE SISKIYOU MOUNTAINS. **BOTTOM:** SCREE SLOPE NEAR PALISADES, HIGH SIERRA.

where space and water permit. The dryland, often alkali-sink flora of the southern San Joaquin Valley has superb drought tolerance, and certain plants like salt bush (*Atriplex*) are both attractive and adaptable to many climates and regimes. Others are unlikely to be chosen for the home garden, owing to their frequently homely appearance.

I have already outlined the effect of elevation in the mountains. Many plants of the Sierra foothills are also those of the interior coastal ranges. Bush lupine (*Lupinus albifrons*) and western redbud (*Cercis occidentalis*) are two striking examples. A few, like bush anemone (*Carpenteria californica*), are truly unique. Most—again, excepting plants of streamsides and shady canyons—are notably drought and heat tolerant. However, many are also adaptable to milder regions and regimes, perhaps with some sacrifice of vigor or flowering. Redbud, for example, seldom flowers as profusely near the coast as it does in its native haunts, though it grows well. The streamside and canyon plants are particularly easy to cultivate, often in full exposure, near the coast.

The middle elevations of the Sierra (and of the higher interior Coast Ranges) are often clothed with diverse forests. Their weather is warm in summer, cool to cold in winter—the effective lows often moderated by the forest itself. There is nothing obvious about this region that should make its plants difficult to grow, but lowland gardeners have had only limited success with them. Perhaps many are intolerant of higher root temperatures or unusually susceptible to the pathogens these temperatures promote.

The moist ranges of far northern California present a special case. Here high precipitation overall and occasional summer rains create lush, deep forests and an amazing abundance of flowing water. Temperatures are also mostly mild to cool, even in summer. I have

found plants from this region generally easy to grow near the coast. Plants of rock outcrops and gravelly spots, like the lewisias, need special attention to soil drainage, and those of the forest floor, like the lovely *Phlox adsurgens* and longleaf mahonia (*Berberis nervosa*), need shade and moisture even in coastal settings. Others thrive in ordinary garden circumstances, with moderate to regular watering. These are generally not good candidates for the hotter interior or for southern California.

When one reaches the higher elevations, some additional features are introduced. Slopes are usually steep. Soils—if one can even call them soils—are often rocky or sandy, and near the ridgetops they are reduced to the packed gravel known as scree. Daytime temperatures are mostly mild in summer, with low to moderate humidity and unpredictable bouts of cold. Winter temperatures are mostly well below freezing. Precipitation is held on the ground as snow and ice until summer. This enforces a distinct pattern of winter dormancy and summer growth, quite different from that of the lowlands.

NATURAL MARSHLAND, SAN LUIS NWR, CENTRAL VALLEY.

I have found plants from this region highly variable in their response to culture. Many thrive near the coast, though intense winter rains can rot their roots unless they are grown in gravelly soils. Only a few, like sulfur flower (*Eriogonum umbellatum*), perform well in hotter-summer areas. Another specific problem, even near the coast and in full exposure, is a failure of some species to flower, though they make good vegetative growth. One possible explanation is a need for higher levels of ultraviolet radiation, as is found in the thin mountain air, to stimulate flower bud formation. Another may be the need for a pronounced winter chill. This is probably true, for example, of *Phlox diffusa* and other high mountain phloxes. For all this, I find myself taking up the challenge again and again, simply because so many plants of this region are so spectacularly beautiful.

Desert plants are another matter altogether. Plants of all areas except the deeper canyons and washes, where there is a little extra water and perhaps some shade, are adapted to excruciating drought and parched air, plus searing summer heat. Many, like the cacti, can be grown with little effort in the same desert areas; simply try to avoid the temptation to provide more than very occasional irrigations, except in the driest years. A few, like the mint-shrub *Hyptis emoryi* and the agaves, seem amenable to culture outside their native haunts, mostly in southern California. Others, like ocotillo (*Fouquiera splendens*), are nearly impossible to maintain in areas with more generous winter rainfall.

The Basin and Range area east of the Sierra presents a less severe version of the same challenges. However, it shares more of its flora with other areas—ponderosa pine (*Pinus ponderosa*) and antelope bush (*Purshia tridentata*), for example. Many of its characteristic plants, like big sagebrush (*Artemisia tridentata*), are amenable to careful cultivation near the coast, even more so in the interior.

Choosing and Placing Your Plants

Armed with the kinds of information outlined above, you can approach your planting decisions from two different perspectives: You can browse successfully for native plants adaptable to your conditions, including those of a specific spot you would like to fill; or you can begin with a plant you admire and determine where it will be most successful (or, in extreme cases, create an acceptable site from scratch).

The typical garden site is a composite of several potential plant habitats. The front yard

RIDGE ABOVE VIRGINIA LAKES, CENTRAL SIERRA. SOME SURPRISINGLY ADAPTABLE PLANTS ARE FOUND HERE.

is often quite exposed to the elements. If your housing pad is elevated, perhaps there is also a noticeable slope or bank here. This would be an ideal spot for sun-loving trees like Catalina ironwood (*Lyonothamnus floribundus*) and for shrubs like the various manzanitas that will appreciate the enhanced drainage of water away from their crowns. It is also a fine place for a naturalistic meadow and the wealth of natives that delight in such a setting: bunchgrasses like the needle grasses (*Nassella*), brodiaeas and other "bulbs," herbaceous perennials like the blue-eyed grasses (*Sisyrinchium*) and sunshine daisies (*Eriophyllum*), and—given careful soil

preparation and weed control—an endless variety of spring annuals. The immediate house front is more challenging, because of reflected heat from walls, water shed from the roof, and constraints of space, especially around windows and doors. Tough and tolerant shrubs, like the holly grapes (*Berberis aquifolium* and *B. pinnata*), are good choices here, though they thrive in more protected sites as well.

Fences between houses can create awkward, narrow strips, often shaded part of the day by the fences themselves. These are actually ideal plots for borders of smaller and medium-sized perennials, like the fleabanes (*Erigeron*) and columbines (*Aquilegia*), the actual mix being determined by the degree of shading and availability of water.

The back yard of an older house might include both more open, exposed spaces and substantial areas in the shade of overhanging trees. These features, along with the likely ability to have total freedom of design, make it a place to garden with abandon. Shady corners, where many plants of exposed habitats refuse to grow, can become a refuge for ferns and woodland perennials as diverse as trilliums and wild gingers (*Asarum*). Areas beneath the outer canopy of a typical shade tree will support an amazing variety of native plants, drawn from a range of habitats, from canyon bottoms to hillside chaparral. The sunniest exposures may be treated like those of the front yard.

Of course, you may not be so fortunate. You may sit on a forlorn island of empty space, exposed on all sides to sun and wind. This is not good, but neither is it hopeless. The first wave of planting, if it is confined to the toughest, most adaptable shrubs (mountain mahogany (*Cercocarpus betuloides*) and native redbud are two that come to mind), will begin to improve the site as they take root and grow. Their branches will begin to cast some shade, cooling the ground and providing new habitat for smaller plants. The addition of an outer border of taller, screening shrubs like the larger ceanothus will have an even more pronounced effect, even softening the gales a bit.

But you can do something more dramatic, something once recognized as indispensable

Chrysothamnus nauseosus var. *albicaulis*, a beautiful and common shrublet of our higher mountains.

to any garden: plant a tree—or better, several trees—and begin to build an overstory. Any tree large and full enough to cast a little shade has a remarkable effect on the ground beneath and around it. The shade itself lowers both air and ground temperatures. Transpiration of water by the canopy results in further cooling. For a dramatic demonstration of these effects, simply drive the tree-lined streets of the "old quarter" in any

Central Valley town. A sizeable tree also provides home and forage for any number of animals, from insects to squirrels, and a friendly plant habitat beneath its canopy—or more often, a variety of habitats from canopy center to edge.

There are other ways—most of which involve some minor engineering—to modify your garden sites for a wider variety of native plants. Beg or buy a load or two of soil being gouged from another homesite, if it is not too clayey, and build a large berm or mound (or several). Now you have not only expanded your planting area, but also provided a place for more sensitive plants (those of the chaparral and mountain slopes, for example) that might otherwise sulk and rot in winter rains. A really sizeable mound will also have different exposures, which can be exploited for plants from different habitats.

As the garden is placed further inland or in otherwise harsher surroundings, a sort of scale of diminishing exposure is required. By lowering temperatures at both foliage and root levels, shade may be used to compensate for higher summer temperatures, at least until growth and flowering seriously decline (at which point you may have to give up your fond dream of growing a particular plant). This is the only practical alternative I know to some massive feat of air conditioning.

THE MATTER OF FIRE

One of the less obvious siting considerations, of far more importance to the gardener than to the plants involved, is danger of fire. As described in the introduction, some natives—particularly chaparral shrubs—have evolved in the presence of recurrent fires. Rather than developing fire-resistant tissues, many have followed the path of regenerative root-crowns or burls, or hard-walled seeds that must be physically damaged to germinate. In some cases

the plants themselves are loaded with flammable resins and volatile oils and may nearly explode when heated by an advancing blaze. It is the latter, including such popular shrubs

TOP: EFFECTS OF AN OVERSTORY: HEUCHERAS UNDER OAKS, SANTA BARBARA BOTANIC GARDEN. BOTTOM: NATIVE SAGES: BEAUTIFUL BUT FLAMMABLE.

as the ceanothus and salvias, that pose a particular danger to human structures in fire-prone areas. The sensible country gardener with a hilltop home would no more plant a large grouping of shrubby salvias directly below the house than scatter cans of gasoline carelessly about. However, in the typical urban or suburban setting, and especially in mixed plantings, these plants present no more danger than many popular exotics. Few shrubs are truly fire resistant.

SPACING

One of the great sins of commercial landscaping is deliberate overplanting for immediate effect (this is not necessarily an indictment of landscapers, but more often of their well heeled but impatient clients). Its earliest effect is simple crowding of plants. Then low shrubs begin to rear up like frightened horses. Smothered lower branches defoliate and die prematurely. Where moisture is retained between leaves and branches, fungus diseases set in, sometimes destroying large branches or even whole plants. At best, many plants may have to be removed with considerable effort, leaving the landscape scarred for some time.

Assuming that you know something about each plant's potential spread, this scenario is entirely avoidable. Avoiding a dense tangle of vegetation is also an aesthetic imperative. One of the most distinctive and attractive features of the California landscape is its open, airy quality. This is captured in the garden simply by ensuring that there will be an open border around each plant, while the plant itself fills in to become a respectable mass. If you turn out to have underestimated a particular plant's size, judicious pruning can usually make the finer adjustments. Overall, you will enjoy a more natural effect and have healthier, more durable plants.

KNOWING AND GROWING YOUR SOIL

I have heard a good share of meaningless drivel and contradictory advice when it comes to preparing garden soils to receive native plants. It is common wisdom that clayey soils need to be mixed and worked deeply with some sort of organic amendment (sawdust, bark chips, peat moss, potting soil, or compost) to aerate it and make it penetrable by growing roots. This may serve to get young plants started without rotting away, but the roots of most trees and shrubs will quickly pass the boundary of all the amendment you can possibly afford, only to be faced with the same clayey soil. The fact that they usually succeed is a tribute to the role of roots themselves in opening and aerating dense soils. Excessive amounts of organic material can actually have an effect opposite of the one intended: they can provide a growing medium for opportunistic root pathogens, like *Phytophthera cinnamomi*. These often feast on dead organic matter but, given both high heat and moisture, can invade living roots.

For really sensitive plants, I have come to believe that the most important step is the construction of mounds and berms, as just described. Again, plant roots will eventually have to deal with the worst features of the soil, but at least they have a substantial period of grace, while plant crowns are assured of sitting high and dry.

Remedies for more serious challenges, like a shallow, impermeable hardpan, are the same for the native garden as for any other. These are basically engineering problems, possibly requiring the service of a large commercial auger or the expensive installation of drain tiles. Leaching salty soils may require similar measures.

CONTAINERS: A SPECIAL CASE

Sometimes you may opt to plant not in the "real" garden settings outlined above, but in pots, wooden boxes, or other containers. Perhaps a treasured plant is simply too delicate for your site, or too delicious to some animal resident. Perhaps you need to hold plants while a site is prepared or, more positively, you have a beautiful container that needs an appropriately beautiful plant to contain. So the potted menagerie grows.

Container gardening imposes a special set of requirements on plants, sites, soils, and the containers themselves. Plant candidates should be of slow to moderate growth, with well behaved root systems. Some of our more rampant shrubs, like the larger ceanothus and woody salvias, quickly outstrip even large pots, requiring extravagant amounts of water, losing leaves prematurely and becoming sparse and unsightly. Many succulents and bulbs, in contrast, will thrive for several years in the same container. Presentation is also an important matter. Plants with fountainlike growth and durable foliage, like some yuccas and nolinas, make beautiful container specimens, while others with less pleasing forms or excessive loads of dead foliage do not.

You should be conscious of the effects of exposure. Full sun, especially in the afternoon, may heat the entire root mass to a lethal level, or the extra heat can promote fungus root rots. Materials with good insulating properties, like wood and thick terra cotta, can mitigate these effects, but light shading at critical times is still a good idea.

Drainage and aeration are of vital concern. Both are heavily restricted by the walls of the container, unlike the porous open ground. For this reason, drain holes should be as large and numerous as possible, and your "soil" should be something far more porous than the real thing. Many of the sand and sawdust (or bark) mixes sold in nurseries will suffice. For particularly touchy plants, like summer-dormant bulbs and lewisias, I usually add coarse perlite (a heat-expanded volcanic glass), as much as a third by volume. Avoiding an excessively large container and resulting soil mass is an easy way to avoid chronically saturated soil and root diseases.

If you have time and space, it is even possible to create small plant communities in containers. Obviously, broader containers are called for, and their depth should be carefully matched to the requirements of your community. Small bulbs like the brodiaeas, matting eriogonums and other diminutive shrublets, and perennials like alpine heucheras and saxifrages are especially suited to this style.

THE PLANTING PROCESS

You may be happy to know that there are no unique rules for planting California's native plants. However, as with exotics, some strategies work better or worse, and some work not at all.

RUSTIC BENCH WITH POT OF DUDLEYAS, SANTA BARBARA BOTANIC GARDEN.

Begin with the season. For plants of lower and middle elevations, fall is clearly the preferable time to plant. Temperatures descend, triggering the onset of new growth. In a normal year, new rains will relieve you of all or most of the job of watering. And best of all, root growth made during winter and spring reduces the need for summer irrigation. All that said, most people will plant when they have the time—which might be during a summer vacation—or when plants are available, which is unpredictable. And yet usually it all works, and reasonably well.

As with nonnatives, the roots of trees and shrubs should be examined for signs of coiling around the walls of the container (something unfortunately common with nursery

plants). These should by opened up or—in the worst cases, and only during the cool season—heavy coils should be cut and stripped away. Otherwise the coils will swell and tighten, blocking the spread of new roots; growth will slow; and the plant may fall over suddenly in a strong gust of wind. This is normally not an issue for herbaceous perennials and bulbs, which form new sets of roots along with new shoots on the periphery of each clump.

The plants and their prospective site should both be watered well ahead of planting, with both given some time to drain. Exposing dry roots to even drier air and soil nearly guarantees the death of young root tips, which can retard establishment of the plant or even lead to fungus invasion of the root system. The hole is dug, wider and slightly deeper than the root ball. At this point, opinions on how to proceed diverge. It was once gospel that one should mix soil of the planting site with nursery mix or its equivalent (sawdust and sand, basically) around the edge and along the bottom of a hole to provide a density gradient and prevent its becoming a bathtublike container for water. Many successful landscapers ignore this injunction, and most, I think, would apply it only to really dense, clayey soils (with the first watering, you should be able to see whether there is a problem). The plant should be placed such that the old container soil line is elevated slightly above the new ground level, to prevent water from sitting around the crown and cultivating lethal pathogens. Creating a raised basin larger than the hole is almost mandatory for summer planting, unless you are install- ing spitter-style irrigating heads or soaker hoses that will cover a broad area around the plant. However, you should knock down the basin— or at least a corner of it—when winter rains begin, in order to prevent the retention of excessive moisture. Similarly, there would be no point in creating such a basin for planting just before or during the rainy season. As a last step, give your newly planted treasure a thorough soaking, unless rain is on the way. I have managed to forget this little detail several times, with disastrous results.

TOP: Pre-plant vertical root pruning: Easy and often essential for good long-term root growth. **BOTTOM:** Globe mallow placed with top of old root ball slighly above grade.

AFTERCARE

California would not have its rich carpet of vegetation if its plants were not adept at handling adversity. Of course, what you see is a tiny portion of all the individuals that started life as seedlings in the recent past. Your job as gardener is to tip the odds as far as possible in favor of the plants you have adopted. For most of us, this will be a matter more of forbearance than of constant intervention.

PROTECTING YOUNG PLANTS

Young, newly placed plants present an odd mix of advantages and vulnerabilities. They are usually in a vigorous, active state, with both shoots and roots growing rapidly. However, they are also, quite literally, "soft." This makes them especially prone to damage in sudden heat waves, especially if they are allowed to dry out. Keeping them constantly moist through their first summer will stave off disaster. Young plants are also susceptible to damage in sudden hard freezes. In this case, placing a protective cone of paper over the plants whenever severe cold threatens can work wonders. They are also particularly delicious to deer, rabbits, and rodents of various descriptions. If these animals are present, you will be wise to protect your plants with cones or cylinders of wire netting, firmly planted in the ground. Basically, anything you can do to keep them growing without setback will hasten the time when they can fend for themselves.

MULCHING

Mulching with your own prunings, shredded branches, or bark can help to reduce soil surface temperatures and evaporative water loss in the summer, while inhibiting weed growth around your plants. However, these materials, like other organic matter, are naturally prone to decay and will have to be renewed from time to time. It is important to leave such a mulch as dry as possible in summer, lest it become a haven for pathogenic fungi. Avoid it altogether around new, frequently watered plants.

IRRIGATION

I have already outlined the most basic problem of irrigation for dryland and other sensitive native plants. While plants sitting with inundated crowns may rot in winter, far more are lost to pathogens cultured by summer irrigation. This perhaps more than anything else explains the reputation of native plants as difficult to grow. Watering in late autumn, winter, and early spring is seldom an issue, as normal rains take care of

LEAF LITTER IN THE WILD: NATURE'S OWN MULCH.

the needs of most plants. When it does prove necessary, cool temperatures inhibit the growth of pathogens.

Proper frequency and depth of watering are two of the most difficult concepts to convey to the "purple thumb" gardener, while some of us seem to know instinctively what is right. I think that the key lies in careful observation, something we do almost unconsciously with the things we love. Watch closely for signs of stress in your newly planted shrubs, and attend to them as needed. You can be a bit more relaxed with established plants, which will usually give clear signs of drought stress before any real damage is done: leaves will droop during the heat of the day; growth will slow, and often leaves will become smaller and paler in color; older leaves will yellow and drop prematurely.

The signs of serious overwatering, on the other hand, are often those that directly

precede the death of the plant, as both young and older leaves shift in color from bright green to yellow or olive green and wilt without drying. Then branches begin to die, often one at a time. At this point little or nothing can be done to remedy the condition.

In the later chapters that describe particular plants and plant genera, some standard terms like "occasional," "moderate," and "regular" are adopted as rough guides to watering frequency. Near the coast, this might be translated as monthly or less, twice monthly, and weekly or more, respectively, adjusted for exceptionally warm or cool summer weather. That frequency will need to be increased as the garden moves inland, most dramatically so in the Central Valley and adjoining foothills. The actual quantity given with each irrigation is equally important; many gardeners (I hope not you) have a tendency to "splash and dash." The correct approach is to fill a large basin once to the brim, and a smaller one twice or more times. This increases penetration and reduces the accumulation of toxic salts where water quality is poor.

A more recent technique permitted by the march of technology is found in the great variety of inexpensive spot-watering systems, using small heads of various sizes that spray or drip. These are now available in any large garden center or hardware store, complete with helpful information for building your own modular networks with flexible pipe and simple pressure fittings. The water diffuses downward and outward in a rough cone, encouraging a deeper root system. Because of this application pattern, multiple heads should be installed for each substantial tree or shrub, to cover at least the area of the original root ball near the surface. Recent incarnations of these systems have largely solved previous problems of clogging by mineral scale and bits of odd matter in household water. However, there is still no substitute for regular inspection while the system is operating, to find and fix failed heads, rather than stumbling upon drought-killed plants.

Watering plants in containers is a particularly delicate matter, primarily because of the suddenness with which soil and roots can dry out, particularly in warm weather. Careful observation, which includes testing beneath the surface with the fingers and being alert for any sign of distress, is indispensable to your success.

A VARIETY OF LOW–VOLUME WATERING DEVICES, TUBING AND PIPE.

NUTRITION AND REDRESS

While California's alluvial valley soils can be spectacularly fertile, those of the hills and bluffs from which most cultivated natives are actually drawn tend to be fairly low in nutrients. This is reflected in a variety of adaptive techniques, from slow growth to relationships with mycorrhizal fungi and nitrogen-fixing bacteria, which give many of these plants low to moderate nutritional needs. If you garden in the typical "flatland" setting, you may do well with no supplemental fertilizer at all. If leaf color seems a little pale, yet your water quality is good, try small applications of any mild all-purpose fertilizer, organic or otherwise. If there are questions about your water quality, a wise first step is to invest in a soil-testing kit and determine the pH (acidity or alkalinity) of your soil. Alkaline soil inhibits the absorption of iron and other essential minerals by many forest and seacoast plants, though some plants of the interior are quite lime tolerant. If this is the problem, both extra applications of more easily absorbed chelated minerals and the use of an acidifying compound like aluminum sulfate, commonly sold for use on azaleas and camellias, can work wonders.

An excess of nitrogen is quickly reflected by certain natives, like the ceanothus and penstemons, in rapid, floppy growth and deep leaf color, much like the response to excess shading. This tells you that it is time to use a lighter touch.

A related matter is building the texture of the soil, for aeration and drainage. Earthworms, soil insects, and beneficial microbes do this with natural litter as it accumulates—one of the best arguments against the fastidious raking of every fallen leaf. If you have the space to maintain a compost pile for vegetable waste, you will also find that the end product is a wonderful supplement to the natural litter and hurries the process of conversion along. Our own clumsier attempts to work in quantities of purchased materials, like peat moss, with shovels and mechanical tillers can do some good but also potentially considerable harm: if one is a little too thorough, larger soil particles are pulverized, and the next irrigation results in an even more compacted mass.

PRUNING AND OTHER MAINTENANCE

Pruning, staking, and other plant maintenance are relatively simple matters with California trees and shrubs, while simple removal of dead stems and leaves (or just letting them rot away) is often sufficient for herbaceous plants. A minimalist approach generally yields the most satisfying results.

Start by asking yourself whether the plant already shows the makings of a natural form, something you might expect to see in the wild. If so, you may choose simply to wait and

---

FROM UPPER LEFT: HOMEMADE COMPOST, VARIOUS COMMERCIAL FERTILIZERS, AND MINERAL SUPPLEMENTS.

watch, taking corrective measures only as needed. It is more likely, however, that you will have to begin by undoing the effects of standardized pruning in a commercial nursery (mostly clipping to develop a full, round silhouette). The worst habit many gardeners apply to their shrubs is indiscriminate hacking to limit their size or to impose unnatural forms, like globes and cubes. The result is often a confused tangle of branches, with many crossing awkwardly from edge to center of the plant and beyond. In contrast, careful, directional pruning (in most cases, cutting just above a node that faces away from the center of the plant) can create gracefully flowing forms, much like those we treasure from scenes of the wild. Strategic removal of one member of a pair of opposite branches, in plants like the maples that have them, can accomplish the same. Or directions can be alternated deliberately to develop a more contorted form. Thinning—the removal of whole branches or branchlets—can expose beautiful trunk structures and bark, which are sometimes the most appealing feature of

our shrubby subjects (the currants and gooseberries, for example). None of these techniques requires advanced skills or investment in equipment beyond a good, stout pair of pruning shears and perhaps a lopper or pruning saw for heavier branches.

Removal of incipient growth buds and timely pruning of actively growing shoots are nearly always preferable to remedial pruning of mature growth. Yet there will inevitably be times when a wave of growth has passed you by. In this case, make each cut just above a node (the site of a leaf base or incipient bud), leaving only a small stub. As tissue below the cut dies, healing will take place largely at the node itself. A longer stub is more likely to be invaded by fungus or bacterial pathogens as it dies back.

As with certain exotic trees, you should take special care when removing really large branches (those with a diameter of, say, three inches or more) on native species, especially the oaks. The cut should leave intact any swollen buttress or collar at the base of the branch; this is where callus tissue will be generated to close off the wound.

GARDEN WARS

We nursery folk spend an inordinate amount of money and effort fighting armies of animal pests and diseases. Much of the problem, while economically difficult to avoid, is of our own making. We gather plants of each species or cultivar closely together by the hundreds or thousands and then heavily water, generously fertilize, and frequently prune them

CAREFUL PRUNING FOR A PLEASING, FOUNTAINLIKE STRUCTURE (LEFT) VERSUS HACKING TO SIZE (RIGHT).

to accelerate their progress to market. These conditions, as it happens, also favor organisms that eat or afflict such plants. You can take some hints from our dilemma; indeed, it is possible to opt out of most of the battle, thereby withholding your hard-won income from the companies that so energetically market arsenals of different poisons, traps, and other alleged "remedies."

First, there is the matter of definition. Just what is a pest? If you are willing (and why not?) to make your garden a haven for wildlife, many "pests" simply become food for desirable garden inhabitants, like ladybirds and brown-headed beetles and lacewing flies. These, in turn, provide food for birds and other predators. Such a community is usually self-sustaining and self-regulating, though within broader limits than the fastidious gardener might have in mind. Each spring, for example, aphids appear, sometimes in large numbers, to attack succulent new shoots. Their predators lag a bit behind them, calling for some patience on your part. If you find patience to be lacking, try a daily blast from the garden hose, which dislodges soft-bodied insects and kills a fair number of them. As a last resort, insecticidal soaps and the short-lived pyrethrins, natural or synthetic, provide a relatively friendly alternative to more familiar organophosphates. Whatever you use, it should break down quickly by oxidation or other means, leaving no persistent residues to harm animals other than the target pests.

Soft perennials and bulbs, as well as young shoots of tougher plants like the shrubby lupines, are often ravaged by snails and slugs. These, too, have their predators, though they are not quite so abundant or easy to obtain. Hand-picking, especially at night when snails and slugs are active, can be quite effective. Another traditional remedy involves scattering shallow pans of beer about the ravaged area; snails and slugs are often attracted, climb in, and drown. These methods offer alternatives to toxic baits, which are highly effective but also attractive and deadly to certain pets and wild birds.

Sometimes the most damaging of all creatures to a native garden are the same ones your neighbors adore and encourage—rabbits, hares (jackrabbits), and deer. I am one of those who have come to see them in a less friendly light, as I have watched them attack even tough shrubs so relentlessly that the plants simply give up and die. Many of their predators, like grizzly bears and mountain lions, were long ago extinguished from human settings or have fled the advancing tide of civilization (coyotes, foxes, and weasels are happy

PEST WARRIOR READY FOR BATTLE. YOU CAN AVOID THIS IN THE GARDEN.

exceptions), so it is left to us to deal with them, as gently as possible. Fortunately, there is hope, in the form of inexpensive and nontoxic repellants to spray on endangered leaves and shoots. A foliar spray consisting of a couple of beaten eggs (removing the "string," which clogs spray nozzles) in each gallon of water may be effective by itself, producing sulfur compounds as the eggs slowly decompose. The same mix also provides an excellent long-term "sticker" for more dramatically effective commercial repellants. The most successful consist of concentrated habañero pepper juice or of ammonia in a fatty base. Each spray will have to be repeated about once a month. In the most desperate cases, simply consider omitting the most edible plants from the most vulnerable parts of the garden. First to go (unfortunately) would be such favorites as the ceanothus and native lilies. Fortunately, the browsers seem to find some attractive natives like the sagebrushes (*Artemisia*) and rabbit brush (*Chrysothamnus*) positively distasteful.

Another native mammal, the western pocket gopher, usually concentrates on plant roots (though I have seen it come out of the ground to gnaw off particularly delicious stems). While established trees and shrubs usually survive its attacks, as they do in nature, a gopher can be devastating to soft perennials and young plants of any category. A variety of macabre traps, poison baits, and "bombs" that send poisonous fumes through its tunnels can all reduce its numbers. However, I long ago began enclosing the root ball of any really treasured—and edible—plant in a wire gopher basket. Once you have used the commercial version, you may find it cheaper and relatively effortless to cut and "roll your own" from rolls of half- or quarter-inch poultry netting (use gloves to avoid bloody gouges from the cut wire ends). Eventually, the roots of larger plants must face life in the open ground; however, the most devastating attacks seem to occur soon after planting.

DISEASES

Diseases require a different set of strategies. I have already described root pathogens, which can kill whole plants in an amazingly short time. In addition to these, mildew, fungal and bacterial leaf spots, and various twig blights disfigure plants and reduce their vigor.

TOP: NATIVE CURRANT AS CATERPILLAR LUNCH. **BOTTOM:** TWO APPROACHES TO PROTECTION FROM FOUR-LEGGED FRIENDS: GOPHER BASKETS AND A PEPPER-SAUCE REPELLANT.

Surprisingly, the chemical battles so many glossy ads would have you fight are nearly hopeless in the long term, particularly in a large garden. Chemicals used as drenches against root pathogens, while successful in the nursery, are filtered out by the first inch or two of "real" soil. Foliar sprays that seem manageable on a few small plants become impossibly costly or time-consuming on large groups of shrubs and trees, and they often work, at best, for only a few weeks at a time.

The more effective remedies are nearly all environmental. Start with siting: don't plant sun-loving plants like toyon (*Heteromeles arbutifolia*) where they will be shaded or crowded by larger shrubs or trees. Try to resist the temptation to create solid walls of foliage, and instead provide each plant with ample room to grow. Simple ventilation around exposed foliage is clearly the best protection against any number of fungal and bacterial afflictions.

Elevation of plant crowns, whether within a single planting hole or on larger berms and mounds, can be critically important. This is especially true if the site is level (the most common tract home setting) and water stands on the soil surface during winter rains.

Deep, infrequent irrigation is by far the most effective measure against root pathogens. Putting the water on the soil, not dowsing the plant, reduces the incidence of foliar diseases. Overhead sprinkling, especially of older or crowded plantings, is truly begging for trouble.

For manzanitas, flannel bushes and other plants prone to fungus cankers and other twig- and branch-killing diseases, pruning practices are also important. Never prune such plants during wet weather; this risks invasion of wounded tissues by any of a wide array of pathogens. Also prune precisely, making your cuts near nodes (the points where leaves and side shoots emerge) rather than slashing through leaves and stems.

WEEDS

Weeds—defined by farmers and gardeners as those plants that insist on growing where we don't want them—become a dark obsession for many people. Some are simply untidy, while others, such as foxtail brome, have seeds like little spears that attach themselves painfully to both humans and pets. Still others actually smother garden plants.

So how does one cope? Typically, by rushing out to buy one of the many chemical herbicides found on nursery shelves. Most of these are diluted and sprayed on living foliage. Some are both effective and relatively harmless when applied in open areas, though accidental sprays or wind-drift on garden plants may occur. In tight quarters, they are instruments of mayhem. Hoeing and hand-pulling are far preferable, if a bit more time-consuming, in areas close to garden plants (to eradicate perennial weeds you may have to be vigilant and pull every new shoot that appears, for several weeks or months). More serious caveats concern the use of preemergent herbicides, which are available by themselves or incorpo-

BOTRYOSPHAERIA-KILLED BRANCH ON A LOCAL MANZANITA.

rated in many garden fertilizers. Their purpose is to stunt or kill growth tips of weeds as they emerge from their seeds. This sounds harmless enough, but the same applies to emerging surface root tips of matting shrubs, like the lower manzanitas, and those of many herbaceous perennials. This reduces the potential extent of their root systems, and thus of both drought tolerance and efficiency of nutrient uptake. Remember, too, that the same preemergent effect also applies to any wildflower seeds you might plant. Exceeding the recommended rate, as many gardeners do, usually extends the time these chemicals are active, by a few months to several years (and do not be surprised if the most pernicious weeds return while the area remains a "dead zone" for wildflowers). Even worse, higher concentrations can aggravate the tendency of these herbicides to leach into the upper root zones of established plants, stunting and debilitating them.

The alternatives are surprisingly simple, though they require some attention to timing. Since most garden weeds in California are fall-sprouting annuals, they may be easily plucked or hoed out as young, relatively delicate seedlings in late fall and winter. In large, open areas, they can be mowed occasionally both for appearance and to prevent seeding, then allowed to die a natural death as the ground dries out in late spring. This reduces—though it does not eliminate—future crops but maintains an erosion-resistant cover on bare ground.

As your plants prosper and grow, covering and shading more ground, you will find that weed problems naturally diminish. Many of the most pernicious invaders, like foxtails and other European grasses, need sun and open space to thrive. You may also find that some of your garden natives, like the penstemons and California fuchsias, scatter themselves about and fill some formerly weedy niches with something far more attractive. More deliberately, as you have both inclination and resources, you can plant weedy spaces with attractive native ground covers, like the lower ceanothus, manzanitas, and buckwheats. Reserve the wholesale clearing of ground for the moment when you decide to create a naturalistic meadow or wildflower patch, and save yourself many hours of effort and gnashing of teeth.

PLANTING FOR THE FUTURE

Planting one of our native oaks, a bay laurel (*Umbellularia californica*), or another slow-starting native tree is truly a long-term investment. Most of these are fairly easy to grow but require a decade or two before giving any hint of their potential grandeur. This is where patience and commitment come in. Some spectacular native shrubs and herbaceous perennials, however, quickly run the full course of their lives in the garden. Several popular wild lilacs (*Ceanothus*) flower in their first or second year from cuttings, achieve more or less full size in their third or fourth year, and are already in decline after age six to ten. Penstemons and monkey flowers (*Mimulus*) often produce a dazzling show in their first year but may require frequent hard cutting or replacement (which their own seedlings often provide). A strategic mix of slower- and faster-growing, longer- and shorter-lived native plants will provide both immediate gratification and a chance to watch something more wonderful unfold over time—just as it does in nature. This brings us to a final topic, which involves the culmination of all the efforts I have just described.

Enjoying Your Garden

One of the curious consequences of the American work ethic is that our gardens, too, are often seen as a place to work, not to play. The ground must be kept tidy, free from weeds and litter. Trees and shrubs must be pruned just so, to avoid critical looks from the neighbors. Yet the first flush of bright new growth, the opening and closing of flowers, and the rich shades of autumn all pass us by, while we attend to the things we believe to be more urgent.

I see the native garden as one that invites our presence, as often and as long as possible.

Bursts of growth, the appearance of flowers with their colors and fragrance, the coming and going of birds and butterflies, and even the scrabbling of small animals about the ground are salve for the harried soul—and ones that pass too quickly as the season marches on. Fascinating changes can occur within a few days, whether we are present to witness them or not. And suddenly another spring, another opportunity to be part of something wonderful, is gone.

Once you have assembled a fair variety of plants, with interesting features in different seasons, try approaching them as you might in the wild. Watch for new developments; there will be many. Be alert for visits by new insects, birds, and other animals. If you have done your job well, these will increase over time. If you can enjoy the colors and textures of leaf litter in the wild, why not at home?

As you observe the active life of the garden, you will find yourself noticing both signs of increasing strength and health and signs of distress, usually at a point when you can do something to help. But more than this, you will learn more about the intricate web of life and how it works. It exists in the native garden, just as it does in wild California.

BEAUTY TO SAVOR: IRIS AND FRIENDS AT STRYBING ARBORETUM.

FILLING YOUR GARDEN: PROPAGATION OF NATIVE PLANTS

Having set out to grow the plants of California, you will inevitably want more of certain species or individuals. The expenses of your quest will mount, and before long you will desire an alternative to purchasing every new plant. This is where techniques of modern propagation ride in to the rescue. Not only do they satisfy an eminently practical need, but they can also become an endlessly fascinating pursuit in themselves, one that brings you closer to a basic understanding of what plants are all about. This pursuit is one to which I have devoted a substantial portion of my life, with no regrets.

Propagation, as the term is used here, is nothing more than the deliberate use of natural processes to produce more plants of a particular species, strain, or cultivar. The purposes can be as diverse as enhancing a garden display or revegetating disturbed areas in the wild. The actual techniques I will discuss are the collecting and sowing of seeds, the making of cuttings, and the division of well rooted clumps and mats.

Contrary to popular and even professional myth, California natives are not, as a group, difficult to propagate. Although a few species have proven sufficiently challenging to keep the myth alive, more often several reliable techniques are available to you. Identifying your particular goals will help you select the one most appropriate for each case. How many new plants do you seek? How much effort and material are you willing to expend on the process? What features do you desire in the plants obtained? How much "parent," or original, stock is available, and what is its condition?

COLLECTING IN THE WILD

I have a personal compact with Mother Nature. I relieve her of a few twigs here, a few seeds there. In return, I promise to work diligently to make more of what I have taken and to distribute it generously. If you choose to collect material in the wild, I would urge you to consider a similar arrangement. Let me describe how this works out in practice.

I will not remove whole plants, whatever their numbers—or, for that matter, major por-

---

LEFT: COLLECTING SEEDS IN OCTOBER, HIGH SIERRA. **ABOVE:** SEED CAPSULE OF SPICE BUSH.

tions of any plant. On encountering a plant of particular interest, I look around to see how many others are nearby. If there are none or very few, I will be content with taking a picture. If there are many, a few seeds or cuttings will likely not be missed. In the case of rare plants, I would take *no* material, unless my goal were specifically to help restore a damaged population.

There are also legal issues. National parks and California state parks universally ban collecting of plant material for personal use. Policies of the U.S. Forest Service differ, district by district, but are generally more obliging, sometimes requiring permits. However, a national forest may contain special botanical preserves and study areas that are strictly off-limits to collecting. Private holdings are, of course, subject to the wishes and dispositions of individual owners. In all cases, you are responsible for knowing the regulations that apply, or for asking someone in authority for guidance.

TECHNIQUES OF CHOICE

Let us take a close look at each of the major propagating techniques. I will refer to these repeatedly in later discussions of particular plant groups.

SEEDS AND SEEDING

Seeding offers certain unique advantages. Given the wealth of viable seed set by many plants (sometimes hundreds per pod, with many pods per plant), vast rates of multiplication

may be possible with minimal disturbance either to the parent plant or to the process of natural succession. When one considers this rate, the small bulk of most seeds, and the simplicity of sowing techniques, seeding usually stands out as the most economical among propagating alternatives. I routinely use this method for most native trees (oaks, maples, pines, and bays, for example). It is equally useful for various shrubs, like the snowdrop bush (*Styrax*), and for many herbaceous perennials and bulbs, from penstemons to brodiaeas.

Since, with rare exceptions, no seedling will be genetically identical to the parent, there is always an element of surprise. I often grow a batch of seedlings just to see what might turn up, selecting the most promising as parents for future seedling generations. Seedling variation is also essential for reconstructing a diverse natural population in disturbed areas. Disease- or pest-prone species may acquire genetic resistance through mutation or recombination, ensuring that at least some individuals survive a future blight.

Nevertheless, seeding does have its limitations. Where greater consistency of a specific

AN ARRAY OF SEEDING STYLES. LEFT TO RIGHT: NEEDLE GRASS, A NATIVE SAGE (ABOVE), BUSH POPPY (BELOW), AND PENSTEMON.

feature is desirable—for example, in a hedgerow or formal border—the normal range of seedling variation may be considered too broad. Certain plants like the globe mallows (*Malacothamnus* spp.) tend to produce few viable seeds. Others, for various reasons, germinate slowly or with difficulty. Finally, considerable patience may be required of you for species that take several years to reach a useful size or to produce flowers and fruit.

OBTAINING AND CLEANING SEEDS

Perhaps the most difficult step in seeding is obtaining the seeds. The site where you first admired a plant in bloom may be only a tangle of dried vegetation when you next visit. Perhaps the seeds are already shed, or the pods eaten or filled with insect larvae in place of seeds. Careful observation and timing are critical for seed collection. Once flowers begin to fade, you may need to visit the same site repeatedly—every few days for some

small annuals, every week or two for many herbaceous perennials, and perhaps once a month for large-fruited shrubs and trees. Small plants can be marked with bits of colored yarn or tape. For pods that explode, like those of the lupines, or open widely, spilling their contents, bags of cheesecloth or other small-mesh netting can be tied over the stems, catching seeds as they are released. By the time pods dry and change from green to yellow or tan, the seeds may already be ripe inside.

Extraction is usually the next step. Place the pods or whole flowering stems in paper or other porous bags to finish drying as necessary. Plastic should never be used, since it traps moisture, leading to the growth of molds that can quickly destroy both pods and seeds. Some pods, like those of the columbines (*Aquilegia* spp.), will open like urns or salt shakers when dry and the seeds will pour out. Others remain closed, or nearly so, and these can be crushed or simply rolled between thumb and forefinger to split them along their seams. Hard pods, like those of the penstemons, are crushed with a rolling pin, jar, or other smooth, hard object (not a hammer).

Seeds generally should be separated from pod fragments and other chaff, for organisms involved in decay of the litter can also attack unsprouted seeds and seedlings. There are various techniques. Hand-picking will suffice for small lots. Screens and sieves are useful where fragments of chaff are either much smaller or much larger than the seeds. When all else fails, pour the mixture into a cup or pan, tilt it, and tap it repeatedly from beneath. The seeds, normally heavier than the chaff, should filter to the bottom (though there are plenty of exceptions).

An easy method for extracting seed from pulpy berries, like those of the toyons (*Heteromeles* spp.), involves putting them in a bowl or jar, barely covering them with water, and allowing them to ferment a bit, softening the skins. After thoroughly mashing the berries, swirl the mixture in successive rinses of water, each time pouring off the lighter skins and pulp.

LIVE OAK ACORNS, BUCKEYE SEEDS, MADRONE BERRIES.

STORING SEEDS

The seeds of many natives ripen and are collected during the spring and summer months. Fall and winter, however, are normally the preferable times for planting. Many, though certainly not all, of our natives will germinate only in the presence of both moisture

and cool temperatures, having adapted to a climate with fall and winter rains. Summer-planted seed may sit idle until fall or simply rot away (this is particularly true of plants from the high mountains, like the matting penstemons). Therefore, you will be concerned with long-term storage. Porous bags or envelopes, placed in a cool, dry, shaded spot, are usually ideal for this purpose. Heat, moisture, and bright light all contribute to a loss of viability. Seeds that ripen in fall and winter, in contrast, may—and often must—be planted immediately. Large fleshy seeds, like those of the oaks, deteriorate rapidly in storage.

ASSEMBLING YOUR MATERIALS

While waiting for sowing time to arrive, assemble your materials. Clay seed pans or other shallow pots make ideal containers for small seed lots, while larger plastic or wooden flats are suitable for larger quantities, as well as convenient for sowing smaller batches of several species side by side. Avoid deep vessels. Typically, young seedlings draw water only from the top inch or two of their medium, and the rest of the medium may become soggy and decay, rotting any roots that enter it. Any of a wide variety of porous materials or blends can serve as a sowing medium. I personally prefer commercial potting soils or other mixes that incorporate sawdust or other organic material and sand. To these, I usually add perlite or coarse sand, roughly 25–50 percent by volume. The organic components in the mixture retain moisture, while sand and perlite keep the particles separated, helping to drain away excess moisture and providing better air circulation about the roots.

SEED TREATMENTS

The sowing process can take several routes. In order to germinate, some species need pretreatments that mimic the effects of natural elements. Chaparral species germinate following fires and often have hard, impermeable coats, sometimes further dressed with a

---

TOP: SOME COMMON SEED COLLECTING AND STORAGE MATERIALS. **BOTTOM:** SOWING FLATS AND POTS, MIXES, PENCIL FOR LABELING AND PLASTIC BAG FOR REFRIGERATION.

layer of wax, as in the bush poppy (*Dendromecon*). Larger seeds can be abraded with a file or sandpaper; smaller seeds respond to various heat and chemical treatments. Burning over a seeded area with a layer of pine needles or straw is a traditional method, still used occasionally for plants like the matilija poppy (*Romneya*). If the fire is too hot, though (something often beyond your control), it simply incinerates the seeds. Fortunately, there is evidence that soaking the seeds in an extract of burned leaf litter confers some of the same benefits without the liabilities. (Although commercial extracts are now available, their cost may be unaffordable for small-scale use.) Seeds with heavy wax coats can be shaken first for a few minutes in white gasoline to dissolve the wax, though finding a brand without toxic additives has become nearly impossible. Seeds of redbuds and other shrubby legumes are commonly placed in hot, though not boiling, water (150–160°F is often recommended); they should be taken immediately off heat and allowed to soak overnight to imbibe water.

Although hydrochloric acid has been prescribed to simulate the effects of the digestive juices of animals on the seeds of edible berries, like those of the holly grapes (*Berberis*), I have successfully germinated the same seeds by simply subjecting them to a natural or artificial winter. The latter technique, in fact, is mandatory for some high-elevation natives, and it can assist in the germination of others. Mix the seeds with several times their volume of moist (*not* saturated) sand or perlite, place the mixture in a plastic bag or jar, and store this container in a refrigerator for a few weeks to a few months. Many bulbs—for example, the brodiaeas and calochortus—and some trees and shrubs, like the maples, may actually sprout while still under refrigeration. If this occurs, they should be removed and planted.

SOWING SEEDS

The final sowing is a simple process, though one requiring attention to detail. Fill your chosen container with the sowing medium to one-quarter to one-half inch below its rim, to permit adequate watering. Level it as well as possible (a ruler or other straight object can be useful here). Next, distribute the seeds thinly and uniformly over the surface, to reduce root tangling and give each seedling as much growing space as possible. Large seeds (acorns of the oaks come particularly to mind) may be pressed into the medium, while small ones are better shaken from a folded paper or by hand. I often take a pinch of seeds between

STEPS IN SOWING YOUR SEEDS (LEFT TO RIGHT): SCATTERING THEM ON THE SOWING MEDIUM, COVERING WITH MORE OF THE MEDIUM, TAMPING AND SMOOTHING THE SURFACE.

thumb and forefinger, then rub them out with circular motions. Or they can be mixed with a larger volume of sand or sowing medium and distributed in almost any manner. This is especially valuable for tiny seeds, which are difficult to spread evenly.

Next, barely cover the seeds with more of the sowing medium. The amount varies with the size of the seeds, but it is usually essential that they be surrounded by moist medium until they germinate. If you know or suspect a particular species to be prone to "damping off" (a fungal disease that causes young seedlings to wilt and fold over), a final dressing of shredded sphagnum moss, coarse sand, or very small (under one-eighth inch) diameter gravel will help keep the offending organisms at bay.

Gently water the completed seed flat or pot until it is thoroughly moistened. Too much force or volume will wash the seeds out of their container or into dense clumps around the edge. Finally, label the container to prevent later confusion and set it away in a shady, protected spot to await germination.

The time required for germination varies by species and even individual source plants, from several days to several months. In the interim, keep the surface of the medium constantly moist. Be alert for signs of rummaging by birds and beasts, protecting the containers with netting, if necessary. Once the seedlings appear, the containers may be allowed to dry just a bit (*never* to the point of wilting) between waterings.

When sowing seeds directly into the open ground, as you would for massed displays of annuals, the same general rules apply. Work up the soil well. Either scatter the seeds and rake them in, or push them into the ground. Barely cover them with a light mulch, using straight soil or a mixture of soil and an organic amendment (or gravel, in the case of really temperamental species). Again, the surface must be kept moist prior to germination, and watering should be only gradually reduced as the seedlings become established. Unless you have great quantities of seeds to share, protective measures such as fencing may be necessary against birds, rodents, and insects (or you might let them gorge on more dispensable seeds). A new plot of succulent seedlings is like a beacon, drawing everything that flies or crawls, as I have learned by devastating experience.

Transplanting Seedlings

Unless seedlings are terribly crowded or showing patches of disease, they should remain in the sowing containers until they are firm and reasonably easy to handle, usually

half an inch or more tall. If you want to speed the process along, you can apply a complete fertilizer at about half the strength recommended for established plants. Transplant the seedlings, when they are ready,

The transplanting process: Trimming young roots and planting the seedlings in small pots.

to intermediate containers to prepare them for the open ground. Traditionally, small pots or compartmentalized trays (like the familiar bedding plant six-packs) are used, but your own imagination may suggest many alternatives. Deep, narrow tubes or even old milk cartons are useful for tap-rooted trees and shrubs, reducing the coiling and binding of roots around the edge of the container.

Begin the transplanting process in a sheltered spot, with a good supply of potting mix on hand. I use a medium much like the sowing mix but with a little less perlite. First, moisten the medium; seedling roots are quickly killed by contact with dry soil. Tease the seedlings apart and select stronger, healthier individuals for planting. In the case of trees and shrubs, tip-prune the roots to promote branching (I do this even for tap-rooted trees like the oaks) or cut them back, as necessary, to get them into their new containers without coiling or folding. Herbaceous plants generally do not require this step. If the roots are trimmed severely, tops must also be cut, or the plants heavily shaded and protected from breezes for a few days to prevent wilting. Pot the seedlings, taking care to get the stems upright and not to bury them much beyond the junction of roots and shoots. Gently tamp the medium around the plants, and water them immediately.

Shelter the young transplants well at first. Then gradually expose them to drier air and brighter light until they have filled their containers with roots and are well acclimated to outdoor conditions. A good indication of success is that the plants become physically "harder" and usually bushier. Water them more and more frequently, especially in warm weather. Regular—though light—fertilizing can also be beneficial. One more container stage sometimes provides an added assurance of survival, though there is a wealth of conflicting evidence on this point. Conventionally, a one-gallon can or deep six-inch pot is used. This time, both planting and growing can take place in full exposure—except, of course, for shade-loving plants—if you live near the coast. Covering them with cones of shade cloth or other open-mesh fabric is still advisable in hotter climates.

The final planting-out is the least controllable stage and deserves the most favorable conditions possible. Even if the transplants are established at midsummer, it may be better not to risk planting in the summer heat. Many natives make extensive root growth during fall and winter, and little at other times, making the cool season by far the preferable time for planting. In any case, both the container and the soil of the planting hole should be moist. Dry soil can dehydrate young roots and kill them almost on contact. If the weather is warm, and there are not too many individuals, protect the plants from sun and wind for a few days with cones of newspaper, foil, or other flexible material. Construct small cages of fencing material or netting to discourage animal depredation above ground and baskets of small-mesh poultry netting or hardware cloth below the plants to fend off gophers and moles, if these are a problem for you.

You should take care to plant out your seedlings with their old soil line at or above the grade of the surrounding soil, to prevent rotting of the crowns during wet weather. More disease-prone natives like the flannel bushes (*Fremontodendron* spp.) and blue curls (*Trichostema*) should even be planted on raised mounds. A raised berm of soil, creating a basin for watering, is useful in summer but should be knocked down promptly with the arrival of autumn rains. Your plants will thank you for attending to these bothersome details, by thriving and becoming more beautiful with each passing year. In time, you may find that tinkering with seeds becomes a fascinating pursuit, far beyond its original purpose.

VEGETATIVE METHODS OF PROPAGATION

Now let us turn our attention to vegetative methods of propagation, which make use of stems, leaves, roots, and specialized vegetative structures such as bulbs and corms. The primary advantage of propagating from these parts is consistency, though it is also useful for those few species or individuals that simply fail to set appreciable quantities of viable seeds or for those whose seeds are difficult or very slow (in some cases taking two years or more) to germinate.

The plants that result from vegetative techniques are genetically identical to the parent plant. Within the limits imposed by climate, soils, and other cultural factors, they will faithfully express the parent's individual traits. Over the years, I have stumbled on many individuals, ranging from trees to herbaceous perennials, that had some special feature not shared by their neighbors and seemed (at least in my eyes) worth preserving for garden use. It is for these that I regularly employ vegetative techniques. Let us consider the alternative methods of cuttings, layering, and division.

CUTTINGS

Cuttings are simply lengths of stems, usually with some leaves attached. Properly treated, they form roots and shoots, becoming whole new plants. Propagation by cuttings is usually the least injurious to the parent plant and may even assist in its rejuvenation. Cuttings work on a wide assortment of plants, woody or herbaceous, though success often requires judgment developed through careful observation and occasional disappointment. This technique is particularly appropriate for many-branched shrubs, like the currants and wild lilacs, and for a variety of leafy perennials like the penstemons, buckwheats, and many perennial daisies.

First Steps

In taking material from a parent plant, you should have in mind a clear image of the final cutting. The model for many plants will be a portion of a shoot from the current or just-completed round of growth, still in a relatively active state. It will normally include at least two—often four or five—nodes, or points of attachment of leaves or side branches. While the shoot tip may be soft and pliable (this portion will be cut out if necessary), there should be some fully expanded leaves, and the base should be firm, though preferably not yet "barked over." Cuttings in an overly soft state are often lost through wilting of the tops or shriveling at the base (a common cause of failure with the ceanothus, for example). If shoots seem too soft and watery, simply revisit them when they have matured a bit—or take a knowing risk, if a return visit is impossible. Overly hardened cuttings may yield few survivors simply because of a lack of active tissue.

A VARIETY OF PREPARED CUTTINGS, SHOWING THE PORTIONS REMOVED.

If possible, each cutting should have a definite node at the base, as this is often the site of greatest rooting activity. Some cuttings will produce roots only at this site. Finally, and perhaps most importantly, all portions of the prospective cutting should be in obvious good health, neither yellowed nor showing dead spots or other sign of disease. Under moist propagating conditions, even apparently minor health problems can quickly lead to decline and death of the cutting, for fungi and bacteria multiply at an astonishing rate. This is strikingly true of dryland plants like the shrubby sages (*Salvia* spp.) and flannel bushes (*Fremontodendron* spp.). It is also best to choose only the most vigorous plants as source material, unless you are making a desperate attempt to salvage a treasured specimen.

Now, picture yourself standing before the parent plant, sharp knife or pruning shears in hand (dull instruments will crush or shred tissues, reducing your chances of success). This may be an opportunity to improve the shape or structure of the plant, through judicious pruning. Wherever branches are congested or cross at awkward angles, selective removal will expose the remaining shoots to more light and air. Otherwise, take only a little more than you need for the final cutting, and make each cut just above a node. In woody plants, at least, the cut stem will heal faster and resist fungus invasion better than one left with a large stub above the node.

Next comes the question of storing the cutting material. If you are tramping the wild, far from home, you can preserve cut shoots in a healthy state for several hours or days by storing them in sealable plastic bags. If storing for longer periods, pour water daily into each bag, agitate to rinse the shoots, then pour off the excess. If water is not available, blow into the bag and seal it quickly; this provides at least a humid atmosphere for the cuttings and reduces dehydration. Place the bags in as cool and shady a spot as possible, preferably a cooler. If you have no option but to store them in a backpack, make sure they are protected from being crushed by heavier objects. It is wise to rinse the cuttings daily, both to freshen them and to remove spores of pathogens before they germinate.

Materials

When you arrive at home, assemble some shallow pots, seed pans, or flats, as described in the preceding section on seeding, and an ample supply of a medium at least as porous as that used for seeding, perhaps a bit more so. Coarse sand works, but propagating-grade perlite, mixed with 10–25 percent screened peat moss (by volume), is preferable and now readily available in retail nurseries.

Rooting hormones speed up the process but are seldom essential. Weak formulations (for example, 0.1–0.3 percent indole butyric acid or its equivalent) serve nicely for

softer, more juvenile shoots. Stronger concentrations (as much as 1 percent indole butyric acid or equivalent) are useful for harder, more mature stems. The powders and liquids commonly available in retail nurseries are quite weak, while potent blends available from grow-

CUTTING MEDIA, CONTAINERS, ROOTING HORMONES AND SHEARS.

ers' supply houses are usually offered only in packages large enough for several thousand cuttings. You might consider a cooperative purchase with friends.

Examine the collected shoots again for disease and physical damage, especially if they have been carted around for several days, and discard any questionable pieces. Assemble your materials in a shaded spot, free from strong drafts, to minimize dehydration while the cuttings are exposed. Fill your pots or flats with cutting medium, pack it lightly, and gently moisten it.

Preparing the Cuttings

You are now ready to prepare the cuttings. Remove soft shoot tips that might wilt under propagating conditions, from both the main shoot and side branchlets. Make a cut just below what is to be the bottom node. If the cutting is a side shoot of a larger branch, you can pull it away with a "heel" of older stem attached, trimmed as necessary for easy planting. Cut large leaves partway back, to avoid wilting and to get a reasonable number of cuttings in each container without crowding, which can quickly lead to problems with disease. Cut or strip leaves and branchlets from the portion to be stuck in the medium (it should be one-half to one inch long), taking care not to damage the stem. Now dip the base end of each cutting in the rooting hormone, if it is being used. Make a hole or slot in the medium, and plant the cutting just deep enough to keep it upright when watered, lightly tamping the medium around it. As each pot or flat is filled, gently water the cuttings and set them away in a lightly shaded spot where they are protected from drying winds.

The cutting medium should never dry out, nor should it be kept saturated, a state that will quickly lead to fungal rots. Finding the right maintenance state for your conditions may require some experimentation (and perhaps some losses during your first attempts). The tops of larger, more recent cuttings should be sprinkled lightly at least every day or two, more frequently if they begin to wilt. If signs of disease develop, remove the diseased cuttings immediately to prevent infection of the rest.

Completing the Process

Avoid the temptation to check frequently for roots. Each time a cutting is lifted, bits of callus (the soft, irregular tissue that generally precedes the roots and performs similar functions) and incipient roots may be torn off. However, resistance to a gentle tug is a fair

---

LEFT TO RIGHT: DIPPING A CUTTING IN ROOTING HORMONE, DIBBLING A HOLE IN THE MEDIUM, AND PLANTING THE CUTTING.

indication of rooting activity. When most or all of the cuttings resist even a moderately firm tug, or when roots emerge from the drain holes of the container, you can begin a staged withdrawal of protection similar to that described for seedlings. Each change should be made in moderate weather, and you should be ready for a quick retreat if signs of wilting or scorching occur. Transplanting through a series of container sizes and the final planting-out should be handled largely as it is for seedlings. The difference is that most rooted cuttings, especially large-leaved shrubs like the currants, will be larger and easier to handle than typical seedlings. Often they can be planted in larger containers and proceed more quickly to the open ground.

A few variations on the cutting theme are worth noting, though you might make only occasional use of them. Root cuttings are successful for an odd assortment of plants—chaparral pea (*Pickeringia montana*) and the willows (*Salix* spp.) come to mind. In this case, accessible sections of roots, usually of pencil thickness or more (enough to have substantial nutrient reserves) are dug and laid out horizontally in flats or pots. They are then covered

shallowly with cutting or potting medium and kept moist until new sprouts appear. Stouter sections may be shallowly planted directly in the open ground.

RELATED TECHNIQUES

Some shrubs, while difficult to propagate by conventional cuttings, can be handled successfully by *layering*. Here, branches that are sufficiently long and flexible are pegged to the ground. Shallow notches are cut in the appropriate nodes, and the branches are covered with soil or potting mix. If the pegged branches remain healthy, they produce roots and shoots. The resulting plants may be dug and replanted elsewhere in the open ground.

Under protected conditions, *air layering* can be a useful technique for trees and shrubs (I have been tempted to try it with some favorite oaks, but have somehow never put thought into action). Notch the stem at what you intend to be the basal node, then tie a bag or pot of porous medium around the node and a few inches of adjacent stem, making sure to keep it moist. This aerial technique has the advantage of avoiding the introduction of soil pathogens into wounded tissues.

DIVISION

Division is the simplest of the techniques I will describe here, requiring only a little care and a sharp knife, trowel, or spade. Plants amenable to this technique include many clumping, herbaceous perennials (erigerons are a good example), some matting shrubs that take

SUCCESS! TRIMMING ROOTS ON A WELL ROOTED CUTTING, TRANSPLANTING TO A SMALL POT.

root as they travel, and various suckering trees and shrubs, like the dogwoods (*Cornus*).

Most failures using this technique can be traced to excessive water loss and the subsequent collapse of plant tissues. Choose a period of cool or at least mild weather to do your work. High heat and drying winds can be devastating to newly divided plants. If possible, avoid times of particularly rapid, succulent growth, as plants in this state are highly prone to wilting. Water the plants well before division.

Approach the plant to be divided and determine where it is rooted into the ground by feeling about the base. Some plants root freely wherever they touch the ground, especially under moist conditions. Others, including apparently broad clumps and mats, may spring from a narrow base, or even a single trunk or taproot. For these plants, try seeding or cuttings instead of division. To divide a plant, carefully dig and lift it, keeping plenty of roots intact. Look for branching points where groups of shoots can be separated easily. Cut or pull each section apart into successively smaller—still amply rooted—pieces until you arrive at the desired size and quantity of divisions.

Next, cut back large, leafy tops or shoots that have few roots attached, to minimize water loss. It is also wise to soak, or at least rinse with clear water, the pieces you have obtained. If you are dealing with disease-prone or otherwise delicate plants, trim any ragged tears to promote faster healing.

The final step of replanting the divisions should be tailored to their particular size and condition. Pot and protect those with few or small roots, much as you would young seedlings. In most cases, you can replant strong, well rooted pieces directly in the open ground. Water them regularly until they are well established, then gradually wean them to the regime practiced with the parent plant.

TOP LEFT: CANDIDATES FOR DIVISION: *HEUCHERA* HYBRID, *FESTUCA*, *ANTENNARIA*. **RIGHT, TOP TO BOTTOM:** PULLING THE PLANT INTO ROOTED SECTIONS, POST-DIVISION SECTIONS, PLANTING THE DIVISIONS INTO SMALL POTS, AND LABELING.

Bulbs, Corms and Tubers: A Special Case

Division is an especially important technique for propagating bulbous, cormous, and tuberous plants. Applied to brodiaeas and other really prolific "bulbs," it permits multiplication rates that approach those of seeding, with only a short wait for first flowering. It is preferable to mark the plants in growth or bloom and dig them while they are dormant, usually in late summer or early fall. Assuming that foraging rodents have left you something to divide, simply pull away individual bulbs, corms, or tubers at their natural points of division. Depending on the size and condition of your new divisions, they may be replanted in the open ground (with ample protection against foraging birds and rodents) or grown on for a season or two in pots.

PARTING THOUGHTS

Don't be surprised if propagating native plants becomes a new passion in your life. With subjects so infinitely varied as the California natives, there will always be new problems to solve and new variations on the cycle of rebirth and growth to witness. At the same time, remember that success is never guaranteed. Be ready to try new approaches following every failure, and to tinker with every detail. This is what the art of successful propagation is all about.

A FEW OF
MY FAVORITE THINGS
· ·
THE TREES

ODE TO AN OAK

. . . .

Genus: *Quercus*
Family: Fagaceae, the Oak or Beech Family

Oaks are not mere elements of a wild California landscape, even major elements. Rather, they *create* a landscape and give it character. The shade they cast and the water shed beneath their canopy generate habitats for whole communities of plants and animals. Their branches are resting and nesting spots for birds and homes for many other creatures. And their vast annual crops of acorns are one of the great food bonanzas for everything from deer down to the lowly seed weevil.

Oaks are no less impressive from a human perspective. Seen from a distance, they weave whole tapestries with clouds and ribbons of deep green set against the spring greens or summer gold of open hillsides. At close range, we marvel at their massive trunks and contorted forms. Their wonderfully textured bark and clean, often shiny leaves, frequently more beautiful still in fall color, capture our fancy. And of course, they provide welcome shade from a relentless summer sun for the foot traveler—sometimes the *only* shade for miles around.

Inviting an oak into the garden is another matter, and one that poses some troubling questions. Yet with a careful choice of site and species, nearly everyone interested in making a native plant garden can enjoy at least one of the oaks at home.

COMMON FEATURES

The oaks are prominent members of the beech family, Fagaceae, which, scattered over much of the globe, also includes the familiar beeches (*Fagus* spp.) and chestnuts (*Castanea* spp.). The oaks themselves (genus *Quercus*) constitute up to six hundred species, the number still a subject of debate and continually swelling as new discoveries are made. They are well distributed around the Northern Hemisphere and into South America. California boasts but nineteen species, yet they are vastly more important than this figure would suggest, given their sheer numbers, size, and familiar presence.

Oaks occupy and often dominate an amazing range of habitats. You will find them occasionally sitting on coastal bluffs and forming large tracts of woods nearby. In the coastal valleys—wherever they have not been shoved aside for building sites

LEFT: MIXED OAK WOODS, HENRY COE STATE PARK. **ABOVE:** FRAMEWORK OF TRUNKS, VALLEY OAK. **PRECEDING PAGES:** BLACK OAK (*QUERCUS KELLOGGII*) IN THE SANTA LUCIAS.

or agriculture—they are at their most magnificent, reaching great heights and breadths. They line the banks of streams throughout the state. In conifer forests, they often define the forest margins or are scattered in a middle story, with smaller trees and shrubs beneath. As one approaches the high peaks and desert edges, they become shrubby and low, sometimes forming impenetrable thickets.

Their numbers and distribution have been drastically affected by human activities. First came the clearing of slopes and valleys for grazing and the harvesting of oak wood for construction, furniture, and firewood. More recently, oaks have been removed by the millions simply to make way for increasingly dense human habitation. While it is still not difficult to view healthy populations of most species in the wild, a few, like the southern scrub oak (*Q. dumosa*), may soon survive only in tiny, protected islands of open space.

Botanically, the California oaks occupy three subgenera, commonly called the white oaks, black or red oaks, and (for lack of a better term) the "intermediate" oaks. Even for the nonbotanist, these categories help to make sense of the many forms one finds in the wild and to suggest the parentage of abundant natural hybrids.

Physically, the oaks include some of our most massive trees, with heights of up to one hundred feet and even greater spread; several of more modest—though still substantial—proportions; and shrubs of many sizes and shapes, in some cases hugging the ground. All are strongly woody, with one to several sturdy trunks from the base. Different individuals of a

given species can show remarkable variation in branching patterns, often due to the conditions under which a tree begins life. In the shade of other, taller trees, many oaks produce a single trunk that reaches up until it finds a break in the canopy, then begins to form a "head" of spreading branches. Given more exposure, multiple trunks will form at an early age, leading to the spreading, graceful forms we humans so admire. Whatever the overall pattern, events such as drought and insect attack, not to mention the basic inclinations of the trees themselves, often lead to a continual overtaking of dominant shoots by their side branches, making the branches twist and turn in unpredictable directions and giving each tree a unique and interesting silhouette.

There is much more to admire. Each branch is covered by distinctive, often beautiful bark. That of the white and "intermediate" oaks is usually

TOP: NEW LEAVES IN SPRING, CALIFORNIA BLACK OAK. **BOTTOM:** BLACK OAKS IN AUTUMN, ELK MOUNTAIN.

pale gray and somewhat rough even when young, becoming more textured as the trunk or branch expands with age. The black oaks have smooth (or nearly smooth) gray to brown younger bark that darkens and develops vertical fissures and often smaller horizontal "checks" as it ages.

Oak leaves are distinctive and beautiful as well. The species known collectively as "live" oaks are essentially evergreen, hanging on to one season's leaves at least until those of the following season are in place, and sometimes for two full seasons. Others are deciduous each fall. A few, like the common black oak, *Q. kelloggii*, have fall colors approaching those of the eastern oaks in brilliance (though fiery scarlets are rare). Still others are autumn-deciduous in wetter years but may drop their leaves earlier in response to drought, thereby gaining protection from further dehydration. Drought-stressed blue oaks (*Q. douglasii*), for example, are sometimes leafless by late summer.

Leaf details vary widely both among and within species, and occasionally even on the same tree. Oak leaves may be less than one inch long in some of the shrubby species, or up to six inches long in the black oak. Leaves produced in the shade are often much larger than those facing the sun, even on the same tree. Their surface varies from smooth and shiny, at least on the upper surface, to densely hairy and dull. They are of simple oval form in the live oaks and some scrub oaks, with or without visible teeth or bristles along the margins. Others are reminiscent of the leaves of eastern oaks, with deep, pointed to rounded lobes (recent immigrants from the other coast will recognize these immediately as "real" oak leaves).

Watching the annual cycle of oak leaves is always a treat. As the shoots emerge in spring, they are tightly clustered and often felted with dense, soft hairs. Sometimes they are also highly colored, showing bronze or pink to red shades that change continually as they expand. The newly expanded leaves are often highly lacquered and bright green, darkening and becoming somewhat duller as the season advances. I have already mentioned fall color, which can be—though it is not always—breathtaking. Even after they have fallen, the leaves make beautifully patterned carpets on the ground.

I suspect that few people think of oaks as having true flowers, though of course they do. Indeed, in spite of their small individual size and lack of petals, they can be quite showy, appearing in spring with or just preceding the new leaves. The sexes are separate, though on the same tree. Male flowers are borne in catkins that may hang from the stems like little strands of beads; they may be painted in bright pink to copper shades, complementing the yellow of the abundant pollen, which blows freely on the wind. The female flowers are small buttonlike structures with dense cups of tiny bracts. These develop after wind-pollination into the familiar nuts we call acorns, which consist of a roughly torpedo-shaped shell around

TOP: LIVE OAK IN FLOWER AT THE INDIANS. BOTTOM: ACORNS ON A LOCAL LIVE OAK.

the actual seed and a much-expanded basal cup. The acorns of most of the black and "intermediate" oaks need two seasons to develop, while those of the white oaks are shed in their first fall. In either case, they create vast stores of food for a great variety of animals (and sometimes humans), while their interesting shapes and attractive tan to mahogany shades make them appealing in dried floral arrangements. Producing a bountiful crop seems to take a toll on the trees; often the following season's crop is quite meager.

LIVING WITH WILD OAKS

The first thing I see when I awake in the morning, and the last before I fall asleep on a moonlit night, is the arching tracery of an old live oak that nearly surrounds the rear corner of my house. It has made good days even brighter and provided comfort in times of trouble, always there like a beautiful painting to behold. This is probably the best one could ask of an oak. I have simply enjoyed it, avoiding any attempt at cultivation save the occasional trimming of a branch that scrapes the roof. Seedlings appear all around the yard. I confess to removing some of them to clear the way for others to grow. Local deer seem to find my garden shrubs much more interesting fodder, though they attack young oaks with relish elsewhere.

This, or something like it, may be a familiar refrain to those of you fortunate enough to have found a place in the country among the oaks, and furthermore to have avoided that all-too-common temptation to thin or remove them to "create a view." (What better view *is* there than that of the gnarled trunk and graceful canopy of an oak?) You will find it hard to improve aesthetically on Nature's arrangement of oaks in the landscape, except perhaps

to carve out a small plot for a garden. If it seems a bit too shady, simply try removing a strategic limb here and there, rather than an entire tree.

Unfortunately, vast numbers of oaks are removed in the building process, without any thought of the future, simply to make access and movement of equipment more convenient or to cut costs. Another practice nearly as destructive is the piling of soil around oak trunks, whether to create a level surface or to dispose of waste. This and the deliberate compaction of soil within the drip line (canopy edge) of the trees interferes greatly with the drainage of water and flow of oxygen about the roots and often leads to attack by a variety of fungus pathogens, of which oak root fungus (*Armillaria mellea*) is one of the most virulent. By the time its clusters of golden mushrooms appear, the battle is probably lost. Your role as a responsible homeowner is to insist that these practices be avoided during the construction process, and to inspect work as it progresses. If you stumble upon a still-living oak with a partially buried trunk, it is worth all you can afford to arrange for careful excavation.

Building also frequently leads to elevation of the terrain

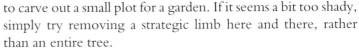

AT HOME WITH AN OLD OAK.

surrounding existing oaks, leaving large wells in which water can accumulate for weeks at a time in winter. Either cut channels for drainage or regrade the area, if you value your oaks.

Finally, recognize that the very existence of healthy oaks is evidence of their success in an all-natural setting. Avoid the temptation to fuss with them, and particularly to provide extra summer irrigation or applications of fertilizer. Branches that invade a living space or threaten damage to a costly structure should be trimmed only during dry weather, to avoid fungus invasion before the cuts have healed. The removal of large broken limbs requires careful attention, both for your own safety (oak wood is hard and heavy) and to avoid ripped and shredded surfaces.

The issue of planting under oaks is often raised, for it also poses a potential threat to established trees. Nothing that requires regular or even moderate garden watering should be considered within the drip line of your trees. Each irrigation in the heat of summer is an invitation to the growth of pathogenic fungi, which are kept at bay primarily by drought. However, a walk in almost any oak woods should tell you that many options are still available. If you feel you must blanket the ground with green, native blackberries (*Rubus ursinus*) and exotic ones, like *R. calycinoides*, revel in summer-dry shade. Our native iris (whose spring flowers—need I say?—are among the most glorious of our wildflowers) can fill the same role en masse, though each plant may spread only two or three feet. Heucheras like *H. micrantha* and *H. maxima* enhance such a display with their attractive foliage clumps and exquisite tiny flowers. More structural effects may be had from shade-tolerant bunchgrasses like *Festuca californica*. As medium to taller understory, the currants and gooseberries (*Ribes*) are beautiful shrubs, offering the bonus of breathtaking floral displays in late winter and spring. Mahonias fill a similar role. There are many more such choices, some of them described in this book.

You will need to make decisions about "acceptable risk" in watering. Most of the understory plants mentioned here will look more presentable, especially by late summer, with occasional deep irrigations. In most cases, once a month, avoiding times of extreme heat, should not be life threatening to the oak above them, unless large areas of solid planting are involved.

Uses and Culture

Given the construction practices outlined above, plus the increasing prevalence of large, fully cleared subdivisions, you may well arrive at a scene devoid of oaks and want to grow them. This is not difficult at the outset, but there are several issues you should ponder, the alternative being considerable frustration and perhaps the premature death of perfectly good trees.

First, how do you want to use the trees? Given the sheer size and elegance of many native oaks, it makes sense to plant just one as the dominant feature of a front or back yard. Only where you measure your space in the hundreds, rather than the tens, of feet can you hope to achieve the effect of a small oak grove. And only then, too, would the most massive of the oaks, like valley oak (*Q. lobata*), be appropriate, even as lone individuals. Others, like the coast live oak (*Q. agrifolia*), are not only smaller but more easily controlled by pruning, at least in their youth. Some of the shrubby forms of otherwise larger oaks, like *Q. chrysolepis* and *Q. wislizenii*, are nearly ideal trees where space is limited. They can be pruned as youngsters to encourage a more treelike form—if that is even desired (you may find them perfect just as they are). Finally, there are the true shrub oaks, which may be used in place of other large to medium-sized foliage shrubs, at far lower cost in terms of water, fertilizer, and pruning. Each of these has its own distinctive features, though you will need some patience to raise young seedlings to presentable size.

An important function of any oak, beyond ornamental use, is to encourage the presence of wildlife. Oaks provide not only cover but also abundant food for a great variety of animals, from insects to the birds and mammals that eat them in turn. Squirrels, mice, and other small creatures feast on the acorns in fall.

The culture of deliberately planted oaks, like the benign treatment of existing oaks, invites forbearance rather than the continual care showered on bedding annuals and many perennials—the only exception being at the outset. It is important to select a species that will tolerate the conditions of the site. For example, black oak (*Q. kelloggii*) would be a poor choice for a flat yard that remains waterlogged most of the winter. Valley oak (*Q. lobata*), which revels in just such conditions, would be similarly inappropriate for an exposed, rocky bank. The oaks are similarly variable in their tolerance of shade and of extreme heat.

If you are purchasing a plant, rather than growing your own, you should give extreme care to its selection. Only strong, obviously healthy plants should be considered. If possible, gently tap the plant out of its container and examine the root ball for large, tightly coiled roots; these should lead to automatic rejection, for reasons laid out below. Unless the plant is quite large (unlikely) or your garden is devoid of deer, rabbits, wood rats, and field mice (only slightly more likely), you should also purchase some small-mesh wire poultry netting, and perhaps some stakes or rods, to fashion a protective cage around the trunk.

Now you are ready to plant. The kind of amendment, with sawdust and other materials, often suggested to remedy poor soil drainage for smaller plants will be of only temporary use for a tree whose taproot will rapidly descend to a depth of thirty feet or more, far beyond the amended column. Planting sensitive species on raised berms is useful simply for preventing the collection of water about the crown. It is particularly important, if your plant is coming from a nursery container, to make your hole deeper than the length of the roots, and to gently unwind coiled roots if possible; those that remain coiled will simply form larger, tighter knots of wood as they expand, unable to support the weight of the mature tree or shrub. Unfortunately, unless the plant is very young—in its first or second year—cutting heavy roots is not a viable remedy. The cut roots will heal slowly or not at all, and the plant may be quickly lost.

Take care not to bury the existing base of the plant; so doing can easily lead to fungus attack. Build your protective cage to a height of at least two feet around the plant to discourage gnawing by rabbits and rodents, or cage the entire plant if there are deer about.

New plants should be watered whenever the soil begins to dry out, possibly every week. As roots extend out and down, this schedule may be reduced, though each watering should be sufficient to provide a deep soaking. Assuming that you have not chosen too thirsty an oak for your conditions, it will be able to fend for itself by the third or fourth year. While it is becoming established you should continue to protect at least the base of the trunk from animal attack.

What else is there to do? Unless your soil is truly impoverished (as evidenced by poor color and growth on most common garden shrubs), little or no supplemental feeding will be necessary or desirable, except perhaps during the first year or two, and then only to maximize the rate of growth and promote rapid establishment. If the plant as you found it was poorly formed (particularly if a single trunk was run straight up a nursery stake), you might do a bit of occasional, light pruning to encourage a more natural formation of trunks and branches. Otherwise, it is hard to compete with the artistic talents of Mother Nature.

It seems odd even to speak of pests among the oaks. Rather, every tree is a large habitat (one might say hotel and cafeteria combined), with many creatures living on and in it, being eaten in turn by other creatures, and so on up the line. Few of them seriously damage the trees, though the fastidious gardener may be driven slowly mad by all the essentially unstoppable activity. Of those that actually feed on the oaks, many are sucking insects, like aphids, treehoppers, scale insects, and whitefly. The sap that exudes where they have punctured stems and leaves with tiny beaks rains down more or less continually on objects like parked cars and is difficult to remove. Twig girdlers burrow inside young stems, often killing them. Tent caterpillars (furry) and oak moth caterpillars (smooth and striped) can sometimes skeletonize large branches and whole trees, eating the leaves to the hard midveins. They seem to have a particular fondness for coast live oaks. Other caterpillars, some of which become very beautiful butterflies and moths, do far less damage. Waging biological warfare with preparations of *Bacillus thuringiensis* is sometimes effective on small, easily sprayed trees. However, it results in the death of *all* kinds of caterpillars, both "good" and "bad."

California's oaks have complex relationships with the fungus world. Mycorrhizal fungi envelop the roots and greatly extend their reach, possibly even warding off attack by disease-producing fungi. They occur naturally in the soil where oaks are present and can successfully colonize even isolated plantings, given generally healthy soils (the scraped subsoil left behind in many newer developments is unfortunately not "healthy" in this sense, lacking the organic matter to support fungus growth). Of the pathogenic fungi, only a few are of real concern, and their control is mainly preventive and environmental. I have already described the promotion of *Armillaria* and a few other virulent root pathogens by burial of the trunks. The decay of heavy wood mulch also favors them, particularly under excessively moist conditions. There are also fungi such as the bracket fungus (*Inonotus* and others), which attack the wood above ground, rotting and killing the branches. These often enter through open wounds left by large cut and torn branches. The wounds themselves are easy, at least for a tree surgeon, to dress and seal when they first occur.

Powdery mildew can deform young shoots and cover them with white "powder" (the fruiting bodies). In this case infected shoots can simply be cut out behind the visible infection and destroyed; they are usually few in number. Fungus leaf spot diseases seem to come and go with wet and dry years but have mostly cosmetic effects.

All that said, a "new" fungus disease, first noticed in the mid-1990s and apparently spreading in several Bay Area counties, is potentially lethal to huge numbers of oaks in California. Popularly known as sudden oak death disease, or SOD, it is caused by a previously unidentified species of *Phytophthora*, possibly though not certainly introduced into California. Its symptoms include the oozing of dark sap on oak trunks, wilting of new shoots, and ultimately death of entire trees. The same organism causes lesser symptoms, from leaf spots to twig dieback, in other trees and shrubs, including madrone (*Arbutus*), huckleberries (*Vaccinium* spp.), and bay laurel (*Umbellularia*). Its primary modes of transmission are still a matter of debate. Pending better information, anyone living among healthy oaks should take all possible measures to avoid assisting the spread of the disease. Some common recommendations include not using oak firewood from unknown sources, buying oak seedlings produced only within uninfested areas, and disinfection of shoes and clothes after hiking in areas with dead and dying trees.

Finally, it must be admitted that most of the larger oaks are somewhat untidy in their habits, more or less continually raining down spent leaves, bits of sap, and of course quantities of acorns in the fall. The litter that accumulates provides habitat for an amazing variety of small creatures and beneficial fungi. It is also a valuable mulch, whose only bad feature is a bit too much acid for some plants. This can be addressed by occasional dressings of ground seashells or other mild lime. When siting an oak tree, try to visualize its mature breadth. Either plant it where it will not overhang a driveway or other "clean" area, or resign yourself to frequent sweeping unless, like me, you are happy with a more "natural" look.

PROPAGATION

Surely you will have heard the verse "From the humble acorn a mighty oak tree grows." One might suspect, from seeing the paucity of oak seedlings around established trees, that there is something inherently difficult about growing oaks from seeds. Actual experience with gathered or purchased acorns paints quite a different picture, however. It turns out that, nearly throughout California, both domestic livestock and—following the slaughter of preda-

tors—unnaturally high populations of deer, feral pigs, and other animals not only harvest most of the acorns produced but eat nearly every seedling at an early age. Those that evade the first wave of predation may be girdled as they form more substantial trunks.

One has a choice of two basic strategies, neither of them particularly exotic, to follow in rearing oaks to a self-sustaining size. Both begin with the step of gathering small numbers of acorns in fall from beneath a healthy tree or trees, examining the shells for the exit holes of acorn weevils, which usually indicate that vital parts of the seed inside have been eaten. A further sorting can be accomplished by placing the acorns in a large bowl or pan of water, then discarding those that float (usually, though not always, the undamaged acorns sink, while the partially eaten ones float).

At this point you may choose to plant your acorns directly in the ground, allowing the taproot that emerges to drill down as deeply as possible during its first season. You might even plant two acorns in the same spot, to allow for early mortality and nonviable seeds. Each acorn should be barely covered with soil, to provide enough moisture for germination. The drawback to direct planting is that the acorns or young seedlings may be attacked and eaten almost immediately by mice and other animals. Building a small cage (at least a foot high to allow for the first season's growth) to protect each plant will greatly enhance its chances of survival. If winter rains fail to keep the soil moist, an occasional deep watering is also important.

YOUNG LIVE OAK SEEDLINGS IN DEEP TUBES.

Some acorns, like those of the coast live oak, will sprout as soon as moisture is absorbed; others, like the black oak (*Q. kelloggii*), need a more extended winter chill to break embryo dormancy. Once the seedlings are up, continue their protection, and do not let the soil about them dry out too severely; usually a deep watering every two weeks or so will be adequate in their first summer, unless they are in a hot, exposed site. Once they reach the limits of their first cage, you may need to build another, taller one, though if deer are absent, just unfolding the top of the first cage to protect the first foot or two of young stem may by enough.

An alternative technique, used in commercial nurseries, is to start the acorns in narrow, deep (often one- to two-inch by eight- to twelve-inch) cartons or other containers. Those with embryo dormancy, particularly those from high elevations, may be refrigerated for one to two months in plastic bags of moistened sand, perlite, or similar medium before planting. It is important not to let the fleshy taproots coil around the sides or bottom of the container.

Once they are established, plant the stronger seedlings in the ground, with care to excavate a hole as deep as the length of the roots, or deeper. The base of the stem should be more or less level with the new soil. With luck, this step will occur in the first fall following planting, and some early effort will be avoided (you can delay it as needed simply by transplanting to larger containers). A well grown tree will reward you with rapid growth, each year considerably faster than the last for several years, and early branching and development of a pleasing shape.

Species of Interest

Let us have a closer look at the features of individual oak species in California, segregating them roughly into trees and shrubs.

The Trees

Quercus agrifolia. Coast live oak (black oak group). Of the many blessings I have enjoyed as a lifelong "country boy," I would have to count life among the live oaks as one of the greatest. In fact, it is difficult to conceive of their absence. In spite of habitat removal on a vast scale, they persist, filling canyons of the coastal hills, making dark green patches on meadowy slopes, and even joining the redwoods and Douglas firs where their shade is not too dense. They are widespread in the Coast Ranges from Mendocino County to Baja California.

This is typically a medium-sized tree, growing twenty to eighty feet high, with sturdy, arching to widely spreading trunks and profuse smaller branches that may reach down to touch the ground. The bark is smooth and dark to pale gray, even silvery on trees well exposed to sun and wind. It eventually splits into vertical bands and ridges with narrow horizontal checks. Providing a thick, billowy canopy are masses of dark, shiny leaves. These are roughly oval

Q. agrifolia in flower, Santa Barbara Botanic Garden.

bare, rocky slopes, at elevations of up to 6,000 feet. The plants stump-sprout to make small colonies. These may present themselves as thickets of upright, white-barked trees up to fifteen feet high or as broad, low mounds and mats. They are truly a wonderful sight when they light up otherwise bare slopes with pink, orange, and red shades in fall.

Oregon oak is a stately tree for the spacious country garden and large commercial landscapes. However, it may be too robust for the rest of us. Brewer oak, in contrast, while slow to get started, is well within scale for the typical garden. In hotter areas both will need either more protection or more irrigation than blue oak and others, though they are otherwise content with minimal care.

Q. kelloggii. California black oak (black oak group). This is a truly grand tree for every season. In winter it shows an elegant fountain of main branches issuing from its sturdy trunk, and often nearly horizontal tiers of secondary branches spreading from these, all covered in blackish bark. In spring, as the young shoots emerge, there is a wonderful interplay of pink to scarlet and pale green, while the male flower tassels glow golden yellow in the afternoon light. Later it carries a rich cloak of large, dark leaves. And when fall comes to the mountains, it creates great puffs of gold, sometimes with a bit of orange and scarlet thrown in for good measure.

Q. kelloggii in fall color, Lake County.

California black oak is found from Oregon to nearly our southern border and from the outer Coast Ranges—away from the immediate coast—to the Sierra Nevada, at elevations up to 8,000 feet. It can grow to over eighty feet in height, though it is usually considerably less. It often has a single, upright trunk when young, slowly branching to form a broad crown. The bark is quite dark, smooth at first but becoming divided as the trunks and branches expand into deep, narrow ridges. The leaves are deciduous, up to six inches long, with deep, sharply pointed lobes. They are often painted in rosy shades as they emerge, becoming deep green as they expand. Even more stunning are the golds and occasional oranges and scarlets they adopt in fall. And there is still more to delight us: The showy male catkins of spring are up to three inches long, while the acorns are up to one and a half inches long and barrel-shaped, with conspicuously large cups. They have the best flavor of any California oak acorn.

This is surely one of the most beautiful of all California trees. While its ultimate size will be a concern for many gardeners, I have seen whole populations of very moderate scale; you might be wise to collect your acorns from beneath such trees. Also, for any given height, black oak tends to occupy less horizontal space than several other species. It prefers reasonably well drained soil but is a notably adaptable tree.

Q. lobata. Valley oak (white oak group). As badly as the coast live oak has suffered at human hands, the plight of the valley oak is even sadder. As its common name implies, it finds its home in the valleys of California, where ample water collects (or used to collect) in winter to percolate and nurture its deep roots through the long, dry summer. It is these very valleys, of course, that are most tempting to modern developers. Even where there is secure open space, regeneration of this species from remaining older trees has been hampered by browsing, foot traffic, and other factors yet unexplained.

Valley oak occurs naturally from the North Coast Ranges to the San Fernando Valley. In deep, fertile soils it can rise to as much as one hundred feet in height, and exceed that figure in spread. This is a truly majestic tree, with massive trunks up to four feet thick and arching branches that may reach down to touch the ground. Every tree is differently formed, and symmetry is a rare feature. The older bark is thick, with sinuous vertical fissures and irregular horizontal checks, the younger bark satiny; the wood beneath is tan to yellowish. Each year there is a fresh crop of two- to four-inch leaves with deep, broad, rounded lobes. When expanded they are deep green and nearly smooth above, light green and distinctly fuzzy beneath. Fall color is not one of their great virtues, though some pleasing soft yellows may appear among the dull greens prior to leaf drop. The acorns are up to two inches long and broadly conical in outline, with rounded, very knobby cups.

Bark detail on Q. *lobata*.

I believe that anyone occupying former valley oak habitat and having sufficient space (it need not be the maximum quoted above) should plant at least one or two individuals of this great tree, in part to restore the extensive habitat it offers for birds and other wildlife. Gardeners with small lots should probably not consider it, however. Where soils are deep and the water table not too low, the valley oak is quite drought tolerant. Yet it can also stand actual inundation during times of winter flood (don't let this happen in summer!). All in all, it is a wonderful tree to have and behold, if the practical obstacles can be overcome.

Q. tomentella. Island oak (intermediate group). I have admired this oak both in the wild and in botanic gardens but have never had an opportunity to grow it. Still, it deserves mention, just in case you find acorns or seedlings available. This is one of the "intermediate" group, along with canyon live oak. It is found on Santa Cruz and other islands off our southern coast, in canyons and on slopes.

Island oak may have one or several trunks from the base and forms an attractive rounded head, twenty-five to forty feet high at maturity. The older bark is made up of broad, thin gray-brown scales, reddish brown where the inner bark is exposed. The leaves, reminiscent of those of the tan oak (*Lithocarpus densiflora*), are evergreen and leathery, up to four inches long, roughly pointed-oval in form but conspicuously toothed, with a deep, featherlike pattern of veins. They are deep green and softly shiny above, lighter and covered with soft tan hairs beneath. Acorns, which ripen in the second year, are up to an inch long, broad and rounded, with shallow cups.

Island oak is showy enough and of sufficiently moderate size to have wide appeal among gardeners, particularly in the south. It thrives under more moist and protected conditions than most of the mainland oaks and may not be a good candidate for the Central Valley. Its ultimate hardiness is unknown.

Q. wislizenii. Interior live oak (black oak group). This is a close relative of the coast live oak, taking up residence where that species leaves off and even hybridizing with it where their ranges overlap. It is found from Siskiyou County in the north to Ventura County in the south, from the foothills of the Sierra to the Coast Ranges, and at elevations from near sea level to 5,000 feet. Like coast live oak, it occupies many different sites, from wooded canyons to open valleys and slopes. In its typical variety, *wislizenii*, it is a dense, full tree, thirty to over sixty feet high. It has attractive smooth, gray bark, which darkens and develops irregu-

Q. wislizenii **in flower.**

lar fissures in age. The head is rounded, often broader than tall, and well filled by one- to three-inch-long evergreen leaves. These vary in outline from lance-shaped to broadly oval, are noticeably flatter than those of *Q. agrifolia*, and may be with or without marginal teeth or bristles. Their surface is dark green and shiny above, usually lighter but equally shiny beneath. Though small (one to two inches in length), the male catkins can be quite showy in spring, with bright blends of orange or red and yellow. The acorns, which ripen in the second year, are up to one and a half inches long, narrow and pointed, with rather deep, rounded cups.

The variety *frutescens*, often found in open chaparral, is shrubby and considerably smaller (usually six to twenty feet), with shorter, sometimes stiffer branches, but it otherwise closely resembles the typical variety.

Interior live oak is a beautiful tree for the garden. By taking care to select acorns from populations of smaller trees, one may have plants adaptable even to the smaller garden, with a bit of judicious pruning. This is a rugged tree, enduring considerable drought, heat, and even cold though requiring reasonably well drained soil in order to thrive. The variety *frutescens* might be an even more satisfactory plant for smaller gardens, if it proves equally easy to grow. However, there is little experience with it outside botanic gardens.

SHRUBS AND "UNDECIDEDS"

Q. berberidifolia. Scrub oak (white oak group). This is the most common and widespread of the shrubby oaks, found from Tehama County in the north to Baja California in the south, and in the Coast Ranges, Transverse Ranges, and Sierra Nevada foothills, in both chaparral and open woods. Many of us have known it as *Q. dumosa*. Under a recent taxonomic scheme, however, that name was restricted to plants occurring only in coastal southern California.

Scrub oak is an extremely variable shrub, a result of both genetics and circumstances. It grows three to ten feet high and is nearly round to widely spreading in form. It can be quite dense or rather sparse and awkward, with long stiff "arms." The bark is smooth and gray, or even silvery in exposed sites, showing its white oak alliance. The leaves are evergreen and leathery, broadly oval in outline or expanded near the tips. They may be strongly or barely toothed, slightly lobed, or smooth-margined. They are deep green and shiny above, gray-green, dull, and somewhat hairy beneath. The acorns are one-half to one inch long, broadly pointed-oval in form, with rounded cups.

Q. berberidifolia **laden with acorns.**

Scrub oak is often more useful for habitat restoration than as a garden ornamental. However, there are whole populations of attractive, well formed shrubs in the wild, which could easily provide suitable material to grow. This is a tough, adaptable shrub, best in sun, with reasonably well drained soil and occasional to no watering once it is established. It is often subject, in its northern locations, to extreme cold and should be one of the hardiest of the evergreen oaks.

Q. durata. Leather oak (white oak group). This is almost a signature plant of the serpentine soils of California, not only found there in abundance but often dominating the landscape. Its typical variety, *durata,* occurs in the Coast Ranges, well away from the immediate coast, from Trinity County to San Luis Obispo County and in portions of the northern Sierra foothills. The similar variety *gabrielensis* is found on non-serpentine (granitic) soils in the San Gabriel Mountains of southern California.

Spring flowers on *Q. durata.*

Leather oak varies from about three feet to (rarely) almost ten feet in height and is often broader than tall. This is a closely branched shrub, with short, stiff branches and smooth, pale gray bark similar to that of *Q. berberidifolia.* The branches are often nearly hidden by masses of leathery, evergreen leaves one-half to one inch in length. These are oval in outline, rolled down and toothed along their margins. Their surface is dull green, gray-green or yellowish green above, lighter and densely hairy beneath. Masses of bright yellow male catkins can create a striking display in spring. The acorns are up to an inch long, broad and pointed, with rounded, knobby cups.

Leather oak is a shrub some will like instantly, while others will dismiss it as too plain. The unusual coloring and dull surface of its leaves are a bit startling to those who associate the oaks with deep and glossy greens. However, it is not difficult to blend the leather oak with more dramatic shrubs in mixed plantings. The slow early growth of the seedlings requires some patience, though this characteristic makes the species a natural candidate for bonsai. Otherwise, it is a tough, undemanding shrub, well able to make the leap from its unusual native soils to the garden and delighting in any sunny, reasonably well drained site. Plants from at least the northern locations are extremely cold-hardy.

Q. sadleriana. Deer oak, Sadler oak (white oak group). Your first encounter with this unusual shrub is likely to leave you baffled. It *must* be some oak relative, but what? Sadler oak is endemic to the Klamath Mountains of far northern California, where it is found in broad thickets on open slopes and as an understory shrub in conifer forest. It grows from three to perhaps eight feet tall, often with greater spread. Several trunks angle out from a common base.

The leaves are three to occasionally six inches long, thick and evergreen. They are roughly oval in outline with neat rows of deeply set veins and teeth along the margins, much like the leaves of chestnuts (*Castanea*). Their surface is deep green and shiny above, paler beneath. The acorns are less than an inch long, nearly triangular in profile, with nearly hemispherical cups.

This is a most attractive shrub, probably best in light shade. I have grown it without trouble in the nursery but never in the garden. I would not expect it to persist in areas with chronically hot summers. It is nearly sure to require well drained soil. All that said,

Q. sadleriana.

coastal and mountain gardeners might find it a surprisingly easy plant to grow, well worth some experimental effort.

Q. vaccinifolia. Huckleberry oak (intermediate group). Huckleberry oak is always a treat to encounter in the wild—unless you are attempting to thrash your way cross-country with backpack and gear. It is a common and sometimes dominant plant of mountain chaparral, occurring from the Siskiyous to the south-central Sierra at elevations of 3,000 to 10,000 feet. Often it takes root in the fissures of bare granite slabs. Usually growing no more than five feet high (a result, in part, of annual beatings by snow), it may spread to ten feet or more, making low mounds and mats. The leaves generally resemble those of the closely related

canyon live oak (*Q. chrysolepis*), though they are smaller and never strongly toothed. They are basically pointed-oval in outline, leathery and evergreen. The upper surface is dark green and shiny, while the lower is gray-green, usually with scattered hairs. The new shoots are particularly beautiful, emerging lacquered and painted in shades of bronze to scarlet. The acorns, which ripen in their second year, are short (about half an inch), quite fat and rounded, with short scaly cups.

Huckleberry oak is a most attractive shrub, for foliage and mounding form. I have grown it without difficulty, though not in my own garden (a lack

Q. vaccinifolia **in the Trinity Alps.**

that should be remedied soon). It thrives on the coast and obviously in the mountains, with well drained soils and moderate to occasional watering. In hot-summer areas I would expect it at least to require shading and more frequent irrigation, though it may not thrive even with these measures.

MADROÑO

. . . .

Genus: *Arbutus menziesii*
Family: Ericaceae, the Heath Family

Each year in late October, I venture out to nearby mountains in search of seeds and berries. This is my time to renew old acquaintances with some of my favorite colonies of trees: valley oak, bigleaf maple, and most of all, madrone—or, as the Spanish called it, madroño. In the particular gathering I have in mind, every madroño is of a different size and shape, with contorted branches and bark that peels in jigsaw-puzzle patterns; large, almost tropical-looking leaves; and masses of decorative fruits that suggest small round strawberries. I have passed many pleasant hours simply wandering among the trees and contemplating their spectacle.

Madroño is a wanderer. Its range extends in a north-south line from San Diego County to British Columbia, and you are equally likely to find it in the deeper folds of chaparral-covered hills, oak woods from the coast to the Sierra, open flats, or shady coniferous forests, sites representing a wide variety of soil types. All of this suggests that it should be one of our easier native trees to grow. Unfortunately, that is often not the case.

COMMON FEATURES

Madroño's form is plastic, very much molded by its environment. In open flats and swales it is relatively short and stocky, often with multiple trunks nearly to the ground. As a forest tree, in the shade of taller conifers, it reaches for the light, with one or a few slender trunks snaking upward as much as a hundred feet. The trunks are fascinating for both their sinuous patterns and wonderfully smooth, satiny, cinnamon-colored bark. This bark peels away in papery curls to expose patches of pale tan to greenish underbark. Only near the base do we find the sort of dark, roughened surface one expects of the bark of trees. Beneath this thin shell lies some of the hardest, densest wood to be found among our native trees.

The foliage is equally distinctive. Loosely set near the ends of the younger shoots are oval leaves up to six inches long (occasionally more), dark green and often shiny on their upper surface, pale and grayish beneath, giving the tree the appearance of a giant rhododen-

MADROÑO IN FRUIT, SANTA LUCIA MOUNTAINS.

dron. Older leaves drop more or less continuously but most heavily in fall and winter, making beautiful carpets of mixed tans, earthy pinks, and pale yellows. In spring or early summer the branches are adorned with small white or pinkish urn-shaped flowers, arranged in broad pendant clusters at the shoot tips. These have a sweet, almost honeylike fragrance and can perfume the air many feet away. Following their brief show come roundish berries a quarter to half inch in diameter, with odd puckery skins, which take on orange to scarlet hues by fall. The berries are edible but too bland to excite the palate. Depending on the force of early storms and the arrival of waxwings and other hungry birds, the berries may have vanished by mid-November or persist into the new year.

Uses and Culture

The question is, what does one *do* with such a tree? Like several of the oaks, madroño is a tree of character, valuable for its distinctive form and textures. Also like the oaks, it is amenable to pruning when young, in the event gardeners feel they must give it their own personal brand. Heavy cuts on older trees are much riskier, healing slowly and providing points of entry for disease. Then there is the matter of litter from leaves, bark, and berries. Planted in the front yard of a typical tract home, under the scrutiny of fastidious neighbors, a madroño would surely try the patience of any gardener. For larger quarters with a little protection from sun and wind, however, it can be a beautiful addition. As in nature, it mixes harmoniously in the landscape with oaks and other larger trees. Gardeners who are enchanted by its appearance but short on space might try it as a sort of giant bonsai, in a large container. Certainly in the nursery it tolerates considerable binding of roots, though hard root-pruning, should this become necessary, might be less successful.

"Unpredictable" probably best characterizes madroño's performance in cultivation to date. As with the more familiar manzanitas and blueblossoms, susceptibility to disease is the main limiting factor, for otherwise the plant is vigorous and fairly adaptable. Madroño has well documented relationships with mycorrhizal fungi, which assist in uptake of nutrients and may provide physical or chemical defenses against root pathogens (though this is still a matter of debate). In any case, the problems that plague it in the landscape seem relatively rare in nature, except in times of severe stress. Combining a hot, exposed location with frequent summer irrigation nearly guarantees its demise, for this practice promotes the growth of several virulent root-rotting fungi. A sheltered spot among other trees and weaning by the second season to a regime of deep, infrequent irrigation (near the coast, perhaps even none) offer the plant at least a decent chance of success.

Madroño seems to have broad tolerance for various soils and climates, though it is said to resent the salty or alkaline conditions that prevail in many populated portions of southern California.

Propagation

Madroño is one of the easiest of our native trees to start from seeds, and seeding has been the primary means of its propagation. A high proportion of the seeds are viable, and several are contained in each berry, so there is no point in collecting more than a few berries unless you intend to cover a hillside. Simply pick them after they have developed

full color and begun to soften—
usually by mid-November—or
gather fallen berries from the
ground. Mash them by hand or
roll over them with a glass or coffee cup, then swirl the resulting
pulp in a pan of water; the seeds
will tend to settle to the bottom,
and you can easily pour away the
lighter debris. Plant the seeds,
barely covered, in a well drained
medium and keep them moist
until they sprout. The young seedlings are quite small, but they grow
rapidly and can easily be a foot or
more tall by the end of
the first season, if you
successively transplant
them as soon as their
roots fill the container.

Damping-off (sud-
den wilting or folding
over of previously
healthy seedlings) can

be a problem with younger seedlings if they are overcrowded,
poorly ventilated, or kept too moist. Avoiding these conditions is the most effective remedy you can provide. Larger
plants in containers should be shaded during summer's blast
to hold down root temperatures.

Vegetative propagation—particularly by cuttings—has
some exciting possibilities, permitting the selection of indi-
vidual clones for disease resistance, smaller size, fruiting characteristics, and other desirable
features. Although this is one of my own fantasy projects for the future, I am unaware of
anyone now employing it commercially. Other, more popular species and hybrids of *Arbutus,* however, are routinely propagated in this manner; they tend to root slowly but are not
difficult to handle.

COUNTERCLOCKWISE FROM TOP: MADROÑO COLONY IN THE WILD, NEW SPRING GROWTH,
DETAIL OF BARK.

THE SHRUBS

IN PRAISE OF THE WILD LILAC

. . . .

Genus: *Ceanothus*
Family: Rhamnaceae, the Buckthorn Family

Some of my brightest moments with native plants involved the ceanothus, or wild lilacs, and the great drought of 1976–77. Ceanothus were among the horticultural stars of that period, eagerly sought for their spectacular performance under parched conditions. A few brash enthusiasts, myself included, combed the wilds for horticulturally promising forms and rushed to market with new selections. Gardeners' memories of that drought quickly dimmed, and interest in the ceanothus faded with them. The longer though less severe dry period of the 1980s did surprisingly little to revive that interest. Nonetheless, a few isolated cultivars, like Carmel creeper (*C. griseus*, formerly var. *horizontalis*), entered the horticultural mainstream and are currently used in vast numbers in commercial landscapes. Others have gained at least a small and enthusiastic following. The present may be an ideal time to judge the horticultural value and limitations of this group, for we have now seen them through many more years of cultivation and some wild extremes of weather, including lesser droughts and historic deluges.

COMMON FEATURES

Those of you who prowl California's back roads in spring and summer will recognize the ceanothus as prominent, often spectacular members of the chaparral and coastal scrub communities that together span much of the state. You probably have also found them to be a confusing and variable lot. Botanically, the genus falls into two large groups, providing at least modest assistance in sorting out the species. The subgenus *Ceanothus* includes plants with relatively slender and flexible branches and alternate, usually thin-textured leaves. The subgenus *Cerastes* includes plants with mostly stout, rather rigid stems and generally opposite, thick-textured leaves (though there are, of course, puzzling exceptions in both categories).

Within each group, the species range in size and shape from low mats to multitrunked trees as much as twenty-five feet tall. Whatever their height, most spread widely, sometimes at an alarming rate. Branching patterns vary from narrowly erect through gracefully arching to trailing or stiffly prostrate, and from sparse to quite congested. Smooth, pale bark is an additional feature of several species.

Leaves in the subgenus *Ceanothus* range from nearly round to linear in outline. They also vary in surface from flat to deeply veined or warty, smooth and shiny to densely hairy. Leaves encountered among the *Cerastes* range from narrow to broadly oval or wedge-shaped, and they are often conspicuously toothed. The flowers, usually tiny but carried in incredible profusion, are arranged in clusters that vary from small buttons to large branched plumes

---

LEFT: *Ceanothus cuneatus* in March at Pinnacles National Monument. **preceding pages:** *Carpenteria californica* 'Elizabeth' at Santa Barabara Botanic Garden.

(*thyrses*, in botanical terms). The blossoms are also interesting at close range, boasting colored sepals; slender-stalked petals with broad, cupped tips; and conspicuous stamens. Flower colors include some of the richest blues and purples of the plant world, though they also extend to azure, lavender, pink, and snow white. Often there is a glittering contrast between white to maroon floral bracts and the flowers themselves.

After the flowers have faded, small, hard, rounded seed capsules, often with odd horns or ridges at their summit, develop in their place. The capsules are frequently shiny and tinged with red and can be decorative in their own right. As they dry, they often rupture explosively, flinging the seeds for several feet in all directions.

USES AND CULTURE

The ceanothus have had many uses in the landscape over the years, and they might have still more, were it not for their wandering tendencies and certain cultural quirks that I will discuss shortly. The most treelike species and hybrids are dramatic features of large commercial landscapes. With care, some can be adapted for use as small trees in home gardens. Plants of medium height are often grouped in large bank and hillside plantings, creating breathtaking spectacles in spring. Potentially, these are also the plants of most interest to home gardeners. Unfortunately, their moderate height is often coupled with a most immoderate spread. The same is true of many low to prostrate species and hybrids. Although these are among the

most beautiful of all the large-scale ground covers, they need, at the very least, frequent pruning to be contained in small home gardens. The development of smaller-scale selections is a fertile field for hybridizers interested in this group, but few have taken up the challenge.

Whatever their size, the ceanothus blend beautifully with many other native shrubs and perennials, and with plants of other Mediterranean climates as well. The rich, deep greens of their foliage are set off nicely by the grays of various manzanitas, shrubby sages, and the Mediterranean rockroses. The vivid blues and violets of their flowers are even more stunning when cast against the yellows and golds of the flannel bushes (*Fremontodendron* spp.), daisies both native and exotic, and California poppies.

This brings us to questions of culture, beginning with the prospects for paring down the scale of normally rambunctious plants. As you will find in the descriptions that follow, response to pruning varies by species and even by individual cultivar. A few simply refuse to be bound, responding to each cut with several feet of new growth. Others, notably *Ceanothus impressus* and its presumed hybrids, have tissues that mature quickly and regenerate poorly

---

C. MARITIMUS 'LEISER'S DARK BLUE', RANCHO SANTA ANA.

after damage of any sort. Happily, a fair number respond well to occasional cutting, at least in the short run, provided that one avoids cutting into older and heavier stems. An ideal strategy for these plants is to pinch out shoot tips during active growth and to thin out the younger branches each year for better lighting and ventilation of the remaining shoots. You should by all means avoid hard pruning during the rainy months, when unhealed wounds may be invaded by fungus pathogens that kill stems or even entire plants.

Susceptibility to disease determines still more basic cultural requirements and is primarily responsible for the reputation of the ceanothus as temperamental and short-lived. Though most will grow luxuriantly for a time in heavy soils with abundant watering and fertilizing, these conditions usually lead to an early demise as the plants are overtaken by root-rotting fungi. The more closely you can approach their natural setting of lean, well drained soils and the more you can restrict summer watering to occasional, deep soakings (assuming that the plants are established through at least one rainy season), the greater your success is likely to be. Gardens in coastal communities are particularly favored spots for the coastal species and their hybrids, which account for most of the cultivated ceanothus. Moderate summer temperatures keep soil fungi at bay and reduce the need for summer irrigation. Gardeners in hotter interior valleys face a special problem with coastal selections, which tend to be the thirstier ceanothus; yet satisfying their thirst tends to encourage lethal high-temperature root rots. Summer problems can be offset to some extent by planting on mounds and berms and by mulching around the plants with bark and clippings to reduce surface temperatures.

Further issues relate to climatic adaptation. *Ceanothus griseus* and some other strictly coastal species seem to resent high heat. Even if the plants evade fungus pathogens for a time, they are often stunted and off-color under consistently hot summer conditions. Some of these same plants are sensitive to cold, particularly to temperatures below 15–20°F. It is wise to know some rough hardiness estimates for particular selections in advance and to compare these to your own rock-bottom winter lows.

Given even the best of conditions, many ceanothus decline after five to ten years in the landscape. They may pile up on themselves, suffocating their own lower branches. Older stems may lose their leaves and die, leaving increasingly distant tufts of live shoots atop unsightly "brush." At some point it is preferable simply to replace overaged plants. For this reason, the ceanothus have been roundly condemned by those who feel that "permanent" is necessary to the definition of a shrub. Personally, I accept their frailties in the same way I do those of some showy herbaceous perennials, like the penstemons. If one can enjoy such beauty for even a few years, why feel betrayed when the show is over? All this being said, some ceanothus are genuinely long-lived.

No discussion of the ceanothus would be complete without a frank admission of their attractiveness to browsing mammals, particularly deer and rabbits. They are an important food source for these animals in the wild, though damage is usually confined to the young shoot tips. The lush, soft growth encouraged by the gardener's generosity, however, sometimes results in one's favorite plants being stripped almost to the ground. Some very effective repellants are now available and easy to use as foliar sprays; country gardeners should employ them regularly. Apart from these nibblers, a few insect pests like aphids may be a temporary nuisance on new growth but are not difficult to banish. Scale insects are sometimes a more serious affliction of *C. griseus* and its cultivars, particularly when they become overly congested.

PROPAGATION

The ceanothus are strikingly variable in nearly every feature of interest to gardeners. Unusually beautiful forms are sometimes discovered in the wild, and some crop up as garden volunteers. For these reasons, most plants used for ornamental purposes are maintained as specific cultivars through vegetative propagation. Cuttings provide the most practical method, for they can be taken at almost any time, assuming they can be adequately protected from dehydration. Current or just-completed shoots are used, and usually only mild rooting hormones are called for. Dehydration can be minimized by making cuttings only during the cooler months and by placing them in a shaded, wind-protected spot. Though rooting takes a little longer under these conditions than in a heated greenhouse, the outcome is far more predictable.

Where seedling variation is acceptable, propagating from seeds is technically easier and more economical. Watch the fruits closely as they ripen and capture the seed before their capsules explode. If this is impossible, you can tie a bag of cheesecloth loosely around a seeding branch to collect the seeds. Once collected, the seeds are generally stored until fall, then planted as the weather cools.

To begin the planting process, immerse the seeds in a cup of hot water, then allow the mixture to cool and sit overnight, to soften the seeds' hard coats and make them more permeable to moisture. Then you can plant them outdoors in pots or flats of a well drained medium, taking advantage of winter's cold nights to stimulate germination.

Plants propagated by either common method should grow quickly and can be transferred quickly to successively larger pots (*never* allow them to become rootbound) until either their size or the time of year is appropriate for planting out in the garden. Like many other natives, they become established more quickly and require less intervention if they are planted as the weather cools in fall. Root and, in many cases, shoot growth continue throughout the winter.

SPECIES AND HYBRIDS TO TRY

When examining a group as large and variable as the ceanothus, it is easy to become mired in confusion. While no organizing scheme is entirely satisfactory, I use three rough size-and-use categories here to help keep our subjects straight. Since a majority of species belong to the subgenus *Ceanothus*, I will note only the exceptions (i.e., those belonging to the subgenus *Cerastes*) in what follows.

TREES AND LARGER SHRUBS

No firm boundaries between trees and shrubs exist among the ceanothus. Even the largest plants have multiple trunks, and most are closely branched. Given different cultural conditions, their size and shape varies remarkably, even for plants of a single clone. With careful thinning and shaping, the largest plants will eventually become picturesque small trees, somewhat resembling little oaks. Hedging and tip-pruning encourage more stems and more congested foliage, which in turn may lead to premature leaf fall and slow decline of the shaded branches. The shrubbier plants work well in loose rows as screening shrubs, although again, overcrowding should be studiously avoided.

Ceanothus arboreus. Catalina ceanothus. This plant is found on Santa Cruz, Santa Rosa, and Santa Catalina Islands off the southern coast. Growing as much as twenty-five feet tall, with stout, shapely trunks, it often resembles a small live oak—except, of course, in spring, when its flowers create breathtaking clouds of lavender to blue or occasionally white. The foliage is also distinctive. Leaves are up to three inches long, quite broad and rounded at the tips; they are nearly smooth and medium to pale green above and covered with whitish wool beneath, giving the entire plant a grayish cast. The flower clusters are closely branched and up to six inches long. Catalina ceanothus has proven fairly adaptable to heavy soils and reasonably heat-tolerant, though widely variable in cold hardiness. Some of my own selections from Santa Cruz Island in the 1980s were damaged significantly at 20°F. Others, like the venerable 'Trewithen Blue' in England, have fared much better. A spectacular and nearly indestructible garden hybrid that reputedly combines this species with *C. griseus* is 'Ray Hartman', described below.

C. 'Blue Buttons'. This hybrid of uncertain parentage was introduced long ago by the Rancho Santa Ana Botanic Garden. It is rigidly branched, becoming a sturdy small tree up to twelve feet high, with equal or greater spread. The leaves are small and dark, forming a thin veil over the purplish younger twigs and light green older branches. In midspring the plant is covered with small, round clusters of light blue flowers.

'Blue Buttons' has thrived for many years in a variety of settings, with moderate to occasional summer irrigation. It survived temperatures in the low teens in December 1990. Like *C. arboreus*, it is most attractively displayed as an individual specimen tree, its picturesque form well exposed. Unfortunately, this is one of many fine cultivars that received only a lukewarm reception and now is difficult to find.

C. 'Frosty Blue'. This is one of my personal favorites among the many introductions by the Rancho Santa Ana Botanic Garden. It is an almost spherical shrub-tree, up to twelve feet high and wide. The leaves are up to an inch long and closely set. They have a glossy, crinkled surface, deep green in color. Its most distinctive feature, for which the plant is named, is the glittering contrast between the white bracts of the bud clusters and the bright blue flowers, which are borne profusely in midspring.

'Frosty Blue' has been a reliable, garden-tolerant ceanothus. It is easily pruned to expose the graceful, smooth-barked trunks, or even lightly sheared for a denser effect. Somehow it captured the public fancy only briefly, mostly in the late 1970s and early '80s, though it has never faded altogether from view.

C. 'Gentian Plume'. One can hardly avoid a mixture of admiration and disdain for this garden hybrid. Despite being sparsely branched and given to rampant, weedy growth when young, well grown larger specimens have gracefully arching trunks up to twenty feet tall. The leaves are exceptionally large, broad, and wonderfully shiny. Though somewhat sparse in bloom, its branched clusters may reach ten inches in length, loosely set with brilliant gentian-blue flowers.

C. **'Gentian Plume', flowering branch.**

Planted as a garden specimen, 'Gentian Plume' has shown reasonable tolerance of heavier soils and summer watering. However, its cultural limits are not well tested, for it has been grown only sparingly since the late 1970s.

C. megacarpus var. megacarpus. Bigpod ceanothus. Subgenus *Cerastes*. This species much resembles a tall *C. cuneatus* (described below), even mingling with that species in the mountains of Santa Barbara County. It is visually distinguished, however, by its more erect habit, attractive fissured bark, and larger flowers. It grows around twelve feet tall, with arching trunks. The thick, oval to wedge-shaped leaves, up to one inch long, are often alternately set along the stems rather than opposite, as in most of the other *Cerastes*. Individual flowers measure as much as half an inch across. They are white overall with large, dark centers and have a powerful honeylike scent. The bold red-tinged pods that follow are also decorative.

The variety *insularis*, found on Santa Cruz and Santa Rosa Islands, is more distinctly treelike, with a spreading canopy. It has generally larger, mostly opposite leaves. Plants of both varieties are attractive overall but have a somewhat "wild and woolly" look that may not endear them to the more fastidious among us. Although country gardeners try them as rugged small trees, their more common use, like that of *C. cuneatus*, is for bank and slope cover, erosion control, and wildlife forage. Their garden tolerance and ultimate cold hardiness need further testing.

C. 'Mountain Haze'. This was a popular garden hybrid from the 1950s to the 1970s. Since then it has faded slowly from view, owing less to its performance in the landscape than to its rampant youthful growth, which makes it difficult to handle in the nursery. It is dense and nearly round in form, quickly reaching its mature dimensions of six to ten feet by eight to twelve feet, even more in fertile, well watered ground. The roundish inch-long leaves are dark green in color, crinkled but shiny on the surface. In most locations, the lavender-blue flowers are freely produced in long (to six inches) branched clusters; however, this cultivar can be oddly reluctant to bloom in fertile soils.

'Mountain Haze' is a fine specimen shrub for the commercial landscape, where its rapid early growth is a valuable asset. Keeping it in bounds for the average home landscape may be a struggle. It has shown excellent tolerance of heavier soils and summer watering, as well as heat and some drought.

C. oliganthus. As originally conceived, this was a southern species, common from San Luis Obispo County almost to our southern border. With the recent incorporation of the former *C. sorediatus*, it can now be said to cover nearly the length of the state, usually dotting mountain slopes.

This is a stout, bushy shrub, growing from five to fifteen feet high, with stiff green to reddish stems. The leaves are about an inch in length, dark and

C. oliganthus var. *sorediatus*.

conspicuously veined, with pale, hairy undersurfaces. The flower clusters are one to two inches long and colored deep to pale blue, purple, or lavender. The typical variety, *oliganthus*, has redder stems and hairier leaves than the more northern variety, *sorediatus*, though the two are otherwise quite similar. Both, wherever they occur, have some strikingly ornamental forms. They have performed well, given at least reasonably well drained soil and careful summer watering, in several botanic gardens. However, they remain almost unknown in private cultivation.

C. **'Ray Hartman'.** Gardeners even passingly familiar with the genus will recognize this plant, reputedly a hybrid of *C. arboreus* and *C. griseus,* as *the* common tree-form ceanothus in private and commercial landscapes. The plant begins life as an erect, somewhat arching shrub, then thrusts out rapidly in all directions to as much as twenty feet. Its leaves are lush and attractive, suggesting the *C. arboreus* parent in shape and size but more polished on their upper surface. In spring, the stems droop under their burden of large, branched flower clusters. Pink bud-scales are intermixed with bright blue flowers to give an overall impression of glowing lavender. A large plant in full bloom is a truly breathtaking sight.

'Ray Hartman' can require careful and frequent pruning (which it tolerates well) to be kept in scale, even as a tree, for the smaller home landscape. Yet it is in all other respects one of the most satisfactory ceanothus hybrids ever discovered. It has proven itself in heavy soils with summer watering, high heat as well as winter cold to 10–15°F, and some drought. You can see it spectacularly combined with hybrid flannel bushes (*Fremontodendron* spp.) in bank plantings along Bay Area highways.

C. **'Sierra Blue'.** For many years one of the most popular large ceanothus, 'Sierra Blue' is a hybrid reputedly involving *C. cyaneus.* Certainly it exhibits some of that species' best features. The plant is nearly erect in habit, quickly reaching a height of at least ten to twelve feet, with similar spread. Smooth green bark provides a generally youthful appearance. Still more striking are the highly polished, oval leaves and profuse spring clusters, each up to eight inches long, of bright true-blue.

'Sierra Blue' is cast most frequently in the role of specimen shrub in both commercial and home landscapes (the latter with frequent pruning). Like 'Ray Hartman', it tolerates a broad range of garden conditions and has proven one of the better hybrids for southern California.

C. **thyrsiflorus.** Blue blossom. This familiar ceanothus roams the coastal hills and valleys from Santa Barbara County to southern Oregon, changing character and hybridizing with other species to produce a confusing and fascinating array of forms.

Blue blossom is commonly encountered as a round to nearly vase-shaped shrub or smooth-barked tree, ranging from four feet to over twenty feet tall, with equal or greater breadth. The stems of recent years' growth are smooth and green, forming an attractive backdrop for darker green leaves of variable size, shape, and spacing. These are often quite shiny on their upper surface. Compound blossom clusters, two to sometimes four inches or more in length, held on even longer stalks, transform a plant into a cloud of pale to deep blue, occasionally even white, for several weeks each spring.

Whatever its guise, blue blossom is one of our most ornamental native shrubs. Its taller forms may be adapted, through various degrees of pruning, to both smaller and larger landscapes. Its attractive trunks are easily shaped and exposed as desired. Lower forms may be individually displayed or grouped as a billowy cover for large open spaces. It is reasonably long lived and tolerant of a broad range of soils and watering regimes (in hot-summer areas it requires supplemental irrigation for good health). Although the species is considered most at home near the coast, various selections have endured both searing heat and freezes of 10°F.

Two cultivars occupy the largest size category. 'Millerton Point' was popular in the 1970s and early '80s, following its introduction by the Saratoga Horticultural Foundation, though it is little known today. It is treelike in form, with a round, full crown of shiny foliage, growing to at least nine feet tall and twelve feet broad. The plant is wreathed in spring with large clusters of white flowers. 'Snow Flurry', selected by Joseph Solomone, has long been my personal favorite among white-flowered ceanothus. It is of widely variable size, depending on cultural conditions. The lacquered foliage forms a beautiful backdrop for masses of snow-white blossoms.

MEDIUM TO SMALLER SHRUBS

Among the ceanothus, moderate height does not necessarily imply moderate spread. Some plants in this category extend even farther laterally than the treelike species. Response to pruning is all-important in determining their suitability for the home garden. They may be used as free-standing specimen shrubs, massed on banks and slopes, or—in a few cases—lined up and pruned as screens and informal hedges.

C. 'Blue Jeans'. Subgenus *Cerastes*. I was enchanted by this plant on my first visit to Rancho Santa Ana Botanic Garden in Claremont in the 1970s. It had a brief moment of glory a few years later, then was largely forgotten.

'Blue Jeans' is a nearly round shrub, up to six feet high and wide. The stems are rather slender and densely set with deep green leaves, each up to three-quarters of an inch long, shallowly toothed, and having a glossy surface. In spring, the entire plant is painted over in bright chalky lavender. When one adds to these characteristics superior tolerance of heavy soils, summer heat, and garden watering, 'Blue Jeans' would seem to have all the elements necessary for popular acclaim.

C. 'Concha' is a venerable cultivar, selected by Charles Sams and probably involving *C. impressus* and *C. papillosus* var. *roweanus* as accidental parents. It is a shrub of four to six by up to nine feet, occasionally more, with gracefully arching branches. The leaves are densely and symmetrically arranged, narrow in outline, and about an inch in length. They are colored a rich, deep green and beautifully textured. 'Concha' is a dependable and heavy bloomer, making a dazzling display for several weeks each spring. Deep blue flowers combine with reddish buds to render an overall impression of shimmering purple. It is sometimes short-lived but generally superior to other hybrids of its presumed parentage in garden tolerance.

C. cuneatus var. cuneatus. Buckbrush. Subgenus *Cerastes*. Common to the chaparral nearly throughout California, this is a stout, stiffly arching shrub, three to nine feet high and usually broader than tall. Some plants become small parasol-shaped trees. Older branches weather an attractive silvery gray. The branches are lined by short spurs, each loosely set with wedge-shaped leaves one-quarter to three-quarters of an inch long. In early and midspring, the plant is massed with short clusters of white to pale lavender or pinkish flowers, whose rich perfume—combining honey, musk, and more esoteric elements—can be almost overpowering.

Buckbrush has been employed largely as a utilitarian cover for roadbanks and bare slopes, where its relish for heat, drought, and impoverished soils is almost unequaled except by desert plants. It is ornamental in this role as well, offering pleasing colors and textures. You might also try it, with careful pruning to accentuate its trunk and branch structure, as a small specimen tree. It needs well drained soil and a sunny site but is otherwise an undemanding subject.

C. cuneatus **var.** *fascicularis*

C. cuneatus **var.** *fascicularis* (formerly *C. ramulosus* var. *fascicularis*). As I have seen it both in the wild and at public gardens like Rancho Santa Ana, this ceanothus has always struck me as a plant that merits greater attention. It inhabits portions of the south-central coast, growing on hills and mesas. The plants are distinctly smaller than those of typical *C. cuneatus*, growing three to five feet high with sometimes greater spread, and generally more compact. The leaves are also narrower and clustered at the nodes. Generous masses of blue to lavender flowers adorn the plants in spring. It has performed well in occasional cultivation to date, but needs much broader trials to define its tolerances.

C. cuneatus **var.** *rigidus*

C. cuneatus **var.** *rigidus* (formerly *C. rigidus*). Monterey ceanothus. This plant, common in the foothills near Monterey Bay, is one of my local spring delights. It is a dome-shaped to mounding shrub, usually three to six feet tall and about twice that in breadth. The slender but stiff and intricately branched stems bear many small, hard, mostly wedge-shaped leaves. The flowers are borne profusely in small, often brightly painted clusters. Typical colors include deep to pale blue and violet to chalky lavender, plus an occasional white.

Monterey ceanothus has many ornamental possibilities but has been only sparingly cultivated in recent years. The one well known cultivar is 'Snowball', a whimsical shrub that, while domelike and nearly six feet tall in some sites, in others flattens itself into low drifts up to fifteen feet broad. It is particularly admired for its masses of snow-white flowers.

'Snowball' has thrived in a wide range of landscape conditions, though the combination of heavy soils and frequent summer watering should be avoided. With light clipping to restrain its spread, it might even accept the confines of the home garden.

C. 'Dark Star'

C. **'Dark Star'.** One of the most impressive hybrids of the 1970s, 'Dark Star' was selected by Kenneth Taylor of Aromas, and I was privileged to bring it to the gardening public. It is believed to be a chance cross of *C. impressus* and *C. papillosus var. roweanus*. Out of bloom, 'Dark Star' is a spreading mass of tiny, dark green, stippled leaves. It reaches four to six feet in height by seven to ten feet in diameter, sometimes even more. For over a month in spring, it becomes a dense mass of cobalt-blue flowers borne in small round clusters.

The home gardener will appreciate 'Dark Star' for its dazzling floral displays and foliar texture, though a hearty struggle may be required to keep it in bounds. This cultivar

C. **'Dark Star'.**

is clearly most at home in large country or commercial landscapes, where it can roam at will. In its youth, it seems a little more garden tolerant than the better-known 'Julia Phelps', which it resembles. Yet it is only marginally longer lived in most sites.

C. foliosus. Wavyleaf ceanothus. This is a highly variable species, found on dry slopes of the Coast Ranges nearly throughout the state. It is usually spreading to mounding in habit and grows from around two feet high, in the variety *vineatus*, to six feet in the variety *medius*, frequently more in cultivation. The twigs are quite slender and clad with small, usually glossy, wavy-edged leaves (the latter feature is less pronounced in the variety *vineatus*). The blossom clusters, while small, offer some of the most brilliant blues and purples of the genus.

I once found a very congested, small-leaved form on a neighbor's ranch and named it (after the ranch) 'Berryhill'. It is usually less than two feet in height and five feet in breadth. The leaves have a lacquered surface, and the flower clusters, though quite small, are bright blue in color.

These are rugged plants, tolerating considerable drought, heat, and cold (probably to 0–10°F). They are admirably suited for decorating summer-dry banks and slopes and should certainly be considered for highway plantings in hot-summer areas. Their response to irrigated garden conditions, however, has varied from good to poor.

C. gloriosus var. exaltatus. Navarro ceanothus. Subgenus *Cerastes*. The typical guise of *C. gloriosus*, Pt. Reyes ceanothus, is that of a large mat or mound. The variety *exaltatus* is a taller, stouter version, found farther inland on chaparral slopes and ridgetops. Its branches arch to form a dome up to six feet high by fifteen feet broad (usually a good bit narrower). The leaves are of variable size, up to one and a half inches long, and distinctly toothed. They are usually deep green above, pale beneath. Flowers are often presented in generous masses along the stems and range in color from pale lavender to violet and deep blue.

Shapely habit, good response to pruning and fair to good tolerance of heavier soils and summer watering should make it a desirable shrub for the average garden. All that being said, only one cultivar, 'Emily Brown', has achieved widespread use. It usually grows three feet or less in height, but may spread to as much as ten feet in diameter. The branch scaffold is just open enough to expose attractive grayish trunks. In midspring, this plant creates a stunning display of glowing blue-violet blossoms. 'Emily Brown' has proven easy to grow under average garden conditions, even far from its coastal haunts. It has survived short bursts of 10°F temperatures unscathed; further testing may reveal still broader tolerance.

C. griseus. Carmel ceanothus. Most gardeners are familiar with this species only by way of its formerly (no longer) recognized variety *horizontalis*, the Carmel creeper of the ground cover trade, though the more typical forms have much to recommend them. They are usually seen along the northern and central California coast as round to spreading shrubs, three to nine feet high and six to twenty feet broad. Their supple green branches are clothed with narrowly oval to nearly round, deeply veined leaves up to two inches long. These are shiny and rich green on their upper surface and light green to grayish beneath. The dense flower clusters range in hue from white to deep true-blue.

Carmel ceanothus is admirably suited, by its often massive size, for large commercial landscapes and highway plantings. Yet pruned early, often, and lightly, some forms can serve as large specimen shrubs for the home garden. It is most at home near the coast, requiring supplemental summer irrigation and sometimes falling prey to root diseases in warmer climates. Its hardier forms have survived winter lows of 10–15°F in the garden.

C. griseus 'Louis Edmunds' is an old but mostly forgotten cultivar that deserves greater recognition. It combines the features of dark, glossy foliage, long blooming season, bright blue flowers, and excellent performance in heavier soils and with summer watering. The main branches spread widely, while the side branches stand nearly erect to form a mass up to six by twenty feet. It seems reasonably tolerant of summer heat.

C. impressus. Santa Barbara ceanothus. This species is found in the fast-vanishing coastal scrub of Santa Barbara County. From a distance, it presents itself as a billowing mass three to eight feet tall and six to fifteen feet broad, its branches nearly hidden by deep green foliage. A closer look reveals pleasing textures in the intricately branched, slender stems and tiny leaves, which are crinkled and rolled at their margins. In spring, all this is hidden beneath a blanket of deep blue, violet, or lavender, the small blossom clusters nearly overlapping.

This fine shrub is not for everyone. Its considerable spread and variable, sometimes poor, response to frequent pruning put it beyond the bounds of many home gardens. The stresses of high summer heat, winter cold below the high teens, or overly wet or heavy soil can render it an unsightly pile of brush. It has few peers, however, for the decoration of large banks, open slopes, and other spaces where it can spread without restraint, at least near the coast.

Only a few cultivars are distinguished by name. 'Puget Blue' was selected many years ago for its floral displays, superior garden tolerance, and hardiness. It is currently making a modest comeback in California after two decades of neglect. This selection is moderate in size, reaching four by eight feet, more in very rich soils. The flowers are a pleasingly bright lavender-blue. My own 'Vandenberg' is a more compact, lower growing form, selected from the Air Force base of that name during a native plant salvage operation. The leaves are quite small and crowded, the flower clusters also small and fairly bright blue in color.

C. integerrimus. Deer brush. In its typical form, this is a plant of mainly utilitarian virtue. At its best, it is distinctly ornamental. Deer brush is encountered in mountains nearly through-out the state as an openly branched shrub growing three to twelve feet tall and four to fifteen feet broad.

This is one of the few winter-deciduous ceanothus in California. The thin-textured leaves are roughly oval in shape and up to three inches long, usually much less. They are colored bright to pale green or blue-green above, pale beneath. Flower clusters are usually long-stalked but otherwise strikingly variable in size. Those of plants in our far northern ranges, once segregated as the variety *macrothyrsus*, may be up to six inches long. Flower color ranges from pure white (or all too commonly off-white) to bright true-blue, lavender, and even pink.

Deer brush has been used extensively for erosion control and revegetation of disturbed areas. It can withstand high summer heat, cold to 0°F or less, impoverished soils, and drought. Even in its typical form, it is attractive en masse as a slope and bank cover where the use of less rugged plants is precluded. Some of the large-flowered northern forms are genuinely ornamental but have been roundly ignored (my own efforts have come to nothing thus far).

Perhaps its most intriguing potential is as a hybrid parent, imparting greater heat, cold, and drought tolerance to the current hybrid swarm.

C. 'Joan Mirov'. This is among the best of several collections from the wild by Roger Raiche at the UC Botanic Garden in Berkeley. It has grown up to six feet tall and ten feet broad in various landscapes and may prove even larger in time; in any case, it has good potential as a large-scale bank cover. The slender stems are neatly lined by very dark, shiny half-inch leaves. Deep blue flowers in smallish clusters make a lavish display in spring. It responds well to pruning and has shown good resistance to disease, at least near the coast. A disappointing performance at Rancho Santa Ana suggests that its tolerance of summer heat and irrigation needs more rigorous testing.

C. 'Joyce Coulter'. This popular plant originated as a garden hybrid, thought to involve *C. papillosus* var. *roweanus* and *C. griseus* (formerly var. *horizontalis*) 'Yankee Point'. Left to its own devices, it forms a rather dense mound, three to occasionally six feet high and up to fifteen feet broad. The branches are closely lined by nearly rectangular dark green leaves that possess a crystalline texture and sheen. Large, medium-blue flower clusters, while seldom entirely covering the plant, make an impressive show that lasts for several weeks in spring.

C. 'Joyce Coulter'.

'Joyce Coulter' is admirably suited for covering large spaces, whether on sloping or on level ground. It also responds sufficiently well to pruning to be considered as an ornamental shrub or a low hedge for the home garden. Its tolerance of heavy soils and summer watering is outstanding (in fact, water is required for good performance in hot-summer areas). I have seen it respond variably to hard freezes, with eventual recovery after dips into the low teens.

C. 'Julia Phelps'. Despite a temperamental disposition, this garden hybrid has probably been more planted and admired than any other bush-form ceanothus. It grows fountainlike to dome-shaped, roughly four to eight feet tall and up to twelve feet broad—even more, on occasion. It has short, crowded branches, densely packed with stippled dark green leaves, each half to one inch long. In midspring, small roundish blossom clusters merge into a solid blanket of glowing blue-violet.

'Julia Phelps' is at its best near the coast, planted on sandy slopes, and left to its own devices in summer. It is one of the great spring spectacles along the highways of the San Francisco Bay Area. It is perhaps unfortunate that this selection is also highly prized by home gardeners, for it seldom persists for long without excellent soil drainage and summer drought. Evidently many gardeners feel that even a brief reign justifies their efforts with this dazzling plant.

C. papillosus. Wartleaf ceanothus. Defying neat description, this species is equally at home in redwood forest, oak woods, and chaparral. In the typical variety, *papillosus*, it ranges from four to sixteen feet in height and may grow erect or mounding, rangy or compact. Its most constant feature is its long, narrow, warty-textured leaves, which are often sparkling and deep green on their upper surface. Flower clusters, though of variable size, are generally a deep true-blue in color.

A particularly attractive version of this species is its variety *roweanus*, distinguished by smaller, denser plants overall, with quite narrow and closely set, square-tipped leaves. The flowers are usually colored an intense blue, with no hint of purple. Plants from seed collected on Mt. Tranquillon, in Santa Barbara County, were once sold as *C. roweanus* and produced such outstanding hybrids as *C.* 'Joyce Coulter' and 'Julia Phelps'. Now all forms of the species are available only from native plant specialists.

Garden use and tolerance for this species will vary with the individual plants selected. More compact forms—especially within the variety *roweanus*—are particularly attractive. Since these forms inhabit primarily dry chaparral, they should tolerate both heat and drought, but probably *not* heavy soils and summer watering. Winter hardiness is likely to vary with the origin of the plants in question.

Flowering branch of *C. purpureus*.

C. purpureus. Hollyleaf ceanothus. Subgenus *Cerastes*. Hollyleaf ceanothus is scattered among the summer-scorched hills of Napa County, where it is rapidly giving way to the march of development. This is a boldly textured shrub with an eventual size of three to six feet in height by four to ten feet in breadth. It may be round and compact or sprawling, with stiff, rather heavy stems. Crowded to rather widely spaced along the branches are thick, deep green leaves up to an inch long, rounded in outline and edged with sharp teeth. Even an average specimen is dazzling in bloom, its stems and foliage hidden under a mass of lavender to deep blue or purple blossoms.

Although hollyleaf ceanothus was cultivated as early as the 1920s, no serious effort appears to have been spent on the selection of superior forms. Thus, its reputation for short life and intolerance of garden conditions may reflect only our ignorance of its possibilities. Its better forms might provide spectacular shrubs for planting in California's interior hills and valleys.

C. thyrsiflorus 'Skylark'.

C. thyrsiflorus. Blueblossom. This species has some very attractive shrubby forms. 'Skylark' is a plant of obscure, possibly hybrid, origins and somewhat atypical features, though it resembles plants I have seen on the Mendocino coast. It is quite compact, usually growing only four to five feet tall and perhaps seven feet broad. The stems are unusually stout for this species, and the leaves are quite dark and resinous. Its dark blue blossoms appear after nearly all other ceanothus have finished their show. There are other relatively low (under six feet) but more widely spreading selections, including my own 'Arroyo de la Cruz'. This is a mound four to five feet tall by six to ten feet broad with densely set, lacquered leaves and abundant medium-blue flower clusters. All cultivars seem quite cold-hardy, and 'Skylark' has already shown its mettle in hot summer areas. All have responded well to pruning. Their only annoying feature is the prominence of old, dead flower stalks, which remain firmly attached to the plants for years.

C. 'Wheeler Canyon'. This cultivar was introduced in the 1980s by Dara Emery at the Santa Barbara Botanic Garden. Since then, it has slowly gained an enthusiastic following. It grows four to occasionally eight feet tall and six to perhaps twelve feet broad. Overall, the plant much resembles C. 'Concha' in form and foliage, though the branches are a bit stouter and the leaves a little larger. The flowers are bright blue, not as dazzling as those of 'Concha' but perhaps even more generously produced. It has

C. **'Wheeler Canyon'** at Santa Barbara Botanic Garden.

proven to be one of the most durable and easily grown of the "warty-leaved" hybrids.

LOW AND MATTING CEANOTHUS

The obvious use for most of the plants in this group is for ground and bank covers. Several species and cultivars are suitable only for commercial landscapes and roadbanks, where they have plenty of room to ramble. However, a few are of small to moderate size overall, making them candidates for gardens with limited space.

C. diversifolius. Pine mat. This charming plant of forest edges in the Sierra Nevada and North Coast Ranges lies nearly flat on the ground and drapes down banks and cliffs. It spreads slowly to perhaps six feet, taking root as it travels. The small, furry gray-green leaves give the plant a soft, pleasing texture. Sky blue flowers in round clusters decorate it during middle to late spring.

This would seem a worthy candidate for small-scale ground cover. Given a little shade—except near the coast—and moderate summer watering, it has thrived at sea level. I have also found it a choice subject for containers. At the same time, its hardiness makes it particularly useful in mountain gardens.

C. gloriosus var. gloriosus. Point Reyes ceanothus. Subgenus *Cerastes*. Of all the low-growing *Cerastes* ceanothus, this is by far the most rapid and luxuriant in growth. It is planted extensively as a commercial ground cover near the coast, where it is found in scattered locations from Marin to Mendocino County.

Point Reyes ceanothus grows as a loose mat or low mound, ranging up to three feet high by eighteen feet in breadth. Its branches are closely lined with deep green, toothed leaves, three-quarters to two inches long, with an attractive sheen on their upper surface. Small round clusters of pale to deep blue or violet blossoms are paired along the stems in the leaf axils in spring.

Used properly, Point Reyes ceanothus is a massive and beautiful cover for large landscapes. Some forms might even be sufficiently restrained for the average home garden, as the plants respond well to light pruning and shearing. They relish the cool, moist climate of the immediate coast and thrive there even in heavy soils, with moderate to occasional summer irrigation. However, plantings rarely succeed for long where summers are hot; because frequent watering is required under these conditions, the plants may fall prey to fungus root and stem rots.

Most of the plants grown today appear to belong to two or three unnamed cultivars, all characterized by rampant growth, lush foliage, and disappointingly pale flowers. 'Anchor Bay', introduced by the Saratoga Horticultural Foundation, is more moderate in growth than these, but not as full and lush. The leaves are an inch long, quite broad and thick, and the flowers are a few shades darker than the norm. Most interesting for home gardeners, I think, is 'Heart's Desire', recently introduced by Phil van Solen. This is a plant of unusually delicate appearance, with slender, intricately branched stems and smallish, glossy leaves. The flowers are colored an attractive lavender-blue.

C. griseus, prostrate forms. Carmel creeper. Along a short stretch of the coastline south of Carmel you will find more or less prostrate, widely spreading forms of *C. griseus*, once classified as the variety *horizontalis*. (Although the *horizontalis* designation is no longer accepted in botanical circles, it may linger forever in the nursery trade.) These plants—which resemble other forms of the species in foliage, though the leaves are usually larger and rounder—are used in vast numbers for large-scale ground and bank cover. Typical commercial clones grow one to four feet tall (much more when crowded) and spread as much as thirty feet. They have flexible bright

C. griseus **south of Carmel. Inset: Detail of foliage.**

green stems, large satiny leaves with attractive veining, and usually pale true-blue flowers. Excellent large-scale ground covers near the coast, they are much less reliable in the hot interior, where they are nevertheless used in vast numbers. 'Carmel Creeper', as well as being the common name, is often used as the cultivar name for one or more of these giant selections. The two or more clones commonly sold under the name 'Yankee Point' are taller, more compact, and darker in both leaf and flower. Though reputed to be more heat-tolerant than other cultivars, they are still only marginally suitable for use wherever summers are chronically hot.

All of these cultivars need plenty of room to roam. Their response to crowding is to rise up into unsightly piles, although judicious pruning and thinning can restrain them somewhat. They are also distinctly more sensitive to cold than more northerly forms of the species.

C. hearstiorum. Hearst's ceanothus. This is a most unusual shrub, found on the Hearst Ranch in San Luis Obispo County. It lies quite flat, with limber branches radiating from the base to form a loose, dark green mat less than one foot high by up to eight feet broad. The narrow leaves are warty in texture, like those of *C. dentatus* and *C. papillosus*. The small, round flower clusters are light to deep blue in color.

The most obvious use for this species is as a ground and bank cover, providing a much more refined texture than Carmel creeper (described above). While plants might be spaced close enough to permit intermeshing, and thus make a more or less solid cover, it would seem a shame not to expose the attractive starlike pattern of growth. This species tolerates ordinary garden conditions near the coast, at least for a few years, but it has not been well tested inland.

C. maritimus. Hoover ceanothus. Subgenus *Cerastes.* This beautiful and potentially very useful ceanothus is native to a small section of our south-central coast, near San Luis Obispo. Like *C. gloriosus*, it occurs as a mat or low mound, usually less than two feet in height, though it is far more moderate in rate of growth and ultimate width. At close range, the thickly set, toothed leaves present a striking contrast between the deep green upper surface and nearly white undersurface. From a distance, the overall impression is one of gray-green. Small deep blue or violet to white flower clusters line the stems in spring.

C. *hearstiorum* at UC Santa Cruz Arboretum.

A trial of several hundred seedlings at the University of California, Davis, yielded only one unnamed cultivar. This is a particularly tall (to at least two feet) form with unusually gray leaves but disappointingly pale lavender flowers. David Fross has recently made two additional introductions. 'Frosty Dawn' grows up to two feet tall and six feet broad (often less) and has flowers of a rich lavender shade, while 'Pt. Sierra' is distinguished by its somewhat larger size, more arching habit, and smaller leaves carried on flatter sprays of branchlets. Further trials at Rancho Santa Ana may broaden the available range of habit and flower color.

Hoover ceanothus has proven surprisingly adaptable with regard to soils and climates (though it is still more reliable and long-lived near the coast), thriving with moderate summer irrigation. It has also endured freezes of 10°F.

C. prostratus. Squaw carpet. Subgenus *Cerastes.* Squaw carpet is a common and distinctive sight at middle elevations in the mountains of northern California, where it makes a perfect deep green mat, just a few inches high and three to eight feet broad. The stems spill over rocks and stumps and take root as they spread. Its leaves are small and toothed, resembling those of a miniature holly. In early summer, the mat is dotted with small, flattish clusters of light to deep blue or violet flowers. The reddish seed capsules that follow are also quite attractive.

C. *prostratus*, Mt. St. Helena.

Squaw carpet is useful for erosion control and, where it is at home, as an ornamental ground cover. It stands considerable summer heat and drought in its native ranges. Plants grown at sea level, however, even pampered with gritty soil and careful watering, often succumb to fungus root rots (not an uncommon experience with mountain natives). There may be better hope of success with plants once dubbed *C. prostratus* var. *occidentalis*, which descend to 2,000 feet or lower from Sonoma to Mendocino County. I maintained cutting-grown selections of this form for several years in nursery containers but never quite extended their trial to the open ground.

SO MANY MANZANITAS

· ·

Genus: *Arctostaphylos*
Family: Ericaceae, the Heath Family

Few native plant groups are as symbolic of the California landscape as the manzanitas. Even for the casual traveler, they conjure images of the chaparral at its flowery best in early spring, and of its soft colors and textures at other times. I have had a privileged relationship with these interesting plants for most of my life. As a boy I marveled at their contorted forms, colorful bark, and rockhard wood in the hills of Sonoma County. It was only natural that they should be among the first native plants I would work with early in my nursery career. Searching for them took me to many beautiful places and introduced me to some of the most interesting people in native plant horticulture—a process that continues to this day.

COMMON FEATURES

Known botanically as the genus *Arctostaphylos*, the manzanitas comprise one of the major groups of woody plants of California and of their botanical family, the heath family (Ericaceae). Some fifty-seven species are described in Philip Wells's treatment in *The Jepson Manual*. They are distributed over the entire length of the state and occur in many plant communities, at a wide range of elevations, though they are particularly abundant in coastal scrub and chaparral.

Manzanitas are equally conspicuous in California horticulture. Of all the thousands of plants native to this state, they and the wild lilacs (*Ceanothus*) are by far the best known and loved by gardeners. Together these two genera account for a sizeable majority of all native plants grown and sold for ornamental use in California.

Also like the wild lilacs, the manzanitas are a botanically confusing group. The sheer number of species is daunting enough, but it is compounded by great variation within species. The result is a welter of subspecies and varieties, and a rather unrestrained tendency to hybridize where several species meet.

There is a dark side to this rich diversity. Fully half of the species presented in *The Jepson Manual* are described as endangered. Several reasons can be given, not all of which spell

---

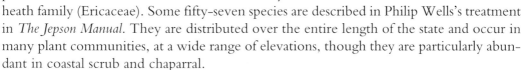

ARCTOSTAPHYLOS MANZANITA IN THE WILD, NAPA COUNTY.

95

disaster. Some small populations, possibly pioneers rather than vanishing relicts, have only recently been discovered and awarded species status. Some occur on isolated geologic formations with unusual soils. Yet the disappearance of habitat under man's heavy hand is undeniably the critical element.

Manzanitas are a wonderfully variable lot, in nearly all the respects of interest to us as gardeners. Some form absolutely flat mats or snake along the ground under other shrubs. At the opposite end of the scale, several are picturesque small trees, reminiscent of the oaks in form. In between lie many mounding to upright, usually billowy shrubs. Whatever their scale, nearly all have beautifully sculptured trunks, though some species hide them under masses of foliage. Some species have a woody basal structure, usually hidden underground, called a burl, from which multiple trunks arise. This adaptation facilitates resprouting after damaging chaparral fires and is conducive to a broadly mounding style of growth. Bark is another ornamental feature. Manzanita bark has a wonderful range of earthy colors, maroon and cinnamon shades being particularly common. The older bark often flakes off in little curls, exposing attractive green to grayish underbark.

Stems and leaves are similarly variable and highly ornamental, as in *A. manzanita*, with its smooth, shiny, nearly hairless stems and leaves, or *A. canescens*, whose foliage is felted throughout with tiny hairs. The abundance of hairs in turn affects plants' overall color and texture, from bright green and bold in the smoother versions to ghostly gray and soft in the hairier examples. A surface dressing of wax can render a silvery impression. Leaf shapes are always simple, usually some variation on a pointed-oval theme, though they may be nearly round or quite narrow.

Although I associate manzanita flowers particularly with the month of March, they may be seen from mid-December to May (later in the high mountains), depending on the species or hybrid. Within the wider-ranging species like *A. manzanita*, season varies according to both latitude and elevation. There are also wide individual differences within any large population. Often quite small (usually not much over a quarter of an inch), manzanita flowers usually occur in good-sized clusters at each shoot tip. The clusters may be simple or branched, forming small sprays. From a distance, set against the darker foliage, they give a glittering effect. At closer range, one can savor their honeylike fragrance and the form and coloring of the individual blossoms. Each flower is an exquisite pendant urn with waxy finish, painted pure white or one of several shades of pink and often shaded dark to light from base to tip. It is always a bit sad to see the floral parade pass on, sometimes in less than a month. However, the berries that develop over the summer are interesting and often showy in their own right. When ripe, many resemble tiny apples, even in their reddish blush—thus the plants' common name, from the diminutive of the Spanish *manzana*, or apple.

Uses and Culture

The overwhelming majority of manzanitas under cultivation are used for ground cover, where the popular ideal seems to be that of a perfectly flat mat. I find this unfortunate, for it ignores much of the basis of their rugged beauty. Even the lowest manzanita can cascade gracefully over rocks and mounds, lending greater interest to the landscape. More interesting still are the billowy patterns of the more substantial shrubs, which can lead to a visually pleasing, if unorthodox, version of ground cover as plants spread and undulate to weave a complex tapestry. Manzanitas can also make a pleasant foil for more dramatic plants, like the fremontias. Given their natural density of growth and good response to at least moderate pruning, midsized and larger manzanitas can be fashioned into lovely screens and informal hedges as well. A few, like the ubiquitous *A. densiflora* 'Howard McMinn', will take even relatively brutal treatment in stride and are often seen as formal hedges, though this seems to me a terrible fate for a plant with such rugged, individualistic natural beauty (better a boxwood or privet, if a formal hedge is needed at all).

All of these uses, of course, focus on foliage. There is another broad category of use—that of "specimen shrub" (meaning that plants are shown off individually)—in which attention is given instead to their beautiful trunks. Manzanitas of all sizes, from rock-garden miniatures to small trees, can be thinned to emphasize their structure and expose their beautiful bark to view.

Manzanitas also have their utilitarian side. The same dense, billowy growth that makes them so attractive helps to cut the force of rain on the soil surface, while the rooting in of lower branches that occurs with many spreading species helps to bind soil particles together. Both functions assist in erosion control. Many manzanitas, particularly the larger ones, provide important services to birds and other wildlife: abundant refuge beneath their branches, edible foliage (sometimes perhaps *too* edible, if you live among deer), and equally edible berries.

Where their basic requirements are met, many manzanitas are rugged, undemanding, and long-lived shrubs. Remember, though, that they hail from distant corners of California and are adapted to many different habitats. At one extreme, several species inhabit dry, rocky slopes, where shallow soils are underlain by sandstone, shale, or even serpentine, while others occur on windswept coastal dunes and plains. Some species thrive in relatively benign settings, like the margins of oak woods or redwood forest. What these diverse sites tend to have in common are well drained soils, usually low in nutrients, and plenty of sun. Species of the interior ranges must endure considerable summer heat and drought; frequently their regime also includes biting winter cold. Those of the coastal strand, in contrast, may be bathed in summer fog and rarely experience frost.

This gives us at least a starting point for cultural recommendations: Coastal species do indeed tend to perform best in cooler-summer climates and to tolerate, even require, more summer irrigation than the interior species. Yet species such as *A. hookeri*, Monterey manzanita, and some individual cultivars, both from the wild and from garden hybrids, have been found to have far broader tolerances than one might predict.

A more serious issue under cultivated conditions is the host of common diseases to

A. UVA-URSI 'RADIANT' IN A LANDSCAPE SETTING.

which manzanitas have little natural immunity. In well mulched, well irrigated, and well fed landscapes, a variety of pathogens such as species of *Pythium, Phytophthera,* and *Rhizoctonia* become established, first as decay organisms and later as active, opportunistic plant parasites. The result for some manzanitas, as for dryland natives in general, can be sudden, apparently random collapse and death as tissues are invaded and killed at the soil line. Less deadly but certainly disfiguring are a variety of fungal and bacterial leaf-spot diseases. The logical remedies for these blights are largely preventive: Give manzanitas the best soil drainage possible, by whatever means are available. Avoid excessive congestion and shading of branches, particularly of ground-hugging plants. Avoid overhead irrigation as much as possible, especially during warm weather; instead, water plants deeply and infrequently at the root zone.

Not everything that troubles the manzanitas is caused by poor culture, however. Afflicting them even in the wild is an organism known scientifically as *Botryosphaeria ribis,* whose progressive symptoms include spotting of leaves and stems, the death of individual twigs, and finally loss of larger branches. Species with hairy stems and leaves (which trap more moisture) are the most susceptible to this blight, but few are exempt. Cultural remedies are essentially the same as those for fungal root rots, with particular emphasis on avoidance of overcrowding, whether of plants, branches, or foliage.

A less serious affliction from the wild is that of aphid galls. The insect in question injects irritating fluids into leaf tissues, which respond with a sort of tumor, often bright red in color, that forms a protective feeding chamber. The most effective remedy is to prune out the affected branches or pick the infested leaves and dispose of them.

It is fair to say that no manzanita requires heavy feeding, while some species and individuals actually cannot tolerate it, particularly when it comes to phosphates. The first indication of distress, above all in the presence of excess lime, is chlorosis, or yellowing of portions of the leaves and shoot tips. This symptom indicates interference with the uptake of iron and other essential minerals. Scorching and gradual death of the leaf margins and shoot tips suggest more serious excesses. These signs are particularly common in portions of the Central Valley and southern California where irrigation water is alkaline or high in sodium and other toxic salts. A good leaching by winter rains can alleviate the problem, which may otherwise lead to the death of entire plants and plantings. Watering with solutions of iron sulfates and chelates can also help.

Pruning is a negotiable matter for most species and cultivars. Manzanitas are easily shaped as they grow by selective pruning and thinning of branches, especially when the plants are young. Tip-pruning of the ground-covering types helps to develop a sufficiently dense mat to prevent overgrowth by weeds. Later in life, the forms manzanitas adopt with no assistance are often the most beautiful. Although some plants will tolerate extensive clipping, there are two important cautions to remember (aside from aesthetic issues): Congested foliage is an invitation to the invasion of leaves and stems by pathogens during extended winter rains or overhead summer irrigation; and pruning should never go beyond healthy, well colored leaves. Bare stems left behind by careless hacking will almost certainly die to the base, promoting invasion by diseases that can spread to healthy parts of the plant.

Timing of planting deserves special mention. Like many native shrubs, the manzanitas make substantial root growth during the cool months. Planting them in the fall gives them the maximum time possible to extend their roots, reducing their need for summer irrigation. Summer planting guarantees that the plants will need frequent watering to survive and carries a risk of losses to high-temperature root rots.

PROPAGATION

Propagation of the manzanitas is surprisingly simple, if a bit slower than that of some other popular natives. In fact, this is a group where some nursery propagators might do well to take a few lessons from ordinary dirt gardeners, as some of the modern nursery techniques they have come to consider routine offer little advantage.

Cuttings provide both the fastest route to new plants for the garden and a way to perpetuate the features of ornamentally superior individuals. Cuttings are most easily handled outdoors during the cooler months, an approach that minimizes the need for frequent overhead watering. Use either just-matured shoots (firm to the touch) or the more mature portions of the current season's shoots, cutting well behind the soft shoot tips, which dehydrate easily. Prepare pieces with at least three or four healthy leaves. A mild rooting powder, if you have it, usually results in faster rooting, though it is seldom critical for success. Plant the cuttings in a porous medium, and place them in a cool, shady spot, watering them only enough to keep the medium moist. *A. uva-ursi* may form roots in two months or less under these conditions, while larger, heavy-stemmed manzanitas may take four months or more. Once rooted, the young plants will grow rapidly and should be transplanted to successively larger pots. Many will be ready for the open ground by the end of their first growing season.

Seeding is of particular interest for revegetation of wild sites, to promote maximum diversity in any setting, or just to see what interesting new forms may crop up from hybrid parents. The berries hang on the plants until ripe, often longer, and are easy to collect (assuming your animal friends have left some behind). The flesh surrounding the large, hard seeds may be pulpy or dry and mealy. In both cases, the seeds are fairly easy to extract, either by squeezing them between your fingers or rolling over them with a coffee mug or similar object. The problem is that the hard, thick seed coats make an effective barrier to the moisture needed for germination. Unless you are prepared to wait several years for these coats to rot away, you will want to soften or abrade them a bit. Placing them in hot water, then allowing them to soak awhile is one common technique. Attacking them with a file to remove part of the hard coat is another. The seeds may then be planted outdoors in pots or flats of any porous potting mix and kept moist through a natural winter. If you live in a particularly mild climate, refrigeration for a few months in containers of moist sand or a similar medium before planting may be more effective. Germination may take a few months, or as long as two years. Once they are large enough for transplanting, the seedlings may be handled much like rooted cuttings.

ROOTED CUTTINGS OF *A. DENSIFLORA* 'SENTINEL'.

SPECIES AND CULTIVARS TO TRY

The manzanitas offer us a rich—for some of us, confusingly rich—abundance of candidates for the garden. Among species and natural hybrids from the wild, many are yet to be tried. There have also been numerous chance hybrids in public and private gardens, thanks to the unrelenting efforts of bees and other insects, manzanitas' own propensity for hybridizing, and the good judgment of some interested human enthusiasts. These "volunteer" manzanitas have provided some of the most gardenworthy and popular of all California's native shrubs.

Given manzanitas' extreme variability, I will organize this review by three rough categories of size and growing habit, which also correspond to broad categories of use in the garden, as discussed earlier: the treelike manzanitas; intermediate and smaller, bushy types; and the low and matting species. Since most manzanitas flower in the months of February, March, and April, I will mention the season only where it begins exceptionally early or late or extends over a particularly long period.

THE TREELIKE MANZANITAS

A. glauca. Bigberry manzanita. This impressive manzanita occupies a wide range of habitats in the mountains of Central and Southern California. It is encountered as a stout shrub or

small tree, up to twenty feet tall. The trunks are beautifully formed and covered with satiny reddish brown bark. Set along them are broad blue- to gray-green leaves up to two inches long.

Bigberry manzanita has a broad range of flowering seasons, from January to April. The flowers are relatively large (about a third of an inch long) and mostly pure white. They are followed by shiny half-inch berries that make a fine display for several months each year. It is incredible to me that a plant as common and beautiful as this has, with rare exceptions, been generally ignored by commercial grow-

A. glauca with berries.

ers. With so many ornamental features and undisputed heat and drought tolerance, it would seem promising for use in the Central Valley and foothill regions.

A. insularis. Island manzanita. Inhabiting the chaparral of Santa Cruz Island, island manzanita often resembles an arbutus more than it does other manzanitas. The plants are usually treelike, growing ten to fifteen feet tall, though shrubbier forms are also encountered. The trunks are bright, often cinnamon brown, the leaves broad and colored an unusually bright green. Island manzanita flowers as early as December, carrying pure white to light pink flowers in loose clusters.

The most noteworthy selection to date, 'Canyon Sparkles', was made several years ago by Dara Emery at the Santa Barbara Botanic Garden. It is distinctly shrubby, growing five to six feet tall under most conditions. Mahogany trunks, bright shiny leaves and pure white flowers well justify its name. This selection seems reasonably garden tolerant, though it was damaged in several recent winters here in northern California. 'Canyon Blush' is a second, pink-flowered selection, somewhat lower but spreading widely. Considering the many small trees of *A. insularis* seen in the wild, there is surely room for further work with this species.

A. manzanita. Parry manzanita. This manzanita, though a common (but never tiring) sight in northern California and the namesake of the whole group, is still not well known. Like *A. glauca*, it has stout, often picturesque trunks, rising as high as twenty feet. They are clothed in beautiful smooth, reddish brown bark, silky to the touch. Rather loosely set along the stems and held in a conspicuously vertical plane are broad leaves up to two inches long and bright green to gray-green in color. Generous clusters of white to pale pink flowers make a beautiful display. The large reddish berries that follow are also quite decorative.

A. manzanita.

Like *A. glauca*, too, this species has outstanding heat and drought tolerance. Its reputation for difficulty stems from the limited tolerance of many individuals to summer irrigation. However, both 'Dr. Hurd', a very stocky, green-leaved introduction by the Saratoga Horticultural Foundation, and my own 'St. Helena', with grayer foliage, have performed well in a wide variety of landscape settings.

The former *A. elegans*, common in Lake County, is included by Wells under the *A. manzanita* umbrella. This is essentially a stouter version of the species, with larger, bright green leaves. Since it is encountered in areas with particularly hot, dry summers, it would seem worth exploring for Central Valley and foothill gardeners.

A. pringlei ssp. drupacea. Pink-bracted manzanita. I have been enchanted by this plant since the early 1970s, though my efforts to propagate and grow it have been disappointing. It is a large, sturdy shrub or small tree, up to fifteen feet high, with beautiful mahogany trunks. The younger stems, flower stems and berries are all conspicuously hairy. The leaves, which are up to two inches long and nearly that in width, are colored a striking gray-green. The flowers are presented in large clusters with pink, leafy bracts. Individual flowers range in hue from white to deep pink. Berries are red and noticeably sticky.

Tolerance of lowland conditions by this species is not well tested, though it clearly favors the warmer, drier climate of southern California over that of the North. It has performed well in at least some botanic garden settings.

INTERMEDIATE AND SMALLER SHRUBS

A. andersonii. Santa Cruz manzanita. One finds this plant widely though thinly scattered in the Santa Cruz Mountains. Some forms once considered to belong to this species have achieved separate species status in Wells's new scheme: *A. regismontana*, near Woodside; *A. imbricata*, from the San Bruno Mountain area; and *A. auriculata*, from the Mt. Diablo area.

In general, these are not massive shrubs, though *A. imbricata* has some beautiful low, densely mounding forms. *A. andersonii* itself and *A. regismontana* have relatively few, thick branches that are held nearly erect, rising as much as fifteen feet, though usually half that height. Young stems are well covered by short, stiff hairs. The leaves are up to three inches long—exceptionally large for a manzanita—with a nearly stalkless base that appears to clasp the main stem.

Santa Cruz manzanita often begins to flower in January, extending its show through March. The flower clusters tend to be quite large, branched, and rather loose, showing a good range of colors from pure white to deep pink.

I once began trials with various selections of this species and found them promising. However, I neglected them too long and will have to repeat the trial.

A. bakeri. This lovely shrub, occupying a small portion of Sonoma County near Occidental, was once considered a variety of *A. stanfordiana* (see below), which has a much broader distribution. The plants are well branched, usually growing three to six feet tall, with smooth reddish brown bark and slender stems. The leaves are elliptical and dark green to gray-green in color. Flowers are tinted various shades of pink and presented in medium-sized clusters. Colorful reddish berries follow them.

A couple of commercial selections made in the 1950s account for nearly everything we know of this species in cultivation. Only 'Louis Edmunds' is generally available. It grows five to eight feet high and has upswept, rather slender branches, gray-green leaves, and bright pink flowers. This is a lovely shrub that has performed well in many landscapes, especially in northern California. Since the natural stands are disappearing quickly under a wave of settlement, it would be good to examine more closely the little that remains.

A. canescens. Hoary manzanita. This manzanita was one of my regular companions in the inner hills of Sonoma County (it also extends much farther north, and south into Santa Cruz County). An extremely variable shrub, it presents itself as anything from a three- by six-foot mound to a small tree, with purplish to reddish brown bark. Hybrids with *A. manzanita* and others compound the variation.

This is one of the truly gray manzanitas, both the younger stems and leaves being covered with soft white hairs. The leaves are up to two inches long, often closely set and variably shaped. White to pale pink flowers are carried in simple or branched, often rather small clusters.

I once avoided working with this species for its presumed susceptibility to disease, as one of the "fuzzy" manzanitas. I did, however, enjoy an apparent hybrid between it and *A. manzanita* for many years.

A. densiflora. Vine Hill manzanita. Whether a pioneer species or a relict of earlier times, Vine Hill manzanita exists as a wildling only in a tiny piece of Sonoma County, near Sebastopol. It is generally mounding in habit, growing three feet high or less in its native haunts, though more in cultivation. The trunks are rather slender and intricately branched, with dark reddish or purplish bark. Perhaps most striking are the bright, shiny green leaves, elliptical to lance-shaped in outline and up to an inch long. Small white to pink flowers in crowded clusters grace the plants in early spring.

The few existing commercial cultivars date mostly from the 1940s and '50s. One of them, 'Howard McMinn', has been a truly adaptable shrub, planted successfully in light and heavy soils, from the coast to the Central Valley. Lately it has suffered a disturbing rise in incidence of diseases in the nursery; whether these will persist in the landscape remains to be seen. Although it was once described as topping out at three feet, well tended plants can

A. densiflora 'Howard McMinn'.

easily reach six feet or more. In this respect it seems quite atypical of the species. It would be interesting to return to the original stand and try some of the more diminutive clones.

A. glandulosa. Eastwood manzanita. Here is a plant that has many interesting features but is thoroughly ignored by horticulturists. It is a complex species, some of which is absorbed by the current scheme into *A. tomentosa.* It is usually encountered as a nearly round, bushy shrub, four to eight feet high, covered with sticky, glandular hairs but nevertheless bright apple green of leaf and stem. The leaves are up to two inches long and relatively broad.

A. glandulosa on Cone Peak.

Eastwood manzanita flowers from January to April. The flower clusters have conspicuous leafy bracts and normally white blossoms, followed by attractive sticky berries. Plants I have seen in the wild seemed fairly free of disease, though their performance under cultivation is currently anyone's guess.

More attention has been directed to the plants once called *A. glandulosa* var. *cushingiana*, now considered simply part of the complex subspecies *glandulosa*. Often less than three feet tall, with pretty, bright green foliage, these have been in and out of cultivation for many years. Another, known at times as the var. *cushingiana* forma *repens*, is a thoroughly confusing, probably hybrid complex. Some of its members resemble *A. edmundsii*, at least to the nonbotanist. I am particularly interested in the subspecies *zacaensis*, which I have seen from the Santa Lucia Mountains south. It includes beautiful dense mounds of varying size, often with striking gray-green leaves.

A. 'Greensphere'. I was fascinated by this shrub on my first visit to Rancho Santa Ana Botanic Garden. It was one of John Dourley's selections, which he thought to be a deviant *A. edmundsii*. This may be half true, but it almost certainly has a second parent. In habit this selection is truly a little sphere when young, usually topping out at three to four feet and spreading slightly in age. The stems are short and stiff, the leaves up to three-quarters of an inch long and pointed, tinted with bronze in new growth. With its bonus of good garden tolerance, it is a fine candidate for smaller gardens. Oddly enough, it has never garnered much enthusiasm among California gardeners.

A. **'John Dourley'.** Here is a cultivar narrowly saved from oblivion. Mike Evans, of Tree of Life Nursery, rescued the plant for trial after a decision at Rancho Santa Ana to abandon efforts with it. It is a sturdy little shrub, spreading in habit, with broad but smallish blue-green leaves suggestive of *A. pajaroensis* and similarly colorful in new growth. It has a long blooming season, the pink flower clusters and wonderful purplish red berries sharing space for several weeks. It is still too early to assess its long-term performance in the landscape.

A. 'John Dourley' with artemisias, Rancho Santa Ana.

A. **nummularia.** Beginning with my first visit to its native haunts, this has been one of my favorite native shrubs. It is simply pretty, combining (in its original conception) small size, billowy growth, slender, hairy stems, broad shiny leaves and small sparkling flower clusters. Wells's treatment demands a new view of the species, given that the more robust form formerly known as the variety *sensitiva* has joined the ranks of the species proper. In this guise the plants are up to six feet tall and often nearly round. Their leaves are pointed-oval in outline and up to an inch long, and the flower clusters relatively large and many-flowered. Meanwhile, the more diminutive, smaller- and rounder-leaved form inhabiting the pygmy forests near Mendocino (and including most of the cultivated material) has been reassigned to *A. mendocinoensis*.

These are among the most garden tolerant of all manzanitas, though they are sensitive to lime and should have a moderately acid soil. They also cannot cope with extended drought. They do, however, tolerate some shading, and even need it to thrive in hot-summer areas.

I have long grown a particularly nice, apparently unnamed clone originally from Tilden Botanic Garden. It forms a low mound, with relatively large, round lacquered leaves and pure white flowers. I have also tried local selections of the former *sensitiva*, several of which developed into rather massive and extremely floriferous plants. Some of these clearly deserve further trial.

A. **pajaroensis.** Pajaro manzanita. One of several species endemic to the Monterey Bay region, Pajaro manzanita is rapidly disappearing as the sandy hills around the bay are developed. It is quite variable in habit, making dense low mounds or rounded shrubs up to ten feet tall. Its stems are loosely covered with stiff hairs and lined by nearly heart-shaped leaves up to two inches long. The leaves are shiny and painted in brilliant red and orange hues in new growth, dull in surface and blue-green to deep green in color when mature.

Pajaro manzanita may show its first flowers as early as December, with later clusters opening through February or March. The flower clusters are exceptionally large and bright, with floral shades including some of the deepest pinks found among the manzanitas. All these features are epitomized by 'Paradise', a stout, medium-sized selection and for many years the only one known. It

A. pajaroensis **'Myrtle Wolf'**.

has deep, bluish green leaves and flower clusters that are exceptionally large and dark even for this species. More recently Roger Raiche gathered together some lovely selections with various habits at the UC Botanical Garden in Berkeley. One of these, 'Warren Roberts', is now offered commercially. This is a more closely branched shrub than 'Paradise', with more slender stems and grayer leaves. Garden performance of both selections has been good near the coast, though they seem to suffer in hot summers.

A. pungens. Mexican manzanita. This is one of the most far-flung of the genus, occupying a huge range stretching from the Gabilan Range in San Benito County to Baja California and Arizona. In appearance it is much like the taller forms of *A. hookeri*. The plants are variable in habit though often quite bushy, growing as much as ten feet high. They have interesting dark reddish brown trunks and deep green, shining, conspicuously pointed leaves, each up to one and a half inches long. Sparkling white flowers in smallish clusters offer a beautiful contrast to the dark foliage.

This species shows a marked preference for exposed sites in the wild and should have considerable potential for gardens in hot-summer areas; however, I have not seen it tried in California outside botanic gardens.

A. rudis. Shagbark manzanita. This is one of my longtime favorites of the genus (though as you may have already gathered, I have many). As I first saw it on the mesa at Vandenberg Air Force Base, it ranged from three- by six-foot mounds up to nearly round shrubs six feet high and eight feet across. The older bark is pale brown and hangs from the trunks in shreds, while the younger bark is an attractive reddish brown. The stems are neatly lined by bright to pale green leaves of variable width, up to one and a half inches long. Showy white to pink flowers dot the plant in round, dense clusters.

The selection I brought to market, unimaginatively named 'Vandenberg', was one of the larger ones in the wild, though it has reached only three feet by six feet in my own garden after eight years. It is a bushy, spreading shrub with cinnamon bark, light green leaves, and pretty pink flowers. David Fross has made and named the selection 'Greenheart', with shiny, bright green leaves and showy berries. Both selections have shown good garden tolerance near the coast. I would expect other selections to be offered in the future, particularly among the lower-growing forms.

A. stanfordiana. Stanford manzanita. Few who have ever seen this shrub can resist its charms.

It is widely distributed in the North Coast Ranges, often on exposed rocky slopes. It is a bushy shrub of moderate size (usually six feet high or less), with smooth reddish brown trunks. The stems are well clothed with lacquered bright to deep green leaves, which measure up to two inches long. Flowers of this species are perhaps the most stunning of the genus, ranging from light pink to purplish rose and carried in generous clusters. They are followed by ornamental reddish berries.

With this species lies one of the sadder tales of horticulture. Although it is unquestionably one of the most ornamental of all manzanitas, it is quite common to see even natural stands, in the height of bloom, riddled with *Botryosphaeria* and other leaf and stem diseases. Several admirers have selected clones that hinted at resistance to these maladies, only to lose them to summer root rots. Wayne Roderick's selection, 'Trinity Ruby', with its elegant form, dark foliage, and lavender-pink blossoms, is probably the most beautiful to date. However, it was difficult to maintain even in nurseries and seems to have vanished from the trade. One of my own selections, 'Palisades', is a bushy, heavy-blooming individual with bright pink blossoms. It holds up reasonably well and has at least some promise for infrequently watered landscapes. Certainly no plant of this species should have trouble enduring high summer heat and drought.

A. viscida. Whiteleaf manzanita. I have always considered this a most promising shrub for gardeners in the warmer valleys and foothills, though it clearly does not enjoy life along the coast. This species makes nearly solid stands, stretching for miles in the Sierran foothills and interior coastal ranges, where it is nearly always encountered as a stout, neat, and densely foliaged shrub. It may grow as tall as fifteen feet, but is usually seen in the four- to eight-foot range. The bark is an attractive dark reddish brown, and the leaves, up to two inches long, are often nearly round and strikingly gray in color. The flowers are borne in rather loose clusters, their color ranging from snow white to some nice pinks.

I have made and tried several selections from the hot hills of Lake County, each of them stunning in the wild. These have lived and grown, but the leaves blister and spot in our coastal winters (apparently less from disease than from excessive hydraulic pressure). The former *A. mariposa*, a plant of the southern Sierra, is considered a subspecies of *A. viscida* in Wells's treatment. It has hairier stems than the typical species, sometimes more spreading habit and extremely showy pink flowers. Both forms deserve more attention from inland gardeners and commercial growers.

LOW AND MATTING TYPES

A. edmundsii. Little Sur manzanita. One can still encounter this fascinating shrub on bluffs facing the sea in the Big Sur area, where it closely hugs the ground, making beautiful dark mats. In the more benign setting of the garden, it forms wonderful billowy carpets that clamber over anything in their path, including other shrubs. It is profusely branched and has slender hairy, often pinkish stems that darken with age. The stems are closely set with broad, often nearly round leaves up to an inch long, painted bronze to scarlet in new growth.

Little Sur manzanita is one of the earliest of the manzanitas to flower, often starting its show in December and continuing for several weeks. The flower clusters are small but show up well against the foliage, particularly in the case of the better pinks.

This species has performed well near the coast but variably inland. In good health, it makes a truly elegant ground cover, dense enough even to suppress weeds. A few selected forms are available. 'Carmel Sur', with relatively narrow, gray-green leaves, is now fairly popular and has also shown relatively good garden tolerance. Perhaps the prettiest of the current lot, though less tolerant of abuse, is 'Bert Johnson', introduced by Tilden Botanical Garden. This is a perfectly flat mat with crowded grayish green leaves, bronze in new growth, and mostly white flowers. Undoubtedly many other choice individuals could be found in the wild.

A. 'Emerald Carpet'. With this plant comes one of the happier tales of native plant horticulture. In the mid-1970s John Dourley, then superintendent of horticulture at Rancho Santa Ana Botanic Garden, freely offered material of several of his favorites to nurseries.

A. 'Emerald Carpet' draping over wall.

'Emerald Carpet' (at that point still unnamed, though thought to be a hybrid of *A. uva-ursi* and *A. nummularia*) was the most exciting of the lot. Its promise has been fulfilled, and it has joined the mainstream of ornamental ground covers in California, used by tens (perhaps hundreds) of thousands of gardeners each year. This is a tidy plant of matting to mounding, symmetrical growth. The slender stems are closely lined by small, dark, narrow leaves. Pretty white flowers are carried in small clusters.

Though not one of the drought-tolerant manzanitas, 'Emerald Carpet' has shown excellent tolerance of ordinary garden watering. Its only major drawback, for landscaping purposes, is a marked sensitivity to alkaline soils and water. However, generous doses of iron sulfate usually provide a fast, inexpensive remedy.

A. hookeri. Monterey manzanita. As a prowler of the hills around Monterey Bay, I am regularly treated to the sight of this showy manzanita. It is still well distributed in the region, though fast disappearing under the bulldozer's blade. This species has been exploited primarily as a low ground cover. However, some of the most attractive individuals I have encountered are hemispheres three to six feet tall. Most are profusely branched, with crooked trunks and dark purplish to reddish brown bark. The leaves are broad and pointed, up to an inch long, usually shiny and bright green in color. The flower clusters are small, though the white to pale pink blossoms are quite pretty at close range.

There are several cultivars of this species, some dating back many years. 'Wayside', the tallest traditional selection, failed to impress me until I saw it pruned up to expose beautiful crooked trunks. 'Monterey Carpet' is perhaps the best-known carpeting selection, pressing close to the ground and spreading to six to twelve feet. It has closely set, dark green leaves, about three-quarters of an inch long. 'Ken Taylor' is a little more open and larger-leaved, while 'Buxifolia' is more congested and smaller-leaved. The subspecies *hearstiorum*, a disjunct population from the Hearst Ranch, might yield some true miniatures, appropriate even for the rock garden.

A. **'Indian Hill'.** Wild-collected at Sand Creek in Monterey County, this plant was grown and introduced by Rancho Santa Ana Botanic Garden. It closely resembles *A. edmundsii* in its broadly matting growth; broad, shiny half-inch leaves; and colorful new shoots. The flowers are shaded white and pink. Though it has been offered commercially since the 1980s, it remains on the fringes of the nursery trade. It has shown good garden tolerance near the coast and in much warmer surroundings at Rancho Santa Ana, with moderate summer irrigation.

A. nevadensis. Pinemat manzanita. This mountain dweller is found on open and lightly wooded slopes at elevations as high as 10,000 feet. In appearance it suggests a large-leaved form of the bearberry, *A. uva-ursi;* however, to date it has proven as difficult to grow at lower elevations as that species is easy. The plants are mounding to matting in habit, often spreading several feet. They have attractive reddish brown bark and rather closely set, variably shaped bright green leaves, each around an inch long. The flowers appear with the coming of spring in the mountains, from May to July, and are presented in dense clusters, usually white and showy. The brown berries are merely interesting.

   Although some adventurous propagators have produced pinemat manzanita in large numbers for planting in the Sierra, I have yet to hear any long-term success stories from the lowlands. My own trials have been inconclusive. Still, it makes beautiful mats and thrives in much harsher conditions than the coastal *uva-ursi*.

A. **'Pacific Mist'.** Another of Rancho Santa Ana's many fine introductions, 'Pacific Mist' is a perfect illustration of the beauty of billowy ground covers. It refuses to lie flat like popular selections of *A. uva-ursi*, but instead makes a more variable, widely spreading mound. It has dark older trunks, pale younger stems, and rather long, narrow gray-green leaves. With an exceptional record of garden tolerance, it is one of the few gray-leaved manzanitas now available for ground cover.

A. **'Pacific Mist', Rancho Santa Ana.**

A. purissima. I first encountered this species on a beautiful windswept coastal mesa at Vandenberg Air Force Base, one of its last refuges. The best of the plants were widely spreading, tidy mats or broad, dense mounds (though some forms grow erect to as much as twelve feet high). They have fuzzy, nearly round, apple-green leaves up to an inch long. White to pale pink flowers are borne in small clusters with leafy bracts.

   I still grow one selection from the Vandenberg site, dubbed—curiously enough—'Vandenberg'. It is a neat, bright mat with pretty pure-white flowers. It has thrived for several years with minimal care in my own garden and others near the coast. I cannot, however, vouch for its heat tolerance inland.

A. **'Sandsprite'.** This is one of a quintet of Rancho Santa Ana introductions ('Sea Spray', 'Indian Hill', 'Windswept', and 'Winterglow' are the others) that closely resemble *A. edmundsii* in their matting habit, small roundish leaves, and colorful new growth. I gave up after a year or two on all but 'Indian Hill' and 'Winterglow' (described above and below, respectively) after recurrent disease problems in the nursery. However, friends like David Fross have had good results with 'Sandsprite'. Its ornamental features include broadly mounding to matting habit, dense growth, bright red to bronzy new growth, showy pink flowers, and attractive reddish brown berries.

A. uva-ursi. Bearberry or kinnikinnick. This is simply "the" manzanita for many California gardeners. Certainly it is one of the most planted of all shrubby ground covers in the state. Bearberry is found mostly on the central and northern coast in California but extends north to Alaska and around the globe in northern latitudes. It makes dense, low mounds or mats that take root as they travel and flow gracefully over rocks and mounds.

Their dark older bark is often hidden from view, but the younger stems may be attractively tinged with pink or red. Closely lining the stems are oval leaves one-half to one inch long, dark green and shiny above, paler beneath. White to rather bright pink flowers are carried in small clusters, sometimes obscured by the leaves. The scarlet berries that follow are often even more decorative than the flowers. Certain individuals flower sporadically throughout the year, especially

A. uva-ursi 'Pt. St. George' at Tilden.

in cultivation, so that it is not uncommon to have a sprinkling of flowers and fully formed berries on the same plant.

There are many cultivars of bearberry, made both within and outside California. Most of these selections perform beautifully near the coast. The problem is that architects and landscapers insist on using them in places like Sacramento. 'Radiant' makes particularly lush carpets with bright green leaves and abundant large berries. Unfortunately, it may suffer from chlorosis and various leaf and stem blights when subjected to high temperatures and overhead irrigation. 'Pt. Reyes' is an old standby with dark, leathery leaves and fewer berries. Though less exciting than 'Radiant' ornamentally, it tolerates a broader range of conditions. I have tried other selections like 'Haven's Neck' and 'Anchor Bay', reputed to have good heat tolerance, but all had other serious problems, mostly with disease. 'San Bruno Mountain', which I received from Ken Taylor a number of years ago, shows considerable promise in this respect. It also has unusually large, thick leaves and large, bright berries. Perhaps the prettiest selection I have seen to date is 'Pt. St. George', at Tilden Botanic Garden. Forming an exceptionally low, dense mat, this plant spreads rather slowly and makes a continuous display of pink flowers and bright red berries. Its response to cultivation has been mixed.

Afternoon shading improves the performance of all selections in hot-summer areas, a point all too often missed even by professional landscapers.

A. **'Winterglow'.** This is my favorite among the Rancho Santa Ana quintet mentioned with 'Sandsprite' above. It forms neat mounds up to two feet high, with a dense covering of broad light green half-inch leaves. The new growth is lacquered in appearance and has a wonderful mixture of red and orange tones. It is extremely floriferous, with light pink flowers in small clusters. The reddish berries are also ornamental.

'Winterglow' deserves far more attention than it has received. Its garden tolerance has been generally good in both northern and southern California.

FURTHER THOUGHTS

Those of us who work commercially with California natives are ever fond of looking for new opportunities, even as the gardening public cries out, "Not *another* manzanita!" It should be obvious from the preceding descriptions that there is currently no lack of good material with which to work. Yet it is unevenly distributed among sizes, shapes, and tolerances. Several creative challenges remain.

We have legions of attractive ground-covering manzanitas, yet the palette of medium-sized and larger shrubs is still quite limited. Systematic testing of climatic adaptability—especially of heat tolerance—is sorely needed, as is comparative testing of disease resistance under high-temperature conditions. Tolerance of irrigation, which is also primarily a matter of disease resistance, would seem an equally obvious topic. Yet this may be a blind alley as water becomes more chronically scarce in California, forcing us all to curb our extravagant use of this precious resource. Whatever the future holds, manzanitas will no doubt continue to play a starring role in the garden.

CURRANTS AND GOOSEBERRIES

Genus: *Ribes*
Family: Grossulariaceae, the Gooseberry Family

Alate winter's walk in the woods brings unexpected pleasures, beginning with the soft colors of the last leaves to fall and the leaves' earthy smell as they return to the soil on the moist forest floor. Then there are the beautiful traceries of bare branches overhead, and the warm tones and textures of bark, which go largely unnoticed in summer when green is all around. But least expected are bright flowers, called forth by the imperceptible warming of the air and lengthening of the days. Chances are, if the owner of these flowers is a shrubby plant, it will be one of the wild currants or gooseberries. The scene is repeated later, nearly throughout the mountains of California, as other members of their clan burst forth with blossoms close on the heels of the receding snows.

COMMON FEATURES

Both currants and gooseberries are members of the genus *Ribes,* which includes (depending on the botanists one consults) 120 to 150 species widely scattered over temperate portions of the Northern Hemisphere and in southern South America. Of these, just over 30 are found in California, typically in somewhat protected sites—in and at the edges of woods, along streams or in canyons, and on seepage slopes—though a few venture onto open slopes and flats as well, usually where a little extra moisture collects.

The genus is made up entirely of shrubs, most of them of small to medium size, with many different growth habits, from matting to stiffly upright. Often the trunks follow attractive zigzag paths as they grow, creating a picturesque winter scaffold in the deciduous species. They have bark of many different descriptions—smooth and glistening, furrowed, shredding—and ranging in color from nearly white or silvery to dark brown. In the species commonly called gooseberries (sometimes separated into the genus *Grossularia*) the stems are armed with one or more sharp spines at each node, and several have additional prickles (sometimes quite intimidating) along the stems. Those species we call the currants have unarmed stems and are far more pleasant to handle, though not necessarily more beautiful.

RIBES SPECIOSUM IN FLOWER, *R. ROEZLII* VAR. *ROEZLII* AND *R. CEREUM* VAR. *CEREUM* IN FRUIT.

A few members of the genus—though in California only *R. viburnifolium*—are entirely evergreen. Some species drop their older leaves just as new growth commences in late winter or spring, while others are entirely (if sometimes only briefly) deciduous. The leaves themselves are quite decorative: they are usually three- to five-lobed and often conspicuously veined, with a smooth to velvety surface. Resinous hairs make both leaves and stems of some species sticky to the touch and pleasantly aromatic. Fall color can be quite delightful, with both soft and vibrant yellows, oranges, and even shades of red.

Wherever they occur, currants and gooseberries are among the first plants to flower each year. They may be enjoyed as early as January in the lowlands, or as late as June and July in the high mountains. The flowers are carried in racemes, or simple clusters, at each node of the previous season's growth. In some species the clusters are pendant and extend gradually into long tresses, displaying dozens of flowers over a period of several weeks. In others, including most of the gooseberries, the flowers are borne singly or in small clusters. Individual flowers are reminiscent of fuchsias, both in their pendant bearing and in form. Their structure includes a basal tube of varying length, spreading or reflexed sepals, and an inner ring of petals that usually extend beyond the tube. Though small—most are under half an inch in breadth and length—they can make a stunning show through sheer numbers. Colors range from white or pale green to pink, red, yellow, and even brown. Some of the gooseberries have particularly striking combinations, such as white on the inner petals set against the maroon of sepals and basal tube.

When the flowers have withered, small berries develop in their place. Those of the currants are usually smooth and painted blue or scarlet to black, while those of the gooseberries are often spiny and tinged with red when mature. The fruits of some species in both groups are quite delicious when ripe. Others have an odd musky or resinous taste.

Uses and Culture

California's currants and gooseberries have much to recommend them for the garden. They include large, thicketing shrubs like *R. aureum* (golden currant), capable of filling substantial spaces; more moderate vase-shaped shrubs like *R. sanguineum* (red currant) that fit easily into the average garden; and small shrubs like *R. roezlii* (Sierra gooseberry) that will happily occupy odd leftover nooks. Their twiggy growth and masses of (usually) softly colored leaves allow them to blend well with other shrubs, both native and exotic, in mixed plantings. They are also amenable to grouping in loose, informal screens. Some of the lower species can assist in covering bare banks, though I would hesitate to lump them in the category of ground covers (which in California usually implies solid carpets and suppression of weeds). One species, however, *R. viburnifolium* (Catalina perfume or evergreen currant), is widely, if sometimes inappropriately, used for this purpose. Some of the more ferocious gooseberries fill an unusual niche usually assigned to the barberries (*Berberis*): that of barrier shrub, placed to discourage traffic by humans or animals. Keep in mind that the barrier will apply to you, too.

Happily, several of the most decorative and useful species are easily grown in the garden, thriving in a variety of soils and exposures. Many do well in light to moderate shade with little irrigation, especially near the coast, making them particularly useful to those of us who garden under oaks. Usually the same species can also be grown in higher exposure, again particularly near the coast, though they will require increased summer irrigation as light and heat levels rise. Most ribes are decidedly less susceptible to high-temperature fungal root rots than are the wild lilacs and manzanitas. However, Central Valley gardeners should be cautious, leaning toward the use of shading rather than extra watering to get plants safely through summer's heat. There are also some gooseberries (*R. speciosum*, the fuchsia-flowered gooseberry, is a prime example) with a pronounced summer dormancy, which they may announce by simply dropping their leaves. It is best to water the plants only occasionally—or not at all—during this time.

Species from the high mountains, adapted to snowy winters, with little or no free water at the root zone, can be difficult in the lowlands, where the combination of rains and relatively mild temperature easily lead to rotting during the plants' winter dormancy. The only straightforward remedy is to plant them on raised mounds, in very well drained soil, though if you're really devoted you might cover smaller plants in winter with tents of some sort.

Alkaline soils and water are not appreciated by most species. Dressing with aluminum sulfate or iron sulfate is usually effective if plants begin to suffer (as revealed by yellowing of the younger leaves).

In other respects, nearly all of the currants and gooseberries are undemanding shrubs. They have their own distinctive forms, which they readily adopt on their own, though a bit of judicious tip pruning on young plants may help to fill and balance their structure. They require little in the way of supplemental fertilizers.

Few pests trouble the ribes. Mine have been largely left alone even by the same deer and gophers that constantly browse other native shrubs in my garden. Diseases other than root rots are also seldom a significant problem—although lately I have found one of the rusts (fungal diseases that produce small pustules on the leaves) on my plants of *R. malvaceum*, the chaparral currant. Rust can also affect other species, but seldom to the point of defoliating them.

In the end, most currants and gooseberries will be more than adequately hardy for the vast majority of California gardeners. Even several of the lower-elevation species are grown successfully in regions with much harsher winters—one notable exception being the evergreen *R. viburnifolium*, though even this species has endured short bouts of the mid-teens.

PROPAGATION

Currants and gooseberries are among the easiest of our native shrubs to propagate. Your choice of techniques will depend on the quantity and variety of new plants desired.

Seeding may happen in the garden with no effort on your part. Birds and other animals eat and digest the berries, passing out the seeds in ready-to-plant form. If your garden is sheltered by overhanging trees (thus retaining more moisture between rains), volunteers

R. SANGUINEUM 'ICICLE' FLOWERING AT THE NURSERY.

will probably pop up here and there. You can either leave them in place or transplant them—ideally during cool weather—to preferred locations. If you are not so blessed, or want to take an active hand in the process, begin by collecting ripe berries in the fall. Crush them and then extract the seeds by rinsing them with water and floating off the lighter pulp and skins. Sow the seeds outside in pots or flats while they are still moist. For species from higher elevations, refrigerating the seeds first for a couple of months in containers of a moist, porous medium will help simulate a more rigorous winter. Keep the surface of the seeding medium moist until spring, when the new seedlings should appear. They will grow rapidly and should be ready to begin transplanting to small pots within a couple of months. Many will be ready for the open ground by autumn.

Cuttings provide a ready means of perpetuating favored individuals or simply accelerating progress toward new plants of flowering size. While I have had at least some success with cuttings taken at any time of year, you can reduce the risk of loss and avoid the need for frequent misting and other measures simply by handling cuttings during the cool season. Sections of perhaps three to five nodes, taken from shoots recently matured, tend to be most successful. Mild rooting hormones, though not essential, can speed the rooting process a bit. Bottom heat is unnecessary. Your cuttings should thrive outside, in a shady and wind-protected spot but otherwise exposed to the elements. You will be surprised by both the number and size of the roots formed. The rooted cuttings can be rapidly moved through a succession of pot sizes, and into the open ground by fall.

Species of Interest

I would like to describe a few (certainly not all) of the species that merit cultivation. To make the list a little less confusing, I will observe the distinction between the two subgroups, currants and gooseberries.

The Currants

Ribes aureum. Golden currant. This plant is widespread in California and much of the West, usually along streambanks. Oddly, I have seen very little of it in my wanderings, though I enjoy it at home.

Golden currant is a sometimes massive shrub, often growing six to eight feet high and spreading laterally by suckers. The stems are rather slender and arching, usually smooth and covered in light gray to tan bark when mature. The leaves are up to two inches long (usually less), normally three-lobed, and light green in color. From February to April the plants are blanketed with clusters of golden flowers, each a quarter to half an inch broad, carried up to a dozen per cluster. Those of the variety *aureum*, whose range extends to the Rockies and beyond, have a rich, spicy perfume, and the petals turn orange as they age. Those of the variety *gracillimum*, resident mostly in the Coast Ranges of California, are odorless, and the petals age dark red (differences that seem scant grounds for varietal distinction). The berries range in color from bright red or orange to black.

Spring display by *R. aureum* var. *gracillimum*.

Golden currant is a distinguished and easily grown shrub, adaptable to either sun or shade, assuming that the garden is large enough to contain it. It does seem to respond well to pruning, though losing some of its natural grace in the process. Near the coast it is even moderately drought tolerant, particularly if shaded.

R. cereum var. cereum. Wax currant, squaw currant. If you travel regularly in the mountains of California, you are sure to encounter this currant. It occurs at elevations of 5,000 to over 12,000 feet, in moist sites and dry, shaded and exposed. Its small clusters of white to light (occasionally bright) pink flowers appear just as the forest comes to life in June or July. Then comes a lush crop of bright green, fragrant half- to two-inch leaves, nearly round in outline with shallow lobes. By late summer it offers a generous crop of scarlet quarter-inch berries. These can be quite sweet and spicy, though they vary markedly in flavor from plant to plant. In autumn, every plant seems to adopt a different shade of yellow, from creamy pastels to deep gold.

Wax currant is a bushy, pretty shrub, though its flowers can be rather plain (all the more reason to choose from among the showier forms). I have found it easy to maintain in containers but difficult in my own, admittedly fungus-riddled garden. However, it is un-questionably a fine shrub for mountain sites, where it is more at home.

R. malvaceum. Chaparral currant. I have firmly etched in memory some striking scenes of this shrub on barren serpentine in late winter and early spring. All else is quiet around it, and the leaves of its neighbors a tired yellow-gray. Yet there it stands, a large shimmering pink dome, defying the elements. The rest of the year it might easily be missed, blending into the silktassels (*Garrya*) and manzanitas around it.

This is a shrub of medium size; I have seen a few around ten feet high in the wild, but most are four to six feet. It is closely branched in full exposure but grows more sparse and spindly when shaded by taller shrubs and trees. The branches are nearly always held erect. Older branches are dressed in attractive chocolate to reddish brown bark that shreds and peels as it ages. Sticky hairs cover stems and leaves of the new growth, lightening their apparent color and giving them a strong, pleasantly resinous fragrance. The leaves are one to three inches across, broadly lobed and heavily textured. In the more widely distributed variety *malvaceum* they are light green above and considerably paler beneath. Leaves of the variety *viridifolium*, found in Southern California, are deeper green throughout. Chaparral currant is basically deciduous in late summer or fall, yet I have seen individuals already in new growth by the time the old leaves fall.

Sometime between December and early March, seemingly oblivious to rain and cold, chaparral currant erupts in a striking display of rose to white blossoms up to half an inch broad, held in dense, spreading to drooping clusters and opening over a period of several weeks. Some plants of the variety *viridifolium* have flower colors approaching that of mara-schino cherries. The inner petals are often lighter than the sepals and tube, giving the flowers a glittering effect. Given enough pollinators (something that depends mostly on the weather), strings of dark purple berries will follow. These are often musky or insipid in flavor, though birds seem to relish them.

There are several cultivars. 'Wunderlich', from the variety *malvaceum*, is one I introduced many years ago. This is a bushy, floriferous selection with gray-green leaves and bright to light pink flowers in three-inch clusters. One with much longer clusters (to twelve inches), discovered by Bart O'Brien and others on San Clemente Island, was introduced by Rancho Santa Ana Botanic Garden as 'Dancing Tassles'. 'Montara Rose' is an extremely dark flowered form, also of the variety *malvaceum*, discovered on Montara Mountain by Roger Raiche. Bart and I have both introduced robust red-flowered forms of the variety *viridifolium* from the Ortega Mountains, dubbed 'Ortega Ruby' and 'Ortega Beauty', respectively.

R. nevadense. Mountain pink currant. This close relative (detractors would say, poor cousin) of *R. sanguineum* is common from about 4,000 to 7,000 feet in the Sierra Nevada and other major mountain ranges, from the San Jacinto Mountains north. The plant itself is quite pretty, growing three to six feet high, with well branched trunks and bright green, three- to five-lobed leaves, each up to three inches broad. The flowers are a little less interesting, on the average, though pretty in a quiet way. Usually a uniform pale pink, they are narrowly bell-shaped, only about a quarter of an inch long, and held in spreading to drooping clusters of up to twenty each. They appear with the leaves from April to July, depending on elevation.

This is a beautiful shrub for mountain gardens, where it should require little care. However, attempts to grow it at lower elevations have not always been successful, probably because of our wet winters. Interestingly, having dismissed the species for lowland use, I tried an unnamed cultivar from Forestfarm in Oregon and found it not only enchanting ornamentally (it is quite floriferous and has good flower color), but as easy to maintain as the popular cultivars of *R. sanguineum*. It clearly merits further trial.

R. sanguineum. Red flowering currant. This species is treasured throughout the temperate world. Its typical form, the variety *sanguineum*, is found in the North Coast Ranges of California and north to British Columbia, usually at the edges of forests, on moist slopes and beside streams. It is narrowly erect to bushy in habit, described as growing up to twelve feet high, though usually half that or less. Mature stems are clothed in grayish to dark brown, sometimes fluted bark. Neatly spaced along the stems are bright to deep green, usually deeply veined leaves, paler and commonly hairy beneath; these range in breadth from one inch to nearly three inches. The leaves are nearly round in outline, with three to five lobes.

Red flowering currant dazzles all who see it in early to middle spring, with arching clusters of up to twenty beautifully colored flowers at every node of the previous season's growth. They range in hue from the rare snow-white through bright, clear pinks to cherry red overall. Often the petals are lighter and create a sparkling contrast. The berries that follow are nearly black, with a thin veil of white wax that makes them appear bluish or purplish. At their best, the flavor is rather good.

Let us not, however, forget the variety *glutinosum*, pink flowering currant, which coastal gardeners from Humboldt to Santa Barbara Counties are likelier to see in the wild. This is often a more graceful shrub, with—on the average—lighter green leaves and longer, distinctly pendant flower clusters that give a more elegant impression, color notwithstanding. The

R. sanguineum **var.** *glutinosum* **'Spring Showers'.**

color is light to quite bright pink, often changing with the weather (more saturated hues reign during cool, cloudy periods).

It is not surprising that there have been named cultivars of this species for many years. More has been done with the variety *sanguineum*. Although most of these are not of California origin, they are worth mentioning, as you are likely to find them in local nurseries. 'King Edward VII' is perhaps the most popular. It is a rather stiff, stout shrub of moderate size, with unusually large, bright red flowers. 'Pulborough Scarlet' is taller, with nearly red (*not* scarlet) tube and sepals and contrasting white petals. 'White Icicle', introduced by the University of British Columbia Botanical Garden, is a bushier, more graceful shrub with pure white flowers.

The one native cultivar you may encounter is 'Barrie Coate', selected by its namesake, one of California's notable plantsmen, near the Geysers in northern California. This is a well formed shrub with attractive reddish younger stems, deep green leaves, and masses of very deep pink flowers.

There are fewer selections of the variety *glutinosum*. The earliest of which I am aware was my own 'Spring Showers', distinguished by neat, bushy habit and flower tresses up to eight inches in length. The flowers are bright pink in cloudy weather, fading during bouts of early heat. 'Claremont', one of several cultivars from Rancho Santa Ana Botanic Garden, is a similar, slightly more open shrub with similarly long clusters but brighter pink flowers, with contrasting light centers. Some stunning selections from the wild by Roger Raiche seem not to have made the leap into commerce, though perhaps they will someday.

Whatever their distinctive features, nearly all forms of *R. sanguineum* are among the easiest of the genus to grow. They do their best with either light shading or moderate watering and acid to neutral soils.

R. viburnifolium. Catalina perfume, evergreen currant. This species is endemic to Santa Catalina Island, a bit of our far southern coast, and parts of adjacent Baja California. It is so distinct from the other Californians that one has to wonder how it came to be.

Catalina perfume is a scrambling shrub, with many slender, reddish stems that arch out and down, often taking root where they touch the ground. Set rather neatly along them are thick, evergreen, broadly oval to nearly round leaves. The leaves are deep green and shiny on their upper surface, paler and sprinkled with resin-producing glands beneath. The resin is spicily and pleasingly aromatic, though difficult to remove from skin and clothes. Beginning usually in January or February, the plant carries small clusters of odd brownish purple flowers with shallow tubes and spreading segments. The berries are red and potentially decorative, though I have yet to see them in good quantity on cultivated plants. Several unnamed clones are sold in California. One of them, offered by Tree of Life Nursery, is particularly distinguished by its large, dark leaves.

R. viburnifolium.

I have never quite understood the popularity of this shrub for large-scale ground cover. Without frequent pruning when young (a practical impossibility in many commercial landscapes), it remains sparse and straggling and may soon be overtaken by weeds. Yet when given the necessary tending (more feasible in home gardens), it is certainly attractive, and valuable for planting under oaks. This species, though easily grown, is the least hardy of our native currants, showing some damage at 15–18°F.

THE GOOSEBERRIES

Ribes californicum. California gooseberry, hillside gooseberry. Of all the gooseberries, this is the one you are most likely to meet in the wild. It is distributed over much of the length of the state, mostly in the western ranges at lower elevations, being particularly common in clearings and at the edges of woods. The plants are extremely variable, beginning with their size. I have seen them over six feet high with much greater spread, and also half that height, growing more narrowly erect. They are usually well branched, with slender zigzag stems, armed at each node with a triplet of sharp spines. The leaves are broad in outline, generally half an inch to an inch in length, three- to five-lobed, and conspicuously toothed. They are deep green and often shiny on the upper surface, paler beneath. I have seen them at times in late summer with striking scarlet and crimson shades, much like those of the poison oak nearby.

R. californicum in fall color.

Beginning in February, the plants will be seen dotted with small, variously colored flowers, usually borne singly at the nodes. The short tube and turned-back sepals are painted light green to deep red, while the petals are usually white. The berries that follow are pendant spiny globes up to half an inch long, turning reddish when mature and making quite a spectacle. The flesh can be quite sweet, for the intrepid few who venture past the spines.

The southern variety *hesperium* is distinguished from the typical variety *californicum* by its hairy leaves and normally red sepals and tube.

California gooseberry is an attractive shrub just for form and foliage. Though often not very showy in bloom, it offers many happy exceptions, and the flowers are always pretty at close range. The plant is not difficult to grow in reasonably well drained soil, with only occasional irrigation in summer.

R. menziesii. Canyon gooseberry. This is often one of the least attractive gooseberries in form, though its flowers provide ample reason to grow it. It is found along streamsides and in woods of the coastal hills from San Luis Obispo County to southern Oregon.

The plant is upright to arching, up to eight feet in height, though usually less, and rather sparsely branched. Besides the customary triplet of spines at the nodes, the stems are thickly set with smaller, less intimidating prickles throughout their length. The leaves are both lobed and conspicuously toothed, from a little over one-half inch to over one and one-half inches long and broad, bright green above, paler and furry beneath.

One to three rather large blossoms are presented at each node in March or April. Maroon to purple sepals fold back over a short tube, showing off the shorter white petals and protruding stamens. The berries that follow are similar to those of *R. californicum*.

This is an interesting and, at flowering time, decorative shrub for shady nooks of the garden. Near the coast, it is a good candidate for planting under oaks. Inland, it may need more frequent irrigation than this use allows.

R. quercetorum. Rock gooseberry. I first encountered this species as a scattering of mysterious dark green mounds along the walls of Kern Canyon. Later it showed up in many other sites (its range extends from Colusa County to Baja California), but nearly always at the edges of oak woods. The species name, in fact, means "of the oaks." It is mounding to prostrate in form, growing up to five feet tall and closely branched. The stems are arching but stiff, clothed in pale grayish bark and closely set with deeply lobed, toothed half- to one-inch leaves. Nestled among them in early spring are small, bright yellow bells with tiny white petals, borne two to three at each node.

This is a neat, pretty shrub, reputedly not difficult to grow (though I have failed thus far to propagate it) in reasonably well drained soil, with sun near the coast, possibly light shade inland, and moderate to occasional watering.

R. roezlii. Sierra gooseberry. This is my personal favorite of the gooseberries. Its common name gives no hint of the actual range of the species, which extends north to south from the Oregon border to the Palomar Mountains and east to west from the high Sierra to the outer Coast Ranges. It grows from one to about four feet high, with sturdy trunks and slender, arching to spreading younger stems that often create a tiered, oriental effect. Three- to five-lobed, toothed leaves, up to an inch broad, closely line the stems, along with one to three sharp spines at each node. The leaves are smooth and shiny, deep green above and paler beneath in the more westerly variety *cruentum*, fuzzy beneath and sometimes gray-green above in the more interior variety *roezlii*, and crowded with white hairs beneath in the variety *amictum*. The same differences in hairiness are seen in the half-inch flowers, which hang singly or in pairs at each node. The maroon to purple sepals curve back, nearly covering the similarly colored tube and exposing white to pale pink, inrolled petals. The contrast is most appealing, and the overall impression, truly elegant.

It is surprising to me that this little shrub has drawn so little attention to date. I am currently working to remedy the situation with trials of some promising wild selections of the variety *cruentum*. The plants are easy to fit into even a small garden and would be useful in the foreground of mixed plantings. They will need reasonably well drained soil, with sun or light shade near the coast, some afternoon shading inland, and moderate to occasional watering.

R. speciosum. Fuchsia-flowered gooseberry. This species creates some stunning scenes both in the wild and in cultivation. When in flower, it is the sort of spectacle that forces one to stop the car in the middle of the road and rush back for a closer look. It may be seen at the edges of woods, in canyons, and even in open chaparral, from Santa Clara County to Baja California. The plants are of various forms, from nearly round to low and spreading, growing up to six feet high—rarely more, and usually less. Their branches are ferociously studded

R. speciosum **'Rana Creek'.**

with sharp bristles and set at the nodes with triplets of wicked spines up to an inch long. The leaves are roundish, up to an inch and a half broad, deep green and shiny above and paler beneath. They may fall completely in summer or persist until new growth commences in late autumn.

Beginning as early as January or as late as April, clusters of up to four one-inch blossoms are hung all along the stems, creating a dazzling display. Scarlet to crimson sepals closely surround the similarly colored petals, forming a tube from which the much longer stamens protrude. The berries are a bit under half an inch broad and often red-tinged.

I have already mentioned the use of this shrub as a living barrier. It is even more prized for its ornamental features. Fuchsia-flowered gooseberry thrives in sun or light shade near the coast, part shade inland, with moderate to occasional watering, and it grows more beautiful each year.

HOLLY GRAPES, OREGON GRAPES

Genus: *Berberis* (formerly *Mahonia*)
Family: Berberidaceae, the Barberry Family

T he mahonias, holly grapes, barberries—whichever of their various common names you choose—are perfect shrubs for the demanding "black thumb" gardener: they are beautiful by anyone's standards; they have many different uses in the landscape; and most of the species currently cultivated in California gardens are adaptable to a wide variety of soils and climates.

COMMON FEATURES

Mahonias occupy many different habitats in nature, from desert washes through open chaparral to (more commonly) woods and shaded canyons where a bit of extra water collects. They take many forms, from scattered colonies of foot-high stems to stout, massive shrubs reaching ten feet or more. The stems usually stand erect. They often branch well above ground while rhizomes creep unseen beneath, forming thickets. Closely set along the younger stems are large leathery leaves, each divided pinnately (like a feather) into several roughly oval leaflets with marginal teeth or spines. The upper surface (except in the desert species) is often glossy, and the young shoots may be painted in shades of bronze to scarlet. Small cupped, bright yellow blossoms issue in fountains from the shoot tips or are borne in smaller clusters in the leaf axils. These are followed by grapelike

berries, green at first. When they ripen, most are tinted blue to nearly black with a "bloom" of whitish wax; those of the desert species range from yellow to deep red or reddish brown. The berries are not only decorative but edible, sometimes even quite tasty.

USES AND CULTURE

Landscape uses for the various mahonias are naturally sorted out according to plant size and ornamental features, and somewhat less so by cultural requirements. The larger mahonias are striking shrubs, with something to offer in every season. Displayed as individuals,

BERBERIS AQUIFOLIUM VAR. *DICTYOTA*, UC DAVIS ARBORETUM.

121

they may be left to form natural thickets or pruned to develop definite trunk structures (the individual trunks, showing smooth, light bark, are quite attractive). Plants may be grouped to fill large areas, planted in rows as screens and tall borders, or even formally hedged (though I cringe at the thought of such destruction of their natural lines). Plantings of some species will in time make formidable barriers to unwanted traffic, minus the liability that would result from more dangerously spiny shrubs.

The smaller mahonias find their primary use in the landscape as ground and bank covers. I have even seen them recommended for erosion control, though I would think only such dense thicket formers as *B. aquifolium* 'Compacta' would serve this purpose well. Other attractive uses include low hedges, shrubby borders, and a role as foregrounds for the larger mahonias and other substantial shrubs. *B. nervosa*, being a forest dweller, is a fine plant for shady sites where many other shrubs grow spindly and pale. The rest of this group will thrive in partial (though not deep) shade, with some sacrifice in abundance of flowers and berries.

Mahonias are in general no more difficult to grow than the common junipers and photinias that once dominated California landscapes. They thrive in a variety of soils, from well to rather poorly drained (with the possible exceptions of the former *B. dictyota* and *B. repens*), acid to moderately alkaline and even, as in the Los Angeles Basin, mildly saline. In areas with high summer heat all but the desert species should have at least light afternoon shading; elsewhere they are adaptable to sun or shade. Moderate to infrequent, deep watering suits them well. The combination of heavy clay soils and consistently heavy watering may lead to attack by fungal root rots.

The matter of feeding is negotiable. For really rich green leaves, moderate and occasional applications of balanced fertilizers are helpful, at least in poorer soils. Also, light applications of iron sulfate or chelates help to stave off chlorosis in alkaline or saline soils.

Occasional light pruning will keep the plants lush and leafy. If they are healthy and well established, selected stems may be cut to the ground to be replaced by new growth. Judicious digging and pulling will keep the thickets in bounds.

A major problem encountered with several mahonias is skeletonizing of the leaves by loopers (caterpillars identified by their odd, "looping" style of locomotion). Usually these pests are few in number and easy to remove by hand, if natural predators fail to take their toll. Hosing with plain water is an effective remedy for aphids, which occasionally cluster on new shoots.

PROPAGATION

There are several ways to propagate the mahonias. All species are easily reared from seeds, though you should not expect immediate results. The first step is to collect the berries after they have ripened fully (as confirmed by generous size and sweet taste). Once extracted from the juicy pulp, the seeds should be either planted immediately outdoors or refrigerated in a moist, porous medium for at least two months, then planted out in a protected spot. They usually sprout as the weather warms in spring, though germination can be erratic. The young seedlings are easily transplanted once they have their first or second true leaf beyond the initial pair of seed leaves, or cotyledons.

Two methods are available for the vegetative propagation of superior clones. Once the plants have produced new shoots from rhizomes, these may be dug up with as many roots as possible attached. The rhizomes should be cut cleanly and leafy shoots trimmed back to reduce dehydration. The other method, favored where even larger numbers are desired, is that of stem cuttings. Shoot tips with at least two or three leaves are chosen just after a growth cycle has ended and the stems are firm to the touch. These are treated with mild rooting hormones, placed in a protected spot, and kept moist until new roots are formed. This may take as long as three or four months. The plants that result, however, are quite precocious, often flowering and fruiting in their first year.

SPECIES OF INTEREST

Now let us have a look at the species found in California, beginning with the larger shrubs. These generally have the most diverse landscape applications. The smaller species and cultivars are particularly suitable for ground cover and perhaps border plantings. I will grudgingly follow the new taxonomic assignments reflected in *The Jepson Manual*, though something inside me rebels.

THE LARGER MAHONIAS

Let us begin with a few of the larger species, which coincidentally are those with the broadest landscape applications.

Berberis aquifolium. Oregon grape. By far the best known of the mahonias, Oregon grape is the one you will meet in any local nursery. In its typical form, the variety *aquifolium*, it is only marginally a California native, inhabiting our most northern counties and fanning out over much of the Northwest to British Columbia.

Oregon grape is highly variable in all ornamental respects. The generally erect main shoots may be well or sparsely branched and range from less than three feet to over ten feet in height. The leaves are divided into five or more leaflets, which are nearly flat to conspicuously wavy-edged, with prominent to barely discernible spines. The most desirable cultivated forms have glossy, dark green leaves and orange to red new growth, though both these features are extremely variable. Winter color is often a rich plum purple. Size and density of the flower clusters and size and coloring of the berries vary widely.

There is an obvious opportunity for selection of superior cultivars or seedling strains within this species; however, few growers have risen to the challenge. The dwarf cultivar 'Compacta' will be discussed with the smaller mahonias.

B. aquifolium **var.** *dictyota* (formerly *Berberis dictyota* or *Mahonia californica*). This denizen of the chaparral and open woods follows the interior ranges from north to south. The plant may be open and straggling but is usually well branched, growing as much as six feet high, usually less. It has pale bark and exceptionally thick, leathery leaves with up to seven large leaflets. The extremely wavy leaf margins are armed with stout, sharp teeth. They range in color from deep to pale green or blue-green above and often chalky greens and grays beneath. The flowers are showy, though presented in less massive clusters than those of other forms of *B. aquifolium*. Berries are typically purple with a pale waxy "bloom." In my own garden, this has been an exceptionally well behaved shrub, requiring almost no maintenance for good appearance.

B. 'Golden Abundance'. Like many other plant introductions by the Rancho Santa Ana Botanic Garden, 'Golden Abundance' arose as a chance seedling. The proud parents were conjectured to be *M. aquifolium* and the former *M. amplectans* (now *M. aquifolium* var. *repens,* according to *Jepson*). It is a textbook example of hybrid vigor, growing about eight feet tall and having sturdy, well branched stems. The leaves are up to ten inches long, with up to nine broad leaflets. Nearly flat and heavy-textured, they have a dark, glistening upper surface. Masses of large flower and berry clusters add to this plant's distinction. The berries are dark purple and covered by the typical waxy "bloom". 'Golden Abundance' has performed well in many California landscapes, yet has attracted only moderate attention.

B. nevinii. This is a rare and unusual mahonia, now surviving only in a few widely separated stands in southern California. It is a robust, bushy shrub, sometimes reaching fifteen feet high and wide, more often eight feet. The older stems are cloaked in attractive pale bark,

B. nevinii, **a great spectacle in spring.**

while those of the young shoots are blue-green or tinged with purple. Against these are set pale green to chalky blue-green leaves, each two to four inches long, with up to five lance-shaped, sharply spiny leaflets. Though only about two inches long, the axillary flower clusters make a striking display en masse. The orange-yellow to bright red berries that follow are also quite decorative. A similar species, unfortunately almost unknown outside botanic gardens, is *B. fremontii.* This denizen of the Mojave Desert and scattered portions of the Southwest is distinguished visually by more rigid stems and leaves, often strikingly blue leaf color, and berries that range in color from yellow to deep purple. Both species offer impressive specimen shrubs for those gardens large enough to contain them. Both have performed surprisingly well in northern California.

B. pinnata. California holly grape. Though hardly a rare plant, California holly grape is always a treat to encounter in the wild. It occurs unpredictably in a range of habitats, from shaded canyons to open chaparral slopes of the Coast Ranges, from the north end of the state to the south. Older plants form thickets often many feet across. The stems are usually well branched and dressed with beautiful three- to ten-inch leaves. Each leaf is divided into five to eleven or more leaflets, the basal pair crowded against the stem. The leaflets are wavy-edged, sometimes elaborately crisped and curled, with conspicuous spines along the margins. They are polished on both surfaces and colored bright to dark green above, lighter beneath. The new growth is often spectacular, with a truly lacquered surface and brilliant shades of red to orange. The flower spikes are densely clustered but quite variable in size. The berries are blue with a heavy "bloom" of wax.

The subspecies *insularis*, from the Channel Islands, is distinguished by broad, nearly smooth-edged leaflets. Though it is described as open and straggling, I have seen at least one beautiful, bushy individual at Rancho Santa Ana and others at the UCSC Arboretum.

Two cultivars of the species are commercially available. 'Ken Hartman' is inclined to be a bit straggly when young, but fills in nicely with some pruning. Eventually it forms broad, lush thickets, with individual stems four to six feet tall. The leaves are typical for the species, three to six inches long, shiny, strongly crisped, and red in new growth. 'Skylark', which I discovered in a batch of nursery seedlings, is more profusely branched and makes dense thickets. The individual stems grow six to eight feet tall. The leaves are five to nine inches long, the leaflets broader and flatter than usual, and the color dark green on mature leaves, brilliant red in new growth. It is a stunning specimen overall.

The Smaller Mahonias

***B. aquifolium* 'Compacta'.** Compact Oregon grape. Nearly as popular as the species itself in California, 'Compacta' may be either a mutant form or a hybrid involving something like the former *B. repens*. In any case, it is certainly distinct. Even a young plant is constantly at work sending out new rhizomes in all directions, each producing multiple shoots. This quickly results in dense thickets that can cover reasonably large expanses of ground. The main stems are usually one to two and a half feet high, rather stout, and closely set with stiff, dark green leaves. These have a satiny surface and show less red or purple shading than one typically sees in the species. The five to nine leaflets are narrowly oval in outline, wavy-edged, and lined with formidable-looking but flexible spines.

For all its vegetative energy (or perhaps, in some sense, as a tradeoff for it), compact Oregon grape blooms somewhat erratically and often sets no berries. However, its ground-covering capacity and attractive foliage are ample reason to grow it.

B. aquifolium* var. *repens (formerly *Berberis* or *Mahonia repens*). Creeping mahonia. This interesting shrublet enters only the northeast corner of California, though it is found over much of the interior Northwest and the Rocky Mountains. It has branched or simple stems usually under two feet tall and arising at variable intervals from the ground. At their tips are clusters of three- to ten-inch leaves with several broad (often nearly round), rather thin-textured leaflets. The leaflets are duller in surface than those of most mahonias, and often bluish green with lighter undersides. In winter they are often painted bright

B. aquifolium var. *repens*, Warner Mountains.

plum-purple throughout. Short, dense sprays of flower clusters are carried at the shoot tips in spring, later forming showy blue berries.

Now included with this variety is the former *B. pumila*, with much broader distribution in northern California. It is distinguished by more conspicuously veined leaves and usually darker, more purplish berries.

Both are counted among the tougher mahonias, tolerating both heat and drought if lightly shaded. However, more generous treatment, including some early pinching of growth tips, may be necessary to encourage an acceptably thick ground cover.

B. nervosa. Longleaf mahonia. Nearly anyone will find it easy to distinguish longleaf mahonia from any of our other native species. It is one of the characteristic understory shrubs of

B. nervosa **in the Siskiyou Mountains.**

moist coniferous forest, encountered first very sparingly, then more abundantly and in more diverse circumstances as one proceeds north from Monterey County to the Oregon border. In the wetter Northwest, it forms lush carpets even in open meadows bordering the forests. Longleaf mahonia is usually seen in loose colonies of solitary stems, a few inches to perhaps two feet high, though I have encountered seven-foot specimens in virgin redwood forest. It multiplies freely in cultivation, but seldom forms the dense thickets typical of *B. aquifolium* 'Compacta'. This is not necessarily a drawback, for its beauty lies in the form, texture, and coloring of the individual leaves. These leaves are indeed long, as the common name suggests—up to eighteen inches—and may have over twenty broad, satiny, dark green leaflets with conspicuous veining and only small marginal teeth. The leaves take on striking red to purple hues in winter. The flowers are presented in impressive sprays, up to eight inches in length and held nearly erect. The berries are large and of the typical mahonia "blue" (actually dark purple with a dusting of white, waxy powder).

I find it puzzling that this plant, while popular in the Northwest, is almost unknown here, even among coastal gardeners. There are few shrubs or ground covers more attractive for shady nooks in the garden.

THE FLANNEL BUSHES

. . . .

Genus: *Fremontodendron*
Family: Sterculiaceae, the Cacao Family

One of our great spring spectacles is provided by the fremontias, or flannel bushes, in flower. Whether scattered over exposed, rocky mountain slopes or planted along our major highways, they make great clouds of gold, often visible for miles.

It seems natural that they should share a prominent spot in the manmade landscape with wild lilacs and other showy native shrubs. And so they do, in large public and commercial plantings. Homeowners, however, face some serious hurdles, beginning with their search for plants. Otherwise knowledgeable native plant enthusiasts and nursery people often consider the fremontias to be nearly impossible to grow. This claim cannot be fairly dismissed as myth, for there have been plenty of puzzling failures over the years to bolster it. Yet neither is it entirely true. Most of the flannel bushes' quirks may be understood in terms of obvious features of the plants and their native haunts.

COMMON FEATURES

As with many other natives, the official identity of the flannel bushes has changed during my acquaintance with them. The old genus name, *Fremontia,* has been replaced by *Fremontodendron,* according to taxonomic rules of precedence, though it survives as an alternate common name. The genus is distributed widely over the state, from Shasta County to south of the Mexican border and Arizona, and from the outer Coast Ranges to the Sierra foothills. Most of that range is occupied by *F. californicum.* The second species, *F. mexicanum,* barely crosses the Baja California border into southern San Diego County. Plants are seldom seen in large congregations and tend to occupy rather inhospitable sites: exposed, rocky, or gravelly slopes, sometimes nearly devoid of other vegetation but more commonly identifiable as open chaparral. Their adaptation to these surroundings does much to explain their need for sunshine, their considerable tolerance of drought and heat, and, on the negative side, their lack of natural resistance to pathogens common in the garden.

Fremontodendron 'California Glory' and iris at Strybing Arboretum.

Like many other plants with broad geographic ranges, fremontias exhibit considerable variation, though they share several distinctive features. Most are large shrubs to small trees. *F. mexicanum* grows erect, with upswept branches, while *F. californicum* takes many different forms, often with arching or widely spreading branches. When tortured sufficiently by the elements, some even adopt the picturesque forms of small oaks. Bark in older shrubs is often grayish. Younger stems and leaves are densely coated with short, brown to whitish hairs. This characteristic is the source of the common name flannel bush, though that is something of a misnomer. Unlike flannel, the hairs are unpleasantly sharp and have a way of working their way inside one's clothing, mouth, and nose, causing hours of irritation if the plants are handled in dry weather.

The leaves are thick-textured and usually around two inches long and broad, though they may be anywhere from less than one inch to over three inches in length. They are roughly maplelike in outline, having three to seven lobes, and colored dark to pale green above and tan to grayish beneath.

Fremontias are most treasured, of course, for their flowers, which are borne in one great burst by most forms of *F. californicum* and more sparingly, but over a period of several months, by *F. mexicanum*. Individual flowers measure about one and one-half to three inches broad. They may open widely or remain cupped, with five broad, thick, petal-like sepals and a central tube of stamens reminiscent of the mallows. Their color varies from tawny orange to lemon yellow.

Uses and Culture

There is no denying the beauty of the fremontias. The question is where and how to use them. The country gardener with a large lot will find them ideal for individual or group display on open slopes and banks, where they require very little care, once established. Taller selections are useful as living screens, as long as they are not crowded. The flatland suburbanite can enjoy one or a few plants, planting them on raised mounds to ensure good soil drainage.

The more limited your space, the more difficult it is to use the flannel bushes. There is a good range of sizes and shapes in the wild, but the material commonly available is dominated by larger, more vigorous plants. Having adapted to lean soils, they also tend to overrespond to luxury levels of nutrients. While the plants can be restrained for a few years by frequent pruning, this will eventually result in a woody, stunted appearance. Still, it is possible to select the less rampant individuals from seedling lots.

This brings us to the problem of culture. Like many other shrubs of the chaparral,

F. CALIFORNICUM 'MARGO' AT REGIONAL PARKS BOTANIC GARDEN, TILDEN.

fremontias perform best when given full exposure to the sun, planted in well drained soil, and left nearly alone, once established. Pampered with normal garden watering or fertilizing, and shaded or crowded the least bit, they produce lush, heavy top growth with a weak root platform and are prone to blowing over in heavy winds. More seriously, these conditions all favor a variety of fungus root rots and twig blights, to which these plants have no natural resistance. It is common for well-tended plants to collapse suddenly after a glorious burst of bloom.

Nearly the same is true of heavy pruning during the wet season. Open wounds serve as ready entry points for fungus pathogens. If all this sounds a bit discouraging, remember that the "correct" thing to do is often nothing at all. Once established, fremontias will thrive and maintain good appearance with no more than an occasional tip-pinching and a few deep waterings each summer (or none at all). The gardener who insists on placing them in a more luxurious setting will have to be content to enjoy them while they last.

PROPAGATION

Success in propagating fremontias sometimes seems to be an art bordering on witchcraft. One might sail through a round or two with virtually no losses, using commonly accepted propagating methods, then suffer total failure under apparently identical conditions. Fortunately, given their substantial size, one is unlikely to seek vast numbers of new plants.

Seeding is the easier route. Most plants set copious quantities of viable seeds. Fall planting, followed by a winter chill, is probably best, though I have had good success at various times of the year. The most challenging step of the operation is to crush or pull apart the tough, usually partly opened seed capsules without poking hundreds of stiff, sharp hairs into the skin. Leather gloves and long sleeves are essential in this effort. Once you have extracted the seeds, place them in a bowl or cup, cover them with hot (not boiling) water, and set them aside to soak for a day or two. This makes the dense seed coats much more permeable to moisture and speeds germination. Sow them on a very porous medium (even coarse sand or crushed lava will do) and barely cover with the same. Having sprouted, the seedlings should be grown in a bright, well ventilated spot to avoid damping-off diseases, which cause apparently healthy seedlings suddenly to fold over near the soil line. If possible, shelter the pots or flats from excessive winter rains. The seedlings that survive will grow rapidly and can be moved up through a succession of pot sizes until large enough to plant out, usually in their first year.

Cuttings provide the obvious route for propagating selected clones, but they are notoriously unpredictable. The most reliable material consists of perhaps three- to five-node sections of young, active shoots, mature enough so that the base node is firm to the touch and preferably with new side shoots just beginning to form in the leaf axils. Treat the cuttings with mild to moderate-strength rooting hormones and plant them in any well drained cutting medium. Periodic mist or enclosure in a plastic bag or case may be necessary, to avoid dehydration and wilting. I have taken to placing the containers on a shaded bench outdoors during the winter months, when the air is usually cool and moist. In any case, within a few weeks the cuttings often begin to defoliate. This is not necessarily a sign of impending death; young axillary shoots should help carry the rooting process to completion. Rooted cuttings grow with astonishing vigor, yielding strong plants within a few months.

SPECIES AND CULTIVARS OF INTEREST

Fremontodendron californicum. California flannel bush. Always a spectacle, California flannel bush comes in a wonderful variety of sizes and shapes, most of them at least interesting and many quite ornamental.

The subspecies *californicum* may be a moderate-sized (five to six feet) shrub or a tree of twenty feet or more. The branches arch or spread widely, and they are often attractively contorted. The foliage varies from sparse to quite dense. Individual leaves are one-half inch to perhaps three inches long, lobed or not, dark to pale green above and densely tan- to white-hairy beneath. The flowers, similarly variable in size and coloring, generally open over a short time in a massive display. The subspecies could itself provide many useful selections, varying in size, form, and floral features. One beautiful, cascading selection from the wild, dubbed 'Margo', has been introduced by the Regional Parks Botanic Garden at Berkeley's Tilden Park. It has rather small, dark leaves and broad, brilliantly colored flowers. Unfortunately, it has proven difficult to propagate and grow on a commercial scale. That said, it certainly deserves some extra effort.

F. californicum among boulders, Santa Barbara BG.

The former subspecies *napensis*, now included in the subspecies *californicum*, is found in Napa, Lake, and Yolo Counties. It tends to be smaller and twiggier than typical forms, with relatively slender stems. The leaves are small and often barely lobed or nearly entire, while the blossoms are small (one to one and a half inches) and variously colored. My own brief trials with this subspecies failed at the propagating stage, as did friends' selections of similar material from the Santa Cruz Mountains; nevertheless, it certainly merits further attention.

Perhaps the oddest variant of *F. californicum* is the subspecies *decumbens*, from Pine Hill in Eldorado County. It is typically mounding in habit and under four feet in height, with spreading to trailing stems and closely set, gray-green leaves. The blossoms are cupped and painted unusual orange or tawny shades. Unfortunately, they tend to be obscured by the foliage, unless the plants are elevated and viewed from below.

Plants of this species seem unusually susceptible to disease, even by flannel bush standards, perhaps largely because the branches lie amid decaying organic litter. However, it has shown considerable promise as a hybrid parent along with more upright forms, producing plants of intermediate size and habit, with interesting flower colors.

F. mexicanum. Mexican flannel bush. Barely a Californian (at least in the modern political sense—remember that California was once part of Mexico), this species crosses our southern border only in San Diego County. It has stiff, V-angled branches rising as much as twenty-five feet. The leaves resemble those of *F. californicum*, though they are usually more deeply and sharply lobed. The plants carry a scattering of blossoms over a long period in spring and summer. The flowers are large, generally cupped, and colored deep yellow overall, with orange to reddish backing. Plants of this species may be as resistant to heat and drought as most forms of *F. californicum*, but are less cold-hardy and usually not as spectacular in flower.

At least five hybrid fremontias, each with distinctive ornamental features, are commercially available from time to time. Rancho Santa Ana Botanic Garden is responsible for three

introductions involving *F. californicum* and *F. mexicanum* as parents. 'California Glory', described as a "presumed" hybrid, was introduced in the early 1960s. It can grow twenty feet or more tall and even more in width, with the stiff branching habit typical of *F. mexicanum*. The leaves are large and broadly three-lobed, with a dark, shiny upper surface. It bears masses of cupped, lemon-yellow blossoms each three inches or more across in spring. Lighter flowering continues in coastal climates through the summer months.

F. californicum ssp. *decumbens* hybrid at Ken Taylor's test plot.

'San Gabriel' and 'Pacific Sunset' were deliberate hybrids introduced by the Garden in the 1970s. Both are gigantic at maturity—up to thirty feet tall, with even greater spread—though somewhat controllable by pruning and drought. Both have similarly large, dark leaves, more deeply lobed than those of 'California Glory'. The flowers are painted a bright, medium yellow in 'San Gabriel' and deep golden yellow with an orange blush in 'Pacific Sunset'. In my experience, 'Pacific Sunset' has been the easiest of the trio to grow and propagate.

A completely different tack was taken in hybrids between the existing hybrid 'California Glory' and *F. californicum* ssp. *decumbens*. The object here was to produce plants of moderate size with arching to spreading habit and new flower colors. A group of seedlings from crosses by Richard Hildreth, at the Saratoga Horticultural Foundation, were planted out at Ken Taylor Nursery in the mid-1970s. These had a wonderful range

F. 'California Glory'.

of sizes, shapes, and leaf and flower characteristics. Various selections were made for further trial. My own favorite, which I named 'Ken Taylor', grows four to five feet tall in most settings (over ten feet in one favored site), with a spread of eight feet or more. It has drooping branches and closely set, shallowly lobed, gray-green leaves. Flowers are cupped like those of *decumbens* but larger, with shadings of tawny orange and gold. Unfortunately, this cultivar has proven difficult to propagate. Another similar selection, 'Eldorado Gold', is the one cultivar of this type now rather widely grown, presumably because of its greater ease of propagation. It also seems to be more disease-resistant and longer-lived than the others. Still another promising cultivar of this group, 'Dara's Gold' from the Santa Barbara Botanic Garden, has recently made its debut. It combines a gracefully flowing habit, moderate growth, and heavy production of bright golden flowers.

WESTERN REDBUD

Cercis occidentalis
Family: Fabaceae, the Legume Family

I never tire of witnessing the western redbud's wakeup call to spring. One week, the hills are painted all in soft, drab greens and grays. The next, a vague purplish haze of rapidly emerging buds appears. Then come bright clouds of purple to pink, dotting the hillsides and lining canyon floors of the hinterlands. The sight can be breathtaking.

The common presence of western redbud in gardens throughout its range hints at another side of its nature: happy acceptance of life in captivity. It is among the least difficult and most rewarding of California's many shrubs to grow.

COMMON FEATURES

Western redbud is a variable shrub, sometimes fairly consistent in its more obvious features within populations, but often differing widely among populations. In portions of Lake County, for example, are found stands of distinctly treelike plants, with arching canopies ten to fifteen feet high or more, reminiscent of *C. canadensis* in the eastern United States. Nearby are whole populations of considerably shorter, many-trunked shrubs. All are easily identified, however, by smooth-barked zigzag branches, which present a beautiful tracery in winter when the plants are leafless. Bark of the older stems is grayish tan to silvery, while the younger stems are often heavily tinged with purple. Round to kidney-shaped leaves are attractive throughout the growing season and spectacular when they first emerge, often polished and bronze-tinted, in spring. When fully expanded, they generally measure one and one-half to three inches across and are dark green to blue-green above, paler beneath. Their usual fall color is a bright, cheery yellow, though it can vary to orange, scarlet, and even maroon.

Flowers alone are ample reason to treasure this plant. They roughly resemble those of

LEFT: *CERCIS OCCIDENTALIS*, FLOWERING BRANCHES IN SPRING. **ABOVE:** A TYPICAL WILD PLANT, CANYON WEST OF WALKER RIDGE.

the peas and lupines in form, though the rather narrow "wing" petals (lower petals) are swept up beside the banner (upper petal). Individually, they measure less than one-half inch long, but they are clustered at every node and nearly hide the bare stems. Their colors include glowing rose-purples to silvery pinks. Friends have described populations in southern California and the central Sierra with uniformly white flowers, though I have yet to make their acquaintance. The drooping, flattened seed pods expand to two to four inches in length and take on reddish and purple hues by late summer, finally drying to beige, cinnamon, or deeper shades of brown. They are held through much of the winter, sometimes well into the following season, and are oddly decorative.

Such variable ornamental features make some deliberate selection worthwhile, at least at the level of seedling strains. Rancho Santa Ana Botanic Garden once introduced a cultivar called 'Claremont', described as "exceptionally heavy flowering and with fine deep color," and an equally beautiful white-flowered clone, designated only as belonging to the wild form *alba*. I once offered a shrubby cultivar with deep rose-purple flowers from Lake County, and currently maintain a seedling strain distinguished by vivid orange to red fall color. Dr. Steve Edwards, at Tilden Park's Regional Botanic Garden, has discovered and propagated plants whose leaves maintain rich red and purple tones throughout the growing season. I hope that these will find broader circulation in the future.

USES AND CULTURE

Western redbud is a rugged, undemanding shrub. It thrives in a variety of exposures, though shading will significantly reduce flower production. It also tolerates many soils. Once a plant is established, it requires very little supplemental irrigation; however, it responds to

more generous treatment with enhanced growth and larger ultimate size. It thrives in searing summer heat with a little afternoon shade and should, if taken from northern populations, endure occasional winter lows of 10°F or less. One climatic limitation should be noted: while western redbud grows vigorously near the coast, it tends to flower less impressively there, lacking either sufficient summer heat or winter cold (or both) for proper bud formation.

Landscape use will be governed to some extent by cultural regime. Given average garden watering and fertilizing and occasional pruning of basal sprouts, western redbud makes an attractive small tree for the front yard. Planted in rows along a property line and allowed to roam, it can form tall, informal screens. With minimal watering and feeding, it is easily maintained as a medium-sized shrub. Where space permits, I would use it as it appears in nature—in irregular, open drifts over banks, hillsides, and open fields.

Given its robust root system, western redbud is not really appropriate as a container subject, though I have maintained a pet plant in this fashion, terribly root bound but healthy, for several years.

SHOWING OFF ITS BEST FALL COLORS.

PROPAGATION

Should you desire additional plants of western redbud, there is no particular obstacle to its propagation. The seed pods are easily opened to extract the seeds. Like those of many legumes, the seeds have hard, dense seed coats that imbibe water poorly until softened or abraded. A simple, reliable method is to drop the seeds into a cup of hot (but not boiling) water and allow them to cool and soak for a day. Refrigerating them for a couple of months, or planting them outside in fall to sit in the elements through winter, assists in their germination. In either case the seedlings should be transplanted to separate pots or the ground when quite young to avoid damage to the vigorous taproots.

Where clonal propagation of a particular individual is desired, stem cuttings are an obvious route. These should be taken during active growth, and each cutting should have at least two or three fully expanded leaves. The challenge is to avoid wilting at an early stage if the weather is warm. A shady location will help, but either periodic misting or protection of the cuttings in a closed plastic bag or case may be nearly essential.

Grafting is frequently employed with other *Cercis* species, and should be successful if one has patience and knowledge of this technique.

MOCK-ORANGES AND THEIR KIN

Genera: *Philadelphus* and *Carpenteria*
Family: Philadelphaceae, the Mock-Orange Family

Whether wandering in a grassy meadow or poking about the native garden at home, one cannot help appreciating the glory of a California spring. Yet all too soon, the show is over. By late April, the native landscape begins to show subtler shades of tan against the rich green of oaks and various leafy shrubs. Still, all is not lost for native plant gardeners who long for the sight of flowers. The subjects of this chapter take the floral stage as spring gives way to summer, and give the gardener much to admire at other times as well. These are the mock-oranges, *Philadelphus*, and bush anemone, *Carpenteria californica*.

COMMON FEATURES

Philadelphus, *Carpenteria*, and a few other shrubby genera are now considered to make up the family Philadelphaceae, though for many years they were gathered with groups as diverse as heucheras and wild currants (*Ribes*) in the saxifrage family, Saxifragaceae. Common features of their "new" family include woody stems, opposite (paired) leaves, and four- or five-petaled flowers with ten or more, often showy stamens. Besides *Philadelphus* and *Carpenteria*, the California representatives of the family include two other ornamental genera, *Jamesia* and *Fendlerella*, which are more difficult to grow, and a more homely but useful little plant, *Whipplea modesta*. Let us examine our chosen few a little more closely.

Philadelphus lewisii. Wild mock-orange. This is a common but delightful sight along creeks and hillside seeps in the mountains of northern California and mingles in my mind with scenes of rushing water in the Marble and Trinity Mountains. Wild mock-orange revels in the sunshine, where its glittering combination of bright green foliage and snowy flowers is shown to best advantage. Botanists once distinguished two subspecies with overlapping ranges, *Philadelphus lewisii* ssp. *californicus*, supposedly the more northerly and somewhat larger flowered, and the ssp. *gordonianus*, with more distinctly toothed leaves. This distinction held up better in the

Philadelphus lewisii 'Goose Creek' flowering in my garden.

textbook than in the wild. *The Jepson Manual* now places them together as part of a single, highly variable complex.

These are robust shrubs, growing six to ten feet tall and often producing many strong,

---

arching shoots from the base. The main trunks are openly branched, with short, leafy, flow-ering shoots that appear in late spring or early summer, followed by vegetative branches. One usually sees a combination of more slender, willowy side shoots and much thicker, elongated, suckerlike growths, usually produced lower on the plant. Ovate (roughly egg-shaped) leaves up to three inches long are paired along the stems. They are conspicuously veined, often toothed, and painted bright green above, paler beneath.

Showing up beautifully against this backdrop are several- to many-flowered clusters of pure white, usually four-petaled blossoms, which are further decorated by dense central brushes of yellow stamens. The individual flowers measure about an inch, occasionally al-most two inches, across and fill the air around them with a delightfully fresh, fruity fragrance.

There is considerable variation in every ornamental feature of this species, suggesting opportunities for superior garden selections. In the middle 1970s Ray Collett discovered a bushy plant with fully double flowers near the Smith River and introduced it as 'Goose Creek'. It is reminiscent of several exotic cultivars like 'Minnesota Snowflake'. My own selection, 'Covelo', made near the town of that name in the early 1980s, is a robust, broad-leaved plant with generous clusters of single flowers, each up to two inches across. These two selections by no means exhaust even the more obvious possibilities.

Philadelphus microphyllus. Little-leaf mock-orange. This is a smaller shrub, usually under six feet high, and globe-shaped to hemispheric in form. It inhabits rocky sites in the ranges bordering our southern deserts and those of Arizona and Nevada to Texas, though I suspect that its presence indicates more moisture than is obvious at the surface, as it thrives with

ordinary irrigation in the landscape. The trunks are more slender than those of *P. lewisii* and more profusely branched. The leaves are also smaller (up to an inch long), narrower, and more closely set. They are covered with fine hairs, giving them an attractive gray-green cast.

The flowers are generally, though not always, smaller than those of *P. lewisii* and borne singly or in few-flow-ered clusters. Nevertheless, the plant makes quite a re-spectable show, sometimes blooming for several weeks. A wide variation in fragrance seems to exist among indi-vidual clones. My favorite among a batch of Arizonan

P. microphyllus, **a more delicately tex-tured mock-orange.**

origin, received from Ginny Hunt, has a delightful per-fume suggesting grape and cinnamon candies. I hope to make further selections within this species, and encourage others to do the same.

Carpenteria californica. Bush anemone. A first encounter with this plant, flowering in the wild, is a memorable experience; there is, quite simply, nothing else like it. It inhabits only a small region in the Sierra foothills near Fresno, forming scattered colonies along streambanks, in canyons and swales, and even on exposed slopes.

Bush anemone is a sturdy, nearly round shrub growing six to ten feet (occasionally more) tall. New stems have a waxy, dark, often reddish cuticle, which gradually gives way to pale, grayish tan bark that shreds with age. Tapered, leathery evergreen leaves, each up to six inches long, are paired closely to rather distantly along the stems. They are dark green and softly shiny on their upper surface, grayish with tiny hairs beneath. Unfortunately, they cling to the stems long after they wither, demanding either tolerance or extensive hand maintenance from the gardener.

Clusters of three to many beautiful white blossoms are displayed at the tips of the previous season's shoots in early summer. Individually, these blossoms measure from a little over an inch to more than three inches across, with a varying number of broad, often cupped petals. Many threadlike stamens radiate from the center of each blossom, forming a showy corona. The seed pods, which slowly develop once the floral show is over, resemble little acorns. Unfortunately, they become a bit unsightly as they change from green to tan, though they are easily pruned out.

Carpenteria varies widely in form and compactness of growth, overall plant size, and flower size and abundance. Thus it is unsurprising that the British, who so often appreciated our natives long before we did, were growing selected cultivars as early as the 1920s. Here at home, the first selection to achieve much attention was 'Elizabeth', collected by Wayne Roderick in the late 1960s but not commercially grown until the early '80s. 'Elizabeth' is a reasonably compact and very

Carpenteria californica **at Tilden.**

floriferous plant, displaying up to twenty smallish flowers per cluster. Others with particularly large flowers or other distinctive features have been offered from time to time.

USES AND CULTURE

With decidedly different sizes, shapes, and textures, the two native mock-oranges and the bush anemone present somewhat different, though overlapping, possibilities in the garden. *Philadelphus lewisii is* the most rambling of the group, and a healthy plant is capable of covering a large area. It has been described, perhaps not quite fairly, as a "filler" shrub, and indeed, it is admirably suited to this role, with bright, lush foliage from spring to fall and attractive pale bark in winter. However, with a little pruning and thinning to encourage a fountainlike form, it is also suitable for more prominent display. By clipping young shoots (particularly the strong, thick ones) and occasionally pruning the plants hard to rejuvenate them, one might even have an attractive informal hedge, as is seen occasionally with the larger spiraeas. *P. microphyllus* is useful anywhere a smaller shrub is desired, assuming the site is reasonably well drained. Like its larger sister, this species takes clipping well, though at the expense of some of its natural grace.

Bush anemone has perhaps the broadest potential in the landscape, but it can also be a

DISCOVERING THE GLOBE MALLOWS

Genus: *Malacothamnus*
Family: Malvaceae, the Mallow Family

E ven for those jaded urbanites who dismiss the chaparral as drab and dull, there is something intriguing about the globe mallows. Their puffs of gray amid the deep greens of chamise and softer tones of the manzanitas are as dramatic as those of the silver lupines, while their silky, softly colored flowers have an almost otherworldly beauty.

It took me many years to become well acquainted with these interesting plants—perhaps not too surprisingly, since habitat destruction has nearly extinguished several species and threatens others in the wild. Those that remain tend to be thinly scattered over large areas, usually on dry, sunny slopes and flats, from Mendocino County to the Mexican border and beyond. The globe mallows have had various taxonomic identities over the years, being included at times with *Malvastrum* and *Sphaeralcea*, the desert mallows, but now the eleven or so species are accorded their own genus, *Malacothamnus*. All but one of them are native to California.

COMMON FEATURES

The globe mallows are a variable and sometimes confusing lot. Some of them are true shrubs, while others are woody only at the base. New shoots arise at intervals from the shallower roots and in time can form substantial thickets. Their trunks are generally erect, with rigidly upright to spreading, willowy branches, closely or densely set. Both stems and leaves are typically clothed—sometimes densely so—with tiny hairs branched in starlike patterns, which are distinguishable only with a magnifying loupe. These lend an overall impression of soft gray-green, tan, or even ghostly white. The leaves are often three-lobed and sometimes toothed, in the manner of certain maples. The flowers may be clustered at intervals along wandlike or rather rigid stalks, or grouped into dense heads at the shoot tips. Their five broad petals are white to deep pink in hue, spreading widely or cupped to form the "globe" of the common name. Often they possess a beautiful silky sheen, as well as a light, sweet fragrance. At the center of each flower sits the bundle of many fused stamens typical of the mallows. The blossoms make their appearance mostly from May to October, their season varying by species and individual but lasting in any case for several weeks.

USES AND CULTURE

These are beautiful shrubs for well drained sites, and particularly appropriate for open banks and meadows. Their bushy habit and unusual foliar shades make them striking accents

---

MALACOTHAMNUS FASCICULATUS 'CASITAS' IN MY GARDEN.

in open meadows or plantings of lower, plainer shrubs. As a bonus, they often flower when little else is stirring in the native garden. The taller species may be employed in the background of informal shrubby borders.

Although globe mallows are sometimes condemned for their invasive potential, the young root-sprouts are easy to pull or cut out (a service provided all too often by gophers in my garden). Again, well drained soil is important for success with most species, particularly in mixed plantings with regular summer irrigation. They do best, however, with only occasional, deep summer watering.

While aphids, whitefly, and certain caterpillars may disfigure the new shoots from time to time, the chief afflictions on these plants, in my experience, are those with four feet and fur. Gophers greedily devour the roots and lower stems; deer and rabbits will happily remove every young leaf and stem not protected by a barrier. Established plants usually hold their own, however, becoming a sort of ornamental forage crop. I have lost portions of some plants to fungus rots during recent relentlessly wet winters. Nonetheless, some piece has always survived to produce strong new shoots the following spring. Most of the globe mallows are quite winter-hardy, easily enduring temperatures in the teens, or even less.

PROPAGATION

I have already noted that the globe mallows are adept at spreading themselves about, but if you desire still more of them, you will find them easy to propagate. During the cooler months, you can simply (though carefully) dig up the recent root-sprouts, each with a generous clump of both older and newer roots attached. This approach might be successful even in warmer weather, if the leafy shoots are cut back hard to reduce water loss, but the addition of heat stress makes wilting far more likely.

I have had little difficulty with stem cuttings, particularly during the cooler months (hot weather can necessitate misting of the cuttings, which unfortunately favors invasion by various fungus rots). The leafy portions of recent shoots, especially side shoots, provide the ideal cutting material. Usually two or three leaves will sustain the cutting while not drawing too much water. A mild rooting hormone may speed the rooting process but is not necessary. Lay the pots or flats away in a shady spot, and water the cuttings lightly as needed. Once initiated, the roots grow rapidly, and you should not delay potting the cuttings into containers of a suitable size, trimming the roots lightly to promote branching.

I have not tried raising the globe mallows from seeds, and many plants consistently set none at all. However, if you have fresh seeds at hand, you can plant them with no special treatment as the weather cools in fall. A porous medium will be essential to avoid damping-off and other fungus blights.

SOME SPECIES OF INTEREST

Malacothamnus clementinus. San Clemente globe mallow. This plant, one of the showiest of the globe mallows, literally begs for a place in the garden (a temptation complicated by its status as an endangered species). It occurs naturally only on San Clemente Island. The plants make impressive thickets only two to four feet high in the wild, but often more in cultivation. The young shoots are set with lobed leaves up to two inches broad, green to gray-green above, grayer and hairy beneath. The flowers are crowded at the nodes of slender, wandlike stalks, opening widely to a diameter of about an inch. They range in color from pure white to light pink. Flowering time extends from April to July.

Malacothamnus clementinus.

This species has performed well in both sun and light shade, the latter preferable in hotter-summer areas. Its winter hardiness is not well tested, but I would not expect it to be as cold-tolerant as species of the interior. Propagation from plants already in public gardens should make it more widely available without harming wild populations.

M. fasciculatus. Chaparral mallow. This is a highly variable entity, confusing botanists by hybridizing and intergrading with other species. It is widely distributed, running mostly near the coast from Mendocino County in the north to Baja California. The plants are usually stout and well branched, growing strongly upright from three feet to over fifteen feet high. The leaves vary from less than an inch to four inches in length and breadth. They are pointed-oval to nearly round in outline and have sharp to rounded lobes, or none at all. Both leaves and stems are covered with white hairs. Beginning sometime between April and August, flowering stalks with tight, well separated bud clusters extend from each shoot tip. Their many cupped pink blossoms, each up to one and a half inches across, open over a period of several weeks.

M. fasciculatus, **detail of flowers.**

In its best forms, this is a truly stunning plant, whether in or out of bloom. (I was fortunate enough to stumble on such an individual, now dubbed 'Casitas', and propagate it.) It is also one of the more invasive, though the young volunteers are easy to cut or pull out. Its tolerance of garden watering seems to vary, even in the same individual at different locations.

M. fremontii. White-coat globe mallow, Fremont globe mallow. This is one of the species most likely to be encountered in a commercial nursery, though even it is not well known to Californians. Like *M. fasciculatus*, it has a large range—in this case from Tehama County north of San Francisco Bay to the east side of the Sierra and south to the San Bernardino Mountains—though it is thinly scattered over this region.

The plants grow from two to over six feet tall, with well branched stems and nearly round to oval leaves, with or without shallow lobes. All parts of the plant are felted with white hairs. It begins to flower sometime between April and September (the latter, in my own garden). It carries generous displays of silvery pink, nearly tulip-shaped flowers up to one and a half inches broad in small clusters on long, graceful stalks. This is one of my favorite garden shrubs, the ravages of local deer notwithstanding.

M. palmeri. Santa Lucia bush mallow. This species is sparsely scattered over Monterey and

San Luis Obispo Counties. It is the least shrubby of the group in California, each plant producing several heavy, branched stems from the base and forming a broad dome up to eight feet high. Often it produces few or no rhizomes. The leaves may be smooth and dark green or hairy and gray-green on the upper surface, paler beneath, up to three inches broad and shallowly to deeply lobed. One of its most distinctive features is the congested heads of wide-open one-and-a-half-inch flowers, borne from April to July. The typical flower color is rose pink, though it varies to pure white (I am currently working with both forms and find them equally enchanting).

M. palmeri, **an unusual white-flowered form.**

Santa Lucia bush mallow lacks some of the grace of other species. However, it makes a good mass of foliage overall, and the flowers are undeniably lovely. It has been fairly easy to grow, with a little more water than is required by species of the interior.

Several other species are of possible interest. *M. aboriginum*, Indian globe mallow, is now classified as a rare plant, though it is widely scattered in central and southern California. It grows as much as ten feet tall, the entire plant covered by tan to white hairs, and it bears small clusters of pink half- to one-inch flowers along the upper stems from May to September. *M. davidsonii*, sand globe mallow, is also a rare plant, found occasionally from San Luis Obispo County to Los Angeles County. It has stems as tall as fifteen feet, densely hairy leaves, and pink flowers up to one and a half inches broad. *M. densiflorus* occurs in the southern Peninsular Ranges. It is a bushy, small to medium-sized shrub with light green to gray leaves and dense clusters of pink flowers, borne in interrupted spikes. *M. jonesii*, sweet globe mallow, is sometimes encountered in the coastal hills of central California. It is also small and dense, well branched, with pale gray-green foliage and small pink flowers in loose, interrupted clusters. Each species has its own particular charm, and individual variations create a most interesting palette from which to choose.

THE GIANT POPPIES

Genera: *Romneya* and *Dendromecon*
Family: Papaveraceae, the Poppy Family

C alifornia is justly famous for its spring displays of annual poppies (Eschscholzia californica and its kin), which paint the hills and valleys with gold. Only native plant enthusiasts, however, recognize it as home to some of the largest, least typical, and most beautiful perennials of the poppy family. These "giant poppies" are far from the easiest of our natives to manage in a typical garden, yet they are treasured by gardeners for their stunning displays.

At first glance the two genera involved, *Romneya and Dendromecon*, have little in common besides the basic structure of the flowers. But there is more than meets the eye. Let us examine each group in turn.

MATILIJA POPPIES

Matilija poppy is the common name shared by *Romneya coulteri* and *R. trichocalyx,* both of which belong primarily to coastal sage scrub and chaparral communities. *R. coulteri* is scattered from San Diego County to Orange County, while *R. trichocalyx* roams from Baja California to Ventura County. Both form large thickets—often many feet across—from odd underground rhizomes. Each shoot has a woody base that may branch into a shrubby scaffold. The seasonal stems are herbaceous, often well branched, and usually four to eight feet high. Loosely set along the stems are smooth blue- to gray-green leaves up to eight inches long. These usually have three to five flat, conspicuously toothed lobes. Sturdy flowering stalks arise at and near the shoot tips. Each bears a single fat bud that opens into a snow-white, broad-petaled blossom up to eight inches across. The petals lie nearly flat, exposing a large central mass of golden stamens. Each petal is intricately crinkled, much like crepe paper. The total impression is breathtaking, even for people with little interest in plants and gardening. This pageant begins in early summer and goes on for many weeks, especially if the plants get an occasional, deep irrigation. The broadly urn-shaped seed capsules are decorative in dried arrangements.

The differences between the two species are best appreciated by botanists. *R. coulteri* usually has stouter stems, leafy flower stalks, and smooth calyces, whereas *R. trichocalyx* has characteristically more slender stems, nearly leafless flower stalks, and short, stiff hairs on the calyx. Assuming that the division is truly this neat, most of the material now available

ROMNEYA COULTERI 'WHITE CLOUD' FLOWERING AT THE NURSERY.

147

horticulturally as *R. coulteri* is of hybrid origin, with various intermediate characteristics. Of course, this in no way detracts from the plants' beauty.

Although most nursery plants are raised from seed, two superior clones are commercially available from time to time: 'White Cloud', introduced many years ago by Armstrong Nurseries, is a robust plant with stout, loosely branched stems and flowers eight inches or more across. My own selection, 'Butterfly', has more slender, closely branched stems, displaying more and smaller flowers with round, overlapping petals.

BUSH POPPIES

Dendromecon rigida, bush or tree poppy, is another chaparral dweller, found on dry, exposed sites and distributed from Sonoma County south to Baja California. It is a true shrub, up to ten feet or so tall (rarely fifteen feet or more), round to spreading in form, and often closely branched. The slender twigs are clad in pale tan to grayish bark. Lining them are stiff, pale green to gray-green, usually narrow leaves. It flowers much of the spring,

D. rigida **growing from a rock fissure.**

continuing into early summer in wetter years. At times, it lights up whole hillsides with masses of glowing yellow, broad-petaled blossoms. Individual blossoms measure around two

D. harfordii.

inches across and are presented on individual stalks. The two- to four-inch pods that follow are narrowly cylindrical, with tapered ends, and rupture explosively when ripe, flinging the dense, hard-coated seeds in all directions.

D. harfordii, island bush poppy, has been taxonomically separated and merged with *D. rigida* several times. *The Jepson Manual* again treats it as a separate entity. It inhabits the Channel Islands, growing in more or less open chaparral. Plants are similar to those of *D. rigida* but often a bit larger. They also differ in their broad, blunt-tipped, often deep green to blue-green leaves and larger flowers. The species has a generally longer blooming season than *D. rigida*, especially in cultivation. It also accounts for nearly all of the plants available commercially.

Superior horticultural selections have been made of both mainland and island bush poppies. Several reside at the UC Santa Cruz Arboretum and other botanic gardens, as well as at my own and various friends' nurseries. None have been raised, to the best of my knowledge, in sufficient quantities to distribute commercially, owing primarily to difficulties in vegetative propagation. However, seedlings of superior parent plants have given nearly equivalent results, in terms of denser growth, more attractive foliage, and more and larger flowers than the norm.

Uses and Culture

Like all too many of our showier natives, the giant poppies are dubious candidates for the "postage stamp" garden. Once established, a matilija poppy will easily gallop over twenty feet of open ground and overpower any smaller plant in its path. Shoots of my own plant at home continually burst through the asphalt of an adjacent road. Nonetheless, this same feature makes them valuable for covering large banks and untended lots. A sizeable colony in bloom is one of the world's great floral spectacles, and even occasional trimming will produce an attractive show of foliage most of the year.

In the case of the bush poppies, invasive potential is of less concern than the simple dimensions of the shrub. Although some forms of *D. rigida* are relatively restrained, a healthy plant of *D. harfordii* will easily spread eight to fifteen feet.

Only in large country or commercial landscapes, where they can be grouped with the likes of large manzanitas, blueblossoms, and flannel bushes, can plants of either genus be said to blend with other shrubs in the landscape. In smaller plots, they are guaranteed to be the dominant feature and, if unrestrained, ultimately the *only* feature.

All this being said, many gardeners find these plants irresistible and struggle to restrain them by digging out wandering shoots, in the case of *Romneya*, or frequent pruning, in the case of *Dendromecon*. The first technique is reasonably easy. *Romneya* should even be cut to the ground every couple of winters, to keep it lush and to remove dead stems. However, pruning of any *Dendromecon* should be limited to tip-pinching of the younger shoots and thinning of the old, or something resembling a pile of sticks will result.

Cultural tolerances are another matter. Both *Romneya* and *Dendromecon* are dryland plants, adapted to rocky or sandy soils. In cultivation, their drought tolerance is guaranteed, as is heat tolerance for all save perhaps some races of island bush poppy. Once established, *Romneya* thrives in a wide assortment of soils, with a variety of watering regimes. Irrigation simply encourages faster spread. Oddly enough, younger plants (which in most species are the more adaptable) are often lost to fungus rots before they can form their more durable structures, accounting for their reputation as "temperamental." *Dendromecon* is more susceptible to these same organisms at any stage, especially with summer irrigation which is usually unavoidable for establishing plants during their first year in the ground. However, *D. harfordii* seems to be more adaptable than mainland, and especially interior, forms of *D. rigida*.

In other respects, plants of both genera are quite easy to grow. There is no point in pampering them with fertilizers, for they thrive in very lean soils. All are only slightly troubled by insects and animal pests, though spider mites are occasionally a cosmetic problem, discoloring the foliage.

Propagation

Matilija and bush poppies are challenging subjects to propagate, even though both yield abundant material with which to try. Both are usually raised from seeds. Seed capsules of the matilijas are held upright and open at their summit. Hundreds of tiny black seeds—about the size of coarse grains of sand—are easily poured from the capsule when it dries. Pods of the bush poppies fling their shotlike seeds for several feet upon opening. Your best chance of success will be with pods that are yellow to tan in color but not yet dried, plucked whole and put in closed paper bags. In both cases, the seeds have a hard, dense coat that requires physical or chemical abrasion to permit absorption of water. Because this is accomplished by fire in the wild, a traditional technique for gardeners and nurserymen has been to scatter seeds on the surface of flats or pots of planting soil, pile hay or pine needles over them, and apply a match. Both seeds and ashes are then covered with a little more planting mix and kept moist until sprouted. Of course, it is difficult to do just the right amount of damage to most of the seeds, so it pays to start with generous quantities. A somewhat more controllable but only erratically successful technique (I have never figured out why) involves soaking the seeds in drugstore-strength hydrogen peroxide for up to one hour, then rinsing and planting them in the normal manner. In the case of *Dendromecon*, agitating the seeds first in a bath of pure white gasoline (not the automotive stuff, with its variety of toxic additives) will help dissolve a dense wax covering the seed coat itself. Most recently, commercial mixtures of smoke extracts and gibberellic acid, a growth-inducing compound, have given excellent and reliable results. The problem is to find retail sources for them. Whatever the initial treatment, a long, cool period, which is easily provided by fall planting, seems to boost germination.

Once the seedlings are large enough to pot, there comes the hurdle of transplanting. They should be teased apart with care not to break their delicate roots, potted with plenty of soil intact, and put in a cool, shady place to recover from their ordeal. The consequence of broken roots is nearly instant wilting and heavy losses.

A particularly successful method for the matilijas is division. Simply attack an established colony after the onset of cool weather in the fall, dig up shoots with lengths of healthy rhizome attached, and replant them in the ground or in containers. Broken sections of rhizome with incipient vegetative buds, planted shallowly in either soil or a commercial potting medium, often generate new plants. However, this method requires some faith and patience on the gardener's part, as new shoots may not appear until mid to late spring.

If you have a flair for experiment, you might try stem cuttings, using shoots that have just completed a wave of growth and begun to "firm up." Each cutting should have three or four intact leaves and a couple of leafless nodes at the base. If kept moist in a shady, protected spot, some of the cuttings may take root and provide duplicates of superior parent plants. Nursery growers have found the results tantalizing but woefully erratic.

SNOWDROP BUSH

Styrax redivivus
Family: Styracaceae, the Storax Family

Wandering the California chaparral, I am continually surprised and delighted. Beautiful plants pop up unexpectedly at every bend in my path, each time exploiting some nearly invisible change in soil or terrain. Snowdrop bush, or styrax, is one of the most elegant of these unexpected treasures. It might be missed at times, nearly blending with other chaparral shrubs; yet it is truly exquisite in spring flower, and plants in their full autumn regalia stand out vividly against otherwise drab hillsides in October.

California's snowdrop bush once shared its designation, *Styrax officinalis*, with plants of southern Europe and parts of western Asia—a jump made by relatively few California natives. Recently it has been recognized as a distinct species, *S. redivivus*.

The plants are medium-sized to large shrubs, inhabiting a broad range of sites and changing character accordingly. I have seen round, many-trunked bushes five to ten feet tall (maximum is around fifteen feet) growing fully exposed in the barren serpentine soils of Lake County. Elsewhere I have encountered individuals with a few long, gracefully arching trunks and very large leaves, growing under canopies of oaks or streamside maples. In both cases, the trunks and side branches are rather slender, often showing an interesting zigzag pattern. They are clothed in smooth pale tan to grayish bark.

Spaced along the stems are broadly oval leaves just under one inch to nearly three inches long, dark green above and pale beneath. Leaves of the former variety *californica*, inhabiting the northern portion of the range, are smooth on the upper surface, hairy beneath. Those of plants in southern California, once distinguished as the variety *fulvescens*, are usually covered throughout with short hairs. In either case, the leaves are attractive but not actually showy until fall, at which point they take on hues from pale yellow to bright, dappled gold or even orange before dropping to expose an intricate winter tracery of branches.

Following the first flush of leafy growth in spring, nodding white blossoms with brushes of gold-tipped stamens, reminiscent of orange blossoms, tip the young branchlets. The blossoms are sweetly fragrant in some individuals, lightly to not at all so in others. The pendant, roundish seed capsules that develop in summer are also decorative.

USES AND CULTURE

Both forms of snowdrop bush are nearly identical in ornamental features and landscape performance. They are attractive as specimen shrubs, whose size and shape are easily con-

STYRAX REDIVIVUS, DETAIL OF FLOWERS.

trolled by pruning or even shearing. I prune them sparingly to develop an open framework that exposes the trunk structure. They can also be employed in screens and informal hedges, and in fact are often seen in this guise along country streams. They are adaptable as well to container culture, tolerating considerable root-binding as they bloom faithfully year after year. I suspect that they might even prove suitable for the bonsai enthusiast.

As in the wild, cultivated plants of snowdrop bush thrive in a broad range of climates and exposures—interior or coastal, sunny or partly shaded—though one can expect heavier flowering in sunnier sites. They are also adaptable to many soils, as long as reasonably good drainage is provided. Rotting of roots and crowns may occur during the long winter dormancy in waterlogged soils. Although these plants are drought tolerant, they perform best with at least occasional summer watering.

PROPAGATION

Snowdrop bush, in either of its forms, is an interesting and somewhat challenging subject for the amateur propagator. Seeds from superior parent plants (vigorous, well shaped, and heavy-blooming) will yield a high proportion of more or less equally good seedlings. To grow them you will want to collect the ripe, dried pods in fall before they drop. Early to middle October is my traditional time for collecting forays. It is far easier to pluck capsules that still hang on the branches than to scrabble for fallen seeds among the litter beneath the bushes (particularly when they are flanked, as is often the case, by poison oak). The large seeds are easily extracted simply by squeezing the tough husk that surrounds them. Either plant them outside, in containers or directly in the ground, or refrigerate them for a few weeks in bags of a moist, porous medium. Germination is stimulated by constant moisture and cool temperatures. The main problem you are apt to experience is rotting of the large, fleshy cotyledons (seed leaves), for once begun, the process often spreads to the stem and roots. A surface dressing of gravel or coarse sand reduces these losses. The seedlings are robust and should be transplanted before their roots become entangled.

If seeds are unavailable or you wish to propagate a particular individual, cuttings are not particularly difficult. They are most reliable when made from vigorous shoots in active growth. The cuttings should have reasonably firm bases, with two to four leaves extending above the medium. Hormone treatment should be moderate, and the cuttings should be protected through shading, misting, or placement in closed jars or plastic bags to minimize dehydration. Once rooted, they should be transplanted carefully (the young roots are delicate and easily broken) and protected for several days afterward to minimize shriveling. They should be ready for planting in the garden by the end of their first season of growth.

A FLOWERING THICKET IN THE WILD.

FRAGRANT CLOUDS OF LUPINE

Genus: *Lupinus*
Family: Fabaceae, the Legume Family

If you prowl the backcountry of California in spring, you are no doubt accustomed to the perfumed blue carpets of annual lupines. You may be less familiar with their shrubby cousins, which make puffs of color on rocky mountain slopes, sand dunes by the sea and other unexpected places. These create their spectacles as individuals, only occasionally en masse, and are as impressive in the garden as they are in the wild.

COMMON FEATURES

The shrubby lupines are scattered over much of California, from the coastal strand to the high peaks and desert margins, and even the desert floor in better-watered portions of the Mojave. Throughout their range they inhabit exposed sites, usually in poor, rocky, or sandy soils. Like many legumes, they supplement the meager nutrients in these soils with the offerings of nitrogen-fixing bacteria that inhabit special nodules on the roots.

The shrubby lupines can take many forms. Even a single species—silver lupine (*Lupinus albifrons*) being the prime example—can occupy a continuum from treelike shrubs with picturesque, gnarled trunks to matting perennials woody only at the base.

Venerable specimens have dark, shredding bark along their trunks and lower branches. The younger stems may be reddish to deep green and nearly smooth, or completely covered in woolly or silky hairs. Closely set along the stems are decorative leaves of highly variable size. These are held on slender stalks, often longer than the leaves themselves. Each leaf is divided palmlike into several leaflets. In the case of *L. arboreus*, yellow bush lupine, the upper surface of the leaflets may be smooth and dark green. Leaves of the other shrubby species are usually hairy throughout, appearing white to gray, often with a metallic sheen.

Each season the stronger shoot tips expand into long, torchlike clusters, each carrying dozens to hundreds of flowers, which are either scattered or gathered in distinct whorls along the stems. In either case, the flowers open in long succession from the base of each cluster to its tip. Though not large (they vary from under a quarter-inch to a little over half an inch in length), they are as beautiful individually as they are in concert. Each blossom has the classic form of the peas, with a larger upper petal, the banner, sometimes folded back along the sides, and two side petals, the wings, cupped and forming a sort of pouch around the narrower lower petals; the lower petals in turn form a narrow sheath (the keel) around

---

LUPINUS ALBIFRONS, FIGUEROA MOUNTAIN.

the clustered stamens and pistil. The blossoms are painted deep blue, violet, or purplish red to white or yellow overall, sometimes shaded differently from base to tip. The banner of darker-colored flowers is often marked with yellow or white, giving a glittering impression from a distance. As if the visual feast were not enough, a fruity perfume often wafts long distances on a light spring breeze. When the show is finally over, beanlike seed pods develop along the flowering stems. The pods build up tension along a central seam as they dry, then open explosively, flinging their seeds for several feet.

USES AND CULTURE

Some of the landscape uses for the shrubby lupines are strongly suggested by their placement in nature. These are ideal plants for open banks, particularly those laid bare by grading and erosion. They have an uncanny ability to find purchase on steep, nearly smooth slopes, probing quickly and deeply into the soil or crevices in rocks. Just as quickly they then form dense canopies that soften winter rains and protect the soil beneath.

Such is the utilitarian side of their nature. Their billowy growth, softly colored foliage, and vividly painted flowers are also highly ornamental. In form, textures, and colors they blend beautifully with the manzanitas, wild lilacs, sages, and other popular native shrubs. One should avoid the temptation to create a solid mass, however. They are generally intolerant of shading by larger shrubs, and of excessive congestion even of their own branches. As with the manzanitas, more open groupings, including a relaxed variant of the shrubby border, are not only healthier for the plants but visually more pleasing, with soft rounded forms in place of tortured ranks.

Each of the shrubby lupines, whatever its size, is also an attractive plant for individual display. They take on a pleasing domelike appearance with no assistance on the gardener's part, though some judicious pruning of younger plants can help to expose and shape the trunks. Few other plants, save the artemisias, can equal them for pure grays and silvers. And even a single plant can light up—and often perfume—an entire garden with its masses of spring flowers.

Perhaps the main drawback of gardening with the shrubby lupines is their tendency to be short-lived. They grow strongly during their first few years of life, often reaching nearly full size in their second season. By age three, they are at their height of bloom. Then various things can happen. Planted on a steep bank, in rocky soils, plants may persist for many years, becoming more picturesque as their trunks develop. In a more typical garden setting, given heavier, more fertile soil and more than occasional irrigation, fungus pathogens accumulate, rotting the roots.

Sometimes a plant seems to commit suicide through massive seeding. *L. arboreus* is particularly prone to this phenomenon. However, there are things one can do to prolong their lives. The flowering stems should be pruned or sheared off as soon as the flowers fade, letting just a strategic few pods ripen to provide seeds for future generations. The other major contribution the gardener can make is to provide the best possible cultural conditions.

All of the lupines described below thrive in poor, rocky, or sandy soil. Although this need not be duplicated exactly in the garden, it is important to provide the best possible soil drainage. The same amendments that make dense, clayey soils more suitable for other sensitive plants will benefit the lupines (though relatively inert materials like perlite are prefer-able to sawdust and peat, which acidify the soil and encourage fungus pathogens). Planting on raised mounds not only improves soil drainage but gives the planting a more natural appearance. It also allows more native treasures to be gathered together in a small area.

Once established, shrubby lupines need only occasional deep irrigation to keep them looking their best. Planted in hot-summer areas, *L. arboreus* and other coastal species will need more frequent watering than interior species, though this leads to the same dilemma encountered with the coastal ceanothus and manzanitas: extra watering encourages high-temperature root pathogens and shortens the lives of the plants. Coastal gardeners, in con-trast, can enjoy both coastal and interior species. Most soils provide more than ample nutri-tion for the lupines. Supplemental fertilizer applications simply promote rampant, floppy growth, reduce flowering, and shorten the lives of the plants.

High exposure is perhaps the most essential element of successful culture for the shrubby lupines. The sunniest possible spot in the garden will promote compact, sturdy growth and a generous floral display each year. Light afternoon shading may be necessary to reduce summer temperatures for coastal species in interior valley gardens, but heavier shading will only result in less tidy plants and reduced flowering.

Cold hardiness will not be an issue for most California gardeners, though I have seen *L. arboreus* briefly damaged in freezes below 20°F along the coast. Other coastal species would probably suffer at somewhat lower temperatures. Forms of both *L. albifrons* and *L. excubitus* grow well above snowline and could easily be selected for gardens in the higher mountains.

These plants are usually free of common garden pests. Aphids may attack the new shoots in spring but are easily removed with the blast of an open hose. Surprisingly, snails are a far more serious affliction, even in well exposed sites, sometimes stripping the branches bare of leaves. Various caterpillars can have an identical effect and should be removed if the plants suffer excessively (unless, of course, you are raising them to feed local birds).

PROPAGATION

Propagation of the shrubby lupines is not only a way to share them with friends or expand your plantings, it is also a means of ensuring a continual succession in the garden, given these plants' frequently short life spans. Seeding is usually the method of choice.

Collecting seeds requires little effort, but timing can be critical. Whole flowering stems can be cut when some or most of the pods along them have ripened, or individual pods can be snapped off as they reach this condition. At this point, they will not only show obvious bulges from the seeds inside, but will have changed in color from green to yellow. Do not wait for them to dry, for by this time they will have flown apart and flung their seeds away. Place the pods or stems in large paper bags, where they can be contained as they dry.

Fall is the perfect time to plant the seeds, for they germinate best after a few weeks of cool nights. A useful first step is to place the seeds in a cup or dish, pour hot (though not boiling) water over them, and let them stand overnight. This softens the waxy seed coats and makes them more permeable to water. Planting them in the open ground where they are to live eliminates the later step of transplanting, but the young seedlings may need protection, particularly from the ravages of snails. Starting them in containers offers a little extra secu-rity. Consider sowing the seeds directly in deep two- to three-inch pots, one or two seeds per pot. Barely cover the seeds with planting medium, carefully water, and set out in a shaded, protected spot outdoors, keeping them continuously moist until sprouted.

Cuttings are reasonably easy to root for *L. arboreus*, more difficult for some other coastal species, and a definite challenge where the interior species are concerned, for they dehydrate and wilt easily when they are first planted, yet any excess moisture about the leaves and stems promotes fungus rots. If, however, they survive for a month or two, they will produce roots without the need for strong rooting hormones or other exotic treatments. Try sections of the current season's shoots, from near the tips to several inches down the stems, each with perhaps three to four leaves and a basal node. Plant the cuttings in perlite or another porous medium and lay them away in a cool, shady place, never letting them dry out but also avoiding excessive moisture (a delicate balance). Once they have rooted, they should be lifted with sizeable chunks of the cutting medium intact around the roots and transplanted to suitably sized containers.

However you propagate the shrubby lupines, you should never let them become rootbound in containers. Young plants in small but deep containers, transplanted while still lightly rooted and before the onset of hot weather, stand by far the best chance of success in the ground.

SPECIES OF INTEREST

Here are some shrubby species of particular interest. If you garden in the hotter interior, you may want to avoid the coastal types.

L. albifrons, **spring display.**

Lupinus albifrons, silver bush lupine, is surely among the most variable of all lupines. It inhabits sites from the seacoast to the foothills of the Sierra and travels the Coast Ranges nearly from the northern to the southern border of the state, dotting the chaparral, rocky outcrops, and open, meadowy hillsides along the way. Its most typical form, now labeled the variety *albifrons*, can reach eight feet or more in height. At the other extreme, the variety *collinus* forms low mounds or nearly flat mats, woody only beneath a mantle of soft leaves and stems. All but the largest forms are profusely branched, with closely spaced leaves, giving the impression of a solid, billowy mass of foliage. The leaves vary from under one inch to nearly three inches in breadth and are carried on stalks of nearly the same length. Each is divided into as many as ten narrow leaflets usually covered with silky to shaggy hairs, appearing nearly white to metallic silver. Variants with sparser hairs are merely pale green in color.

From March to June, silky flower stems issue from the shoot tips. These expand into virtual towers, up to a foot or more tall, of purple-blue to reddish violet flowers. The flowers measure from a bit over one-third to about two-thirds of an inch long and are generally decorated by a white to yellow patch on the banner. Fragrance is a highly variable feature even within a given population, some individuals having a powerful, sweet perfume while others are nearly unscented.

The species is divided botanically into several varieties, implying neater distinctions than one actually encounters in the field. The variety *albifrons* is the most broadly distributed, the largest in overall growth, and the most variable in details of foliage and flowers. The variety *douglasii*, in contrast, is usually smaller and nearly always silvery in leaf. It also sports smaller flower clusters. This variety follows the central coastline to the San Francisco Bay and is at home in coastal climates. The variety *abramsii*, Abrams's lupine, is a still smaller form, usually growing three feet high or less, with woolly rather than silky hairs on leaves and stems. It inhabits the coast ranges from the Santa Lucia Mountains south. The variety *collinus* is the most distinct. It is found nearly throughout the Coast Ranges and in the Sierra Nevada foothills, nearly always in exposed, rocky places. It makes mats and low mounds of silvery foliage with large, brilliantly colored flower clusters.

Silver bush lupine has been cultivated for many years, though never on a large scale. The variety *albifrons* is best known. On a sunny bank, with only occasional summer irrigation, it can be a picturesque and durable shrub. Less is known about the varieties *douglasii* and *abramsii*, though they should be no more difficult. The variety *collinus* is best under rock garden conditions, always in perfectly drained, gravelly soil, but it is well worth the extra effort: A well grown plant is among the showiest of all lupines.

L. arboreus, coast or yellow bush lupine, is distinct from *L. albifrons* in several respects. It is a less variable shrub, inhabiting a narrow strip within a few miles of the immediate coast from Ventura County north and occurring as an escaped "exotic" in far northern California. It grows three to eight feet tall, usually erect though often beaten into mounding forms by coastal winds. The trunks become stout and gnarled in age. The younger stems are nearly smooth to thickly covered with silky hairs, and often tinged with red. The leaves are similarly variable, though generally deep to pale green above, light green to gray beneath. They are divided into five to a dozen leaflets, each up to two inches long.

L. arboreus at its summer best.

Flowering can start as early as March, peaking on the central and north coast in late spring and early summer. A scattering of flowers may persist throughout the summer. Clusters up to a foot long bear many cheery blossoms, often arranged in distinct whorls. The individual flowers are large—up to two-thirds of an inch long—and painted golden to pale yellow, various shades of lavender, or white. At one time the lavender-flowered forms were segregated as *L. propinquus*. Where lavender- and yellow-flowered forms meet, their interbreeding often produces some interesting—though not always beautiful—intermediate shades and combinations of shades, including pink. Fragrance is also a variable feature. The best forms have a powerful, almost lemony perfume.

Yellow bush lupine is an attractive shrub for coastal gardens. It may need frequent pruning to keep it sturdy and compact, especially under irrigated conditions. Its unfortunate tendency to die after setting a particularly heavy crop of seeds can be combated by shearing off spent flower stems. In hot-summer areas, its susceptibility to high-temperature root rots makes it nearly an annual.

L. chamissonis is another denizen of the seacoast, found on dunes and bluffs from Los Angeles County to Marin County. It can vary much like *L. arboreus* in size, from about two to seven feet, though it is usually smaller and more compact in growth. The entire plant is clothed in soft, silvery hairs. The leaves are closely set and measure roughly one to two inches broad. They form an exquisite backdrop for the flowers, which vary from light or medium blue to chalky lavender, carried in clusters up to eight inches long.

L. chamissonis, detail of foliage.

This is a beautiful shrub in all respects. It is easily grown, at least in well drained soils, near the coast. I would expect gardeners in hotter climates to find it more temperamental and short-lived.

L. excubitus, fondly known as the grape soda lupine, is a familiar sight to travelers in the southern mountains. It inhabits the southern Sierra Nevada and ranges to the south, growing mostly on open slopes at elevations from about 3,000 to 10,000 feet. It is similar to *L. albifrons* in many respects (the new *Jepson Manual* describes them as "± indistinct"). The variety *excubitus* is a roughly two- to five-foot shrub, while the variety *austromontanus* is a low mound or mat, woody beneath, from under one foot to about two feet high. The plants of most forms are quite silvery, like those of *L. albifrons*. The leaves also resemble those of *L. albifrons*, though they vary from under half an inch to around four inches across. Few lupines are as dazzling as these in bloom. The flowers are borne in clusters often over a foot long. They are painted mostly in vivid tones of violet to deep lavender, with bright yellow on the banners. Their delightful, grapelike fragrance is noticeable from far away.

L. excubitus near Lake Hughes.

The variety *excubitus* is found around the borders of the Mojave and in the higher mountains. It is the largest form overall—though not in its flowers—and is nearly round to mounding in form. The variety *hallii*, occurring at somewhat lower elevations, is similar but of more open growth and greener. It has the largest flower clusters of the species. Variety *austromontanus* is found from the Tehachapi Mountains south, often at high elevations. It is a stunning plant, with its vivid, fragrant flower clusters often blanketing a metallic silver mat. Variety *johnstonii* is a similar, sometimes even more ground-hugging plant with a similar range.

Surprisingly, these beauties have been tried very little by gardeners. Excellent soil drainage is a must, as is full exposure. I have grown plants of the variety *austromontanus* for several years on a steep bank. They persist and flower well in spite of periodic ravages by rabbits and snails.

L. variicolor. This coastal lupine is described in *The Jepson Manual* as a "perennial to subshrub." I have seen its full range of forms but have worked with only the shrubbier sorts. It is usually well branched, the stems prostrate or at least widely spreading, making a mat or low mound two to six feet broad. Both stems and leaves are covered with silky to shaggy hairs, giving them a soft gray-green appearance. Leaves are normally one to two inches broad, with up to nine leaflets.

This plant's flowering season begins in April and extends through the summer months. The flowers are distinct from those of the other shrubby lupines in at least two ways: The clusters are relatively short—generally under six inches—and few-flowered, the half-inch blossoms arranged mostly in whorls. Also the individual flowers are presented in a variety of colors, from purple, blue, or pink to white or yellow, usually in bi- or tricolor combinations. Even neighboring plants may have quite differently colored flowers. Apparent hybrids between this species and *L. arboreus* add to this variety with stockier plants and larger flower clusters.

L. variicolor (x *arboreus*?), Devil's Slide.

I have enjoyed the company of this little shrublet and have found it no more difficult to grow than yellow bush lupine. It is sufficiently showy to display alone, and it might be used as a small-scale ground cover, with care not to crowd the plants.

L. littoralis is a very similar species, with overlapping but more northerly distribution, extending to British Columbia. It is supposedly distinguished by shaggier hairs, pale blue to purple flowers, and a later blooming season. Its cultural requirements are presumably the same as those of *L. variicolor*. I have almost certainly grown both as *L. variicolor*, with the same good results.

BLUE CURLS

· ·

Genus: *Trichostema*
Family: Lamiaceae, the Mint Family

The chaparral—*California's dryland pygmy forest*—is not something most Californians cherish. In the popular mind, it is a wasteland, nearly like the desert, where one might go to shoot a gun, ride a motorcycle full tilt up a mountainside, or generally vent the frustrations born of city life without inviting arrest. The few of us who deliberately explore the chaparral, however, know it as a place teeming with life and dotted with unexpected treasures. Some of those treasures are the blue curls. Though they belong very much to the chaparral, they seem to delight in edges and clearings. They do a fine job of colonizing road banks, making them easy for the casual tourist to enjoy, and they thrive in recent burns and bulldozer cuts. Some of their neighbors—the manzanitas, for example—may be more impressive in form and foliage. But in bloom, they create a spectacle rivaled only by that of the much larger wild lilacs, flannel bushes, and bush poppies.

COMMON FEATURES

The plants we know as blue curls belong to the genus *Trichostema*, one of the smaller genera of the mint family. The new *Jepson Manual* lists ten species in California, of which two are shrubs or subshrubs (plants with woody trunks and nonwoody seasonal stems). The rest are annuals (I will describe only the shrubby species here). Like many of the mints, they have leafy stems and neatly paired, opposite leaves. All parts of the plants are pungently aromatic, with various combinations of sweet, resinous, and acid scents. Showy violet or blue to white, irregular flowers, somewhat resembling those of the garden germanders (*Teucrium*), are clustered along the upper stems. They are made even more beautiful by the long, colored stamens that arch out and down, well beyond the floral tubes.

USES AND CULTURE

Given their ornamental features and moderate size, blue curls should have a variety of uses in the landscape. Their main limitations, as it turns out, are cultural. *T. lanatum* has long been known as a fussy and somewhat unpredictable plant; the same is clearly true for *T. parishii*, a plant that few people have even tried.

A steep, bare bank is the perfect site for either species. They blend beautifully with the shrubby sages and sagebrushes, the moderate-sized manzanitas, and wild lilacs, and make fine accent plants for plantings dominated by the much larger flannel bushes and toyons. This assumes that care is exercised to avoid crowding and to keep them well exposed. The

---

TRICHOSTEMA LANATUM, A WHITE-FLOWERED FORM, AT RANCHO SANTA ANA.

TOYON ON MY MIND

Heteromeles arbutifolia
Family: Rosaceae, the Rose Family

Y ou have seen it while walking in the hills on a crisp autumn day or driving through the countryside enjoying a break between winter rains. Barely noticed the rest of the year, toyon suddenly seems to be everywhere, from mountain slopes to freeway banks, a cheery dressing of red on green. Perhaps it has occurred to you that this would be a fine shrub to have at home. And so it is, with a few practical qualifications.

GENERAL FEATURES

Toyon or Christmas berry, known to botanists as *Heteromeles arbutifolia*, is an evergreen, shrubby member of the rose family. Unlike many other native shrubs—most notably the manzanitas and blueblossoms—it is the sole representative of its genus (though it was once included with the photinias, of which there are many). Toyon is distributed from Humboldt County in the north to Baja California in the south, and from near the coast to the Sierra foothills. Though especially common in the chaparral and coastal scrub, toyon often stands alone on rocky or meadowy hillsides or shares the understory of light woods with more shade-loving shrubs. Even more surprising is its tolerance of soils ranging from rich alluvium in canyon bottoms to barren serpentine screes. The latter, in fact, support some of the largest populations and most massive plants I have seen.

Toyon often straddles the boundary between shrub and tree, growing from around six to over twenty feet tall. It nearly always has multiple trunks from the base and is well branched above, though overly shaded plants grow more sparse and straggly. Younger stems are bright green or tinged with red, darkening as they mature. Older branches are clothed in attractive smooth, gray-brown bark. Even more striking are its bold, leathery leaves. These are rather closely spaced, two to at least six inches long, and nearly lance-shaped to broadly oval in outline; most are set along the margins with sawlike teeth. They are colored deep green above, with a satiny to shiny surface, and bright green to nearly chartreuse beneath.

In June and July each plant is decorated with many large, branched clusters of cream to white five-petaled flowers. These are showy en masse, though individually measuring only a third of an inch or less across. They are followed by little green berries that expand throughout the summer and early fall. As the nights cool, the berries begin to change color, finally taking on hues from crimson through vivid reds to an occasional orange or yellow. Throughout their color range, the berries are extremely showy against the clean, dark foliage. They have proven so popular for Christmas decorations that local ordinances have been passed to forbid their collection on public lands. The berries usually drop or are

HETEROMELES ARBUTIFOLIA IN BERRY. PHOTOGRAPH BY WILLIAM T. FOLLETTE.

stripped from the plants by birds by mid-January in colder winters. Following dry, mild winters, however, I have sometimes seen plants laden with fruit as late as March.

Although toyon can be found in many local variations, it has no currently recognized botanical varieties. Yellow-berried forms were once grouped under the variety *cerina*. More recently, plants from San Clemente and Santa Catalina Islands, with berries sometimes twice the normal size for mainland plants, were segregated as the variety *macrocarpa*, but the newer taxonomic scheme reflected in *The Jepson Manual* dispenses with these distinctions.

More surprising, given toyon's many ornamental features, is a scarcity of horticultural forms. Seedlings of the former variety *macrocarpa*, and of yellow-berried variations of the species at large, have been commercially available from time to time. I once offered cutting-grown plants of a spectacular red-berried plant, dubbed 'Berryessa Beauty', but found it difficult to propagate. Recently, some nurseries have begun to distribute 'Davis Gold', selected at the UC Davis Arboretum. This is a robust, bushy plant with exceptionally clean, bright foliage and orange-yellow berries. There should be ample opportunity for future selections based on foliar characteristics, berry size and color, disease resistance, and smaller plant size, with the home gardener in mind.

USES AND CULTURE

Toyon has many of the same uses as some of the more familiar large shrubs, for example the related photinias. In its better forms, it can make a beautiful specimen shrub, forming a centerpiece around which smaller natives or exotics are planted. With careful pruning to expose and shape the trunks, it will become an attractive small tree. It is also beautiful in group plantings, in combination with shrubs such as the larger manzanitas and wild lilacs. One benefit of such a mixture is that one can have a succession of colorful berries and flowers lasting from fall to early summer. Toyon is a star performer for banks and hillsides—and much appreciated for this feature by highway departments—reveling in full exposure and maintaining good appearance even with considerable heat and drought.

The challenge is to bring all these advantages to a typical home garden, where space is severely limited. An unrestrained toyon can easily grow to eight feet or more in height, with an equal or greater spread. Plants do respond well to tip-pinching and moderate pruning—but not to heavy cuts in mature branches, which can lead in time to congestion of the shoots. They also resent excessive shading and retention of moisture around the older leaves. These conditions invite an unfortunate host of diseases, including powdery mildew, apple scab, and a variety of fungus leaf spots that disfigure the leaves and can even kill the younger shoots. For this reason, the hedge-clipping style of pruning should be avoided, and young shoots should be thinned out from time to time.

Foliar diseases are also relevant to the use of toyon in screens and shrubby borders, for example along walkways and around property boundaries. With its mass of clean, dark foliage, it would seem a natural candidate for these uses; however, one must avoid the temptation to create the crowded thickets often seen with photinia or English laurel. Rather, the plants should be spaced so that they barely touch when mature, generally eight feet or more apart.

Though somewhat troublesome as a young plant in the nursery, toyon is ultimately more adaptable than many manzanitas, wild lilacs, and certainly the flannel bushes (*Fremontodendron*). It delights in a sunny site, making sturdy, compact growth, though it will

tolerate light shade. Soil must be at least reasonably well drained. Dense, clayey soils should be amended, or better yet—since organic amendments can promote the growth of pathogenic fungi—plants should be placed on elevated mounds, berms, or banks. Most soils will provide ample nutrients for good growth and foliage color with little if any supplemental feeding. Heavy-handed use of fertilizers will only promote weaker shoots, necessitate more frequent pruning, and shorten the lives of your plants. The same deep, occasional summer irrigation enjoyed by many other native shrubs—perhaps once every two to four weeks after the plants are well established—will suit toyon well. Frequent, shallow watering and continually moist soil about the crowns during hot weather favor rapid growth of root-rotting fungi. Toyon truly thrives on neglect.

This is a plant with few animal pests. Deer have been its one serious affliction in my own garden, stripping off new shoots and leaves of all ages without mercy. Sometimes gophers attack the roots. Insect pests are usually a nuisance only on overcrowded or overly shaded plants. The aphids that sometimes visit the new shoots in spring are easily removed by a well directed stream from the hose.

PROPAGATION

Given the size of a typical toyon, you may never need to raise more plants of the same, except perhaps to give to admiring neighbors. If you do, however, you will find propagation by seeds an easy and interesting process. First, resist the natural assumption that the berries

TOYON IN WINTER, SHOWING HABIT, FOLIAGE AND FRUIT.

are ripe and ready for collection when they first color in the fall. Cutting open a sample berry will reveal that the seeds inside are still quite soft and poorly developed at this point. They should be ready by mid to late December, however. Depending on the quantity of plants desired, either strip a few berries from a cluster or cut whole clusters from the plant.

In either case, place the berries in a bowl or pan (preferably not your best white china), pour in just enough water to cover them, and let them stand until they begin to ferment. Be prepared for complaints from other members of the family about "that smelly mess." Both the skins and the pulp of the berries will now be softened, and it should be easy to squeeze the seeds out by hand. Large lots of berries can be mashed by rolling over them with a cup or jar, and much of the pulp and skin debris can be floated off under a gentle stream of water. Plant the seeds in a porous medium, such as a mixture of commercial potting soil and perlite, and barely cover them with the same, keeping the medium constantly moist until the seeds are sprouted. Usually they will germinate in one month or less. They grow rapidly and, if transplanted at each stage before they become rootbound, can be bushy plants several inches tall by the end of their first season. Sometimes large numbers of seedlings are lost to damping-off and other diseases, usually under excessively moist conditions. Your best defenses against these plagues are to place the plants in a bright, well ventilated spot and to water them with care.

Propagation by cuttings is more challenging, though it offers more hope of perpetuating desirable features of individual plants. Although cuttings of first- or second-year plants will produce roots easily, very young plants often give little hint of their adult features. By the time these features are well developed, however, the plants have gone through physiological changes that may render cuttings from them much more difficult to root. Nonetheless, it is worth experimenting with favorite plants. Some individuals are much easier to propagate than others. Take your cuttings from shoots that have just completed a round of growth, with fully expanded leaves. Prepare them with perhaps three to five leaves. Dip the base end of each cutting into a fairly strong rooting powder or liquid, then plant in moist perlite or other well drained medium. Given the same protection you would provide other leafy cuttings, but probably less frequent watering and certainly more time—as much as four to six months—they should succeed.

ABOVE: *H. ARBUTIFOLIA* 'BERRYESSA BEAUTY', AN OLD FRIEND. **RIGHT:** *SALVIA SONOMENSIS* IN THE SANTA LUCIA MOUNTAINS.

SOUP TO NUTS:
TWO BROADER GENERA

SAGES FOR THE SENSES

Genus: *Salvia*
Family: Lamiaceae, the Mint Family

One day in the early 1970s I found myself thrashing through hard coastal scrub in the hills near Santa Ana, enjoying the pungent smells. Suddenly I was met with the sweet, minty perfume of what later turned out to be black sage, *Salvia mellifera*. Naturally the leaves had to be tasted, then tried in tea (I highly recommend it), and a few cuttings were spirited home. Thus began a love affair with the salvias, one that has only grown with the passing years. My menagerie now includes perhaps a hundred species and cultivars from around the world. Several of the Californians are still among my favorites, admired also by nearly everyone who has tried them.

COMMON FEATURES

The California sages include several true shrubs, some woody-based perennials, and even a couple of annuals (which are discussed later with other annuals). They are scattered over much of California, from the coast to the far interior, often in exposed, rocky places.

Though they vary widely in growth habit, texture, and colors, the California sages are remarkably consistent in basic botanical features. Like most members of the mint family, they have opposite, paired leaves, usually stalked and oval to oblong in outline. The upper surface may be smooth or deeply textured. At least the lower surface is softly hairy; in some species, the entire plant is clothed in white wool. All vegetative parts are strongly aromatic, mixing sweet, spicy, and bitter smells in various proportions. Often, in the same population, you will encounter plants that are deliciously fragrant and others that verge on the unpleasant.

Like the sages in general, ours can be extremely floriferous, making a grand display. When their appointed season arrives, flowering shoots extend from the branch tips, often towering over the foliage and carrying whorls or ball-like clusters of buds at intervals along the main axis. These open a few at a time in each cluster, extending the show for several weeks. The flowers are beautiful both en masse and individually, at close range. Each consists of a basal tube and a free portion, usually shorter, divided into upper and lower "lips." These are formed of partially fused, rolled to spreading segments. The flowers are colored white to deep blue, purple, or rose, sometimes in striking contrast to colored bracts beneath the

---

LEFT: *SALVIA LEUCOPHYLLA* 'PT. SAL' AT THE SANTA BARBARA BOTANIC GARDEN. **ABOVE:** SALVIA 'WHIRLY BLUE' IN EARLY SUMMER.

clusters. Four slender, colored stamens and a central pistil often protrude from the flowers, adding a delicate touch. As each blossom is spent, the tubular, often colored calyx is left behind. Old flower stems can remain decorative for months.

USES AND CULTURE

Few of our native plants are as rewarding of minimal effort as the sages. Though some are short-lived in cultivation, they grow quickly and make lavish displays of foliage and flowers.

In the case of the shrubs, the density and soft colors of their foliage make them ideal subjects for planting in groups, combined with swatches of other bushy shrubs, like the lower manzanitas and ceanothus. This assumes, of course, that you have the space to paint a land-

scape on such a grand scale. However, even a single plant of one of the more spreading forms of *S. leucophylla* or *S. clevelandii* will make a good show, all the more so in bloom. They are similarly attractive in informal hedges and borders, with a couple of quali-fications: You should give them ample space to prevent overcrowding and buildup of unsightly, suffocated branches. And you must avoid the temptation to cut into mature, woody branches when pruning, for these often fail to generate new shoots.

A more controversial use for the shrubby species is that of large-scale ground and bank cover. They are aesthetically ideal for such use, and their cultural demands are few. However, the plants are highly flammable. Large masses may pose a serious threat to nearby buildings, in the event of wildfire. A viable compromise may be to use them in limited areas, surrounded by more fire-resistant shrubs or by open ground.

The less shrubby sages have two distinct uses, reflecting the growth habits of the plants. Small-scale ground cover is most obvious for the dense mats of Sonoma sage, *S. sonomensis*, and the slowly spreading colonies of hummingbird sage, *S. spathacea*, will provide a similar service. Hummingbird sage is also remarkably showy in flower, making it useful for borders and flower gardens.

Native sages in flower provide great feasts of nectar and are wonderful attractors of wildlife—hummingbirds in the case of *S. spathacea* and a wealth of butterflies and wild bees in the others. Some of the shrubby species, like *S. mellifera*, are major commercial honeybee plants. Nor are we humans excluded from the treats they offer. The perfume of the sage garden can be irresistible; some species may be used as culinary herbs in place of the Medi-terranean *S. officinalis*, while others make excellent teas; and dried flower arrangers will delight in the old flowering stems.

S. LEUCOPHYLLA 'PT. SAL' WITH A BACKDROP OF *S. SPATHACEA*, SANTA BARBARA BG.

Salvias' cultural needs directly reflect their natural habitat. Most species are plants of coastal scrub, open chaparral, and barren hills, where they receive sun much or all of the day. While partial afternoon shading is desirable for coastal species when they are grown in hot interior valleys, excessive shading will result in loose, weak growth and few flowers. Salvia habitats commonly include rocky or gravelly soils for a base, or slopes that assist in draining away surface water. Certain selections of *S. leucophylla*, *S. mellifera*, and *S. spathacea* and hybrids of *S. clevelandii* have proven remarkably tolerant of heavier soils; however, most will be short-lived under these conditions, which favor fungal root rots.

Temperature is a surprisingly negotiable matter, considering the origins of some species. Even coastal forms have held up well in high summer heat, given a little afternoon shading. For the desert species, of course, hot weather and drying winds are a routine matter. I have seen some winter damage on coastal selections of *S. leucophylla* at temperatures below 20°F and would expect the same of any salvia from the Channel Islands. Others, however, have weathered bouts of 15°F or less without damage, while sages of the high deserts, like *S. dorrii*, are much hardier still.

A more lethal combination, because it promotes diseases to which California sages have little resistance, is cold and wet. Although several species thrive as far north as the San Francisco Bay region, gardeners along our rainy northern coast may find them a struggle to maintain. Excessive summer irrigation has the same ill effects nearly anywhere.

These plants are particularly adept at dealing with drought. They have robust root systems that, incidentally, make them useful in erosion control. As drought stress increases, older leaves shrivel and drop, leaving tiny clusters of incipient leaves that sit poised to explode when the rains arrive. You will naturally want to keep them a bit more attractive. Occasional deep watering (say, once a month when the plants are established) will serve this purpose nicely. In most soils, little or no supplementary feeding is necessary to keep them in prime condition.

Finally, the California sages have few pests. The same pungent juices that give them their pleasing aromas discourage browsing by deer, rabbits, and most insects (though their nectar is well appreciated). Whitefly and aphids are occasional exceptions, especially near the coast. To the extent that plants are attacked, it is likely an indication of excessive watering, feeding, or shading, all of which reduce their chemical arsenals.

PROPAGATION

The sages are not difficult to propagate, even for the home gardener. Seeding is the more economical method. Sow the seeds in fall to provide a cool pregermination period. Immersing them in hot (not boiling) water, then allowing them to cool and soak overnight before planting, helps soften the seed coats and makes them more permeable to moisture. The medium should be well drained to prevent damping off, and the seeds should be only barely covered and kept moist until sprouted.

An easy way to propagate superior individuals is by two- to four-node cuttings taken from young shoots that are just beginning to harden, with their soft tips removed. In the case of hummingbird sage, the leaves are quite large and should be cut back substantially to prevent dehydration. Treating the cuttings with a mild rooting hormone is beneficial but not essential. They should be placed in a shady, wind-protected spot and kept moist until rooted. Frequent misting is not advisable, as it promotes a variety of fungus diseases. Once roots begin to grow, they quickly form a sizeable mass, enabling them to be transferred to four-inch or larger pots, and soon thereafter to the ground.

Hummingbird sage, *S. spathacea*, may be dug and divided into rooted sections, preferably with at least one aboveground shoot per division to hasten reestablishment.

SPECIES AND CULTIVARS TO TRY

SHRUBBY SAGES

The differences among our shrubby sages are considerably less dramatic than among, for example, those of southern Mexico. Still, they are distinct, both aesthetically and in terms of their cultural tolerances. You will have to decide which of them are best for you.

Salvia apiana. White sage. Common from Santa Barbara County south, white sage is found both near the coast and in interior chaparral. It is variable in habit, from compact to sparse and open, usually three feet high or less, excluding the flowering shoots. Ash-gray leaves up to five inches long are clustered near the stem ends. Above these rise wandlike flowering stalks, as much as eight feet high, loosely branched and set with clusters of white to lavender blossoms, each up to an inch long. The long stamens give a spidery effect. Though less showy in bloom than some of the other sages, white sage is a striking foliage shrub. It may be pruned lightly when young to fill it out a bit, though the open trunks are really quite attractive. Easily grown in southern and central California, it does not appreciate wet northern winters. However, the plants I have grown have proven remarkably cold hardy.

S. clevelandii. Cleveland sage. This species is more narrowly distributed than *S. apiana,* found in coastal scrub and inland chaparral from Riverside County into northwestern Baja California. It is also much more closely branched, making a domelike to spherical mass up two feet to occasionally four feet tall. The leaves are roughly oval to elliptical in outline, about

S. clevelandii.

two inches long, gray-green above and paler beneath. They have the sweetest perfume—and for culinary purposes, the sweetest taste—of our native sages. There is still more to appreciate: Cleveland sage is extremely floriferous in its better forms, presenting its three-quarter-inch lavender to blue-violet blossoms in ball-like clusters, one to several clusters at each shoot tip. Beyond the usual injunction about soil drainage, it has proven easy to grow near the coast from the San Francisco Bay area south, though some forms are notably tender to winter frost.

At least one selected clone and several hybrids of Cleveland sage are commercially available. 'Winifred Gillman' grows three to five feet high, with smallish, unusually green leaves. It usually bears a single flower cluster at each shoot tip and has deep violet blossoms. 'Aromas' was long sold as a cultivar of this species but is now considered a hybrid, probably with *S. leucophylla*. It was grown by Ken Taylor and introduced by the Saratoga Horticultural Foundation. This selection is exceptionally vigorous, growing as much as six feet tall, and has large lavender blossoms. My personal favorite is 'Allen Chickering' (*S. clevelandii* x *leucophylla*), introduced by the Rancho Santa Ana Botanic Garden. (Actually, it is not the original clone of that name—now lost—but a second-generation seedling.) This is a luxuriant shrub at least four feet tall and six feet broad, with several large clusters of violet blossoms on each stalk. More recent, similar offerings are 'Whirly Blue' and 'Pozo Blue'.

Most of these cultivars have shown reasonably good garden tolerance. 'Winifred Gillman' is the most demanding of well drained soil. Cold hardiness is a more variable feature. I have lost whole crops of 'Winifred Gillman' in freezes of around 20°F, whereas 'Allen Chickering' has passed through the same with minor tip damage or none at all.

S. dorrii. Purple sage. This is, in my mind, one of the most stunningly beautiful of all sages. Its range extends from eastern Washington to southern California and Arizona, mostly in the high deserts and the mountains bordering them. (In fact, three varieties share this range, though few gardeners will appreciate their distinctions.) Purple sage is upright to spreading in habit, growing one to three feet high. Gray-green to silvery gray leaves are crowded along the stems. In spring, short, dense flower clusters are carried at every shoot tip. The flowers are painted a vivid, clear blue to violet. Enhancing

S. dorrii in April near Walker Pass.

their impression are the rosy or purple tints commonly shown in the large floral bracts.

This is a fine choice for gardeners in our high desert and mountain areas, where the coastal species would quickly expire. However, I find that it suffers badly in wet coastal winters.

S. leucophylla. Gray or purple sage. Found in dry coastal hills from San Luis Obispo County to Orange County, this is one of the most ornamental and useful of our sages. It is normally bushy, growing six feet tall or more in some populations, three feet or less in others, and often widely spreading. Both young stems and leaves are covered with soft gray hairs, and some plants are nearly white throughout. The leaves are up to three inches long, oblong in outline, with roughly textured surface and scalloped margins. The flowering stalks carry three to several dense clusters of pink to lavender blossoms ("purple sage" has never struck me as a good common name).

This species is generally easy to grow, particularly so in forms selected from near the coast. These same forms, however, suffer periodic cold damage in northern California, except near the coast.

At least four selections are commercially available. 'Pt. Sal'

Detail of flowers, *S. leucophylla* **'Figueroa'.**

(or at least one of the several individuals circulating as 'Pt. Sal') is a massive, widely spreading plant from the site of that name, introduced by Native Sons Nursery. Similar and taken from the same site is 'Pt. Sal Spreader', from San Marcos Growers. 'Amethyst Bluff' is a recent introduction by Santa Barbara Botanic Garden, with beautiful amethyst-colored flowers. All are useful for large-scale ground cover. My own selection, 'Figueroa', was made for smaller size, compact form, and superior cold tolerance. It is also distinguished by nearly white leaves.

S. mellifera. Black sage. This was my first acquaintance among the shrubby sages. It is widely distributed in both the inner and outer Coast Ranges from Contra Costa County to Baja

S. mellifera **'Terra Seca' at Rancho Santa Ana.**

California, growing round and dense in its better forms, sparse and straggling in its worst. The leaves are up to three inches long, oblong in outline, dark to medium green, and rough-textured above, paler beneath. The flowers are arranged in several dense clusters along the main stalk and range in color from blue or lavender to white. Most often they are pale and plain, but showier forms are sometimes seen. An interestingly variable feature of the plant is the aroma and flavor of its leaves and stems: these can be as sweet as in *S. clevelandii* (and with the same culinary uses), musky and bitter, or anything in between. Black sage is easy to grow, tolerating a wide range of conditions in the landscape. Hardy forms could be selected specifically for northern California.

The only cultivars with which I am familiar are prostrate. One found by Wayne Roderick has been known variously as 'Prostrata' and 'Terra Seca' (its preferred designation). It is a dense, low shrub with medium-green leaves and typical off-white flowers. There is also 'Green Carpet' from Native Sons Nursery, with darker leaves and white flowers. A taller, mounding form selected by Charles Christiansen and dubbed 'Shirley's Creeper' is said to be a hybrid with *S. mellifera* as one of the proud parents.

S. pachyphylla. One can encounter this showy sage in the mountains bordering our southern deserts, where it makes a dazzling spectacle in flower. It is spreading in habit, generally two feet tall or less. The leaves are usually under two inches long, broad to rather narrow, and densely felted with white hairs. Crowded flower clusters with showy rose to purple bracts are grouped along stalks up to six inches long. The flowers are about as large as those of *S. clevelandii* and colored deep blue or violet to rose. The plants sometimes rebloom after fall rains.

I found this a thoroughly delightful little plant when I grew it several years ago but can find little data concerning its cultural tolerances. It was raised successfully at Rancho Santa Ana, and John Dourley recommends it in glowing terms, but notes that it "tends to be short lived" at lower elevations. It is unquestionably cold-hardy.

Two other species worth mentioning are ***S. brandegei*** and ***S. munzii***. The first, from Santa

Rosa Island and Baja California, is distinguished by its narrow leaves, rolled down along the margins and felted beneath with white hairs. It has clusters of lavender flowers. Plants of this species may be tender to cold, though they have not been widely tested. *S. munzii*, inhabiting portions of San Diego County and northern Baja California, has more slender stems, smaller and grayer leaves, and true-blue to lavender flowers. Trial and selection work with this species are in their early stages. The better forms should have good ornamental potential, at least in southern gardens.

PERENNIAL SAGES

S. sonomensis. Sonoma sage. I first met this species in the dappled shade of light oak woods, not far from Santa Rosa. Long before I knew it as a salvia it was intriguing for its thick carpets of oddly aromatic, textured leaves. Later I found it equally at home on exposed slopes, growing in poor volcanic soils. Its range ex-

tends, with some breaks, from Siskiyou County in the north to San Diego County in the south. One might expect it to show similar adaptability in the garden. Strangely, though, it is one of the most difficult salvias to grow.

Sonoma sage has prostrate, freely branched stems growing both on and just below the soil surface. These are thickly set with blunt-tipped leaves up to three inches long. The leaves are deep or olive green to nearly white above, pale with soft white hairs beneath. As in the case of several shrubby species, their scent may vary from sweet and spicy to odd

S. sonomensis, a beautiful carpet-former.

and rather bitter. The leaves shrivel somewhat under severe drought stress, but under most conditions the plants are attractive year round. In late spring and summer many leafless flower stems make their way a few inches to nearly one foot above the mats, displaying blue-violet or deep true-blue to pale lavender (rarely white) blossoms in interrupted whorls. Though only about half an inch long, the flowers often make a beautiful display.

Sonoma sage is an attractive plant for ground cover, in a variety of exposures. Typical forms require very well drained soil and only occasional summer irrigation. It will endure considerable heat, particularly if lightly shaded, and forms inhabiting our northern mountains should be quite cold-hardy. Selections might be made for any of a variety of foliar or floral features. I have tried many, with the object of combining superior disease resistance, gray leaf color, and well saturated floral hues. Most have failed, though 'Fremont Peak' and a few others from the mountain of that name have thrived in some gardens.

'Dara's Choice' is a selection first thought to belong to this species but now considered a hybrid. It is named for the late Dara Emery, who made the selection at Santa Barbara Botanic Garden. It is a little taller and more mounding than typical Sonoma sage, with relatively large dark green leaves and lavender flowers on eight- to twelve-inch stems. It has fared generally better than typical Sonoma sage under cultivation. 'Bee's Bliss' is a more recent arrival, discovered by Roger Raiche at the UC Botanical Garden in Berkeley. It captures the matting habit and gray leaf shades of *S. sonomensis*, and produces a wealth of beautiful chalky lavender flowers. Both cultivars have been generally more garden-tolerant than *S. sonomensis* itself, though 'Bee's Bliss' may suffer from powdery mildew at times, and 'Dara's Choice' can be lost unpredictably to various root and crown rots.

S. spathacea. Pitcher or hummingbird sage. Though one of our most beautiful native perennials, this species is still unknown to most Californians. It is widely scattered in the hills of central and southern California, growing at lower elevations and mostly in the light shade of overhanging trees. Plants are closer in appearance to those of some herbaceous European and Asiatic salvias than to other Californians. They spread by underground rhizomes, frequently forming broad carpets. The basal leaves are up to eight inches long, with roughly arrow-shaped blades, carried on stalks often nearly as long. They are deep green to chartreuse in color and deeply textured above, paler and covered with soft hairs beneath. Both stems and leaves are sweetly and somewhat resinously fragrant.

S. spathacea **'Kawatre'.**

In spring (or, under coastal garden conditions, sometimes from spring to fall) a thick succession of leafy flowering stems appears. Each bears several dense, bracted flower clusters at intervals along its axis. Beautiful one- to one-and-a-half-inch blossoms, ranging in color from purplish red to pink or carmine, open a few at a time in each cluster. Even the spent flower stems are ornamental, adding a bold touch to dried flower arrangements.

Pitcher sage is a showy perennial for sun or shade near the coast, partial shade inland. More densely carpeting forms are useful for small-scale ground cover. It is ideal for planting around oaks, as it is seen in nature. Yet it also seems tolerant of moderate watering and ordinary soils.

The endearing features of hummingbird sage invite horticultural selection. My own early effort in this line was 'Kawatre', named for a Girl Scout camp in the Santa Lucias. It is distinguished for its abundance of flowers and interesting flower color, the blossoms changing from carmine to rose as they age. More recently, plants with crimson, orange, and even yellow flowers have been found and circulated to a limited extent.

My thanks to Betsy Clebsch and Bart O'Brien for sharing their experience with the salvias. Betsy is a self-professed "salvia fanatic" and widely recognized for her work with this group. Bart is Director of Horticulture at Rancho Santa Ana Botanic Garden.

BUCKWHEATS I HAVE KNOWN

. . . .

Genus: *Eriogonum*
Family: Polygonaceae, the Buckwheat Family

*A*fter *one spends a few seasons exploring the California outback, certain groups of plants* become old friends, turning up predictably in similar, though distant habitats. Think of the ferns and lilies along shady streams, for example, or the lupines and poppies of sunny meadows. Our wild buckwheats have this same welcome dependability, though in more unusual—and often less benign—circumstances. They are the ridge runners, the cliff dwellers, and the denizens of rocky scree and (fortunately, for the more fainthearted tourist) roadbanks. Some of them literally light up the slopes of the high Sierra and other rocky ranges in summer and fall, dotting them with swatches of gold to crimson, while others create delicate clouds of white and pink in the lowlands. Even out of bloom, they are nearly always interesting in form and foliage, and some are truly spectacular.

COMMON FEATURES

The wild buckwheats, known botanically as the genus *Eriogonum*, are American relatives of the true buckwheat, *Fagopyrum*, of Asia, widely grown as a food crop. Theirs is an enormous genus, currently thought to contain about 250 species, though this is a topic of hot debate. Well over 100 species and many subspecies and varieties are listed for California in the new *Jepson Manual*. These include a few large to medium shrubs, a greater number of lower, mounding to matting subshrubs, some herbaceous or woody-based perennials, and legions of annuals. Yet certain shared features make them readily identifiable, at least at the genus level. Keying out individual species, however, can be a maddening exercise in detail. The leaves of the annual and smaller perennial species are often arranged in basal whorls, and a similar pattern is seen at each node of many intricately branched perennials and shrubs, though some of the latter have their leaves more widely scattered along the stems. Individual leaves are simple (undivided) in outline and usually held on distinct petioles, or stalks. At least the lower leaf surface is normally hairy, and often the entire leaf and stalk are felted with white to brownish hairs, making the foliar mass quite striking.

One of the most welcome features of the wild buckwheats for gardeners is their habit of blooming in summer and fall, after most of our native wildflowers have gone. Only a few annual species are primarily spring-blooming. They also tend to produce their flowers over a

---

ERIOGONUM UMBELLATUM IN A NATURAL ROCK GARDEN, MARBLE MOUNTAINS.

long period, particularly under cultivation. Individual blossoms are commonly less than a quarter-inch long, but generously clustered along, or at the tips of, branched flowering stems. One of the more distinctive styles of presentation, common among the showier species, is that of compound clusters. Dense heads of flowers are held on stems that radiate like spokes from a common base. Each ultimate cluster has an involucre—a flat to conical or bell-shaped circle of bracts—from which the six-parted flowers project on threadlike stalks, opening only partially. Flower colors include white and cream, every imaginable shade of yellow, some true oranges, and pink to crimson. As if this were not enough, the flowers turn rich shades of pink to rust-red when dried, hanging on the plants for many weeks. As attractive as they are to the human eye, the wild buckwheats seem even more so to a wonderful variety of pollinators, including many butterflies and bees, both wild and domestic.

USES AND CULTURE

Uses of the native buckwheats are nearly as varied as the plants themselves. Their main limits are set as much by cultural requirements as by aesthetic considerations. The more finely textured of the larger species combine well with many other native shrubs, such as the bushier manzanitas and smaller-leaved ceanothus. However, *E. arborescens* and *E. giganteum* are inevitably the focal points of any planting they occupy.

Another attractive role for the larger species is in making informal shrubby borders. Formal hedges are not an option, however, for hard pruning and continual shearing result in unsightly dead stubs or even death of the branches, except perhaps in the case of *E. fasciculatum*.

The larger buckwheats might even serve the role of ordinary foundation shrubs, replacing privets, viburnums, and the like along walls and entryways. This use assumes something other than a sprinkler-watered lawn in the adjacent yard, however, for few buckwheats will endure in soggy soil.

Banks and open hillsides have already been mentioned as prime sites for buckwheats of many different sizes and shapes. The taller shrubs combine beautifully with manzanitas and other shrubs, either loosely dotting the landscape for individual display or planted more closely for a billowy, multitextured cover. The lowest forms of *E. fasciculatum*, plus any of the more broadly matting species, serve admirably as ground covers in the traditional sense. They are often less temperamental than the manzanitas and ceanothus widely prescribed for this purpose. Some species will serve the same role even on level ground, given well drained soil.

The smaller buckwheats also have multiple uses. The more easily grown species, like *E. latifolium* and *E. umbellatum*, can take their place with many other perennials in mixed borders. The ones that are fussier about soil and exposure, which also tend to be the smaller mats, are nearly ideal rock garden plants. One of the surprising things I have found about the latter is that even those from

BUCKWHEATS IN PLANTING AT REGIONAL PARKS BOTANIC GARDEN, TILDEN.

high elevations tend to flower well in lowland gardens, unlike many of their companions in the wild. These same species often can be maintained for several years at a time in containers, given a well drained mix amended with gravel or perlite for maximum drainage.

One unfortunate feature of many or most wild buckwheats is the brittleness of their stems. This makes it advisable to place them where they will not be brushed frequently by passing humans or pets, and especially where they are not likely to be mauled by small children.

Successful culture of the native buckwheats involves meeting just a few simple needs. Most delight in a sunny site, but several, including all of the larger species described here, will tolerate light shading at least part of the day. Nearly all require at least reasonably well drained soil. This will be a stumbling block for many lowland gardeners, though the mounding and soil amendment practiced for many other plants of Mediterranean climates serves the eriogonums as well.

The matting types, excluding *E. umbellatum* and *E. siskiyouense*, require placement on banks, with gravel around the base of each plant, or planting entirely in a sand-gravel mix. Generally, however, the buckwheats tend to be more tolerant of other soil and water problems, like salinity and alkalinity, than the more popular manzanitas and ceanothus. The drought tolerance of some species, such as *E. fasciculatum*, exceeds anything encountered in a garden setting. Most of the coastal species will need some summer irrigation in hotter interior areas. Although heat tolerance is less well explored for the coastal and mountain species, some, such as *E. umbellatum* and *E. grande* var. *rubescens*, have performed well in Central Valley gardens, especially with light afternoon shading in summer. Others are simply untested.

Other than root rot in soggy soils, the buckwheats have few pests and diseases. Aphids can trouble the new shoots of the larger shrubs for a few weeks in spring. Some are attacked by caterpillars from time to time, and others by tiny insects that produce stem galls. Often the results are barely visible.

PROPAGATION

Few native plants are more encouraging to the budding propagator than the native buckwheats, though one's choice of techniques is often limited.

The overwhelming majority of plants grown both privately and commercially are raised from seeds. Some of the reasons are superficially obvious. Most species produce hundreds or thousands of flowers per plant each season, and a high portion of these result in viable seeds, if only one per flower. The seeds are easy to collect and—curiously, in the case of species at high elevations—similarly easy to germinate, even with no special preplanting treatment (although moist refrigeration for a month or two often helps). The seedlings also transplant well, and their survival rate is high throughout the stages leading to final placement in the garden.

Collection is a simple matter. Wait until the spent flowers have changed in color to one of several shades of brown and begun to shatter. If you have waited too long, it is still usually possible to sweep up quantities of the tiny achenes (seed cases) from the ground beneath the plants. The seeds are sown in pots or flats of sand or a well drained potting mix and barely covered with more of the same, then kept moist until germinated.

Once the seedlings are up, allow them to dry out slightly between waterings. Most will grow rapidly and need frequent transplanting through their first year, after which the growth rate declines, sometimes dramatically. Shading may be desirable during the summer months to avoid sudden drying, but the plants should be given increasing exposure as they approach final planting out in the garden.

Cuttings are a more challenging means of propagating favorite individuals. It may well be that most perennial species can be reproduced in this manner, but few have been tested. In my experience, the current season's shoots, with at least the lowest node of the proposed cutting firm to the touch, yield the best results. Matting species tend to have several tiny leaves clustered at the ends of very short twigs. Here, the trick is to ensure that there is a basal node. Sometimes this must be accomplished by sacrificing some adjacent shoots and clipping a piece of a larger branchlet with the cutting. In *E. umbellatum* it is often possible to split the node from which several branchlets radiate, making several cuttings.

A typical sand- or perlite-based medium in shallow pots or flats is used. Mild rooting hormones are beneficial, but I have found no particular advantage, even for the woody, matting species, in stronger formulations. If given a protected spot, the cuttings should require nothing more than a daily misting with a laundry sprayer and watering often enough to keep the medium moist. Once rooted, they are easy to transplant and grow through various pot sizes until they are sufficiently robust for planting out.

Some of the broadly matting species take root wherever they touch the ground and can be divided with a knife or trowel into smaller, rooted pieces for replanting. Many mats, however, insist on maintaining one central rootstock that cannot be divided.

Species of Particular Interest

Now, for a closer look. I have grown nearly all of the following species at some time and have wished to grow the rest. Together, though, these species represent only a small fraction of the genus as it occurs in California. Once you have tried a few, you will probably crave each new species you meet. I have deliberately omitted the annuals, of which there are dozens worthy of cultivation. In this case, my limited experience is compounded by confusion over the identities of plants I have met and grown.

The Taller Buckwheats

Eriogonum arborescens. Santa Cruz Island buckwheat. This is a most unusual shrub, found only on a few of the Channel Islands. It exhibits a wide range of sizes, from about two feet to perhaps eight feet, and shapes. It can be hemispherical, parasol-shaped, or truly treelike, with interesting crooked branches. The stems are leafy, though the leaves are retained mostly near the active shoot tips. Individual leaves are narrow and rolled down along the margins. They are one to three

Eriogonum arborescens.

inches long and colored an attractive blue-green or gray-green above, grayer still beneath. The flowers are borne in flattened, yarrowlike clusters up to six inches across. They are cream to pale pink in color at first, aging rust to dark brown. Unfortunately, they are not among the more attractive buckwheats when dried.

This is a fine shrub for large, open banks, though it needs some summer irrigation inland. It is also among the most tender species, damaged at around 20°F.

E. cinereum. Ashyleaf buckwheat. Though grown in California for many years, this species has never been as popular as the island buckwheats. It occurs near the coast from Santa Barbara County to Los Angeles County.

This is an intricately branched shrub, growing two to six feet high, and usually somewhat spreading in habit. The stems are covered with short white hairs, giving them an attractive gray cast. The leaves are up to one inch long, broadly oval in outline and felted, at least beneath, with white hairs. Ball-like clusters of cream to pale pink blossoms are borne on branched flowering stems at the shoot tips in spring. I have not personally grown this species, but it is reputed to be an adaptable plant, at least in mild climates, and desirable for massing on banks.

E. fasciculatum. California buckwheat. This species is nearly as well distributed as its common name implies, found over not only much of central and southern California, but also much of the Southwest. One can encounter it as a six-foot-by-ten-foot shrub, a broad, low mat, or nearly everything in between. The lower forms are more frequent in the variety *fasciculatum*, found along the central coast. The branches of this variety are densely lined by clusters of narrow leaves, bright green above and gray beneath. Plants of the variety *foliolosum* tend to be taller and more upright, with darker foliage. The variety *polifolium*, inhabiting the desert margins, the eastern Sierra Nevada and the Great Basin, has somewhat broader, often strikingly gray leaves. Single or clustered heads of white to pink blossoms are borne at the shoot tips in late spring and summer. Their abundant nectar and pollen make this one of the most valuable of all California natives to beekeepers. The flowers take on beautiful warm, rusty shades when dried.

The better forms of California buckwheat—those of low or compact habit or brighter flower color—are pleasing ornamentals, especially impressive en masse. However, they have their utilitarian side, too. With large, tough root systems and dense foliage to break the rain, they are valuable on banks for erosion control. At least three prostrate cultivars have been exploited as ground covers. These include the older 'Theodore Payne' and a more recent arrival, 'Warriner Lytle'—both of them nearly flat mats—and Tree of Life Nursery's recent offering, 'Dana Point'. The last is an exceedingly vigorous plant, forming very wide, low mounds. The ultimate hardiness of the coastal forms is not well tested, though some have endured temperatures to 15–18°F. Plants of the variety *polifolium* taken from the east side of the Sierra should survive nearly anywhere in California.

E. giganteum. St. Catherine's lace. In its best-known form, the variety *giganteum*, this species is found only on Santa Catalina Island. Two similar varieties occur on San Clemente and Santa Barbara Islands. This is truly the giant of the genus, growing as much as ten feet tall and often broader than high. It is not as tidy a shrub as *E. arborescens*, being more openly branched, with stout, thick stems. The leaves are up to four inches long, broadly oval, often rather crinkled, and gray and woolly throughout. The flower clusters are flat-topped like those of *E. arborescens*, but more open and larger, sometimes well over a foot in diameter; they resemble huge lace doilies. Where this species meets *E. arborescens* in cultivation, the two frequently hybridize, resulting in seedlings with intermediate characteristics, sometimes

Garden plant of *E. giganteum*.

offered commercially as *E. blissianum*. This is one avenue that deserves further exploration; another is simple selection of more compact strains, for more attractive landscape plants.

LOWER AND MATTING SPECIES

I include here an odd mix of true shrubs and semishrubby to nonshrubby perennials. The lines between categories are blurry, even within certain species.

***E. compositum* var. *compositum*.** This is always a surprising sight, dramatically different from any of its neighbors in the wild. One finds it in barren, rocky places, including serpentine scree, from Lake County to our northern border and over much of the Northwest. Stout shoots with bold, lance-shaped leaves up to eight inches long arise from a branched, woody base. The thick, hollow flowering stems stand nearly erect, usually one to two feet tall, and carry at their summit broad, compound clusters of cream to bright yellow flowers. Overall, they suggest a giant yarrow. I have grown this plant many times in containers, just to have it around. It is more difficult to specify its garden use, though it could be spectacular in open bank plantings, and perhaps as a bold centerpiece for the rock garden.

***E. crocatum*.** Saffron buckwheat, Conejo buckwheat. This is an unusual small shrub found only in a small portion of the northern Santa Monica Mountains. It is roundish to mounding in form, growing up to one and a half feet tall and three feet broad, and closely branched. Both the stems and the broad inch-long leaves are completely clothed in white hairs. Tight heads of sulphur-yellow blossoms are

***E. crocatum*, saffron buckwheat.**

presented on branched stalks at the shoot tips, turning cinnamon brown as they age. This is a striking plant, whether in or out of bloom. It demands excellent soil drainage but can be a durable shrub on exposed banks.

E. grande. Gardeners will be most familiar with this species by way of its variety *rubescens*, red buckwheat. The species inhabits rocky, open sites on four of the Channel Islands. It is a semishrubby perennial, making a loose mound
up to three feet tall and as much as six feet wide. It has
broad, often wrinkled leaves, green to gray-green above
and white-woolly beneath. The flower stems are stout and
bare, branching above to form broad clusters of white to
pinkish flower heads. Plants of the variety *rubescens* are typically smaller, with generally more densely clustered flower
heads, colored pink to nearly crimson. These are easily grown
in the garden, useful in mixed plantings or for massing alone.

E. grande **var.** *rubescens.*

E. kennedyi. This was one of the first buckwheats I grew,
and one of my first pleasant surprises with this group. It
inhabits the southern Sierra Nevada and several ranges in southern California, growing
from middle elevations to over 11,000 feet. It forms low, leafy mounds or mats ("buns," in
the parlance of rock gardeners) with white-hairy leaves half an inch or less long. Small,
dense heads of white to pink blossoms are carried above the foliage on stems usually under
six inches tall. The variety (formerly subspecies) *austromontanus* is distinguished visually by
narrower leaves. This is probably the only representative I have grown. It seemed an adaptable plant, growing and blooming well even near the coast. There are other varieties, perhaps equally satisfactory.

E. latifolium. Coast buckwheat. This species is a common feature of coastal bluffs, dunes,
and roadbanks from San Luis Obispo County north to Oregon. It is a bushy perennial,
usually one to two feet tall. The stems are closely
lined by leaves up to two inches long and
broadly oval in outline. A dense coating of
white hairs imparts a pleasing gray-green color.
The flowers are borne in dense, often single
heads, elevated well above the foliage on sturdy
green to gray-green stalks. Colors range from
white to soft pink.

This is a fine garden and bank plant near
the coast, though probably not at home in hot-
summer areas.

E. latifolium, **growing in a coastal dune.**

E. lobbii. An odd little plant, *E. lobbii* is common in rock scree of our higher mountains, in
both the inner Coast Ranges and the Sierra Nevada. It often goes unnoticed, nearly blending into its surroundings. One or a few rosettes of rounded leaves up to two inches long lie
flat on the ground above a short rootstock. The leaves are hairy to smooth and bronze-
colored above, densely felted with white hairs beneath. Prostrate flowering stems radiate
like wheel spokes from the rosettes, carrying relatively large, roundish clusters of white to
deep pink blossoms. This is an ideal rock garden plant, given its small size and distinctive

features. It also thrives in a small container. In either case, it needs both full exposure and perfectly drained soil to last for long.

E. nudum. This has always been a botanically confusing complex, treated alternately as a single species with several varieties and as one of several subspecies of *E. latifolium.* Yet it is one of the most common of the buckwheats, familiar to even the most casual traveler. It inhabits rock outcrops and barren slopes in nature but seems almost to prefer roadcuts and other disturbed sites.

The plant has a stout rootstock, from which come one or a few rosettes of long-stalked, spreading leaves. These have roughly oval blades up to two inches long. Branched, nearly leafless flowering stalks rise as much as six feet—though usually only one to three feet—above the rosettes, displaying airy clouds of white to pink flowers, usually in headlike clusters. From a distance, large colonies give a shimmering quality to an otherwise bare bank. The variety *oblongifolium,* known at one time as *E. latifolium* ssp. *sulphureum,* frequents far northern California and Oregon. It often has sulphur-yellow flowers. Other varieties have their own slightly distinctive features.

Plants of this species are not particularly beautiful at close range. However, they make a wonderful dressing for open banks and hillsides, or perhaps any piece of bare ground shunned by more demanding plants.

E. ovalifolium. Many of the puzzling white mats one sees in the high mountains spanning much of California belong to this species. It has a branched, woody rootstock and an intricate network of small, hard branchlets crowded with leaves. The latter are under half an inch long, roughly oval in form, and completely felted over with white hairs. The flowering stems are usually four to eight inches high, carrying dense clusters of white to yellow or red flowers. There are several varieties, of which *ovalifolium,* with yellow flowers, and *nivale,* with white flowers, are the most common, some of them sharing the same range. Nearly everyone admires these plants, yet few grow them successfully. Perfectly drained, gravelly soil seems to be key to their survival. Some individuals are also disappointingly stingy with their flowers at low elevations.

E. parvifolium. The Latin name for this species has always puzzled me, since many native buckwheats have smaller leaves. In any event, it is a pleasant enough shrub, growing as much as three feet tall and six feet broad—though it is usually much smaller—with many slender stems. The leaves are dark and often tinged with bronze above, whitish beneath, up to an inch long and varying considerably in width. Small heads of white to pale pink blossoms are carried along and at the tips of slender, branched flowering stems. One can find some truly showy forms of this species and apparent hybrids between it and *E. fasciculatum* along the slopes facing the Big Sur coast. Recently I have tried and enjoyed a few with particularly bushy habit and deep pink flowers.

E. saxatile. This is an old favorite of mine, though hardly a plant for the masses. It is found in dry, rocky places at a wide range of elevations, throughout many of the ranges of central and southern California. Often one spots it as a mysterious white object against darker rocks, resolving as one approaches into a small, few-stemmed plant entirely clothed in white hairs. It has clusters of nearly round, wavy-edged leaves, from which the slender flowering stems rise with a scattering of white to pink, sometimes even deep red, flower clusters. This is a striking though usually short-lived perennial for the rock garden.

E. siskiyouense. Confined to portions of the Klamath Mountains, this is a showy and unusual buckwheat. It makes low mats up to two feet (sometimes more) across. The leaves are often green and shiny on their upper surface, but white-hairy below. Round heads of bright yellow flowers are displayed on four- to eight-inch stems. This is one of the easiest of the matting buckwheats to grow, though it does not always flower freely at low elevations.

E. strictum. One of the most widely distributed of the mountain buckwheats, *E. strictum* is found from the high Sierra Nevada north, nearly throughout the Northwest. It forms dense mats up to two feet across (or more, in the variety *proliferum*). The leaves are relatively broad, under half an inch to nearly one inch long, and covered with white hairs. Short gray stems carry multiple clusters of white or yellow flowers, ranging to red or purple in the variety *proliferum*.

This is one of the easiest and most adaptable of the mountain buckwheats, especially so in the case of *proliferum*, which once became almost a pest in the native rock gardens at the UC Botanical Garden in Berkeley.

E. umbellatum. Sulfur flower. Of all the lower-growing buckwheats, this is the one every mountain traveler is nearly certain to meet. It is found in most of the substantial ranges of California, so abundantly in parts of the Sierra Nevada that it colors whole mountainsides. It is also one of the most variable species, ranging from miniature mats to straggling shrubs over three feet tall—differences that are reflected

E. umbellatum, **possibly the variety** *covillei,* **High Sierra.**

in the seventeen varieties listed in *The Jepson Manual.* Leaves are broadly oval to lance-shaped, of highly variable size, smooth and green to white-hairy above and usually woolly beneath. They tend to be carried in whorl-like clusters at the tips of the current shoots. The flowering stems may carry individual, roundish heads or larger, compound clusters. Flower colors include yellow or cream to red. Obviously there is much to choose from.

Most cultivated material appears to be of the variety *polyanthum,* with matting to mounding habit and brilliant yellow to gold blossoms carried in compound clusters. 'Shasta Sulfur' is an introduction of the UC Davis Arboretum, forming a dense, low mound with exceptionally large, bright yellow flower heads. It has performed well in a wide range of climates. 'Alturas Red' is a smaller plant with grayer leaves, reddish buds, and creamy flowers that darken to crimson as they age. Recently I have been enchanted by plants apparently belonging to the variety *covillei,* though getting them through wet lowland winters is not always easy. These are small, bushy shrublets with nearly white foliage and glowing yellow flowers. Further trials are on the docket. Sulfur flower has been arguably the easiest of the mountain species to cultivate.

E. wrightii. Our last subject is yet another complex species, inhabiting much of California and the Southwest. Its largest forms are mounding shrubs, up to three feet tall in flower, while the smallest are two-inch-high mats. Most have short, woody branches and crowded, narrow gray leaves. The flowering stems are slender, either branched or simple, with small clusters of white to deep pink flowers set at intervals along them. I have successfully grown plants of the variety *subscaposum*, a tidy, matting plant with six- to twelve-inch stems. The variety *trachygonum* is very similar.

E. wrightii **var.** *subscaposum*, **flowers.**

RIGHT: *LEWISIA* 'DARK CLOUD', A RECENT HYBRID.

SUBSHRUBS AND
HERBACEOUS PERENNIALS

DAZZLED BY PENSTEMONS

Genus: *Penstemon*

Family: Scrophulariaceae, the Figwort Family, or Plantaginaceae, the Plantain Family

I have admired the penstemons for nearly as long as I have prowled the wilds of California. They seem to revel in all of my favorite places, from rocky roadcuts to high mountain peaks. They have brought me cheer in dark times, and they enhance nearly every experience in the California outback with their unstoppable zest for life and sheer beauty.

Not long ago I would have described them as the showiest members of the figwort family, Scrophulariaceae, a membership they shared with such winsome associates as the monkey flowers (*Mimulus*) and paintbrushes (*Castilleja*). Now their taxonomy is in flux, with demands for placement with the lowly plantains (*Plantago*). Fortunately, their basic features remain the same.

COMMON FEATURES

Penstemons are found in every corner of California. A sizeable majority live in full exposure, on poor, rocky, or sandy soils, though a few inhabit light woods and forest margins. They vary widely in size and form. There are broad, ground-hugging mats like *P. davidsonii*; bushy plants of one to three feet, like *P. grinnellii*; and virtual towers of leaf and flower, like *P. palmeri*, which can rise six feet or more. The stems may be slender and willowy or thick and rigid. Set along them in pairs are generally thick, waxy leaves. Several dryland species have strikingly toothed, lance-shaped to pointed-oval leaves up to four inches long, while those of certain matting species may be under half an inch long and nearly round. The leaves are often attractively tinged with blue or gray; others are deep green, sometimes with a lacquered surface. The leaves just below the flower clusters are frequently expanded and joined into a broad collar around the stem.

Flowers, of course, are the feature for which the penstemons are most admired. They are typically carried at the shoot tips in more or less erect, extended clusters—either simple, with flowers paired along the stems like the leaves, or branched. Sometimes they appear to be whorled around the stems. A particularly floriferous species such as *P. heterophyllus* may display dozens of flowers per stem, opening over several weeks' time. Some of the desert penstemons flower as early as March, while the weather is still benign. More commonly, however, flowers are seen from late April or May in the lowlands to August on high Sierran ridges. Drought and heavy seed production often force an early end to flowering in the wild. Under garden conditions, with spent flower stems removed regularly, many penstemons continue to bloom throughout the summer.

PENSTEMON RUPICOLA, TREASURED BY ROCK GARDENERS AROUND THE WORLD.

Penstemon flowers share several distinctive features. They are tubular in form, narrowly so in some species and bell- to nearly lantern-shaped in others. The "throat" or major portion of the tube is often markedly expanded from a narrow base. Most have a distinctive, two-lipped "face" composed of two upper and three lower, usually spreading lobes. Within each flower are four fertile stamens, the anthers often strategically poised above and below to rub their pollen on any visiting insect. A fifth sterile stamen may be tipped by a brush of hairs. This feature accounts for the odd common name for penstemons, "beard-tongue." I have often wondered about the function of this structure—perhaps it forces a certain path of entry on insect visitors? Flower colors are among the most brash and beautiful in the floral kingdom. There are blues as bright and true as those of the gentians, lavenders, rich violets, wild magentas, and subtler pinks, plus blazing reds and occasional oranges and yellows. Often the face of each flower is a different color from the throat and tube, or the entire blossom is shaded gradually from base to tip. Add to this the wide differences seen among individuals and populations of the same species, and one should never find reason to tire of penstemons. When each long-lasting blossom has faded, a sturdy, usually sharp-tipped seed capsule develops in its place. This may split immediately upon drying or cling to the plant, unopened, for many weeks or months.

USES AND CULTURE

I can barely imagine a serious gardener who, having chanced upon one of our showier native penstemons, would not wish to grow it. The usual barriers are practical—certainly not aesthetic, unless one shies away from bright, clear colors; even then, there are pastel-flowered sorts to choose from. Deciding on an appropriate site in the garden will hinge on a combination of plant size and habit, the original habitat, and whatever is known of cultural tolerances (the surprises in this regard being many). The matting forms and slow growth found in species of the higher mountains naturally recommend them for the rock garden or on banks. Mounding and bushy penstemons are perfect for the middle ground of perennial borders, though they may be substantial and showy enough to hold their own in any mixed planting. The tallest sorts are useful in the backgrounds of borders, or they can create bold spectacles in isolated groups.

There are also incidental benefits of having penstemons in the garden. Many are attractive to butterflies and other native insects, while red-flowered penstemons like *P. centranthifolius* are irresistible to hummingbirds. By combining these species with the fall-blooming California fuchsias (*Epilobium*), you can enjoy visiting "hummers" for six months each year.

The natural habitats of penstemons offer valuable clues for their successful culture. Most of these sites are well exposed, sometimes to the point where one marvels that any green plant can endure. Penstemons from such sites respond to excessive shading, either by overhanging trees or by neighboring plants, with weak, floppy growth and reduced flowering. Happily, some exceptions can be found, like *P. anguineus*, described below, and certain compromises are acceptable for the rest. In the Central Valley and other areas with chronically hot summers, a spot with full morning sun and afternoon shade, for example along the east side of a building, may be useful in holding down soil temperatures while maintaining enough total light accumulation for good growth and flowering.

Soil and watering regimes go hand in hand. Penstemons planted in dense, clayey soils tend to succumb to root rots during periods of heavy winter rain, and again when they are irrigated under high-temperature conditions in summer. Planting them on slopes and artificial berms will alleviate the winter woes. Occasional deep watering, as opposed to frequent shallow irrigation, will help in summer. Well drained—especially gravelly—soils, low

in organic matter, are excellent defenses against soil pathogens. However, they may dramatically increase the need for summer irrigation, if the plants are to be kept growing and flowering. An alternative, visually unacceptable to some of us, is simply to allow them to shrivel a bit and pass the summer in a more or less dormant state, as they do in the wild.

Species of the higher mountains and those of the deserts are special cases. In the case of the mountain dwellers, coastal gardeners are the lucky ones. Mild summer temperatures allow these plants to thrive even in full sun with only moderate to occasional watering. Winter wet can be a problem, because the plants are accustomed to frozen ground at this time; however, it can be overcome by planting in typical rock garden conditions, combining raised mounds with dressings of gravel about the base of the plants. Unfortunately, the mountain penstemons seldom flower as profusely in lowland gardens as they do in their native haunts, where the light is far more intense. These same species may be nearly impossible to maintain in Central Valley gardens.

Species of the deserts and their borders present a slightly different set of problems. Coastal gardeners can enjoy them from spring to fall but may lose them to root and leaf blights during wet winters. Gardeners in the drier interior, particularly in southern California, tend to fare much better with these plants.

Penstemons are among the many California natives with meager nutritional needs. Fertilizing them as one might do a hydrangea simply encourages lush, floppy growth, often reduces flowering, and promotes early decline. A further, curious effect is that many blue-flowered penstemons shift in hue to pink and magenta shades under high-nitrogen conditions.

Native penstemons need only occasional pruning or other maintenance. Simply shear off old flowering stems before the seed capsules develop, to promote further flowering waves (unless, of course, you wish to collect seeds for later generations). Cut the plants back rather hard about once a year—preferably just before the onset of spring growth—to rejuvenate them.

Penstemons are troubled by few pests. Aphids may trouble the new shoots in spring, but they are usually gone in a few weeks.

However you treat them, penstemons tend to be short-lived in the garden, and often even in the wild. There are exceptions, of course. I have been visiting the same mats (or what appear to be the same mats) of *P. rupicola* and *P. davidsonii* in the northern mountains for many years. However, one should feel fortunate to enjoy the company of any individual

---

Penstemon heterophyllus 'Margarita BOP' at Rancho Santa Ana.

plant for three or four seasons. The way to enjoy them for a lifetime is to keep new plants always in reserve, and to plant them out even while the older ones appear to be in perfect health.

PROPAGATION

Propagating the penstemons is an essential part of a campaign of renewal, as well as a way of increasing their numbers. One has a choice of two, occasionally three techniques, all of which yield flowering plants at an early age.

Seeding is a natural choice. With many seeds per capsule and many capsules per plant, you are limited only by time and desire. Collect the capsules as they dry and store them in a dry place until fall. Then take them out, crush any unopened capsules (rolling over them with a stout coffee mug is an effective technique), and separate seeds from chaff as much as possible. Lowland species can be sown directly outside in pots or flats of a well drained medium, protected from birds and rodents. Seeds of the mountain penstemons benefit from (and some require) prior refrigeration for a couple of months in containers of moist sand, perlite, or similar medium. They may be started in midwinter, so that their planting out coincides with diminishing rains. In both cases, the plants will make surprisingly rapid growth, particularly of the roots, in spring. They can be quickly shifted through a series of larger containers—*always* in a well drained potting mix—though even a plant established in a two-inch pot is perfectly suitable for planting out, if watered regularly until its roots have penetrated well into the ground below.

Penstemons are also excellent candidates for propagation by cuttings, particularly where an outstanding individual plant is concerned. Whatever the scale of the plant, a cutting from the leafy portion of a stem, well below the lowest set of flower buds, will serve nicely. Each should have a basal node for rooting and a couple of pairs of leaves above. Rooting hormones may be necessary for the stouter, harder-stemmed penstemons but are only marginally helpful for the rest. Plant your cuttings in flats or pots of a moist sand or perlite medium and set them away in a protected spot. The thick, waxy cuticle of many penstemon leaves will protect them from dehydration, necessitating only minimal sprinkling or misting from above. Once rooted (often in one to two months), they grow rapidly and are soon ready for transplanting.

Matting penstemons often take root where the stems touch the ground. This makes it possible to make vertical cuts in the mats, carefully dig out rooted pieces of the desired size, and simply replant them elsewhere in the garden. This procedure is best carried out during the cooler months, since some root loss is inevitable, and high heat may cause wilting of the divisions.

Whatever the method of propagation, your efforts will be richly rewarded. Young penstemons grow at an astonishing rate and often flower well in their first season.

SOME SPECIES OF INTEREST

I have grown about half the penstemons found in California, learning early in my career to admire most of the desert species in the wild but leave them to gardeners in warmer climates to grow. Thus my list of favorites is skewed in favor of northern and high-elevation species. I would encourage you to collect a few seeds of any penstemon that strikes your fancy and experiment with them. Nearly all are worthy of a place in the garden.

THE LARGER PENSTEMONS

Penstemon centranthifolius. Scarlet bugler. Certain scenes from the wild seem to linger throughout our lives, waiting to be savored again and again. For me, one of the most vivid is a sandy roadside near Idyllwild, lined by this penstemon and an equally dazzling matting lupine, *L. excubitus* var. *austromontanus*. I continue to find *P. centranthifolius* in similarly delightful settings in central California, nearly always in exposed places on sandy or rocky soils. The plant often has an almost ghostly appearance, with ash-gray leaves to blue-green leaves and stems. The stems rise as much as four feet high; they are lined below by stalkless, usually narrow two- to four-inch leaves and extend above into wandlike flowering shoots. The flowers are loosely clustered, narrowly tubular in form, barely spreading at the tips, and colored a brilliant red. It is short-lived in the garden but well worth the effort. Full sun and well drained, gravelly soil are absolute requirements.

Penstemon centranthifolius at home in the Santa Lucias.

P. palmeri var. palmeri. I saw only the dried stems of this plant for many years in our eastern deserts, so to find it in flower recently was a great treat. It occupies scattered sites in the higher deserts, from our own Mojave to Utah and Arizona. The plants grow erect to as much as six feet high. The leaves are up to three inches long, rather broad, toothed, and gray-green in color; those just below the flowers join and completely surround the stems. Sweetly fragrant, broadly bell-shaped blossoms, each about an inch long, are carried in small clusters along the upper stems. The lobes are large and showy, opening widely. Flower color ranges from cream to light pink, sometimes tinted with lavender.

Thus far, I have found this plant less disease-prone than some other desert penstemons, but this may be beginner's luck. Certainly it will overwinter better in the south than in the north.

P. spectabilis. As the species name suggests, this is one of the showiest of all penstemons. It occurs on dry slopes from eastern Los Angeles County to Baja California and is a frequent, always stunning sight along mountain roadsides. The stems are stout and grow erect or nearly so to as much as four feet (sometimes more) high. They are loosely set below with smooth bright green to blue-green leaves, each up to four inches long, with sawtooth margins. Along the upper stems are generous clusters of strongly bicolored flowers, measuring about one inch long, with widely spreading lobes. The tubes are typically lavender, sometimes rose-tinted on their outer surface and nearly white within; the lobes are bright blue to vivid purple. Pure white-, pink-, and blue-flowered forms also exist.

This is a plant most practically grown as an annual in the north, though it can be overwintered successfully in pots of sand and gravel. In the south, it can be relatively easy to maintain, given well drained soil and minimal watering in summer.

SPECIES OF MODERATE SIZE

P. anguineus. This is a common sight at forest edges and clearings, mostly at middle elevations in the Klamath Mountains and extending into Oregon. One would be hard-pressed to
identify the nonblooming plant as a penstemon. It forms densely leafy clumps with broad,
dark, thin-textured leaves. The flowering stems rise one to nearly (and rarely) three feet in
height. They are leafy below, set at intervals above with half- to three-quarter-inch blossoms, tightly clustered on slender stalks. The flowers are pleasing in form, with relatively
large lobes at the tips, and lavender to vivid blue-violet in color. I have grown this plant
without incident for several years, yet have also lost it in the first season.

P. azureus. This is another mountain penstemon, occurring mostly at middle elevations
(4,000–6,000 feet) in portions of the Sierra Nevada, and in the North Coast Ranges as far
as southern Oregon. It is a bushy, woody-based perennial, growing up to two feet high. The
leaves are smooth and bright green to blue-green, lance-shaped to pointed-oval in the
variety *azureus*, quite narrow in the variety *angustissimus*. The showier forms of both varieties carry many small clusters of colorful flowers along the upper stems in early summer. The
unopened buds are often yellow, contrasting oddly with one-inch (or even longer) sky-blue
to bright blue or lavender blossoms, which have broadly flared tips. I have found plants of
the variety *azureus* easy to grow and fairly long lived, though certainly demanding of sun
and well drained soil.

P. clevelandii. This was one of the first penstemons I encountered on my wanderings in
southern California, and it is still one of my favorites. It inhabits lower and middle elevations of the Peninsular Ranges, usually among rocks. The plants grow one to two feet high,
with several erect or upward-arching stems. The leaves are thick, up to two inches long,
smooth-edged or toothed, and dark green to blue-green in color. Those just below the
flowers are widely joined around the stem in the variety *connatus*; in the variety *clevelandii*
they are not. Broad clusters of vividly colored flowers decorate the plant from March to
June. Each blossom is around an inch long and roughly trumpet-shaped. Flower colors
include bright pink to magenta, crimson, and reddish purple.

I have found this species easy to grow during the warmer months. However, it suffers
badly from fungus leaf spots and other afflictions during our wet northern winters and is
much easier to handle in the drier Southland. Recently I have been working with an
apparent hybrid (I would guess with *P. centranthifolius*), which I have found much more
cooperative.

P. grinnellii. This is a delightful penstemon, encountered from the far southern ranges to
the Santa Lucia Mountains. It is often a companion to *P. centranthifolius*, similarly reveling in
sun and sandy or gravelly soils. The plants have sturdy stems that extend as much as thirty
inches high from a branching base. They are loosely set below with channeled, thickly
textured leaves, light green in color and up to four inches long. Above, they carry broad,
loose clusters of large, sweetly fragrant flowers. These have inflated, cream to lavender or
pink throats and broad, usually darker faces. Flowers in the more northerly variety
scrophularioides tend to be more deeply colored throughout, while those of the southerly

variety *grinnellii* are more subtly shaded. In either case, it needs—and well deserves—well drained soil and a careful watering regime.

P. heterophyllus. This is one of the most common and widespread of the penstemons, growing on sunny slopes and flats of the Coast Ranges and Sierra foothills from Humboldt County to San Diego County. The plants are woody and well branched at the base, with more or less erect, slender stems, usually one to three feet high. These are closely lined by narrow blue- to gray-green leaves. Dense bud-clusters are paired along the upper stems, often with cream to yellowish buds. From these emerge many colorful one- to one-and-a-half-inch blossoms. The blossoms are roughly bell-shaped, their tubes expanded from a narrow base and somewhat pinched vertically, and they have nearly flat, broadly lobed faces. They vary in color from deep violet or true blue to pink and magenta, usually with lighter shading on the tubes. The variety *heterophyllus* is distinguished by smooth, green

P. heterophyllus, **an unusual white-flowered form at Rancho Santa Ana.**

to blue-green leaves and stems, often with tight bundles of smaller leaves in the main leaf axils. Plants of the variety *australis*, inhabiting southern California, are similar but hairier; its flowers open from yellow buds. The variety *purdyi*, found in the Sierra foothills and North Coast Ranges, has simple pairs of leaves along the stems.

It is not surprising that commercial seed strains, especially of the variety *purdyi* (often sold as "blue bedder"), have been developed for this species. Some plants from the wild are genuinely easy to grow in any reasonably well drained soil; others die unpredictably from root rots in either summer or winter. I have offered many different strains through the years. Las Pilitas Nursery has introduced a wonderfully floriferous and disease-resistant selection, 'Margarita BOP' (for "back of porch," not a musical genre), with bright blue flowers. There are also occasional white-flowered forms. All should be welcome additions to the native garden.

P. laetus. This species is found mostly at middle elevations of our major ranges, from the Tehachapi Mountains to Oregon and Nevada. It is not unlike *P. heterophyllus* in overall appearance, though often a little more open and spreading in form and usually two feet or less in height. The leaves are quite narrow below, widening somewhat above, and up to two inches long. They are colored a pale green to gray-green. Clusters of bright blue to purple flowers, usually about an inch long, are loosely set along the upper stems. They are a little narrower

P. laetus var. *laetus.*

than the flowers of *P. heterophyllus* and have more deeply and narrowly parted, less abruptly spreading lobes. The varieties *laetus, leptosepalus,* and *sagittatus* are distinguished by the width of the throat, the degree to which the lobes spread apart, and other features of minor interest to gardeners.

This is a pretty plant for sunny banks and rock gardens. Although it seems not to appreciate our wet coastal winters, it is easily restarted from seeds and cuttings.

P. rostriflorus. I have known this plant as *P. bridgesii* for most of my life; however, *The Jepson Manual* decrees otherwise. This is the cheery red-flowered penstemon seen all along the eastern front of the central and southern Sierra in midsummer. It also ranges south and east to Arizona and Colorado. It forms broad mounds, branching freely at the base, with upswept slender stems. The leaves are narrow, usually one to two inches long, and pale green to slightly gray-green in color. The flower stems rise to a height of one to three feet, carrying many clusters of bright red to orange-red blossoms, each about an inch long. They are roughly trumpet-shaped but have a hooded upper lip and narrowly parted, backswept lower lip.

This species is not difficult to grow in a sunny, well drained site. Given moderate watering and trimming of the old flowering stems, it can be induced to flower from late spring to fall.

LOW AND MATTING PENSTEMONS

P. davidsonii var. davidsonii. One of the great floral sights of the high Sierra is a colony of this penstemon, making small carpets on bare rock scree above the Virginia Lakes, backlit by the afternoon sun. It is found more widely in the high eastern Sierra, the Cascades, and Warner Mountains to the north, and in the Klamath ranges to the northwest.

Although this is one of the truly shrubby penstemons, it is perfectly prostrate and so dense that it is difficult to poke a finger between the shoots. The closely packed basal leaves are usually under an inch long, broadly oval to nearly round and deep green in color. Violet to bluish purple flowers are clustered on short stems above the mats; often over an inch long, they seem gigantic in proportion to the rest of the plant.

This is an easy plant to maintain in coastal and mountain rock gardens, given well drained soil and preferably dressed with gravel. However, it never flowers quite as impressively at low elevations as it does in its lofty haunts.

P. newberryi, mountain pride, is one of nature's rewards for the early-season mountain traveler, for it flowers soon after the snows recede. It is a common plant of rock shelves and outcrops at middle and higher elevations, the variety *newberryi* occupying the Sierra Nevada and southern Cascades, while the variety *berryi* (a serious designation, not some bit of humor) occurs in the Klamath Mountains. It forms broad mats with deep to pale green or gray-green, broadly oval leaves, which in the mountain spring are nearly hidden by clusters of pink to rose-red flowers, each about an inch long. The flowers are flared at the tips, with broad upper and lower lips. In the mountains of Sonoma, Lake, and Napa Counties, the variety *sonomensis* is found in similarly rocky habitats but at much lower elevations. This is usually a small mound, rather than a broad mat, with almost cherry-red blossoms.

Penstemon newberryi **var.** *newberryi* **near Tioga Pass.**

All forms are considered difficult to grow, though I have found selections of *sonomensis* distinctly easier than the others. All require rock garden conditions, preferably with gravel all around the plants, and careful watering. Some of the mountain forms flower quite profusely at lower elevations.

P. parvulus. If I were forced to declare two or three favorite penstemons, this would surely be one of them. It is common in the Klamath Mountains and parts of the high Sierra. Plants can be perfectly prostrate, with just a few to many stems, or bushy and ascending, though usually well under a foot high. Gray-green to quite silvery leaves, usually one to two inches long, are closely set along the stems. The flowering stalks are short and carry only a few clusters each, but the half- to three-quarter-inch blossoms are vividly colored, usually bright true-blue to violet, and make a stunning contrast against the grays of the foliage.

This is a fine rock garden plant, though it grows a bit larger in cultivation than in the wild. It seems less susceptible to winter rots in the lowlands than some other mountain species, but is not necessarily tolerant of high summer heat.

P. procerus. This little penstemon is indelibly linked for me to meadows and scree of the high Sierra, though it is found both at lower elevations and over a much larger domain. It forms tight clumps with dense clusters of narrow, deep green basal leaves. Above these, one or more whorl-like clusters of blue to violet flowers are carried on slender stalks. The flowers are usually under half an inch long, but they make a fine show en masse, especially on more floriferous individuals. There are only minor apparent differences between the variety *brachyanthus*, which occupies lower elevations, and *formosus*, the true ridge runner.

This penstemon—at least the variety *brachyanthus*—is not a difficult plant to grow in the north and along the coast. Unlike many species, it actually needs moderate watering to thrive. It is also a good candidate for large pots.

P. purpusii. This was the first of the "little penstemons" I grew, being enchanted by the plant and finding it easy to propagate. It is found in the higher mountains of the North Coast Ranges, usually on rocky slopes, from Lake County to Humboldt County. The plants are prostrate to mounding in habit, woody at the base, with branched, slender stems and curious small, incurved, scallop-edged leaves. Several glowing violet blossoms, variously shaded with bluer and rosier tints, are clustered at each shoot tip. They measure about an inch long and are flared only slightly at the tips. This is a fine little perennial for rock gardens and containers. I have found it decidedly less prone to summer rots than *P. newberryi*.

P. rupicola is one of the penstemons treasured by rock gardeners around the world, though most of the material grown comes from Oregon and Washington. It occurs from the Yolla Bolly Mountains northward, making shrubby mats with closely packed, dark blue-green leaves. Elevated just above the mats in early summer are small clusters of rose-pink to violet blossoms, often well over an inch long, that open a little more widely at the tips than those of *P. newberryi*. I have grown plants in containers for several years at a time, but not in the ground. It requires the same excellent soil drainage, gravel, and careful watering as *P. newberryi*, yet it is less prone to disease.

IRIS ALL AROUND US

· ·

Genus: *Iris*
Family: Iridaceae, the Iris Family

For sheer elegance, few flowers rival those of the iris. They have been celebrated for centuries by artists and poets, and even stylized in the fleur-de-lis as political and architectural symbols. That we should have them growing in abundance around us is one of the joys of life in California. Unlike the manzanitas, wild lilacs, and many other familiar plants of California, the native iris long ago captured the fancies of both amateur and professional hybridizers, with spectacular results. These hybrids, known among enthusiasts as the Pacificas, still retain more visible links to their ancestors than do, say, the modern tea roses. However, their flowers now come to us in colors and forms only hinted at in the natural state.

COMMON FEATURES

The California iris are monocots (having one seed leaf) like the lilies, grasses, and orchids and unlike most familiar trees and shrubs. They are also long lived perennials, producing graceful fountains of evergreen leaves astride a branched rhizome at or just below ground level. The leaves are distinctly flattened, usually rather narrow, and tapered to a point.

Flowering stems arise in spring or early summer, each tipped by two or more bracts from which the flowers emerge. The flowers are smaller than those of some of the Old World species—usually two to four inches in diameter—but still quite showy. The floral structure, though a bit confusing at first, is quite simple. There is a basal tube; three "falls" or downward curving outer segments; three "standards" or upright, inner segments; and three spreading, petal-like style branches that end in forked crests. The style branches hover over the falls and nearly hide the three long stamens. Background flower colors range from deep purple to white or yellow. Often there is an "eye" or central area of contrasting color on each fall. This may be supplemented by a beautiful "spray," or outer tracery of darker veins. When the flowers have faded, large, roughly oval, often wrinkled seed capsules develop over a period of several weeks or months. After drying, they open slowly to spill their many plump, hard seeds.

USES AND CULTURE

The iris of California, whether species or hybrids, are among the most useful of our native perennials. In coastal climates they may be planted in sun or shade. Generally speaking, plants will have their lushest appearance in shadier sites but flower more heavily in brighter light. Like the exotic *Liriope*, or lily turf, and the ornamental bunchgrasses, they

---

IRIS DOUGLASIANA IN THE GARDEN.

make permanent, boldly textured foliage clumps. They are appropriate for formal border use but even more attractive in informal drifts, whether in odd nooks or large areas of the garden. Just as they do in nature, they thrive in cultivation under oaks, where their minimal summer water needs can be met by only occasional irrigation beyond fog drip.

As they are carried into the hotter interior, their need for irrigation, shading, or both for good appearance increases, and their role in the open garden diminishes. Particular problems will be encountered in the Central Valley, where supplemental irrigation becomes mandatory but the combination of high soil temperatures and moisture can lead to crown rotting diseases. It is here that hybrids heavily involving the southern Sierran *I. munzii*, described below, really shine.

In any case, the plants require little active care. Reasonably well drained, acid soil is appreciated, particularly if the plants are to be summer irrigated. Up to the point where leaf tips begin to die back prematurely (this is normal in fall and winter with older leaves), the less supplemental irrigation, the better, for purposes of avoiding disease. Once a year, in late winter, you may want to tidy up the clumps by removing dead leaves, which take a while to rot away. If you find that you have some of the more rust susceptible clones, you have the

choice of removing these plants, giving them more exposure, applying an appropriate fungicide once in a while, or simply learning to tolerate spotted leaves (the disease is almost never lethal). Whitefly have been an occasional nuisance on overcrowded nursery plants but are not normally troublesome in the open landscape. Happily for those of us who tear our hair over attacks on ceanothus, manzanitas, and other edible natives, the iris (or at least their vegetative parts) are normally shunned by deer, rabbits, and even gophers, though flowers and flower stems are occasionally browsed.

Propagation

There are many reasons to dabble in the propagation of Pacifica iris, ranging from simple increase of your plants to the surprise of new floral forms and colors. Two main methods are available, depending on your goals. Seeding is the more exciting—sometimes spectacularly so—since new features emerge with each succeeding generation. If you have specific combinations in mind, you will find the Pacifica iris easy to hybridize. Simply snap a mature stamen (with pollen grains visible on the surface of the anther) from a flower of one parent and rub pollen on each stigma (the point where a small lip juts out beneath the forks of the style crest) of a well opened flower, perhaps one to two days old, of the second parent. Once the blossoms have shriveled, watch the pods as they swell and turn yellow, then tan, and finally split. Gather them up in paper bags to dry before the seeds spill out. If you have no specific plan or want to be surprised, simply let local bees do your work, and gather the seeds when they are ready.

I. 'Wayne's Violet'.

In either case, plant the seeds outside in fall or early winter, using pots or flats of a light, well drained medium. Barely cover them with the same medium and keep them moist. The combination of moisture and cold is essential for germination, which usually takes one to two months. Pot the seedlings separately when they are large and tough enough to handle easily—usually around two inches tall—and grow them on until they are substantial enough to fend for themselves in the open ground. Many will flower in their second season of growth.

To multiply established plants of particular clones, simply dig them up in fall with as much intact root mass as possible and divide the rhizomes at their natural branching points. If they are to be replanted directly into the open ground, it is wise to maintain at least three to four shoots in each new clump. Timing is the most important factor in this process: New root growth begins in fall and proceeds rapidly through winter and early spring. Roots are nearly inactive by summer, and summer divided plants, if lifted without most of their extensive root systems intact, often shrivel badly before new root growth can commence.

SPECIES OF INTEREST

Let us have a look at the ancestral species, each well worth growing in its own right. Four species account for nearly all the wild plants in California gardens, and their contributions have dominated the hybrid mix. Another three or so have made minor contributions to the rich variety we now see, and two stand alone outside the fray. All except these latter two belong to the series *Californicae* within the much larger genus *Iris*. They are remarkably interfertile, making abundant natural hybrids where their ranges overlap. All provide variations on an easily identifiable theme in growth and bloom.

IRIS IN THE WILD

Each of the California species is worthy of cultivation, though some are a bit finicky for the average gardener. Here are a few of the more interesting.

Iris douglasiana. Douglas or coast iris. Douglas iris is the best known of the ancestral species. It is a familiar sight on hills and bluffs facing the coast from beyond the Oregon border to Santa Barbara County. This species thrives equally in woods and coastal meadows, though the more exposed plants seem more prolific in both growth and bloom. It may be encountered as a broad, six-inch-high mat or as a narrow fountain rising two feet or more. In or out of bloom, it is most easily recognized by relatively broad (to about one inch) leaves, dark and shiny on one surface, duller and distinctly paler on the other, and by thick, usually pinkish rhizomes. The

I. douglasiana **near Salt Point.**

flowering stems are simple or occasionally branched, bearing at each tip a pair of two- to four-inch, broadly parted to rather spidery, short-tubed blossoms. Floral shades range from deep violet or the more usual lavender to an occasional white, often with a contrasting white to yellow "eye" toward the base of each fall.

Douglas iris is a fine garden subject. In addition to its beauty, it is notable for its vigor, ease of culture, and (in better individuals and populations) floral form. Horticultural forms have been chosen for a variety of features. 'Canyon Snow' is a white flowered cultivar selected a number of years ago by the late Dara Emery at the Santa Barbara Botanic Garden. This is still one of the most lovely and popular of all the native iris. I have made several commercial selections among the broadly matting, dark-flowered forms found along our north coast.

I. innominata. This iris is only marginally a California native, being found in light woods and the edges of conifer forests in Del Norte County and neighboring Oregon. The plants form profuse clumps, usually six to ten inches tall, of narrow, grassy leaves that are dark and shiny on their upper surface.

The blossoms are borne either singly or in pairs. They are generally a bit smaller than those of Douglas iris, though large in proportion to the plants themselves. The individual segments can be both broad and pleasingly ruffled, traits that are imparted easily to hybrids. There is a wonderful range of colors, although much of it occurs beyond our borders: whereas the Californians are mostly dark purple to lavender, the Oregonians also include pale to deep, golden yellows, often with brown to golden veining on the falls.

While less vigorous and probably less heat tolerant than Douglas iris, *I. innominata* has been responsible for much of the wealth of colors, profuseness of growth, and dwarf habit seen in many modern hybrids. Surprisingly, there seem to be no named cultivars of the species itself in current circulation, though superior forms are sometimes offered according to flower color. Gardeners along the coast will find *I. innominata* as easy to grow as Douglas iris. In the hotter interior it should be grown in protected spots, with at least afternoon shading.

I. macrosiphon and **I. fernaldii** are two very similar species with overlapping ranges in northern and central California, further blurred by their propensity to hybridize and intergrade. They form tight clumps with short, slender rhizomes. The leaves are narrow, usually of dull surface, and blue green to gray green in color. The color of the leaf bases is supposed to be a distinguishing feature, being white in *macrosiphon* and reddish in *fernaldii*, but there are many exceptions.

I. macrosiphon.

The plants in both cases are most often eight to twelve inches tall; however, some charming miniature forms inhabit portions of the range (my favorites are those of northern Lake County). Both have long tubed, broadly parted to rather spidery blossoms borne in pairs. Flower color in *I. fernaldii* is typically creamy yellow, while *macrosiphon* varies from white to deep yellow and, more commonly, pale lavender to deep purple.

Plants of both species prefer a distinct summer drought but are otherwise rather easy to grow. They have played a minor role in the modern hybrids, extending their color range and reducing plant size. Their potential for imparting heat and drought tolerance seems to have received less attention. I have used selected forms of *I. macrosiphon* with all of these features in mind, and have had some pleasing results.

I. munzii. Until recently this species had a limited, though still important, role in the modern hybrid mix. It is found in portions of the southern Sierra foothills, mostly on wooded slopes. The plants form dense to rather sparse clumps with broad leaves, carried more or less erect and up to one and a half feet long. These are colored pale green to gray green and lack the sheen of the last two species described.

The flowers are quite large, with broad segments. Though lavender is the predominant shade, the falls are often marked with bright to light true blue, a color rare among the iris (and flowering plants generally). All of the desirable floral features of this species have carried over into its hybrids. Unfortunately, so have its tendency for less attractive foliage and heightened susceptibility to various diseases, especially leaf rusts. Careful selection of the best individuals is dramatically improving the picture. A compensating feature is superior tolerance of heat and possibly of drought, though the latter is still a matter of some controversy.

LESSER-KNOWN SPECIES

I. hartwegii. One of the gems of the Sierra and adjacent ranges, *I. hartwegii* is often missed except by those who venture into the mountains just as the snows recede. It is a somewhat wispy plant, often consisting of only a few shoots, though occasionally forming substantial clumps. The leaves are narrow, usually eight to eighteen inches long. The flowers, which measure up to four inches across, have somewhat narrow segments, colored creamy to occasionally deep, golden yellow.

There are four recognized subspecies, with distinctions few gardeners would appreciate. They are not considered easy to grow, except in their native ranges. However, a combination of well drained soil, shade, and some summer irrigation may suit them at lower elevations.

I. longipetala. One can encounter this species in moist, open places, mostly near the coast, in central and northern California. It is a robust plant, standing up to two feet high, with three or more large flowers carried on each stem. The flowers are interestingly colored, usually with lavender-blue to purple standards and falls that are paler overall but with darker veining. It prefers a sunny spot with abundant moisture, at least through late spring. Unfortunately, the leaves are often afflicted with rust in a garden setting. Both this species and *I. missouriensis*, below, belong to a separate section of the genus *Iris* from the rest presented here. I do not know whether successful hybrids have been or can be made across these genetic boundaries.

I. missouriensis in a marshy meadow near Bridgeport.

I. missouriensis. Western blue flag. This is the iris you see making great swatches of lavender-blue along the eastern front of the Sierra and as far east as the Rockies during early summer. It is similar to *I. longipetala* in all respects, and debate has periodically raged on the question of whether the two should be combined. However, it is somewhat smaller and fewer-flowered, though the range of colors and patterns is virtually the same. It is not difficult to grow, given plenty of moisture. Unfortunately, it can be reluctant to flower without its customary winter chill.

Colony of *I. purdyi* southwest of Leggett.

I. purdyi. I have been intrigued by this species in the wild for many years, though I have grown it only occasionally. It inhabits the North Coast Ranges and is abundant on lightly wooded slopes and roadbanks in Humboldt County. The plants often make substantial clumps of arching narrow leaves, up to a foot high, and abundant flowers in mid-spring. The flowers tend to be variable in both size and coloring. Common shades are pale yellow and lavender to white, but I have also seen and grown some lovely pinks. The falls are often conspicuously veined with darker colors, including brown. In my experience this species performs best in light shade and resents high heat, though it is otherwise undemanding.

A BIT OF HISTORY

The Pacifica iris have a colorful history of cultivation, involving extensive world travel and generous sharing of plants and ideas among enthusiasts.

As with many other American natives, the first serious work with the Pacificas was done in England, in this case during the early 1920s by William Dykes. He was followed by others whose work seems to have had little impact here. Rather, the ancestry of the modern Pacificas appears to have begun with the work of Fred DeForest and Carl Starker in Oregon during the late 1930s, mostly selecting particularly beautiful forms of *I. douglasiana* and *I. macrosiphon*.

Hybridizing of the Pacificas was truly launched when Sydney Mitchell, at the University of California, Berkeley, received seeds of DeForest's and others' material of *I. douglasiana* and *I. innominata*. He distributed these seeds to enthusiasts throughout California and around the world and made interspecific crosses, distributing their seeds, too. The recipients shared the fruits of their efforts, and the enriching effects of this broad exchange have continued to the present.

Oddly, considering the northern origins of the ancestral stock, the center of hybridizing effort from this point through the 1950s was the Los Angeles region. We probably owe much of the broad climatic tolerances of modern hybrids to this period, since southern hybridizers necessarily selected for tolerance of warmer, drier conditions. Lee Lenz began work with *I. munzii* during this period, eventually introducing a series of beautiful named cultivars. Then came George Stambach and Jack McCaskill, who made and introduced many named hybrids. Their achievements included entirely new color breaks, miniature plant size, and larger, broader, more abundant flowers.

Beginning around 1970, the north began to reclaim "its" iris with an energetic burst of effort that took several directions. Joseph Ghio of Santa Cruz plunged energetically into a breeding program that added local material from the wild to complex hybrids from other sources. His first named introductions came in 1970. When I met him in 1976, he already had a dazzling array of yellows, purples, maroons, whites, and bicolors. Later developments included ruffled flowers, colors ranging from nearly black to copper, blue, pink, and even red shades, elaborate spray patterns, and extremely profuse and floriferous plants.

An example of modern hybridizing trends. Cross by Joe Ghio.

Other actors of interest include Lewis and Adele Lawyer of Oakland, who have sought to combine the true blues of the *I. munzii* derivatives with vigor and garden tolerance previously lacking in that group. Their introduction, 'Sierra Dell', is one of the loveliest Pacificas I have seen, with a profusion of large, soft blue blossoms. Vernon Wood has worked on a broad front, combining material from several sources to produce sturdy, prolific plants and bright, clear flower colors, including rose pinks. Many more enthusiasts begin similar efforts each year.

_____

I wish to thank Joseph Ghio, Lewis and Adele Lawyer, Vernon Wood, and Colin Rigby for their personal interviews, in which they provided valuable information on both the history and current state of Pacific Coast iris hybridizing.

ALUM ROOTS AND CORAL BELLS

· ·

Genus: *Heuchera*
Family: Saxifragaceae, the Saxifrage Family

Few flowering perennials are as enchanting as the heucheras, yet their appreciation by gardeners was long in coming. Recently there has been an explosion of offerings in this country, with seemingly endless variations in foliage and flowers. Yet the Californians are barely visible among them. As we will see, this is not for any lack of endearing features.

COMMON FEATURES

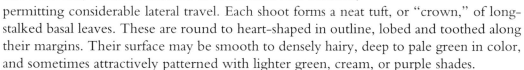

California is host to about thirteen currently recognized species of heucheras, all of which share several obvious traits. Most are found in moist or protected sites, including shady canyons, cliffs, and banks with seasonal seepage in the lowlands. In the higher mountains, they are often found fully exposed, creeping along rock fissures fed by melting snows.

The visible shoots rise from a branched caudex, or rootstock, whose reputedly astringent flavor gives them their common name, "alum root." The branches are often elongated into rhizomes, which in turn take root and form new caudices, permitting considerable lateral travel. Each shoot forms a neat tuft, or "crown," of long-stalked basal leaves. These are round to heart-shaped in outline, lobed and toothed along their margins. Their surface may be smooth to densely hairy, deep to pale green in color, and sometimes attractively patterned with lighter green, cream, or purple shades.

The slender, naked or few-leaved flowering stems appear in spring or summer (or in the case of some hybrids, much of the year). They rise well above the foliage and have numerous slender branches, which often form distinct lateral tiers. Along each branch are displayed myriad small blossoms, of which the most conspicuous portion is often the fused base of the sepals. The petals are small and usually narrow, either widely spreading or forming a little bell. White to cream is their most common color, but they vary to deep rose-pink in some species. Reddish or purple hairs on flower stems and sepals can create a glittering contrast. The stems retain their elegant structure long after the last blossom has faded.

USES AND CULTURE

Garden uses for the heucheras vary with the size of the foliage clumps, texture and color of the leaves, and—to a lesser extent than one would guess from the diversity of

---

LEFT: *HEUCHERA* 'WENDY' AT RANCHO SANTA ANA. **ABOVE:** *H. MICRANTHA* 'PAINTED LADY'.

habitats represented—the cultural needs of the various species and hybrids. The largest and boldest are striking plants for the background and middle zones of the perennial border. They are also effective individually or in small groups, for dressing up drab corners of the garden. A larger colony can take the place of the shrubby carpets that normally fill the role of ground cover, at least over limited areas. Medium-sized (and usually more delicately textured) heucheras are effective in the foreground of a border and are elegant additions to a larger rock garden. The smaller species, usually of the high mountains, are delightful subjects for rock gardens and containers.

Most native heucheras are readily cultivated in a garden setting. This is even true of the alpine species, many of which are associated in the wild with plants that even experienced rock gardeners consider difficult. All heucheras appreciate reasonably well drained soil, preferably on the acid side, though *H. maxima* and its hybrids do tolerate mildly alkaline soils.

As suggested by their natural occurrence on shady banks and among rocks, they thrive best where the roots, at least, are kept cool. Along our northern and central coast, virtually all will thrive, develop their best leaf color, and flower most profusely in full sun, though partial shade is also satisfactory. In our hotter interior (and I would think, almost anywhere in lowland southern California), they should have partial shade at least in the afternoon. Water is a negotiable matter, although the alpines and hybrids involving *H. sanguinea* (the Arizona coral bells) should never go quite dry. *H. maxima* and *H. micrantha* are fine plants for shady spots with only occasional irrigation, and thus for planting under at least the lighter-canopied oaks. However, even these will flower longer and grow more vigorously with moderate watering through the dry season. Regular watering is, of course, a must where plants are confined to pots.

Many different animals find heucheras irresistible. Flower stems are browsed from above by deer and rabbits, while gophers plunder the roots. Only a couple of insects seriously threaten their existence, however. Mealybugs may cluster densely about the bases of the plants and in leaf axils, sucking their juices and debilitating them. Natural predators seem to keep them at bay in the garden, except when plants become too congested. Dividing the clumps regularly, as well as pulling off dead leaves to expose the stems, is the logical remedy for this condition. The larvae of black vine weevils and strawberry root weevils occasionally find the plants and can completely sever the connection of crowns to roots. Digging the plants and surrounding soil and destroying the grubs by hand is the most effective control (often any severed pieces can be treated as cuttings and salvaged).

Certain fungus rots may strike roots and stems when the plants are overcrowded or overwatered, or planted in dense, clayey soils. Better culture and more frequent division of the clumps are the primary remedies. It may be possible to salvage healthy portions of an infected plant and replant them.

Hybrids between *H. maxima* and *H. sanguinea*, Rancho Santa Ana.

PROPAGATION

Heucheras can be propagated by a variety of simple techniques, the more productive requiring a bit of time and patience. Division is the safest and easiest method and one that immediately yields plants of flowering size; this method is also useful for keeping wandering clumps in bounds and rejuvenating older plants. Vertical cuts are made with a sharp spade, generous sections of shoots and roots lifted, and the healthier portions replanted. Division is best accomplished in fall and winter, when dehydration of the tops is minimized by lower temperatures.

Should you desire larger numbers of a particular individual, you can cut or pull many shoots from the main clump and treat the ones without roots as stem cuttings. Trim each piece at the base and strip it of dead leaves. Place the pots or flats in a shady, wind-protected spot and keep them moist until they are well rooted. At this point, you can easily transplant them to individual pots for a final burst of growth before you transfer them to the open landscape.

If you crave a still larger quantity of new plants, you can grow them readily from seeds. Flowering stems with ripened seed capsules are easily dried in paper bags or open vessels, crushed to extract any seeds not yet released, and run through a sieve to remove the coarser chaff. Scatter the resulting mixture of fine seed and other assorted matter thinly over pots or flats of a well drained planting or cutting mix. Mixing them first with a larger volume of coarse sand makes even distribution much easier. Gently water the containers, and keep the surface moist until the initially tiny seedlings have grown large enough to handle easily. A well rooted plant in a two- to three-inch pot should be large enough for successful planting-out in the fall and should bloom the following spring or summer.

SPECIES AND HYBRIDS TO TRY

Let me describe a sampling of the more ornamental heucheras, from large to small. Happily for the interested gardener, all are at least sporadically available from commercial nurseries dealing in California natives, as well as from plant sales of California Native Plant Society chapters and botanic gardens.

Heuchera maxima. Island alum root. The species name is appropriate, for this is truly the giant among heucheras. It dwells in the shady woods, canyons, and on cliff faces of Santa Cruz, Santa Rosa, and Anacapa Islands off the Santa Barbara coast. It is more openly branched than other species in the wild, though well tended garden plants can form reasonably compact, if enormous, clumps. The leaves are strikingly large, with blades up to four inches broad and sturdy stalks as much as nine inches long. They are usually colored a uniform dark to pale green but may have lighter marbling. Attractive orange to red tints appear in colder weather. In early to middle spring, or even throughout the growing season in coastal gardens, it bursts forth with one-and-a-half- to three-foot panicles carrying hundreds of tiny white to light pink buds. These open in lengthy succession, usually into white or cream-colored flowers.

Heuchera maxima.

Island alum root is one of our best native perennials for dry shade, though it also thrives under ordinary garden conditions. Only its limited cold hardiness should give any gardener pause. I have seen plants slightly damaged at 18°F, and heavily damaged below 15°F.

In recent years the Rancho Santa Ana Botanic Garden has introduced a series of hybrids between *H. maxima* and the popular Arizona coral bells, *H. sanguinea*. These not only retain some of the best features of *H. maxima*, but introduce a whole new range of leaf and flower coloration. They also exhibit such elements of hybrid vigor as more rapid growth, even larger panicles carrying more blossoms (a bit surprising, since *H. sanguinea* is relatively few-flowered), and an extended blooming season. These hybrids are now moderately well known in the California nursery trade. 'Santa Ana Cardinal' is remarkable for shiny, deep green leaves and two- to three-foot stems of bright red blossoms, produced most heavily in late spring. 'Genevieve' has bluish green foliage with lighter marbling and makes a nearly continuous show of glowing pink blossoms on one-and-a-half- to two-and-a-half-foot stems. 'Wendy', which emerged from the horticultural shadows only in the late 1980s, has smooth, medium green leaves and delightful soft pink flowers. Closer to the *H. maxima* parent is 'Opal', with cream-white flowers taking on rosy tints as they age. These hybrids are at least a little hardier than *H. maxima* itself, though possibly less tolerant of drought (a feature that has not been sufficiently tested, given that their most frequent use has been in well tended perennial borders).

H. micrantha. This is one of the most charming of the medium-sized heucheras. It is well distributed through the Coast Ranges from San Luis Obispo County north to British Columbia, delighting in wooded slopes, cliffs, and canyon walls (not to mention rocky roadcuts, where even the casual explorer can view it with ease). The variety *erubescens*, differing in only minor respects, extends the range of the species to the central and northern Sierra.

H. micrantha, **bank near the Tuolumne River.**

The caudex is closely branched, yielding more profuse clumps of foliage than those of *H. maxima*. The leaves have blades one and a half to three inches long, heart-shaped in outline and rather sharply lobed and toothed, carried on stalks up to six inches long (usually less). Some are dark green throughout; others add purplish veining and pale green marbling; still others are beautifully overlaid with silvery patterns. Often the undersides are heavily tinged with purple, and the entire plant may take on red and purple hues in winter. During late spring and summer the plants are adorned with one- to two-foot intricately and openly branched flowering stems bearing clouds of tiny white- to pink-petaled blossoms (*micrantha* means "small flower"). Often both the stems and the calyces are tinted red or purple, enhancing the overall impression.

At least two cultivars of this species are now commercially available in California. 'Martha Roderick' was selected in the wild by Wayne Roderick for its generous clouds of deep pink blossoms. I was enchanted by it in his mother's garden and, with his permission, named the plant for her. 'Painted Lady' is my own wild selection, made not for flowers but for its striking silver-patterned leaves with purple undersides.

In all its varied forms, *H. micrantha* is a lovely plant for the foreground of the perennial

border, the rock garden, or containers. Unlike island alum root, this species spans a sufficiently broad geographic and climatic range to offer material that is hardy nearly anywhere
in the state.

H. rubescens complex. Some of our most beautiful smaller heucheras were formerly lumped
under *H. rubescens*, but several have been given separate specific status for features too obscure to interest most gardeners. These are the true mountaineers of the group, happily
colonizing high, rocky slopes or clinging to niches in boulders and cliffs, from the Santa
Rosa Mountains in the south to the Klamath and Cascade ranges in the north. Among
those of particular interest are *H. elegans*, *H. hirsutissima*, *H. parishii*, and *H. rubescens* itself.
All have profusely and widely branched rootstocks that can produce broad mats or serpentine strips along rock fissures. The dark green, sometimes red-tinged leaves are arranged in
nearly flat tufts. Their blades are usually under one inch broad and often much smaller,
round to nearly heart-shaped overall, and lobed but not strongly toothed, with one- to two-
inch stalks. Fuzzy, often purple-tinted flowering stems arise in early summer. These vary
from under four inches to one foot tall and are less intricately branched than those of the
larger species. The individual blossoms are relatively large and conspicuous, with more or
less unequal, pure white to light pink petals. The latter contrast nicely with purplish stems
and calyces.

The alpine heucheras are fine rock garden or pot plants, even spilling nicely over the
sides of a hanging basket. Their slow wanderings are easily curbed with trowel or shears.
They are not very drought-adapted by nature and will need supplemental watering in the
dry months. All are extremely cold hardy.

Rancho Santa Ana has made two introductions of note from the wild. *H. elegans* 'Bella
Blanca' is an extremely tight mat with bright green leaves, six- to ten-inch stems, and snow-
white flowers. *H. parishii* 'Chiquita' is a tiny hummock with
only three-inch stems and small white flowers lightly shaded
with pink.

In an effort that paralleled work at Rancho Santa Ana with
H. maxima, Dara Emery produced a series of hybrids between
our alpine natives and *H. sanguinea* at the Santa Barbara Botanic
Garden. The resulting seedlings combine the small plant size
and dense mats of the natives with larger flowers and a wide
variety of floral hues. Introduced in the 1980s, 'Canyon Delight' offers an incredible wealth of rose-colored flowers on
eight- to twelve-inch stems. The blossoms of 'Canyon Pink'
are similarly colored, but their lighter centers add a glittering
effect. 'Dainty Bells' has delicate pink blossoms.

H. 'Canyon Duet'.

In the 1990s the Garden introduced a new round of hy-
brids. 'Canyon Duet' is my personal favorite. The plant is as dense and small-leaved as those
of the high mountain natives, and it flowers with complete abandon. The combination of
intense deep rose and white gives an even more sparkling impression than that of 'Canyon
Pink'. 'Canyon Belle', with dark, shiny leaves and nearly blood-red flowers, resembles a
small, very dense *H. sanguinea*. It will take several years to evaluate such a wealth of new
heucheras, but it is a process we can all enjoy.

CALIFORNIA FUCHSIAS

. . . .

Genus: *Epilobium*
Family: Onagraceae, the Evening Primrose Family

I have long been delighted by the ironies of the roadbank. That strip of bare earth or rock along the highways, where human crews struggle so valiantly to erase all signs of life, actually offers a wealth of unexpected habitats. Into these habitats descend many plants of cliffs, rock talus, and scree, usually unseen except by the intrepid hiker, to dazzle even the casual tourist. California fuchsias are some of the most common of these "roadbank natives," and happily so. In late summer and fall, when most of their neighbors are scorched by drought, they grace the roadsides with brilliant bursts of color.

COMMON FEATURES

California fuchsias are distinguished members of the evening primrose family, Onagraceae. Well represented in California, this family includes some of our showiest wildflowers, like the evening primroses themselves (*Oenothera*) and the many beautiful clarkias. California fuchsias once had their own genus, *Zauschneria*, with four species in California. However, recent work by Peter Raven and others places them with the fireweeds in *Epilobium*.

As a group, the California fuchsias are distributed over much of the state, from Trinity County to Baja California and from coastal bluffs to high mountain slopes, even reaching out into the high deserts to the east. They occupy exposed sites in sandy or rocky soils and are often seen cascading from crevices in cliffs.

The plants of some forms are completely herbaceous, dying to the ground each winter. However, most are woody at the base or even reach out with a permanent framework of short trunks, covered with thin, shredding bark. They range in habit from tightly matting and only a few inches high to nearly erect, rising as much as three feet. While plants with a single base are not uncommon, many produce underground rhizomes from which new shoots arise at intervals to cover a wide area. This feature is especially pronounced in cultivation, sometimes to the chagrin of the gardener. The stems are crowded with broadly oval to quite narrow leaves, from one-half to two inches long, usually smooth-margined but sometimes toothed. Often the leaves are thickly coated with white hairs, giving them a soft gray-green to silvery appearance.

LEFT: CALIFORNIA FUCHSIAS IN MIXED BORDER, RANCHO SANTA ANA. **ABOVE:** *EPILOBIUM CANUM* 'UC HYBRID'.

Sometime between late June and October, clusters of red-tinged buds appear at each shoot tip. These develop into tubular flowers up to one and a half inches long, with spreading faces formed of four colored sepals and four petals. The flowers vary in color from the common blazing scarlet to deeper reds, occasional coral and pink shades, and the rare pure white. They are a classic example of flowers evolved for pollination by hummingbirds, in their shape, color, and the deep-seated nectaries. As garden plants, they have few equals for attracting these colorful and entertaining birds.

USES AND CULTURE

The garden uses of California fuchsias are varied. Dense foliage and pleasing tones of green to gray make many kinds useful in both formal and informal borders. Their placement from foreground to background depends on their expected height. The same features make them attractive in swatches among plantings of larger, shrubby natives, relieving a monotony of dark green.

The more prolific, widely spreading plants are novel ground covers, especially suited to banks, where they assist in knitting and stabilizing the soil. However, be mindful of their winter appearance: forms that die down in winter should be used in limited drifts, except in the more distant reaches of the garden. The larger, more erect forms serve nicely as substitutes for small shrubs, offering attractive billowy forms as well as beautiful foliage and flowers (again, though, their winter appearance can leave something to be desired). Many California fuchsias can be very effectively combined with large boulders, while the minia-

ture forms of *E. canum* ssp. *latifolium* are at home in the traditional rock garden and in rock walls—though one must be vigilant against roaming "volunteers."

To some bird lovers, these flowers' attractiveness to hummingbirds will be all the recommendation they need. Combined in the garden with *Ribes speciosum* and other hummingbird attractors that flower at different times, plus some of the notable butterfly plants like the sages and milkweeds, they can become part of a useful strategy for capturing some of the last bits of wild California at home.

California fuchsias are not all equally easy to grow. Some individuals adapt well to a broad range of climates, soils, and watering regimes. Certain coastal forms need increased irrigation during hotter weather. *E. septentrionale*, in general, seems to require more frequent summer watering than *E. canum* for good appearance. Some of the interior forms, while remarkably drought-tolerant, need particularly good soil drainage and cannot stand up to warm-weather irrigation.

Light tip-pruning should be all that is required to shape and fill out the plants during the growing season. Plants that become unsightly in winter can be cut to the ground at that time, once they are well established. More important, you may need to restrain your plants

E. CANUM SSP. *CANUM* IN THE GARDEN.

from overwhelming their neighbors in the garden. Fortunately, recent seedlings and the young shoots and rhizomes of older plants are easy to dig or pull out. Not so with those ignored too long.

Other than root rots from excessive irrigation, California fuchsias suffer few diseases and pests. Occasionally, plants are stricken by a disfiguring rust, for which the only easy remedy is to remove the affected parts of the plant. Powdery mildew may attack the foliage of plants grown in excessive shade or overly moist conditions. Among animal predators, aphids may be a temporary nuisance in spring, as are spittlebugs, which make unsightly masses of foam but do little damage. Leaf hoppers are problematic mainly in southern California. In rare instances, tiny flea beetles will attack and skeletonize the leaves, then disappear as quickly as they came.

PROPAGATION

The California fuchsias are outstandingly well equipped for propagation, with or without our help.

Their small seeds are borne many to each cylindrical pod. Capturing them before the pods open is your main challenge, for they are quickly borne away on the wind by silky hairs. Once extracted from the pods, the seeds may be sown at any time (those from higher elevations should be planted in fall or refrigerated for a month or two). Use containers of any well drained potting mix, barely covering the seeds with more of the same. Keep them moist until they germinate. The seedlings grow rapidly and often bloom during their first year of growth.

Stem cuttings can be taken at almost any time during the growing season. Those made during spring and early summer will begin to form roots in as little as one week. Their chief disadvantage is that the tissues are soft and dehydrate quickly, unless the cuttings are misted frequently or maintained in humid surroundings. Those cuttings taken in late summer and fall root more slowly but are more resistant to wilting. In either case, cut pieces near the growing tips, each with several leaves intact. No rooting hormones are necessary. After being transplanted to pots, the rooted cuttings will grow vigorously for the balance of the season.

Simple division, accomplished by the digging and transplanting of single stems or groups of stems with rhizomes and roots attached—or even stemless networks of rhizomes—is also effective for the more prolific forms. Fall and winter are the safest times for this procedure. However, you should be able to lift sections of a growing plant at almost any time of year, with care to capture a substantial root mass. Water the plant well beforehand and cut back the tops a bit to ease the transition.

SPECIES AND CULTIVARS OF INTEREST

Epilobium canum. This is an extremely variable entity and includes all of the better-known California fuchsias. The subspecies *canum* is made up of two former species of *Zauschneria*: *Z. cana*, of the outer South Coast Ranges from Monterey County to Los Angeles County; and *Z. californica* (excluding *Z. californica* ssp. *latifolia*), common in both inner and outer North Coast Ranges, from Lake County to beyond our southern border.

The growth habit of this conglomerate species varies from matting to narrowly upright, sometimes even within the same population. Plants in favorable locations may form broad mounds, with many stems arising from an intricate network of rhizomes. The leaves are often clustered, generally lance-shaped or narrower, and tinted green to nearly white overall, depending on the length and density of hairs.

Flowering begins in the wild sometime between late June and early October and lasts up to two months. However, cultivation has the effect of both hastening the onset of flowering and extending it by several weeks. Some plants are covered with flowers nearly from top to bottom, while others may present them only at the ends of the main shoots. The flowers vary from under one inch to nearly two inches in length, with similar variation in the relative breadth of the flaring "face." Colors include the full range for the group, from the predominant scarlet to white.

Epilobium canum ssp. *canum*.

With such a variety of ornamental features, it is not surprising that many horticultural selections have been made through the years. Several of these have endured in the nursery trade and are at least sporadically available to gardeners. Most are derived from the former *Z. californica*; the plant known for many years as 'UC Hybrid' is not a hybrid, but simply a superior form, possibly wild-collected, from the UC Botanical Garden in Berkeley. (I will shortly describe a "real" hybrid now offered under nearly the same name.) This is a bushy selection, growing one to two feet high and at least four feet broad. It has soft gray-green leaves and bears masses of smallish but intense scarlet flowers from July to November. 'Everett's Choice' is a lower-growing selection originally introduced by Everett Butts at Wapumne Nursery. It has equally brilliant flowers and is reputed to be one of the most drought-tolerant selections. A more recent introduction by Ray Collett and Brett Hall at the UC Santa Cruz Arboretum is 'Cloverdale', which forms mounds six to twelve inches high and up to three feet wide. It has exceptionally broad, gray-furry leaves and large, bright flowers.

An unusual pink-flowered clone, brought out of the wild by Dan Campbell and introduced by Ron Lutsko, is 'Solidarity Pink'. It grows a little over a foot high and at least three feet broad, and has large, pale green leaves and soft pink flowers. The old 'Alba', a smaller plant with somewhat open, unimpressive habit, green leaves, and attractive white flowers, is still sometimes seen.

There are also several offerings derived from the former *Z. cana*. The earliest of which I am aware was 'Hurricane Point', found by Dr. Ray Collett at the location bearing that name south of Carmel. This is a beautiful low, widely spreading selection. It has unusually small, narrow, gray-green leaves and abundant scarlet flowers. My own 'El Tigre', from Santa Cruz Island, is often under six inches high but widely spreading. It, too, has small gray-green leaves and bright but smallish flowers. Also from Santa Cruz Island comes a selection by Warren Roberts, known variously as 'Davis Gray' and 'UC Davis'. This is a taller, very dense, floriferous plant. Most recent is 'Catalina', selected by Mike Evans on Santa Catalina Island;

a robust plant, it grows up to three feet tall, with large, nearly white leaves and spectacular one-and-a-half- to two-inch flowers.

E. canum ssp. latifolium. Plants given this designation were known earlier as *Zauschneria californica* ssp. *latifolia*. This is the mountaineer of the group, occupying rocky slopes at elevations up to 10,000 feet over much of the Sierra Nevada, the North Coast Ranges, and the higher mountains of the south. I have seen it many times as a few small sprigs of foliage tipped by small but pretty clusters of proportionately large, scarlet flowers. Yet it can be a more substantial plant, up to eighteen inches tall and three feet broad. The leaves are mostly paired along the stems, generally pointed-oval in outline and green to gray-green in color. Flowers are of the usual scarlet and borne in mostly smallish clusters. The plants are partially to completely deciduous in winter.

Smaller forms of this subspecies have grown for many years as rock garden plants, though the more benign circumstances of cultivation can increase their size considerably. These are mostly unnamed. 'Brilliant Smith', found by Ray Collett and Brett Hall near the Smith River, is low and dense, with many large, brilliantly colored flowers.

E. septentrionale is the second species recognized under the new taxonomic scheme. It is found at scattered locations in Trinity, Mendocino, and Humboldt Counties, at elevations of a few hundred feet to possibly (so claims *The Jepson Manual*) 6,000 feet. The plants are entirely herbaceous, rising from the ground each season to make low mounds or mats of short seasonal stems. These are lined by lance-shaped to broadly oval, often strikingly silvery leaves, each up to an inch long. Against this backdrop, the one-inch scarlet blossoms make a stunning display.

Several nice cultivars derived from this species are available from time to time. The plant sold for many years by rock garden nurseries as *Zauschneria californica* 'Etteri' appears to belong to this species. It is a silvery, nearly flat mat with flowers decidedly on the orange side of scarlet. 'Select Mattole' ('Mattole River'), found by Ray Collett and Brett Hall, makes thicker mats up to three feet broad, with broader leaves and the

E. septentrionale.

more usual scarlet flowers. 'Wayne's Silver' is a plant I chose from a large group raised from seeds kindly provided by Wayne Roderick. It is a dense, low mound, with strikingly silvery foliage and typical scarlet flowers. A purported hybrid between this species and *E. canum*, selected by Roger Raiche at the UC Botanical Garden, is sold as 'Roger's UC Hybrid'.

LIVING WITH LEWISIAS

Genus: *Lewisia*
Family: Portulacaceae, the Purslane Family

L ewisias are Nature's special treats for the mountain traveler. They pop up at unanticipated moments, lighting up cliffs, rock crevices, and gravelly slopes with gaily colored blossoms, then often disappearing into their surroundings. I have enjoyed their company for many years in the wild, in the nursery, and in my own garden.

COMMON FEATURES

These relatives of the more familiar red maids (*Calandrinia*) and miner's lettuce (*Claytonia*) have several distinctive features. They are perennial plants, usually springing from a stout, trunklike caudex or rootstock, normally hidden from view. They have odd fleshy leaves, cylindrical to flattened in cross section and arranged in rosettes a few inches to perhaps a foot broad, lying close to the ground. Older plants may have many such rosettes in a dense tuft. Blooming characteristics are highly variable. Some species, like the bitter root (*L. rediviva*), put on a brief, intense display in spring or early summer, while others, like *L. cotyledon*, produce a succession of flowering stems over a period of several weeks or months. The blossoms may nestle among the leaves or sit well above them astride branched, leafy-bracted stems. The individual flowers are always beautiful, though some are so small that they require close inspection. They range in size from under one-half inch to over two inches and have a widely variable number of petals, from five to over a dozen. The petals are oval to strap-shaped. They are often enhanced by a silky, even iridescent sheen and range in color from white through pink, yellow, or apricot to deep rose or reddish purple. In some species the sepals are enlarged and colored like the petals.

USES AND CULTURE

Lewisias have been treasured by gardeners for many years, though, oddly enough, far more in Britain and continental Europe than here. Few of our native perennials are as tidy and attractive in their vegetative parts or produce such lavish floral displays on such small plants as these. That said, it must be confessed that both their small size and their cultural requirements limit their uses in the landscape. Their traditional place has been in the rock

---

LEFT: *LEWISIA LEANA*, GROWING NEAR TAYLOR LAKE. **ABOVE:** *LEWISIA COTYLEDON* ON MARBLE MOUNTAIN.

garden, with matting penstemons, sedums, rock ferns, and other small plants from similar niches in the wild. Gardeners fortunate enough to be situated on rocky slopes might try larger groupings for a more impressive floral display. However, few if any species will be appropriate for mass planting in a perennial border, given the heavy soils with which most of us must contend. Another use to which lewisias are admirably suited as as potted plants. In this regard, shallow, unglazed clay pots are preferable, and overpotting is to be rigorously avoided.

Many of the cultural difficulties attributed to the lewisias are easily explained by their habitat and growth cycles in the wild, and have ready solutions. Most species are found in gravelly soils, pure rock grit, or even fissures in boulders and cliffs, where water drainage and air circulation about the roots are excellent and various fungus pathogens are kept at bay by a lack of organic debris in which to multiply. These same pathogens quickly overrun plants set out in heavy garden soils and given "normal" watering. To shift the balance back in favor of the lewisias, it is necessary to add sufficient rock chips, perlite, or similar inorganic material to permit rapid drainage and good aeration. Planting on raised mounds is another useful technique, one nearly essential where water may stand in winter. In any case, the base of each plant should be elevated above the soil line or surrounded with pure rock grit or coarse sand. With a few exceptions, like *L. nevadensis*, that inhabit seasonally moist meadows and lakeshores, the plants should be watered only as the soil dries. Plants of *L. rediviva* and other summer-deciduous species should be dried out completely when the foliage withers and kept dry until the new shoots appear in winter or spring. Plants from high elevations, where they are covered by snow rather than rained on in the winter months, can be maintained in much healthier condition through lowland winters under a rain shelter of some sort. Though it shortens the lives of the plants, regular fertilizing generally yields dramatic increases in both vegetative growth and flower production over the starvation regime that more closely replicates their natural setting. Several species can stand full exposure, but *L. cotyledon* and other evergreen species benefit from afternoon shading where summers are hot. This also helps to keep pathogens at bay by reducing soil temperatures.

Apart from these pathogens, lewisias have few pests. Aphids, whitefly, and other common sucking insects may attack and distort new shoots, particularly the flower stems, but seldom bother the older foliage. More lethal is root mealybug, though lewisias seem less subject than many other succulents to its attacks. Sometimes a plant will have to be uprooted and washed carefully—perhaps even treated with a weak solution of insecticidal soap—then replanted in a fresh mix. Mealybug is far less troublesome in the open ground than in pots, probably because of the activity of natural predators.

PROPAGATION

Lewisias are easy to propagate by any of several techniques. In seeding, the main trick is to capture the seeds when they are ripe but not yet shed. I usually cut whole blooming

L. 'Orange Beauty', an example of modern hybridizing.

stalks when they have begun to yellow, and put them in paper bags for drying. Sometimes the papery envelopes formed by the old ovaries are reluctant to open, but rolling stems and pods between the hands usually releases most of the seeds. My own experience suggests that they rapidly lose their viability after the first season and should be planted the first fall after harvesting. Germination is considerably enhanced, even for *L. rediviva* and others collected at low elevations, by refrigeration in a moist, porous medium for two to three months, followed by sowing in a protected spot. The seeds should be covered barely, if at all, and misted just often enough to keep them moist until sprouted. Often they begin to sprout while still under refrigeration.

Cuttings afford a means of propagating plants that produce new shoots about the original rosette—in which case, strong, healthy shoots are merely stripped from the old crown—and a way to salvage plants that have rotted at the base, by making a cut well above the infected area. In either case, the cuttings are planted, with or without a mild rooting hormone, in a porous medium. They require no misting and only infrequent watering until rooted.

Basal offsets of *L. cotyledon* and other profusely growing species may take root on their own; here, they are simply separated from the main plant with some roots intact and re-planted.

SPECIES OF INTEREST

The following are a few of the best known and most frequently cultivated species, and they serve to illustrate the diversity of the genus.

Lewisia cotyledon. This is the species most popular in cultivation, both in its original forms and in an array of dazzling hybrids. It is encountered on rocky slopes and cliffs from the region of the Trinity Alps north to the Siskiyou Mountains of far northern California and Oregon. It also covers a wide range of elevations. Each plant forms rosettes three to nine inches broad, of flattened, roughly tongue-shaped leaves. These may be smooth or toothed or crisped along the margins. Older plants have several rosettes. Branched and many-flowered stalks, each up to a foot

L. cotyledon **in the Siskiyou Mountains.**

tall, rise from the rosettes in summer and early fall. Cultivated plants often flower in both spring and fall (or, along the coast, in waves repeated at nearly any time of year). The flowers are usually one to one and a half inches across and have eight to ten petals. They vary in color from white to nearly crimson. Often each petal has a pink to yellow or apricot central stripe and white to cream edging. The variety *heckneri*, which inhabits the southern part of the range, is distinguished primarily by broad, toothed leaves. The variety *howellii*, found mostly at lower elevations and to the north, has narrower leaves with wavy, finely toothed margins. I have seen beautiful natural hybrids between *L. cotyledon* and *L. leana* (described below) in the Siskiyou Mountains. These have relatively narrow leaves and vividly colored flowers, intermediate in size between the two parents.

L. cotyledon has long been the darling of rock gardeners and collectors of hardy succulents. Not surprisingly, it captured the fancy of both amateur and professional hybridizers many years ago. Recent hybrids offer almost endless variety. 'Sunset Strain', produced in England by Jack Drake, is remarkable for its wealth of large flowers, and for floral shades that now range to clear oranges, yellows, and wild reds. I have had a delightful time crossing these with some "nearly wild" plants to produce seedling strains with generous bouquets of pink, carmine, and rose-colored flowers.

L. leana. A more delicately detailed lewisia than *L. cotyledon, L. leana* inhabits portions of the south-central Sierra Nevada and a swath from the northern Yolla Bolly Mountains to southern Oregon, at around 5,000 feet and above. The one-half- to two-inch leaves are narrow and nearly cylindrical, distinctly blue-green in color, and held nearly erect. The flower stalks are slender and widely branched, rising four to eight inches (I have seen a few taller still) and displaying many small six- to eight-petaled blossoms. The usual color range is pale pink to deep magenta, though white and cream with pink veining are also seen. This is a truly elegant small perennial, but one easy to lose among larger

L. leana.

neighbors, even in the rock garden. Some dazzling hybrids between it and *L. cotyledon* are seen both in the wild and under garden conditions.

L. rediviva. Bitter root. This is the wanderer of the genus, spanning the distance from the

R. rediviva **in leaf and flower.**

Peninsular Ranges and the Sierra in Mono County north to British Columbia and portions of the Rocky Mountains, at elevations of a few hundred to about 6,000 feet. Often it is seen in nearly barren rock scree, including serpentine. It has very narrow, flattened leaves three-quarters to one and a half inches long, which arise early and often disappear as the flowers open in spring (on a schedule that varies according to elevation, from March to late July). I have often wondered how the plants manage to produce and store adequate reserves for the next extravagant show.

The many-petaled flowers, borne singly on stems barely exceeding the foliage in length, are the largest of the genus, around two inches broad—enormous for so tiny and wispy a plant. They are made even more dazzling by their silky texture and snow-white to deep rose coloration. The sepals are enlarged and colored nearly like the petals. In the variety *minor*, which extends the range of the species south to the San Bernardino Mountains, the flowers are a little smaller and paler in color.

BLUE EYES, GOLDEN EYES

Genus: *Sisyrinchium*
Family: Iridaceae, the Iris Family

When we recall a particularly glorious California spring, it is worth reflecting on the floral actors that contributed to the grand spectacle. Which of them might we use to capture some of the beauty of the vanishing meadows in our gardens, and how? The annuals have their just tribute elsewhere in this book. Here I would like to describe some of my favorite meadow perennials, the blue- and yellow-eyed grasses. I have always thought of their colorful blossoms as little stars, not "eyes," but call them what you like.

COMMON FEATURES

The sisyrinchiums are members of the iris family, scattered over the Americas and numbering about six species in California. Of these, two are clearly easy to grow and garden worthy, and a third may be of interest to gardeners seeking a good challenge.

These are perennial plants, with contracted rhizomes, or rootstocks, from which they produce narrow clumps of shoots resembling those of the bunchgrasses. Their leaves are flattened in the manner of iris, though narrower.

Most species bloom in spring or early summer, but their season may be extended by cool weather and continued moisture along the coast. The blossoms are carried in small, umbrella-like clusters, emerging from pairs of bracts at the tips of elevated flowering stalks.

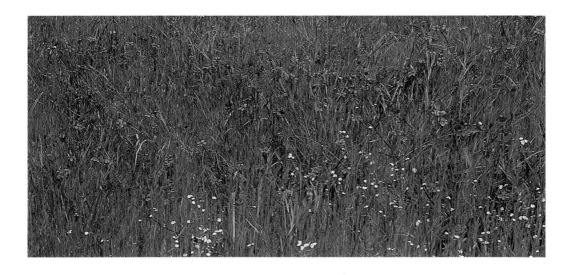

SISYRINCHIUM BELLUM, BLUE-EYED GRASS, IN ITS TYPICAL MEADOW HABITAT.

Though they open only one or a few at a time in each cluster, there are many overall. They bear little resemblance to flowers of the iris, having six nearly identical, petal-like segments that form perfect little stars. Flower colors include a range from deep blue or violet to white, plus yellow. Three stamens are tightly gathered at the center to form a brightly contrasting, golden yellow "eye." Each flower lasts but a day or two, opening in sunshine and closing quickly when clouds appear (at which time it is easy to miss the plants altogether). The roundish seed capsules that follow, though tiny and inconspicuous, spread abundant fertile seeds. Depending on their habitat, plants may be forced by drought into a dormant, even shriveled state by midsummer. With moderate summer irrigation, however, at least some forms continue to grow and flower.

Uses and Culture

Garden uses for the sisyrinchiums will be guided partly by their origins and resulting cultural preferences. *S. bellum*, blue-eyed grass, is a nearly essential part of any naturalistic meadow, combining spectacularly with California poppies, goldfields, lupines, and other spring annuals and often continuing its show after the annuals have gone. *S. californicum*, yellow-eyed grass, is perfectly at home at the edge of a small pond, seep, or any sunny spot where moisture collects at least in winter and spring. *S. douglasii* might be best appreciated in containers, with some shelter from winter rains. All of them are attractive rock garden subjects, though *S. californicum* will quickly edge out less rambunctious neighbors unless it is carefully controlled.

Summer watering is a fairly negotiable matter. If you happen to live along the coast, where summers are relatively cool and foggy, your plants should remain active as long as they are kept moist. Where summers are hot, it is probably wise to give *S. bellum* only occasional waterings, to avoid fungus rots. *S. californicum* should have a little more. *S. douglasii* is a summer grower and requires constant moisture. Keeping it as cool as possible in summer and on the dry side in winter will certainly improve its prospects for survival.

Propagation

I have seldom deliberately grown sisyrinchiums from seed, though they appear continually as "volunteers." Because these plants are so variable, and the superior ones so easily propagated by division, this has been the commercial method of choice. Nevertheless, seeding is certainly economical, and it presents an opportunity to find interesting new variations. Try collecting whole flowering stems before the tiny pods have dried completely and split. Invert them in a paper bag to dry, and sow the seeds thus collected when the weather cools in fall. The seeds are tiny and should be covered with only enough soil or other medium to permit keeping them moist until sprouted. The resulting plants can be potted in a few months, planted out the first year, and enjoyed in bloom during their second spring.

The method I prefer—so useful for capturing the features of certain individuals—is division. Plants are dug from the ground or removed from pots, preferably in fall (timing is not critical, but fall planting minimizes shock and yields sizeable clumps for spring bloom). The clumps are simply pulled apart into groups of perhaps a half dozen shoots each, more if possible, then repotted or planted in the ground. They should be kept moist until fully established. If some are accidentally separated from their roots, they can be treated as cuttings. Simply insert the base of the shoot or shoot-cluster in a well drained medium, like coarse sand or perlite, and keep it moist until new roots have formed.

An interesting twist is that some individuals produce plantlets along their blooming stems. These, too, can be treated as cuttings, preferably planted with a piece of the parent stem attached.

SPECIES OF INTEREST

Sisyrinchium bellum. Blue-eyed grass. Though we may not know it, blue-eyed grass is a common neighbor for many of us. It occurs on meadowy hillsides, roadbanks, and even vacant lots. The species itself is distributed in our coastal hills and valleys from Ventura County north. Various forms, formerly considered separate species by some botanists, occupy more specialized habitats in the Sierra and elsewhere. It forms compact, often many-stemmed clumps, usually in the range of six to eighteen inches tall. Narrow leaves are mostly clustered at the base and colored a rich,

Sisyrinchium bellum, **detail of flowers.**

dark green to pale blue-green. The seasonal stems are commonly branched, with two or more flowering stalks at each node. Over a period of several weeks, many tiny new buds appear, expanding fully almost overnight and opening into gaily painted blossoms up to one inch across. The colors vary from deep violet to true blues and lavenders to white. After a brief burst, they are gone, to be replaced quickly by a new wave.

This is an extremely variable species with respect to size, vegetative and floral profusion, and flower color. Thus it is not surprising that several horticultural selections, both named and unnamed, are now available. Most have flowers in the blue-purple to violet range. 'Arroyo de la Cruz', introduced by the UC Santa Cruz Arboretum, grows eight to twelve inches tall and bears a continual succession of large, almost iridescent violet blossoms through the spring and summer months. Also distinguished by large, dark flowers, coupled with short, dense, relatively broad-leaved plants, is 'Rocky Point', offered by Native Sons Nursery. 'Occidental' is my own earlier introduction, with shorter, densely clustered shoots and remarkably abundant flowers, though its flowering season is relatively short. Also among the "violets" is the half-native 'Wayne's Dwarf'. This was selected by Wayne Roderick, who describes it as a hybrid between *S. bellum* and *S. macounii*, a tiny species from Washington. It forms clumps only three to four inches tall and has dark, broad-petaled blossoms. A lovely dwarf selection, introduced years ago by Western Hills Nursery but never widely available, has finally been dubbed 'Bluette' for its sky-blue flowers. 'H Bar H White' from the UC Santa Cruz Arboretum grows about one foot tall and flowers prolifically with snow-white blossoms. Perhaps the most unusual floral selection seen to date is 'Becky Blue Eyes', selected by Steve McCabe. It grows fountainlike to a foot or more and has large white blossoms with a violet center. In a completely different vein is 'Figueroa', which I discovered on the mountain of that name near Santa Barbara. It has ordinary deep lavender flowers but is distinguished by creamy yellow leaf margins.

S. *californicum*. **Photograph by William T. Follette.**

S. *californicum*. Yellow- (or golden)-eyed grass. Yellow-eyed grass is a denizen of freshwater marshes and seeps. In spite of the draining of wetlands all across the state for agriculture and housing, it has hung on admirably by colonizing roadside ditches. It forms thick clumps with narrow, pale green leaves up to a foot tall, while the blooming stems rise one to two feet. In comparison to *S. bellum,* the flowers of this species are usually not as abundant (in fact, many individuals seem positively stingy in this regard, directing all energy into lush vegetative growth), and they can also seem disappointingly small—often just a little over half an inch—though larger-flowered forms are not hard to find. This suggests an opportunity for selection of superior individuals or strains, though to my knowledge nobody has taken up the challenge. In any case, the bright, cheery yellow of the flowers makes them attractive regardless of size. The plants set a remarkable quantity of seeds that sprout freely, sometimes creating a nuisance in well irrigated gardens.

S. *douglasii*. Barely a Californian, this species occupies the middle elevations of our northernmost ranges and distributed far more abundantly from Oregon to British Columbia. It is generally under a foot tall. Instead of the basal clumps of the preceding two species, it carries its leaves mostly along the stems. Its flowers are the largest among our group, measuring over an inch across. They range in color from rich purple to crimson. This would be a most promising garden candidate were it not for difficulties encountered in adapting it to lowland life, consisting primarily of fungus rots encouraged by mild, wet winters. As a consequence, although the species is cherished by rock gardeners in the Northwest, its appeal in California will be limited to only the most adventurous enthusiasts.

COYOTE MINTS

Genus: *Monardella*
Family: Lamiaceae, the Mint Family

Since the 1980s, perennial mints have been in high fashion with California gardeners. Dozens of different salvias—a few natives among them—are now common garden plants, along with the germanders (*Teucrium*), catmints (*Nepeta*), and many others. The spotlight has yet to shine on many of the mints of California, but clearly it is deserved. I will devote this chapter to one of the most interesting and colorful groups, the coyote mints or monardellas. Their common name is a mystery to me, though coyotes at times consume a number of wild herbs.

COMMON FEATURES

Coyote mints are among those natives that seem to welcome adversity. Casual explorers of the California outback are most likely to meet them on barren roadcuts, sharing space with wild buckwheats, sunshine daisies (*Eriophyllum*), wild brooms (*Lotus*), and lupines. Mountaineers find them a consistent feature of rocky bluffs and scree slopes, from nearly sea level to well beyond timberline. More often than not, they sit fully exposed to the elements. A few species even venture into the high desert, scattering themselves among the pinyons and Joshua trees.

In their more obvious features, at least, the monardellas are all variations on a rather narrow theme. There are both annual and perennial species in California, but just a few of the perennial species will be discussed here. Most of these have short underground rhizomes, from which clumps or small thickets of shoots develop. The stems may be from a few inches to around two feet tall, often branched near the base. The leaves are neatly paired along the current season's shoots. They vary in outline from roughly heart-shaped to quite narrow, and at their margins from smooth to distinctly toothed. Tiny hairs often impart a grayish cast to at least the undersurface. Sometimes the entire leaf is white-woolly. Their most distinctive feature, however, is not seen, but smelled: they are powerfully aromatic, blending sweet, minty fragrances with more pungent elements. The overall balance is nearly always pleasant, especially to those of us who enjoy the scents of wild California.

In late spring or early summer—from May in the lowlands to August in the high mountains—dense heads of flower buds begin to open at the shoot tips. A few clusters may also be spaced along the upper stems. The flowers are irregular, like those of most mints, with a basal tube and five narrow, extended lobes. Usually they measure well under an inch

MONARDELLA ODORATISSIMA NEAR SONORA PASS.

long overall, but by their sheer numbers and cheery colors—from white, through pink and lavender, to violet, crimson, and even orange—they make a fine display. The impression is enhanced by a circle of bracts, sometimes colored almost like the flowers, that sits just beneath each head. The flower heads hold their structure long after the flowers have gone and are attractive in dried arrangements.

USES AND CULTURE

Their modest size, ornamental features, and natural habitat all suggest certain uses for the monardellas. The larger species, like many Mediterranean mints, are fine for sunny, informal borders (by which I mean those not overly crowded or constantly pruned). They are also desirable for adding seasonal splashes of color to open banks and slopes, especially those receiving only occasional summer watering. When combined with other drought-tolerant perennials like the lupines and shrubby *Mimulus*, they act as a colorful substitute for the lawnlike expanses of shrubbery we have come to think of as ground cover. This arrangement, with variety and space between plants, captures much of the charm of the wild setting. Some of the smaller species are equally worthy candidates for rock gardens, and can be displayed effectively in the chinks of rock walls. In each of these sites, their presence will help extend the season of color in the native garden, where many drought-adapted plants are nearly dormant by June.

Most monardellas are sun-loving plants, requiring high light levels for sturdy growth and abundant production of flowers. However, they will tolerate some afternoon shading, and a few, like *M. macrantha* and *M. nana*, will actually benefit from it in hotter areas.

Soils can be quite poor, down to nearly pure gravel or sand for some species. The sort of soil one prepares for a vegetable garden, rich in nutrients and organic matter, has unintended effects on monardellas: they will grow rapidly for a while until they pile up on themselves, whereupon parts of the plants will begin to suffocate and die; and the resulting dead matter can nurture fungus pathogens, which will finish them off. Their one truly nonnegotiable requirement of soil is that it be well drained. This is best achieved by planting on a natural slope, bank, or elevated mound, or by adding copious amounts of coarse sand and gravel to a clayey soil (small amounts have almost no effect). The bark, peat, and other organic materials so often prescribed for improved drainage are often colonized by pathogenic fungi as they decay.

Watering should also follow a spartan regime. Simply give the plants a good soaking as often as it takes to maintain good foliage color and moderate growth—probably once or twice a month near the coast, more inland, once the plants are well established.

Many monardellas tolerate considerable summer heat, though, as mentioned above, light afternoon shading will moderate its effects and benefit some species. Most are also quite cold-hardy, though forms of *M. villosa* and others taken from sites near the coast might prove somewhat tender (even in their case, however, I have yet to see a plant damaged by a hard freeze).

Monardellas need little maintenance in the garden. Shearing off spent flower stems will relieve the plants of the burden of setting seeds and often promote further waves of flowers. The more robust *M. villosa* should be cut back hard once a year or so, to avoid the buildup of woody, less productive stems.

PROPAGATION

Like many other mint allies, the monardellas are easy to propagate. Cuttings can be taken during periods of active growth (spring and early summer in the wild, or a month or two after any hard pruning in the garden). Sections near the base of the stems not only produce roots more freely but, once rooted, are more certain to form new shoots than those taken farther up the stems. This is not unusual in the mint family, where even the leafy portions of flowering stems are often incapable of regenerating vegetative parts. A piece with two or three pairs of leaves intact will do nicely. Usually no rooting hormone is necessary, though it may help with *M. odoratissima* and other high-mountain species. Simply plant the cuttings—preferably outdoors, in a protected spot—and keep them moist. Often roots form within just a few weeks. Once rooted, the cuttings can be transplanted and grown quickly to a suitable size for the open ground.

Seeding is an easy means of increasing most species. Monardellas set great numbers of viable seeds. The heads are collected as they dry and stored until fall in paper bags. Then they can be rolled over with a jar or similar object to break them up and help extract the seeds. The seeds germinate particularly well after exposure to cool winter temperatures outdoors. Seeds collected from plants in the high mountains seem to benefit from refrigeration for one or two months in bags of a moist, porous medium. Once they are large enough to handle, the young seedlings should be transplanted and moved to a bright, well ventilated spot, where they will grow rapidly. In a few months, they should be ready for the open ground.

SPECIES OF INTEREST

Here are a few of my favorite monardellas for the garden. I have grown them all with at least some success, and the most difficult ones were well worth the extra effort.

Monardella macrantha. Scarlet monardella. This is one of the least typical, and certainly one of the most stunning, of the group. Scarlet monardella is widespread but seldom abundant in the mountains of south-central and southern California. It inhabits chaparral as well as the margins of woods, making low, leafy mats. The stems are usually short and closely packed with broad deep green leaves, paler beneath, that measure up to an inch long. Throughout the summer months, or from mid-spring to fall in cultivation, it is decorated by clusters of one- to two-inch scarlet (or even blood red) to pale yellow flowers, perched just above the leaves. The subspecies *hallii* is visually distinguished from the typical subspecies *macrantha* by its furry leaves and more frequently yellow flowers.

M. macrantha 'Marian Sampson'.

Horticultural selections of scarlet monardella have been made for flower size and color and are sometimes available at California Native Plant Society sales and native plant nurseries. 'Marian Sampson', named for the late co-owner of Mourning Cloak Ranch and Botanical Gardens, is more widely distributed. This is a striking selection with small, tightly packed leaves and the most vivid flowers I have yet seen in this species. It also seems to be unusually resistant to disease.

Scarlet monardella is a beautiful plant for rock gardens and containers, if not the easiest to grow. Gravelly soil and perhaps a dressing of rocks about the crown will help prolong its life.

M. nana. A low-lying, often matting perennial, *M. nana* is found in the Peninsular Ranges of southern California. The stems are usually six inches long or less, set with small green to nearly white leaves. The spidery white to light pink blossoms, each up to an inch long, are borne from April to July. My favorite of the four subspecies is *tenuiflora*, a plant I encountered years ago in the San Jacinto Mountains. It forms neat gray mats with mostly light pink flowers. I found it easy to grow as a rock garden or potted plant, though not necessarily long-lived.

M. odoratissima. Mountain pennyroyal. A familiar and welcome sight (and smell) to summer backpackers in the high Sierra and other major ranges, mountain pennyroyal grows in rocky soils and scree at elevations to nearly 11,000 feet. Its scope as a species has been considerably narrowed in *The Jepson Manual* by elevation in status of several former varieties

M. odoratissima **in scree, Marble Mountains.**

to separate species. It has creeping rhizomes, sometimes making foot-wide, many-stemmed mats and mounds. The individual stems are slender but straight, rising a few inches to about one foot high. The leaves are commonly lance-shaped, one-half to one inch long, and dark green to gray-green in color; they have a powerful aroma, spicy and sweet in some plants, bitter in others.

Mountain pennyroyal blooms at the height of the mountain summer, lighting up rocky slopes with puffs of white to purple. What is now called the subspecies *odoratissima*, with mostly purple flowers, is limited to far northeastern California and much of the Northwest. The common form of the high Sierra and all of our higher northern ranges is the subspecies *pallida*, with mostly white to lavender flowers. The most beautiful forms I have seen, with purplish stems, leaves, and floral bracts and deep lavender to violet flowers, are described by the *The Jepson Manual* as hybrids with one of its former varieties, now called *M. glauca*. I have tried some of these and have found them to be dazzling rock garden subjects—for a while. Unfortunately, they succumb easily to winter root rots in the lowlands, where their accustomed snow is replaced by rain.

M. purpurea. This species is thinly scattered over a wide area from the South Coast Ranges to Oregon, at elevations below 4,000 feet. It is branched at the base, with several purplish stems from four inches to a little over a foot tall. The blunt-tipped leaves are up to an inch long and dark green in color. Heads of reddish purple flowers decorate the plants from midsummer to early fall.

I have not grown the species itself, though it is certainly showy enough. I have, however, experimented with what was once called *M. villosa* var. *subglabra*, claimed in *The Jepson Manual* to be a recurring hybrid between *M. purpurea* and *M. villosa*. The plants I have grown, from both my own collections and those received from the Santa Barbara Botanic Garden, are bushy plants growing one to two feet tall. Broad bright green leaves give them a particularly lush appearance, and they bloom repeatedly throughout the summer and fall, if old flower heads are removed. Both *M. purpurea* and its hybrids have basically the same garden uses as *M. villosa*.

M. villosa. Coyote mint. This plant is one of the cheery sights of summer in the hills of central and northern California. It grows in both the inner and outer Coast Ranges from Humboldt County to San Luis Obispo County. It is a woody-based, usually bushy perennial, growing up to two feet high, though usually less. Both the stems and the undersurfaces of the variously shaped leaves are hairy or even white-woolly. The leaves are usually dark green above, though varying to gray. It blooms throughout the summer in many places, even longer in cultivation, giving a generous display of reddish purple, pink, or occasionally off-white flower heads.

M. villosa.

This common shrublet is one of the easiest of the group to grow and has a number of possible uses, including borders, banks, and mixed plantings. My own plant has thrived in the garden for over a decade, growing each season more lavish with its floral display.

THE MAGIC OF LILIES

Genus: *Lilium*
Family: Liliaceae, the Lily Family

Lilies, for me, have always belonged to some magical realm removed from our daily struggles. The way they explode from the ground in spring; their contrast of bold stature and delicate textures; their wonderfully polished surfaces; the varied shapes and hues, the waxy texture, the fragrance of their flowers—these things have enchanted me since childhood, and they have had the same effect on other gardeners and amateur naturalists for centuries.

About twelve species of lilies make their home in California, occupying a wide variety of habitats: forested streams, boggy meadows, oak woodlands, and open chaparral.

COMMON FEATURES

The resting structures of lilies are the classic, true bulbs: shortened, thickened rhizomes covered by fleshy modified leaves called scales. From these bulbs the seasonal shoots burst forth in spring, looking like shiny green rockets as they emerge from the ground. Each shoot elongates rapidly. Narrow, often wavy-edged leaves unfold, either scattered along the stems or arranged at intervals in distinct whorls. With leaves often several inches long, broadly oval to linear and polished vivid green, the plants are showy even out of bloom.

Well before the stems have reached full height, which may be several feet, clusters of flower buds (sometimes only one or two, but frequently a dozen or more) develop at their tips. Often these are set, like the leaves, in tiers. Gradually the main axis and individual flower stems lengthen, and the buds swell until they seem about to burst. Suddenly they part, assuming their familiar forms.

Flowers of our native species do not include the elongated trumpets of the Easter lilies, but all the other common shapes are well represented. Ours also exhibit most of the colors of the lily spectrum, from white through pink to crimson, and yellow to orange and scarlet. Some species have decidedly petite flowers as lilies go—two inches or less across in *L. bolanderi* and *L. maritimum*, for example—but those of *L. washingtonianum* can measure five inches or more. They vary similarly in fragrance: some, like *L. pardalinum*, have only a faint, spicy scent or none at all; others, like *L. rubescens*, are almost overpowering at close range, recalling gardenias. The flower segments are thick and waxy, often with a surface like fine china. Long stamens arch from the center. At their tips are hinged, freely swinging anthers bearing masses of colorful pollen. The floral show may go on for several weeks, the flowers opening in succession from bottom to top. Then large three-chambered seed capsules develop, each containing dozens to hundreds of seeds like flakes of tissue, easily dispersed by passing breezes.

LEFT: *L. PARDALINUM* SSP. *PITKINENSE* IN THE GARDEN. **PRECEDING PAGES:** *LILIUM PARDALINUM* [SSP. *WIGGINSII*], HORSESHOE FALLS, SISKIYOU MOUNTAINS.

USES AND CULTURE

Few gardeners have seen the lilies without feeling an urge to grow them. We in California face some special challenges of siting and soil preparation, but these are usually manageable for exotic and native species alike.

We can take our first clue from the relatively moist, shady spots where several species are found in nature. *L. pardalinum*, the leopard lily, and its kin are perfect plants to grow in the shade of overhanging trees. As in the wild, they combine beautifully with ferns, shade-loving shrubs like some of the currants, and such carpets of the forest floor as redwood sorrel (*Oxalis oregana*) and wild ginger (*Asarum caudatum*). Their height (in the case of *L. pardalinum*, up to six feet) suits them for placement in the background, along fences and walls, where they are easily visible behind many other shade-loving plants. Some form sizeable colonies if allowed to roam, making their display more impressive every year.

Coastal gardeners can grow lilies in a wide variety of sites, including mixed perennial beds and the background of formal borders, in sun or shade. The plants themselves are quite tolerant of sun under cooler coastal conditions, as long as the soil surrounding the bulbs is kept cool; the shade cast by neighboring plants, large or small, will suffice.

Unfortunately, only those of us living in or beside conifer forests are likely to have the perfect soil for lily culture. Generally speaking, it should be not only acid but also porous, well drained, and well aerated. Most of us will need to add peat, sawdust, or other porous organic material, and possibly an aerating agent like perlite or crushed volcanic rock, to achieve proper drainage; or we can create raised beds, as for azaleas. Most lilies have contractile roots that drag the bulbs down, sometimes a foot or more over time, so soil amendment to a similar depth is advisable. Exceptions are some of the streamside growers, whose bulbs remain perched at ground level.

Lilies of summer-dry woods and chaparral are in various ways both easier and trickier to handle. Most can tolerate denser, more neutral soil, though care must still be taken to provide adequate drainage in winter. However, they must be kept on the dry side once the stems begin to wither, to prevent rotting of the bulbs. They are thus difficult to combine with the many shade-loving plants that require constant moisture (though all the more suitable for planting under oaks). Further, although some of these lilies come from exposed sites in the wild, they usually occur in the cooler mountains and so are even less tolerant of high soil temperatures than their streamside kin. Standard rock garden conditions suit them well, but it is aesthetically difficult to combine all but the smallest species (for example, *L. bolanderi*) with typical rock garden plants of diminutive stature.

Lily bulbs are attractive to rodents, and it is wise to line the planting hole with hardware cloth or use commercial gopher baskets. Similarly, all aboveground parts are relished by deer and rabbits. You may need to decide how much you want to share.

For some gardeners, the ideal way to control soils, site, and watering for the full range of native lily species is to grow them in containers, from large pots to planter boxes. Touchier subjects can get a little extra perlite or gravel in their potting mix. Watering can be tapered off in late summer, and the containers moved as necessary from sun to shade. Generally speaking, containers must be shaded in summer to prevent destruction of the bulbs by high-temperature fungus rots. Of course, it is difficult to recreate the charm of their natural setting with colonies of pots.

PROPAGATION

Propagation of the lilies is both easy and interesting. If you don't mind waiting two years (in the case of *L. pardalinum* and other robust types) to as much as five years for flowers, seeding permits staggering rates of multiplication from one or a few plants. To ensure a good seed crop, simply rub some of the abundant pollen from a plucked anther onto the stigma of a flower that has been open for three or four days. Collect the pods when they have turned to yellow or tan but have not opened. Dry them in paper bags and shake out the seeds. Their need for a cool, moist period prior to germination can be satisfied by planting them outside in fall, in flats or pots of a porous mix, and keeping them moist through the winter. An alternative is to refrigerate them for a couple of months in bags of moist perlite or a similar medium, then plant them out in the same manner (they may even begin to sprout in the bags). However they are started, they should be ready for individual small pots sometime between their first summer and the commencement of new growth in the following spring.

An interesting method for propagating superior plants involves individual bulb scales. Lift the bulbs in winter and carefully break off the outer scales, each with its base intact. Insert the lower third of each scale in a well drained medium, and lay the pots or flats away in a shady place outdoors, keeping them moist. In a few months, after small bulblets form, roots and shoots will commence, at which point the young plants can be transplanted to small pots. Often they will flower the following year.

The easiest, though least interesting or productive, method is simply to divide the older bulbs as offsets are formed. The elongated bulbs of such species as *L. pardalinum* can actually be broken into sections of an inch or two in length. These will quickly form plants of flowering size.

SPECIES OF INTEREST

Every one of our native lilies is beautiful in its own way, and some are spectacular. Not all, however, are equally easy to grow. Let us begin with those of distinctly moist sites.

LILIES OF MOIST PLACES

Lilium kelleyanum. Kelley's lily. Of all our native lilies, this and *L. columbianum* (Columbia lily) are most reminiscent in flower of the old-fashioned tiger lily, *L. tigrinum,* and its many modern hybrids. Kelley's lily is found at middle and higher elevations of the Sierra Nevada and the Klamath Mountains. I have seen it nearly always along sunny creeks, seeps, and bogs. It grows up to six feet high, with both whorled and scattered, highly polished leaves, and produces many nodding flowers per stem, each measuring two to three inches across. These have the familiar "tiger lily" form, their segments swept around and back to nearly touch the stalk. They are painted bright yellow to orange overall, with tiny flecks

Lilium kelleyanum.

of deep maroon. I have found it easy to grow near the coast, with constant moisture; however, I would not expect it to thrive in the heat of the Central Valley without special measures to keep the bulbs cool.

L. maritimum. Coast lily. This species inhabits bogs, ditches, and other moist sites along the coast of Marin, Sonoma, and Mendocino Counties. I have seen it as a plant of two feet or less, though it can reach at least twice that height, rising from a rather small (one- to two-inch) bulb. The narrow leaves are usually scattered along the stems rather than whorled. One to several bell-shaped, orange-red to blood-red blossoms with darker spotting, each about two inches across, are presented in early summer.

Some friends have grown this lily successfully for several years. I have lost it more than once to summer rots. Clearly it needs a combination of very well drained soil, cool root temperatures, and, during growth and bloom, constant moisture.

L. occidentale. Western lily. This plant is a denizen of bogs and other moist places of far northwestern California and Oregon. It has been plundered nearly to extinction by collectors. Western lily is similar to *L. pardalinum* in overall appearance, though usually less robust and with smaller bulbs. The leaves are mostly scattered along the stems. The flowers are of similar shape and size to those of *L. pardalinum*, while the coloring differs mainly in the greenish centers and broader orange or red portion of each segment. It is not particularly difficult to grow, though one should be very sure that any commercial material offered is nursery-grown, not collected.

L. pardalinum (*L. pardalinum* ssp. *pardalinum* in *The Jepson Manual*). Leopard lily. This is the lily most often encountered in the wilds of California. It is common along streams and year-round seeps of the Coast Ranges from Santa Barbara County to Humboldt County and in much of the Sierra Nevada.

Leopard lily is a robust plant with elongated, freely branching bulbs, capable of producing large colonies in a short time. The sturdy stems rise three to six feet, with occasional giants of eight feet or more. The narrow leaves are up to eight inches long, both whorled and scattered along the stems (particular plants may show one or the other extreme) and making a beautiful display. Leopard lily is usually generous with its flowers, which are of the familiar "tiger lily" form, and plants with a dozen or more are common. Each segment of the flower is yellow with maroon spots

L. pardalinum ssp. pardalinum.

near the center, shading to orange or red near the tips. Even the long stamens are showy, with their large red-orange anthers.

Now considered a subspecies of leopard lily is the former *L. pitkinense*, Pitkin lily, distinguished, for our purposes, by darker flowers. This plant is restricted in the wild to a single site at Pitkin Marsh in Sonoma County. Through the efforts of Wayne Roderick, it is now well distributed among commercial nurseries. My favorite form of this lily is a three- to five-foot plant with mostly scarlet blossoms, many per stem. I have offered it as 'Fireglow'.

Leopard lily is easy to grow, particularly from material found at low elevations near the coast. It requires only constant moisture to thrive. The bulbs have the peculiar habit of perching at the surface of the ground, so they should receive a little extra protection from foraging animals.

LILIES OF WOODS AND CHAPARRAL

It is natural to associate the lilies with streams, bogs, and seeps, for these are the sites where they are most often found. Even the lush appearance of the plants suggests a love of shade and moisture. However, some of our native lilies have abandoned these haunts for open ground in conifer forests, oak woods, and even chaparral, where they must endure at least some summer drought. Even so, those frequenting the most open sites tend to be found in the cooler mountains of far northern California, and all species have at least their soil shaded by overhanging shrubs or trees. In cultivation, they may be allowed to dry out as the stems wither in summer, but the bulbs must be kept shaded and cool to avoid fungus rots. All are suitable for container culture.

L. bolanderi near Gasquet.

L. bolanderi. Bolander's lily. I think of this as our most diminutive lily, for the plants I have seen were all in the one- to two-foot range, even though it is described as ranging to three feet. This lily is restricted to Del Norte County and southern Oregon, where it is found at forest margins and in open chaparral. It is usually slender-stemmed, each stalk set with both whorled and scattered, narrow, bluish green leaves. The plants are few-flowered, and the funnel-shaped blossoms rather small (usually two inches or less across), yet they are stunning nonetheless. The segments are painted crimson to bright red overall, with darker spotting near the centers. Natural hybrids with neighboring species produce a variety of beautiful color combinations. I have found this species reasonably easy to grow in containers, in a very well drained medium. Similar soil drainage is required in the open ground. I would not expect the plants to tolerate high summer heat.

L. columbianum. Columbia lily. This species, a roadside treat for summer travelers in far northern California, is common on wooded and brushy slopes near the coast. The plants are rather stout, usually in the range of one and one-half to three feet in height, with mostly whorled, medium to light green leaves. The flowers are of the "tiger lily" type, nodding and with all segments swept back and around. They are generally two to three inches broad and vary in background color from yellow to dark red; those with which I am familiar are of light to medium orange, liberally dotted with deep maroon. I have found Columbia lily easy to grow, even tolerating moderate summer watering—a reminder of the heavy summer fog drip and summer showers in its native range.

L. humboldtii (*L. humboldtii* ssp. *humboldtii* in *The Jepson Manual*). Humboldt lily. Found at lower elevations in the southern Sierra Nevada, this is one of the most robust of all our native lilies. Rising from large, many-scaled bulbs, its sturdy stems often stand six feet or more tall, occasionally even reaching ten feet. Large, thick, wavy-edged leaves, frequently tinged with purple, are arranged in whorls along the stems. The flowers may be four inches across and have striking maroon spots sprinkled over an orange to golden yellow background.

Better known than the species proper is the subspecies *ocellatum*, which is sometimes treated as a separate species. It is found in chaparral and oak woods on the mainland, from Santa Barbara County south, as well as on the Channel Islands. It can be even more robust than the type species, but is best distinguished by the red border around each spot on the flowers. I have found summer drought to be nearly mandatory with these plants, making them ideal for planting under oaks. They take several years to achieve their full glory.

L. kelloggii. Kellogg's lily. This is one of the few native lilies I have not been privileged to see in the wild, yet it has long been one of my favorites in cultivation. It inhabits conifer forests of far northern California. The plants are generally of moderate size, three feet or less in height, and have rather narrow, whorled, dark green leaves. Flowers of "tiger lily" form, each only about two inches broad, are borne a few to many per stem. The background color is pale to deep pink, while each segment is decorated with a yellow band and often many tiny maroon flecks. Adding to the impression is a sweet, spicy perfume. In cultivation, this species seems to thrive best in partial shade, even along the coast. Well drained soil is a must.

L. rubescens. Redwood lily. This is an old plant friend for me, first encountered on forested slopes where I grew up in Sonoma County. Following the redwood belt from Santa Cruz

L. washingtonianum, a stunning sight in the wild.

County north, it inhabits both forest and chaparral. The plants are usually in the range of two to four feet tall, arising from surprisingly small bulbs. The leaves are mostly whorled and of strikingly lacquered appearance. Unlike other lilies described here, it bears its flowers erect or nearly so. They are also distinctive in their trumpet-like shape, and most of all in texture, for they truly appear to be molded in china. Their fragrance, reminiscent of gardenias, is almost overpowering at close range. The blossoms open white to pale pink, speckled with maroon, but darken as they age, sometimes nearly to crimson. I grew this species quite successfully as a container plant in full sun until one awful September, when a late heat wave turned the bulbs to mush. The lesson, already stated, is to keep the bulbs shaded and cool. They should also be dried out almost completely as the stems yellow and wither.

L. washingtonianum (*L. washingtonianum* ssp. *washingtonianum* in *The Jepson Manual*). Washington lily. A true denizen of the chaparral, Washington lily is found in the central and northern Sierra Nevada, the Cascades, and the Klamath Mountains, where it is often seen towering above manzanitas and scrub oaks. The bulbs are broad and creep horizontally. The stems commonly range from three to five feet tall, and are set with whorls of light, often bluish green leaves. The flowers, whether few or many, are always a striking sight. They face outward or upward and are broadly trumpet-shaped, often four inches or more across. The segments are colored white to cream, with or without red dots near the center, and have the same chinalike texture as those of *L. rubescens*. There is a subspecies, *purpurascens*, that opens white to pink and deepens with age, also in the manner of *L. rubescens*. My own experience with this species has been inconclusive at best. However, given well drained soil and well shaded bulbs, it should be amenable to cultivation.

HYBRID LILIES: FANCIFUL PURSUITS

As we might expect for plants with flowers so dazzling, lilies have long captured the hybridizer's fancy. To this we owe the enormous range of sizes, shapes, and colors available in garden lilies today. Some of the Californian species have apparently figured in the back-

One of my *L.* Corralitos Hybrids group.

ground of these complex crosses, but few enthusiasts have worked with purely native species to extend their natural variation and improve their garden tolerance. Some time ago, I decided to see where this might lead and began with crosses involving *L. pardalinum* ssp. *pitkinense, L. kelloggii,* and a natural *L. bolanderi* hybrid. Even the first generation showed good plant vigor, often many flowers per stalk, and flower colors ranging from rose to coral, scarlet to crimson. Later addition of a larger *L. pardalinum* brought an even broader range of colors and larger flower size. Fragrance is a frequent bonus. You can easily do the same with your own lilies if you are so inclined, though you may prefer simply to enjoy them in their natural state.

BRODIAEAS AND FRIENDS

Genera: *Brodiaea, Triteleia, Dichelostemma*
Family: Liliaceae, the Lily Family

Among California's thousands of native plants, certain ones never fail to delight the child in us. Such are the brodiaeas. Viewing a sunny meadow from a distance, you will notice spots of cheery color among the grasses. At closer range, some of these spots resolve into clusters of little stars or trumpets. They face the sun on delicate, often glistening stems that sway with the slightest breeze. Even in their smallest details, the flowers are thoroughly enchanting. Those of us who enjoy the company of our favorite natives in the garden will find a welcome surprise in the brodiaeas. For all their delicate features, many of them are quite durable and easy to grow.

COMMON FEATURES

Brodiaeas are showy members of the lily family. They are widely scattered over the West, but are particularly abundant in central and northern California, especially at lower elevations. Grassy meadows suit most species, though a few are commonly seen on scree slopes and rocky outcrops.

These plants have challenged taxonomists over the years. In the time of Willis Jepson they were considered to belong to the lily family, but they were later included in the amaryllis family (Amaryllidaceae), partly on the basis of the umbrella-like flower clusters. After sharing yet another family with the onions and

their kin (Alliaceae), they once again appear, in the new *Jepson Manual* and elsewhere, with the lilies. The old genus *Brodiaea* was broken into three or more groups at various times, reintegrated, and more recently split again into the current *Brodiaea, Dichelostemma*, and *Triteleia*. Newcomers to California's native flora may be spared the trials suffered by some of us who have struggled to stay in step with modern taxonomy. In any event, "brodiaea" persists as a common name for members of all the current genera, and I will use it without apology here.

Brodiaeas are perennial plants that arise from underground corms (fleshy, contracted stems) with dry, fibrous coats. These act much like true bulbs in storing nutrients and water through the dormant season, usually summer and fall. The annual growth cycle begins above ground with the appearance of a few grasslike, smooth, and often shiny leaves from each corm. The leaves may be held nearly erect, arch over, or meander along the ground. Those of *Brodiaea* itself are rolled inward from the edges and may appear to be cylindrical.

LEFT: *TRITELEIA IXIOIDES* SSP. *IXIOIDES* IN A MEADOW NEAR WATSONVILLE. **ABOVE:** *BRODIAEA CALIFORNICA*. PHOTOGRAPH BY WILLIAM T. FOLLETTE.

In *Dichelostemma* and *Triteleia* they are distinctly channeled or folded along a central axis. The leaves often shrivel and dry by the time flowering stems appear, which for most species of *Brodiaea* and *Triteleia* varies from late April to July. *Dichelostemma capitatum*, the common blue dicks, begins its show in the lowlands in March while still in active growth, and others of this genus soon follow.

Flowering structures follow a common theme but vary widely in their details. The main stems are slender, cylindrical, and smooth, but they may stand up, sprawl, or even clamber up through neighboring shrubs, as in twining brodiaea, *Dichelostemma volubilis*. The aboveground portions vary in height from under one inch, in some plants of *Brodiaea terrestris*, to over two feet in the larger forms of *Triteleia laxa*, Ithuriel's spear. At their summit is an umbrella-like flower cluster with a circle of bracts at its base. The pedicels (individual flower stalks) vary from quite short, giving the cluster a dense, headlike appearance, to several inches long, literally resembling the spokes of an umbrella.

The flowers also vary considerably in size—from a little over one-half inch to about two inches—and in shape. The six segments are fused at their base into a tube of variable length. This tube may be bowl-shaped and nearly inconspicuous, with free petal-like lobes spreading nearly flat, like little stars. More commonly it is bell-shaped, with lobes cupped or flaring like the bell of a trumpet. In the firecracker flower, *Dichelostemma ida-maia*, the tube is long and cylindrical, the lobes curling back just at the tip. Common floral shades are violet to bluish purple, lavender, and lilac, yet there are species with snow-white, straw-colored to bright yellow, pink, and even crimson flowers. Often the midrib of each segment is darker than the rest. The effect is further enhanced by a waxy surface that may glisten as if inlaid with tiny crystals. The stamens, though not always conspicuous, are useful for distinguishing both genera and species. A true *Brodiaea* has only three fertile stamens alternated with three staminodia, or sterile stamens. *Dichelostemma* is more confusing, but usually displays just the three fertile stamens. And *Triteleia* has six fertile stamens, with often beautifully colored anthers.

When the flowers have faded, small, narrowly egg-shaped capsules develop, each filled with many tiny black seeds, which rattle in the summer breeze until their contents are dispersed.

USES AND CULTURE

Brodiaeas have long been used in gardens, though only a few species—notably *Triteleia laxa*—have received much attention. Their most natural role, for those of us with ample space and time, is that of decorating a naturalistic meadow. Native bunchgrasses like needlegrass (*Nassella*) and squirreltail (*Elymus elymoides*), other bulbs such as the mariposas (*Calochortus*), and, of course, the showy annual lupines, gilias, clarkias, and poppies are all ideal companions. Many brodiaeas begin to bloom just as most of the annuals fade, prolonging the floral parade. One can combine species for a tapestry of colors. For example, the rich purple *Brodiaea coronaria* might be interspersed with soft yellow *Triteleia ixioides* and white *T. hyacinthina*. The daunting side of such a project is, first, to clear a space of weedy plants, including lawn grasses, then to prevent their overrunning it again (an event actually more threatening to annuals than to brodiaeas and other perennials). My own would-be meadow is the scene of constant battles against encroaching Bermuda and Kikuyu grasses. Fortunately, several brodiaeas, as well as some associated annuals, also thrive in more barren circumstances, such as roadcuts and open banks, where the progress of weedy invaders is diminished.

Given their small size and delicate features, many brodiaeas are prime subjects for the rock garden. Besides its distinctive visual effects, the typical rock garden is a relatively small, controllable space, inviting close inspection. Some of the small, matting eriogonums, monardellas, and penstemons—which tolerate at least some summer drought—are ideal neighbors in this setting. If one is not too fussy about geo-graphic origins, one can also effectively combine brodiaeas with small exotic bulbs, like the South African babianas and tritonias, for a succession of flowers lasting several months each year.

Many of us already grow brodiaeas in pots, which can be laid away in a cool, dry place for the summer and brought out for display—even shifted about at the gardener's whim—during the growing and blooming seasons. Pots can also be used as protective structures, being sunk in the ground in winter and lifted when the plants are dormant.

Brodiaeas are not generally difficult to grow. Indeed, many are adaptable and amazingly prolific; left to their own de-vices, they would quickly fill and overflow any meadow in the wild, or any planting in the garden. However, this is not the usual scenario. Their succulent leaves are relished by rabbits and deer and frequently pulled up by thrashers and other birds in search of soil insects. The corms are prized by gophers, field mice, raccoons, and other beasts (not to mention, once upon a time, the humans who roamed the hills and valleys of California), so that even in the wild mature plants sometimes are left with only one stem—and the wonder may be that even that one remains.

As gardeners, we are entitled to intervene and tip the scales a bit. To protect a single clump or small colony, either a commercial gopher basket or its homemade equivalent is an excellent start. The structure should be closed at the top to prevent entry from above (as has happened to all too many of my own small bulbs). The wire mesh does not impede the growth of brodiaeas' slender shoots, which simply push up along the path of least resistance. A mulch of small rocks gives added insurance against mice. However, neither measure addresses the problem of vulnerable leaves. To protect these, a light spray of one of the common deer and rabbit repellants, performed once a month in dry weather, more often during rainy periods, is quick, cheap, and usually effective in making the plants unpalatable.

A concern in larger plantings, as suggested above, is competition with exotic weeds. Brodiaeas persist remarkably well amid wild oats, bromes, and other annual grasses; in fact, these even provide some measure of protection against their predators. However, larger-leaved weeds cast more shade and can stifle their growth. The time for control is soon after the first fall rains, when unwanted seedlings first appear—and before the delicate shoots of the brodiaeas emerge, lest they be trampled or pulled up along with uninvited vegetation.

Triteleia laxa 'Queen Fabiola', a popular cultivar.

Siting is a negotiable matter. With a few exceptions (described individually below), they prefer a sunny site. Many will grow and even multiply in light—never heavy—shade, but flowering is reduced, and the flowers may not develop their full, rich colors.

Species that inhabit the hills and valleys at lower elevations tend to be tolerant of a wide variety of soils, even including heavy clays. Notable examples are *Dichelostemma capitatum, Triteleia laxa,* and *T. hyacinthina.* Plants from the higher mountains are generally more demanding of well drained soil. Pot culture changes the rules a bit, as it does for many other plants. A porous, wood- or bark-based potting mix, or ordinary soil to which a generous quantity of perlite or volcanic cinders has been added, will compensate nicely for the restriction of drainage and aeration by the pot itself. Brodiaeas' nutrient needs are low. Several species are equally at home in rich valley bottoms and nutrient-deficient serpentine meadows. Richer soils simply tend to produce larger plants, with more and larger flowers, sometimes at the expense of the grace we admire.

Watering is also a relatively carefree matter, particularly in the gardens of northern and central California. Brodiaeas need only for their soil to be moist during active growth, which normally coincides with the rainy season. An occasional irrigation during prolonged dry spells should be all the intervention they require. Southern Californian gardeners may need to be a bit more generous, as they are with other garden plants. Watering should in any case be reduced as the leaves begin to wither in late spring, then suspended altogether after flowering. Brodiaea corms generally tolerate more summer moisture than the mariposas and other *Calochortus* that often share their meadows. However, the combination of moisture and high soil temperatures are an invitation to fungus invasion of any summer-dormant plant, native or exotic.

PROPAGATION

Brodiaeas are among the most prolific of our native bulbs, multiplying at an astounding rate with little care. In a good year, each flower results in a well filled seed capsule containing many tiny seeds, most of which, in turn, are viable. The seeds can be sown outside in the fall, using shallow pots or flats and any reasonably well drained medium, from commercial house plant mix to sandy loam. They should be barely covered with more of the same, gently watered, and kept in a shady spot sheltered from winds. Germination occurs not long after the nights have grown chilly, usually by the end of November. The seedlings often make two distinct rounds of growth in their first year, if kept cool and shaded. Since the young corms are quite small and their roots fleshy and delicate, it is usually wise to leave them in their initial containers until the second season's shoots have appeared. Then they can be teased apart into small groups and planted in individual pots. On commencing their third season, they are ready for a site in the garden, and many will bloom the following spring.

While seeding yields the greatest rate of multiplication, simple separation of the many corms and cormlets gives us plants that flower the first or second season. Several cormlets develop around a mature corm of a *Dichelostemma* or *Triteleia* by the end of the growing season. Those of a typical true *Brodiaea,* in contrast, are produced at the ends of thin rhizomes that extend like the arms of a tiny starfish from the parent corm. This is a good reason not to disturb the plants during active growth. In either case, the clumps are most easily located while something remains of the old shoots, just after flowering. They can be carefully dug, placed in pots or bags, preferably with a little soil to retard dehydration, and laid away in a shady spot until fall arrives once more.

SPECIES OF INTEREST

As explained above, the plants that once all belonged to the genus *Brodiaea* are now sorted botanically into three smaller genera: *Brodiaea* itself, *Dichelostemma*, and *Triteleia*. Let us have a closer look at each group.

BRODIAEA

The new *Jepson Manual* lists fourteen species in *Brodiaea* proper, still the largest of the three groups. Its members share several distinctive features. Their leaves are particularly narrow and grassy, made more so by their inrolled margins. The flowers are upfacing, often richly colored and waxy in texture. Each has a bell- to funnel-shaped tube and six flared to widely spreading, free segments in inner and outer whorls. The three staminodia, or sterile stamens, are often petal-like and lighter colored than the outer segments. They alternate with three usually smaller, fertile stamens. This genus includes some of the most petite of the brodiaeas, and some of the last to bloom, showing up vividly against the tans of dried grasses. The smaller and more wispy species are particularly susceptible to attacks by birds and rodents, but most are otherwise easy to grow. The corms should be allowed to dry out completely when the flowers have passed and the stems begin to yellow.

Brodiaea californica. This is a robust species, found in scattered locations from Sonoma and Napa Counties to Shasta County. It grows in both light woods and open meadows. The plants have narrow leaves up to twelve inches long and flowering stems that rise one to two feet, or sometimes a bit more, from May to July. The flowers are individually large—from one to nearly two inches long—and elevated on pedicels, or flower stalks, up to twice their length. They open less widely than those of other species. Flower color is usually pale lavender to white. The variety *californica* is the typical, larger form of the species. The variety *leptandra* is generally smaller in all its parts and has other minor distinctions not likely to be appreciated by the gardener. Though a little less flashy than some of the species that follow, this is still a plant well worth growing.

B. coronaria. This brodiaea is abundant in the hills of northern and central California, including the northern foothills of the Sierra. One usually encounters it in open meadows. The leaves vary from about three to twelve inches in length and are quite narrow, while the flowering stems grow up to ten inches high. Each carries a few large, broadly flared blossoms, painted in shades of violet to pale lavender, on long pedicels. The flowers may be seen from May to July.

B. elegans. Harvest brodiaea. This plant evokes vivid childhood associations for me: the first hot days of summer, the soft waving of dry grasses, and the beautiful yellow mariposa (*Calochortus luteus*) that accompanies it in June. It is also beautiful in its own right and, happily, one of the most common brodiaeas. You will find it in meadows and open woods, mostly inland, from Monterey County to southern Oregon. Both leaves and stems grow from four to twelve inches high or more. I will have to confess a preference for the smaller forms. Between late May and July, it carries open clusters of broadly flared blossoms, each one to two inches long and rich violet to bluish purple in hue. Protected from marauding birds and rodents, this species can quickly make impressive colonies. It is surely one of the best of all brodiaeas for the garden.

B. jolonensis **at the Indians.**

B. jolonensis. This is a more southerly species, found from Monterey County to northern Baja California. It inhabits open meadows and flats, often in large colonies. Its leaves and stems are from two to six inches high. From April to June it carries clusters of clear violet blossoms, similar in form to those of *B. elegans*, but usually one inch or less in length. The staminodia are violet in color, unlike those of most species, and the anthers are purple. *B. jolonensis* is obviously well adapted to southern climates. It would be interesting to test its winter hardiness in northern California.

B. terrestris. Once included in *B. coronaria* as the variety *macropoda*, this is a petite but prolific, easily grown brodiaea. It is common from near the coast to the foothills of the Sierra, and from the Tehachapi mountains north to Oregon. It has small, very narrow leaves and flowering stems, often barely rising from the ground. The pedicels range from under one inch to six inches long, carrying lavender to blue-violet blossoms similar to those of *B. coronaria*, though usually smaller. It often makes its appearance in late April and May, a little ahead of the other true brodiaeas. This is a charming little plant for rock gardens and pots.

DICHELOSTEMMA

This genus contains some of the most familiar brodiaeas as well as two of the most unusual. The leaves are usually longer and broader than those of *Brodiaea* itself, with a distinct ridge or "keel" below. The flowers are borne in generous clusters, either dense and congested (as implied by two of the species names below) or more open and relaxed, with longer pedicels. They are beautifully colored and glisten in the sun. The floral tube varies in shape from bell-shaped or cylindrical, and in extent from less than half to nearly the entire length of the flower. The free segments are slightly spreading to completely reflexed. One species has six fertile stamens, the others only three; their bases create a conspicuous raised collar. The dichelostemmas are robust, easily grown plants that reward even the beginning gardener with more impressive displays each year. They are generally more resistant to summer rots than other brodiaeas, though it is still a good idea to place them beyond the reach of the hose. Most of them thrive in either sun or light shade.

Dichelostemma capitatum. Blue dicks. It is nearly impossible to tour the California countryside in spring without seeing this plant. It spans the length of the state, spilling into Oregon and Baja California, and occurs from the coast to the Sierra foothills and even portions of the deserts, in various exposures. The few leaves are up to one foot—occasionally more—in length, often sprawling close to the ground. One- to two-foot flower stems appear from March to May, carrying headlike flower clusters. The flowers are broadly bell-shaped, from one-half to nearly one inch long, and painted lavender to violet, or occasionally white or purplish pink. Unlike the flowers of other species, they have six fertile stamens. The variety *capitatum* is the typical representative. This is a strong and adaptable plant, with no special requirements. It multiplies freely and pops up in unexpected corners of the garden. I have not tried the variety *pauciflorum*, found in and around the deserts and usually distinguished by fewer flowers with longer pedicels. It may demand better soil drainage and more pronounced summer drought than the typical form.

D. congestum **near Clear Lake.**

D. congestum. Ookow. This species is found from Santa Clara County, in central California, to southern British Columbia, in meadows and open woods. The leaves can be quite long and floppy. Flowering stalks rise as much as three feet high from April to June, carrying dense, many-flowered clusters, each with a short vertical axis rather than the typical umbel. The individual flowers are a little over half an inch to nearly one inch long and bluish purple in color. This is another robust and easily grown brodiaea, adaptable to a variety of garden settings.

D. ida-maia. Firecracker flower. The sight of a firecracker flower in bloom, especially backlit by the afternoon sun, is a memorable experience. It is often found at the edges of woods, from Mendocino County north to Oregon. It has leaves from one foot to nearly two feet

D. ida-maia.

long, and stems that rise up to three feet high, though usually less. I associate its flowering with that of the native mock-orange, *Philadelphus lewisii*, which is often found nearby, usually beginning in May. Drooping, cigar-shaped buds, carried on pedicels of equal length, develop into cylindrical one-inch blossoms, bright red to crimson in color, with short, reflexed green tips. There is simply nothing else like it among California's many bulbs in form, color, and sheer elegance. Fortunately, it is also easy to grow, preferring a lightly shaded site and even tolerating some summer moisture. Several corms in a large pot make a stunning display. Natural hybrids between *D. ida-maia* and other species like *D. congestum* and *D. multiflorum* were once collectively called *D. venusta*. These combine firecracker flower's distinctive shape with rose to reddish purple coloring.

D. multiflorum. Wild hyacinth. This is another impressive brodiaea, encountered in the central and northern Sierra, the inner North Coast Ranges, and occasional sites near San Francisco Bay. It produces leaves from one to two and a half feet long, and stems of nearly the same length, flowering in May and June. Both the sheer number of flowers and their relatively long individual stalks make the clusters considerably larger than those of *D. capitatum* and *D. congestum*. The flowers are up to an inch long and violet to lavender-pink in color, with usually lighter-colored, inflated tubes. The corms are fairly prolific and will form sizeable clumps in time.

D. volubile. Twining brodiaea. This is both a beautiful wildflower and a bizarre novelty. One meets it unexpectedly on rocky slopes and flats, usually in chaparral, from Butte County to Kern County in the Sierra and from Tehama County to Solano County in the inner Coast Ranges. It is a mystifying sight from a distance, emerging with large clusters of pink flowers from the tops of scrub oaks and other usually drab shrubs. The actual body of the plant includes a few sinuous leaves, often two feet or more in length and lying on the ground, and a flower stem that twines around the branches of neighboring shrubs (or any other support) to a height of two to eight feet. The flowers are under an inch long, with short, fat tubes and spreading free segments. They are bright to pale pink in color. Flowering time is April and May.

Twining brodiaea is not difficult to grow, though it may require a more pronounced summer drought than other species. The problem is how to use it. One might train several stems up a stake or open frame for an interesting display. Unsupported, the stems tend to sprawl or snake along the ground.

TRITELEIA

The triteleias have an airy grace matched by few other native perennials, together with beautiful, often subtle colors. Their leaves are similar to those of *Dichelostemma*, several inches in length and keeled below. The flowers are borne in broad umbels, with long, slender pedicels. The tube is usually funnel-shaped, the free segments flared to widely spreading. There are six fertile stamens, whose colored anthers often add to the beauty of the flowers. The species that follow are all reasonably easy to grow—three of them strikingly so— needing only a spot where the soil dries out well in summer. Other species, particularly those of higher elevations, have additional requirements, like protection from winter rains and sandy or gravelly soil.

Triteleia hyacinthina. White brodiaea. This species is a common indicator of hillside seeps, tiny rills, and marshy swales that bake dry in summer. It graces these spots with puffs of little white, green-centered stars in April and May. White brodiaea is common from Monterey County in the Coast Ranges and Tulare County in the western Sierra, north to British Columbia and Idaho. The plant has narrow leaves up to one foot in length, and slender stems standing one to two feet high. The flowers are borne on pedicels of widely varying length, the longer ones giving a more graceful presentation. Each half- to one-inch blos

Triteleia hyacinthina, **easy and beautiful.**

som has a short tube and widely spreading white segments with green midribs. The corms multiply freely, quickly forming many-stemmed clumps. This is a fine plant for naturalistic meadows, rock gardens and containers, and one of the easiest of all brodiaeas to grow.

T. ixioides. Golden brodiaea. This is one of my favorite neighbors in the hills near Santa Cruz. It grows on both wooded and meadowy slopes, from the Sierra foothills to the coast, and from central California to Oregon. The leaves are from eight to eighteen inches long, and the flowering stems eight inches to well over two feet high. They carry open clusters of golden yellow to straw-colored flowers, usually banded with green or brown along the middle of each segment. The tube is shorter than the free segments, which spread widely, forming a star up to an inch across. Of the four subspecies in California, the two you are likely to find and grow are subspecies *ixioides*, with golden yellow flowers, from the Coast Ranges, and subspecies *scabra*, with straw-yellow flowers, from the foothills of the Sierra and the Cascades. These are beautiful, delicate-looking plants, useful for naturalizing in a lightly wooded setting.

T. laxa. Ithuriel's spear. At one time, this species must have graced vast areas of the California countryside with a soft lavender haze. It is still a common, gregarious plant wherever the twin blights of overgrazing and bulldozing have yet to eradicate it, occurring from San Bernardino County north to Oregon. Like many brodiaeas, it is highly variable in all its parts. The leaves may be broad or narrow and range from eight to eighteen inches in length. From April to June, it bears broad clusters of trumpet-shaped blossoms on sturdy stems up to two feet tall. The individual flowers are roughly one to two inches long and

T. laxa, **stunning in the garden.**

range in color from an occasional white through the more common blue-lavender to bright purple. The anthers are often blue and quite pretty at close range.

Happily, this is one of the easiest brodiaeas to grow. There are even horticultural selections. One of them, 'Queen Fabiola', with purple flowers, is found on the fall bulb racks of many local garden centers. However, none of these is quite as nice, in my eyes, as some of the soft, shaded lavender forms to be seen on a country drive in May. Ithuriel's spear is a fine choice for naturalistic meadows, flower gardens, and containers, multiplying well from year to year. It is best in full sun, though it tolerates light shade.

T. peduncularis. Long-rayed brodiaea. One normally thinks of the brodiaeas in terms of color, and perhaps the shape of the individual flowers. This species, however, is most striking for the structure of the flower clusters. Populations are widely but thinly scattered, from Monterey County to Humboldt County, inhabiting seeps and swales where there is abundant moisture in spring. The plants have narrow leaves up to eighteen inches long, and flowering stems up to thirty inches in height. Many strikingly long pedicels radiate from the summit of each stem, bearing small white to pale lilac, trumpet-shaped blossoms. This is a fascinating subject for either sun or light shade. It is undemanding, except for requiring plenty of moisture in spring, and it resists rotting in summer-irrigated soils.

SMALL MATTERS

THE TROUBLE WITH ANNUALS

. . . .

Every few years, all the forces of Nature line up just so, and the hills, meadows, and desert floors of California become a riot of annual wildflowers. Every open patch of ground seems to erupt in color. The show begins with white puffs of meadow foam (*Limnanthes*) in the wettest spots, bright patches of goldfields (*Lasthenia*) elsewhere. The pace quickens, and great drifts of blue lupines and gold and orange poppies fill one's field of view. In places these are punctuated by carpets of moonlight-yellow cream cups (*Platystemon*), purple phacelias, pale lavender gilias, and many others. In stony soil and dotting rock outcrops are still more, from the phloxlike linanthus to blazing stars (*Mentzelia*). Even after the ground has dried, pink and lavender clarkias stand out against a pale tan background of parched grasses. This is truly a show for the masses, sometimes causing mayhem on country roads as throngs stampede to each new site announced in the evening news. Fortunately, those of us who crave a little solitude can enjoy the same displays—and much more— by taking the effort to hike backcountry trails far from the milling crowds.

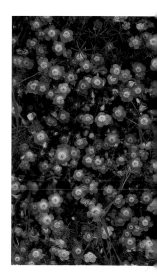

Having filled our souls with the warm glow of such beauty, some of us will begin to wonder whether we might create similar spectacles at home. It is here that the trouble with annuals begins. We forget that Nature's best displays are occasional and unpredictable. We tell ourselves that anything seen over such vast areas *must* be easy to grow. And so they are, in a well tended flower pot. Creating a reliable display in the open garden is more difficult—as I have learned though harsh experience. I will try to explain why this is so and suggest ways in which you can succeed with at least modest aims. We will look to Nature for some hints.

COMMON FEATURES

Simply put, annuals are plants that sprout from seeds, grow, flower, set seeds for the next generation, and die, all in one year or less—sometimes much less. They are found in many plant families. Many share their genus with perennial and even woody species. They range in size from tiny specks to monsters that tower over us, in shape from mats to narrow poles, and in color through nearly the entire visible spectrum.

As a strategy, their life cycle is especially practical in climates like those of lowland California, where any plant standing above ground must cope with several months of drought, often coupled with considerable heat, each year. Some annuals quickly follow their entire path almost regardless of conditions, producing only a single, tiny stem and a few small leaves before flowering and seeding. Others, like some of the clarkias, are opportunists,

---

LEFT: CREAM CUPS (*PLATYSTEMON CALIFORNICUS*) ON CARRIZO PLAIN. ABOVE: BABY BLUE EYES (*NEMOPHILA MENZIESII*), TREASURED IN CALIFORNIA GARDENS.

branching out and increasing their display until parched soil makes further progress impossible.

Some of the same features that protect these plants in the wild can make them seem fickle and demanding in the garden. Their seeds, like those of most plants, require moisture to germinate. However, they have additional mechanisms for preventing disastrous false starts. Often a certain minimum period of continuous moisture is necessary to activate them. Seeds of many species also require a certain number of cool or even frosty nights. Even so, it is not uncommon for vast numbers of young seedlings to wither and die in an extended midwinter drought. Such is the nature of life in California.

Even given favorable weather, success is never assured. Many native annuals, like the poppies and lupines, need abundant sunshine to thrive. Shading and root competition from weedy European grasses and other robust exotics can stifle them. A year or two of relative drought can beat back the weedy competitors a bit; then one really good winter's rains may create spectacular displays. Too many "good" years in a row, or somewhat too generous rains in late winter and spring, can result in a choking growth of the exotics, throttling wildflower displays. It is no accident that some of the most reliable wildflower shows are to be found on roadbanks, some grazed areas, and other sites simply too barren for exotic weeds to prosper.

ANNUALS IN THE GARDEN

Every adverse condition or event just described for the wild has its parallel in the garden, as I have amply proven by my own experience. One year I might manage an early sowing, get promising assistance from early rains, then neglect my unsprouted seeds and seedlings just a little too long when the rains fail. Another year, pressed for time, I might procrastinate until late December or January, then watch in helpless disappoint-

ment as unseasonable heat comes to stay. Or I may be too cavalier about the appearance of grassy weeds until they form a nearly solid canopy over my would-be wildflowers. In each of these cases, spring is heralded by a thin sprinkling of flowers where there should be multitudes. Yet the opportunity exists to weight the odds in our favor, if we pay close attention and maintain a firm commitment to success.

TOP: POPPIES AND GOLDFIELDS IN ANTELOPE VALLEY. **BOTTOM:** LUPINES AND POPPIES AGAINST A WALL, NEAR SONORA.

GETTING STARTED

While a few native annuals can be found at times in bedding plant packs and flats, this is an extravagant way to procure them, and no way at all to capture a good variety of species. Seeds of many species can be obtained at the plant sales of various California Native Plant Society chapters, plant shops of several botanic gardens and arboreta, and a few commercial sources (some of which are listed under "Resources" in the back of this book). Purchasing them in late summer or fall will help to ensure that they are of the current season's crop, rather than stored from a previous year.

You may choose to collect your own seeds, either from a garden or from the wild (the latter *only* where plants are visibly abundant and the amount taken is small, if you would be a good steward of the land). The process is quite simple. Wait, in most cases, for the plants to begin to wither, then cut whole flowering stems before many of the seeds are lost. If there is a long succession of flowers (with different pods ripening at different times) snip off individual pods or seeding heads as they ripen.

If they need to dry further, place the stems and pods in paper bags or between paper sheets. Then either harvest dry seeds directly, if they have fallen cleanly, or crush the pods. The tight heads of many daisies can be pulled apart, or their clusters of seedlike achenes lifted from their receptacle. You need not be too meticulous about separating seeds from chaff (pieces of dry pods and stems). Transfer the resulting material to paper bags or envelopes to await sowing. Writing a clear label on each container may seem unimportant at this time, but you will thank yourself later when you confront a row of otherwise identical bags.

And what is sowing time? It is common wisdom even for established native shrubs and perennials that they should be planted in fall, when the weather has cooled. This is perhaps even more emphatically the case for seeds of native annuals. An earlier start, under drought conditions, means increased losses as seeds blow away, are moved about by animals (including, by careless scuffing, yourself), or are eaten by birds and mice. In irrigated areas, seeds may actually be rotted and destroyed by a combination of continuous moisture and warmth. In any case, do not expect them to sprout. Fall is for planting, as an old nursery industry slogan goes.

SITE PREPARATION

Perhaps the most critical steps of all are choosing and properly preparing a site to receive your annuals. In general, it should mimic a native meadow or scree slope. Begin with full exposure to the sun for at least a good portion of each day. If this is unavailable, you still have a more limited choice of shade-tolerant annuals. This site need not contain the best-textured or most fertile of soils; however, you *must* do something to suppress weedy competitors. One easy way to reduce their ranks is to water the site well and repeatedly as the weather cools, encouraging germination, then till the soil or hoe out the weeds while they are young and vulnerable. Later, unless you are planting very sparsely, you will find it impossible to enter the site to remove the weeds without wreaking havoc on young wildflower seedlings.

If you find yourself tempted to take the easier route of chemical weed killers, you should know that they can have unintended consequences. While the residues of most popular brands are quickly inactivated by oxidation or reaction with clays in soil particles, some can persist—particularly in sandy soils—with disastrous results for young annuals. The worst case is that of preemergent herbicides, which are formulated to kill or stunt young roots as they emerge from sprouting seeds. Their effect is likely to be even more potent against the seeds of delicate wildflowers than against tough, garden-adapted exotic weeds. And they persist, often for many months.

PLANTS AND PLACES

Next there is the matter of matching species and sites. I have already mentioned one constraint, lack of direct sunlight. This particular one can be met by careful choice of shade-tolerant native annuals. Certain species of *Nemophila*, like five-spot (*N. maculata*), fit this description nicely, as do fiesta flower (*Pholistoma aurium*) and some of the Chinese houses (*Collinsia*). There are also similar choices for particularly wet spots (here you might try plants such as the meadow foams), and for particularly clayey or sandy soils. I will mention such tolerances in the plant descriptions that follow.

An issue that might not seem obvious at the outset is the relative size and leafiness of different species. The more robust and leafy annuals, like *Phacelia tanacetifolia* and some clarkias, can visually obscure or even physically overwhelm smaller neighbors, especially those as low and delicate as linanthus and bird's-eye gilia, unless they are sown sparingly.

There are also purely aesthetic choices. If you are enchanted by scenes of well mixed annuals in the wild, you can easily duplicate the impression, either by physically mixing the seeds of different species before sowing or by scattering them in repetitive waves over the same site. However, it is also possible to "paint" with annuals. You might choose to create broad swatches (one would hope not military ranks) of different colors, textures or sizes. In the last instance, you might take inspiration from the traditional perennial border, placing the smallest species in the foreground for easy viewing and a succession of taller species to frame them in the background.

SOWING YOUR SEEDS

In nature, most seeds are simply scattered on the ground and work their way into spaces among small rocks and organic particles. They may also be buried a little by the scuffling of animals, downslope movement of rocks and soil, and new accumulation of leaf litter beneath shrubs and trees. Many are lost, but their sheer numbers help to ensure survival. You will logically want to spend an extra bit of time and effort to improve the odds for your precious seeds.

Given the small size of the seeds of many native annuals, it is no simple matter to distribute them thinly and evenly over a large area. Thus it makes sense to dilute them with a material like sand, soil, or commercial potting mix. A large bread bowl or pan—something with no sharp corners or creases where clumps of seeds can hide—makes a fine container for hand-mixing. Partly fill the vessel with the diluting medium, allowing plenty of space above for lifting and turning the mixture. Scatter the seeds over the top and mix them in roughly like the ingredients of any good pastry, turning the mass in all directions. Assuming that you have picked a relatively windless day for your operation, you can easily scatter handfuls of the resulting mixture over the ground with sweeping motions of one arm.

To help keep the seeds in place, to avoid rapid drying between rains or irrigation, and to reduce predation before they sprout, it may be wise to give them a light covering of vegetable compost, potting soil, or other moisture-retaining medium, then lightly pack it by rolling or careful stepping.

Now it is time for a first irrigation, and for patience and care. It is amazingly easy to dislodge small, shallowly buried seeds with a strong stream from an open hose. Even with the soft, scattered flow from a good sprinkling head, seeds may be floated up and away wherever excess water collects. This suggests that you pass over lightly and repeatedly with whatever device you have chosen, allowing water to soak in completely between passes.

If you live with a community of birds and other small animals, it may be advisable to cover the seeds after planting with screens or bird netting, raised above the ground at least a few inches with stakes or other supports but pegged down carefully around the edges. Loosely piled branches will serve the same purpose. You may have to take more dramatic action against slugs and snails. The object is to get the young seedlings safely past the cotyledon (seed leaf) stage, when they are particularly vulnerable, and apparently delicious, to half the animal kingdom.

There is an alternative to most of the sowing process I have outlined thus far. Where the area to be planted is small, seeds on hand are few, predation is particularly severe, or the species you have chosen are relatively robust, it may be worth the extra effort to start your seeds in large pots or flats, in a protected place. Transplant single plants or clumps of plants to individual pots (two- to four-inch pots are especially easy to deal with). When they are strong and well rooted, transfer the seedlings to the open ground.

AFTERCARE

In the aftermath of sowing, observation is truly the key to success. If the rains should fail to start on time, or when they stop without warning, as they often do, you must be ready to irrigate your plot as often as necessary to keep the seeds continuously moist. A bout of dry Santa Ana–style winds can create a sudden water emergency. The disappearance of seedlings or appearance of little craters where once there were seeds is an urgent signal to bring out the netting or other protection. Rapid growth of weedy volunteers may demand your attention, even if the price of their removal is a certain number of trampled "friendly" annuals. There will come a point—usually about the time the first of your annuals begin to flower—when they will be largely able to fend for themselves. Barring a visit from a neighbor's escaped livestock, you can relax a bit, worry less about the frequency of rains, and enjoy your garden.

Nonetheless, there are still things you can do to enhance and prolong the show. Unless your soil is already fairly rich, you can have larger plants and many more flowers by lightly scattering an all-purpose garden fertilizer when the plants have sprouted and grown for a few weeks. Just as late rains can extend the flowering season of wild annuals by several weeks, you can extend it in the garden with periodic (perhaps once every week or two) irrigations as natural rains taper off.

NATIVE ANNUALS IN CONTAINERS

When all else fails in the open garden—or sometimes for more positive reasons, like the sheer joy of a small but extravagant display—you will find many native annuals easy to grow in containers. Both their generally small stature and their generosity with flowers make pots a nice way to view them at close quarters. Large tubs and boxes can contain whole communities of different species, giving some hint of their diversity in the wild.

The mechanics of pot culture are simple. If the seeds are started in a shady spot, where temperatures are cool, sowing can be delayed by at least a month or two (they will grow rapidly and make up for lost time). Broad, relatively shallow containers are preferable to deeper ones, since root systems are often small and excess soil can remain saturated, inviting disease. The growing medium should be porous.

Fill the container most of the way with your chosen medium. Level and slightly pack the surface. Sprinkle the seeds thinly and evenly over the surface, first mixing any really fine seeds with the same medium or sand to facilitate even distribution. Cover them thinly—enough to ensure that they don't wash away when watered—and pack the medium lightly. Then water them very gently. The soft, broken stream from an ordinary sprinkling can is ideal for this purpose. Place the pots outside, protect them from foraging animals—including (or perhaps especially) slugs and snails—and keep the surface moist until your seeds have sprouted. Then handle them as you would potted plants in general. The only real challenge is to avoid flattening delicate stems with each watering. For most species, full sun will promote heaviest flowering, though it makes more frequent watering necessary and the consequences of an accidental drying-out more serious.

FINISHING THE SEASON

When seeds are set and the plants begin to wither and die, it is time to provide for the next generation. If you feel particularly confident about having stifled weedy competitors, you might just let seeds fall in place the first time around, perhaps giving them a light organic mulch, both to retain moisture when the rains come and to reduce losses to winds and the feasting of insects and other animal neighbors. By the second season, your war with weeds will probably need to be renewed, or your flowery meadow may come to look like those in the wild in the worst years. Thus some careful seed collection will be in order. The challenge will be to harvest each species at a point where seed pods have ripened but only minimal quantities of seeds have fallen or flown away on the winds. This requires frequent observation. If you, like me, are prone to forget such things at times, it is better to make your collections a little early than to arrive at a scene of barren stems and empty pods.

GENERA OF SPECIAL INTEREST

One could go on more or less forever about the hundreds of species of beautiful California annuals. Unfortunately, many are from highly specialized habitats (vernal pools and desert sands, for example). Others are rare or of extremely limited distribution. The following are reasonably common in the wild and often available from specialty sources.

Calandrinia ciliata. Red maids. Portulacaceae (the purslane family). If they were a little taller and larger-flowered, red maids would be among the most dramatic of our native annuals. As it is, the plants are sometimes nearly lost to view as they nestle among the taller grasses.

Red maids are widespread in California and beyond, favoring sunny meadows. They have low stems radiating from a common base and narrow, somewhat succulent leaves. A lengthy succession of wide-open five-petaled flowers is carried at the shoot tips. Each blossom measures up to one inch broad and is colored a vivid purplish red.

Red maids are easily grown in soil rich or poor, holding their own against the weeds, though not always visible.

Castilleja and ***Triphysaria.*** Owl's clover. Scrophulariaceae (the figwort family). In simpler times we knew the owl's clovers (unrelated to real clovers) as *Orthocarpus*, while *Castilleja* was the genus of the paintbrushes, most of them perennial. The distinction is no longer so neat. Both genera are described as root parasites, though they seem to accept a wide variety of hosts (among the annuals, grasses and neighboring wildflowers) and cause them no visible harm.

The species in question are small, delicately textured plants with slender, single or few-branched stems and narrow, often deeply divided leaves. What appear to be dense flower heads at the shoot tips elongate gradually to produce dozens of small tubular, two-lipped blossoms with colored bracts. The upper lip is beak-shaped, while the lower consists of three pouchlike lobes. Two species are particularly common and widespread in California.

C. densiflora, inhabiting meadows of the Coast Ranges from north to south, grows from four inches to (rarely) over a foot tall. It has narrow undivided leaves and divided white- or purple-tipped bracts. The flowers are an inch or less long and range in color from creamy yellow to deep, purplish pink. *C. exserta* is found from the coast to the Sierra. While similar overall to *C. densiflora*, it has very narrowly divided leaves and purple to crimson—occasionally pink—flowers.

Triphysaria eriantha, butter-and-eggs, is a close relative of similar appearance. It is also a common plant in the meadows of much of California. It grows from a few inches to a foot high and has openly branched stems with narrowly lobed leaves. The flowers are similar to those of the last two species, usually purplish on the upper lip and yellow on the lower.

All are easily grown in a sunny mixed planting. Given their small size and delicate features, they are most effective in large numbers, painting colorful swatches over the ground. Once they begin, all seem to continue flowering until the ground dries.

Clarkia. Farewell to spring. Onagraceae (the evening primrose family). When the wild oats and bromes have dried, painting the hills in shades of tan, an odd and rather wonderful thing occurs: sprinkled among the grasses, poking up among rocks on shady slopes and making shimmering tapestries on sunny banks, is a whole new wave of colorful wildflowers, the clarkias. These are slender-stemmed, graceful plants with narrow leaves and beautiful four-petaled, often cupped flowers. Some species have proven to be among the most useful of our native annuals for ordinary garden conditions.

Clarkia bottae. **Photograph by Ginny Hunt.**

C. amoena, often known as godetia (a former genus name), is found from the Bay Area to British Columbia. It generally grows one to two feet high, with branched, leafy stems bearing a long succession of broad-petaled flowers at their tips. The flowers are bowl-shaped or flared, from an inch to over three inches across. The petals are painted pink to lavender, with dark red spots or dots near their centers in the subspecies *amoena*. Flowers of the subspecies *whitneyi*, now nearly extinct in the wild, usually have broad cream-white centers with or without red spots, shading to a bright pink or lavender rim.

Hybridizers have adopted this species and produced hundreds of variations, with many lurid colors and frequently huge, carnation-like double flowers. These have lost all the grace of the original; I trust that you will use them, if at all, in flower gardens with gaudy exotics.

There are other similar species, each with its own particular charm. *C. bottae*, punch-bowl godetia, inhabits both coastal and interior ranges of central and southern California. It is of similar size and habit to *C. amoena* and equally generous with its flowers, which are generally one to two inches broad, white with red dots toward the center, shading to pink or lavender toward the tips. *C. rubicunda* is my personal favorite of the group. This native of the central coast has well branched stems, from which issue a seemingly endless progression of mostly one- to two-inch blossoms. These are rose-pink to lavender overall, much darker at the base. *C. purpurea* is the most widely distributed of this group, occurring over much of the state. It is distinguished (to gardeners, not botanists) by the vivid floral hues of its better forms, ranging to deep purplish red.

These would be enough for any native genus to offer us, but there are other clarkias that would hardly seem related, at first glance. I will name just two. *C. concinna*, red ribbons, is found in central and northern California, often at the edges of woods or in the chaparral. It grows from a few inches to a little over a foot high and has dark, often shiny leaves. The flowers are up to two inches broad and of an elegant form: the petals are narrow toward the base, with flared, lobed outer portions, and one of them (the lower, or "middle") is often longer than the others. Colors include medium to quite deep pink. *C. unguiculata*, wide-spread in northern and southern California, is a more robust plant with equally unusual though less showy flowers, also measuring up to two inches across. Each petal consists of a long, narrow basal claw and a broad, nearly triangular tip. The claws are often bent to one side, giving the flowers a decidedly irregular appearance. Their color is pale pink to vivid reddish purple.

The clarkias are excellent garden plants, tolerating harsh conditions but responding generously to a little extra care. I have had both *C. rubicunda* and *C. bottae* flowering in my garden until November, simply by continuing to water them (though this might be hard to duplicate in hot-summer areas). Most, and especially *C. concinna* and *C. unguiculata*, will thrive in either sun or light shade, and in a wide variety of soils.

Collinsia heterophylla. Chinese houses. Scrophulariaceae (the figwort family). This is a wildflower of more subtle beauty, appearing in middle to late spring. It is widespread in California, usually on shaded banks or at the edges of woods. The plants are slender-stemmed, growing more or less erect to a

Collinsia heterophylla.

maximum of twenty inches tall. The stems are lined by pairs of toothed, lance-shaped leaves and several dense tiers of strongly two-lipped flowers. These are up to three-quarters of an inch long, white to violet overall but often strongly bicolored, the upper lip lighter, the lower darker in color.

Several other collinsias are worth trying. *C. sparsifolia*, also common in more meadowy sites in the north, is a smaller plant with narrower leaves and somewhat smaller, lavender to purple flowers. *C. tinctoria* is a stouter plant up to two feet high, found in open woods in the north. Its flowers are cream to pale lavender in color. *C. heterophylla* is easily grown where weedy competitors are suppressed, and is an excellent choice for shady sites, where many meadow annuals would sulk. *C. tinctoria* will thrive in a similar site but demands better soil drainage. *C. sparsifolia* adds variety to a sunny meadow.

Downningia pulchella. Campanulaceae (the bellflower or lobelia family). This is one of the showiest members of a rich but vanishing California community, the vernal pool. The depressions in valley bottoms where water once gathered, drying slowly in late spring and ringed by colorful wildflowers, are now largely filled and leveled, under the guise of "improvement."

The subject at hand is a branched, leafy-stemmed annual, under one foot high, with mostly narrow, bright green leaves. Borne at each shoot tip in late spring are several lobelia-like flowers up to three-quarters of an inch broad. They are colored deep blue overall, with a broad white central patch, marked with yellow, on the expanded lower lip, and as showy as any garden lobelia.

I found it easiest to grow this little gem in containers, simply because it needs constant moisture to thrive. However, any sunny patch of moist ground in the open garden—if you have such a thing—will do nicely. It is otherwise undemanding.

Eschscholzia. California poppy. Papaveraceae (the poppy family). There are still a few places where one can go in spring to see a natural landscape completely carpeted by wildflowers. In such places, like Antelope Valley and the area near Gorman, California poppies present themselves in their full majesty, forming an incredible orange glow that stretches to the horizon. On a smaller scale, it creates nearly as dramatic a show in gardens and on highway banks over much of California.

Eschscholzia is a genus of annuals and short-lived perennials endemic to the West. They have stout taproots and basal crowns of usually long-stalked, dissected, often blue- or gray-green leaves.

Eschscholzia californica, **our state flower.**

Showy four-petaled flowers are elevated above them on long stalks, and a conical "cap" of sepals is pushed off as the petals expand. The petals are broad and brilliantly colored, from pure yellow to deep orange, often spotted with deeper shades.

E. californica is by far the most familiar, occurring naturally over much of California and beyond. It is a robust, seemingly indestructible plant, either annual or perennial (sometimes depending on the harshness of its environment), varying from a few inches to two feet high and wide. Its attractive smooth leaves may be deep green or gray- or blue-green in color. The flowers are freely produced from early spring to the last drying of the soil. Each is from a little over one inch to nearly three inches across, flared or opening widely. Color varies from bright yellow, usually with a large basal orange spot on each petal, to vivid, deep orange throughout. More succulent gray-leaved, coastal populations with strongly bicolored flowers were once designated as the variety *maritima*.

Hybridizers here and abroad have extended the floral hues of this species to include near-violet, blood red, pink, and cream. You will have to decide their merit for yourself (I have found very few of them appealing).

Each of the other nine currently recognized species is probably worth growing, though the desert species are likely to be difficult in the home garden. *E. caespitosa* is particularly common and widespread in chaparral and on rocky slopes and banks. It is, on average, about half the size of *E. californica*, making dense clumps with similar but smaller leaves. The flowers are usually one to two inches broad and bright yellow, with or without basal orange spots. Those of its commercial seed strains now range from cream to bright red. *E. lobbii*, from the Central Valley and Sierran foothills, is often still smaller, with bright yellow flowers only one-half to one inch broad.

E. californica is truly a plant for any gardener with a sunny patch of ground. While it is most durable in well drained soil, it can tolerate heavy clays for a season. I have found that an occasional irrigation will keep my plants flowering nearly year-round. They also grow and flower in light shade, though the leaves are prone to mildew under these conditions near the coast. *E. caespitosa* and *E. lobbii* are more demanding of well drained soil and are particularly well suited for banks and rock gardens.

Gilia. Polemoniaceae (the phlox family). Gilias often tint the landscape with pastel shades by their sheer numbers, yet they are still more lovely at close range. The flowers are small, beautifully formed, and sometimes intricately patterned.

Gilia tricolor, **meadow near Sonora.**

The plants vary widely in stature according to species and conditions. The stems can be almost threadlike, the leaves often lobed or divided. The flowers are presented singly, in open clusters, or in dense heads. Each has a distinct basal tube and five spreading lobes similar to those of the phloxes.

G. tricolor, bird's-eye gilia, is a common spring sight in much of lowland California. It produces one to many delicate four- to twelve-inch stems, loosely lined with narrowly divided leaves and topped by clusters of beautifully painted quarter- to half-inch blossoms. The broad lobes are pale lavender to violet overall, often with darker tips. A deep purple ring at their base surrounds a bright yellow throat. Pale blue anthers lend a further decorative touch.

G. capitata, blue gilia, is also widespread, with several subspecies, though not as gregarious. This is a more robust plant, sometimes two feet or more high, with similarly divided leaves. At the shoot tips are long-stalked, globe-shaped heads of spidery flowers with protruding stamens and pistils. They range from sky blue to bright blue-violet in color.

Truly anyone can grow the gilias, or at least the common ones. They ask for only a sunny spot and moisture through the winter and early spring. Continued irrigation can prolong their display into summer.

Lasthenia. Goldfields. Asteraceae (the sunflower family). Goldfields are among the first of the annual wildflowers to appear in large numbers, and frequently among the last to go.

Plants in the wild often barely rise from the ground, though in generous circumstances some can grow as high as a foot. They are usually well branched and have paired, sometimes dissected leaves. Carried on graceful stalks at the shoot tips are flower heads that vary with the plants in size, sometimes to an inch or more broad. Each has several bright yellow, mostly narrow rays and a dense, darker disk.

L. californica occurs nearly throughout the state, in many habitats, including the desert margins. It may be branched or single-stemmed, growing four to twelve inches high. The leaves are undivided, the flower heads up to three-quarters of an inch broad

Lasthenia californica **with** *Castilleja.*

with as many as a dozen rays. *L. glabrata* is found in wetter parts of the same range and usually grows a little taller. It has narrower leaves and very similar but larger and showier flower heads, occasionally over an inch broad. Several other species, not as common or widely distributed, are equally beautiful and worth trying.

The only problems you are likely to experience with the goldfields follow from their need for full exposure. They seem to be stifled easily by shading and root competition. Otherwise they are fine wildflowers, most effective in large drifts, since both plants and flowers are small. They will continue to flower through late spring if the ground is moist.

Layia. Tidy tips. Asteraceae (the sunflower family). The layias are among the showiest of our annual daisies. Where they are abundant, they can paint whole slopes an almost blinding yellow.

These are usually more substantial plants than the goldfields, often a foot and sometimes over two feet high. The leaves are narrow and frequently toothed or lobed; in some species they exude a fruity or spicy scent. The flower heads of most species have several bright yellow rays surrounding a dense golden disk. Often the rays are tipped with white; hence their common name.

L. platyglossa is the species you are most certain to meet, occurring in open meadows over much of the state. It is extremely variable, growing a few inches to two feet high and spreading to erect. The flower heads can be well over an inch broad, the rays colored a rich, glowing yellow with or without contrasting white tips. *L. chrysanthemoides* is a similar plant, inhabiting open meadows mostly in the northern half of the state. It is a little smaller than *L. platyglossa* but has similarly large (and colored) flower heads. *L. gaillardioides* is another northerner often found in light woods and chaparral. It is a robust plant, up to three feet high, with fragrant foliage and typical flowers. There are still others worth growing.

Tidy tips are nearly indispensable members of a native annual garden, lighting up any sunny (or, in the case of *L. gaillardioides*, lightly shaded) spot. They should have a weed-free, sunny site but are otherwise undemanding.

Limnanthes. Meadow foam. Limnanthaceae (the meadow foam family). In our wetter springs, weeks before the main floral parade begins, one sees what appear to be white clouds in the low spots of our valleys. These are the meadow foams. How long they continue depends on the generosity of the rains, for they love moisture, but they are beautiful while they last.

The plants grow mostly erect, from a few inches to perhaps a foot high, with long-stalked, rather finely divided leaves, both basal and along the stems. They are often branched above, bearing several rather large, white to bright yellow (or white *and* yellow) flowers. The flowers are usually cupped or bell-shaped, having four or five broad petals that appear cut off at the tips. *L. douglasii* is a familiar sight from the coast to the Sierran foothills in northern and central California. It is a robust species, sometimes over a foot high and often with many half- to one-inch flowers, yellow with white edges in the variety *douglasii*, pure white in the variety *nivea*. *L. alba* is a little smaller on the average, with similar, pure white flowers, darkening as they age.

The meadow foams are easily grown in sun or light shade, as long as they are kept constantly moist. Even a slight drying-out is their signal that the season is over. They make beautiful displays grouped in large pots.

Linanthus. Polemoniaceae (the phlox family). Some of my fondest wildflower memories include the linanthus, dotted over rocky ground where few other showy annuals thrive. Though delicate and small, they shimmer with bright color.

While there are a few perennial and even shrubby species, this is mostly a genus of annuals. They are typically few- and openly branched, with slender, delicate stems loosely set with ex-

Linanthus 'Confetti', a hybrid far removed from the wild. Photograph by Ginny Hunt.

tremely narrow, often several-parted leaves. One to many flowers are carried at each shoot tip from mid to late spring. Often they are arranged in a dense head. Individual flowers closely resemble those of the related phloxes, with a distinct basal tube and five deep lobes ("petals") at its end. The flowers are beautifully colored, with whites, pinks, and lavenders being most common; a contrasting "eye" is often created by yellow in the throat.

L. parviflorus is common over much of California. It is a delicate plant, with threadlike stems two to occasionally ten inches high. White to violet, deep pink, or even yellow blossoms open in succession from dense heads. Though only half an inch or less across, they are elevated on much longer, very narrow tubes. *L. androsaceus* is a very similar species inhabiting the North Coast Ranges. *L. grandiflorus*, found sparingly in rocky or sandy spots in the Coast Ranges of northern and central California, is occasionally over a foot high but usually much less. Its white to lavender flowers can measure over an inch across and are borne in dense heads.

Few wildflowers have such delicate grace as these; certainly they are worth a bit of extra effort. They should have full exposure, at least reasonably well drained soil, and—most important—complete freedom from weedy competitors. They are ideal choices for rock gardens and for containers, if one can solve the problem of watering them without knocking down the plants. Continued irrigation can extend their display for weeks or months.

Lupinus. Lupine. Fabaceae (the legume family). In California's legendary scheme of blue and gold, much—sometimes all—of the blue is provided by the annual lupines. In spite of our massive disturbance of the land, they still form fragrant sheets that can stretch to the horizon.

Lupinus succulentus.

Botanists currently recognize over sixty species of lupines in California, of which just over a third are annuals. These occupy many different habitats, including portions of the deserts. All are similar in certain basic features. The stems are lined by stalked leaves that are palmately divided (like the fingers of a hand); these may be smooth or hairy, even silky. Each shoot is tipped by an extended cluster of flowers, often arranged in interrupted whorls. These are typical of the legumes, with a large upper petal, the banner, usually turned back laterally, and two lateral petals, the wings, forming a sort of pouch around the two lower petals, which in turn form the keel enclosing the stamens and pistil. The flowers are often gaily colored, and sweet fragrance is a common feature. The explosive seed pods that follow are much like those of the beans.

Nearly all the annual lupines in California are worth growing, though some are found in rather specialized habitats. Perhaps the most familiar is *L. nanus*, found in open fields and on meadowy slopes over much of California. It grows from four inches to (rarely) two feet high, with erect, hairy, leafy stems. The flower clusters are up to eight inches long, with typically several distinct whorls, the individual flowers up to half an inch long. They are usually bright blue, with a white basal patch and frequently other markings on the banner, and wonderfully fragrant. Easy to confuse with the smaller forms of this species is *L. bicolor*, miniature lupine. Adding to the confusion, the two often occur together throughout their range. *L. bicolor* is usually distinguishable by smaller overall size, fewer flowers in fewer whorls, and smaller flower size.

Some other species are bolder variations on the same theme. *L. succulentus* is a common inhabitant of exposed sites in the Central Valley and Coast Ranges, north and south. It is a robust plant, sometimes reaching three feet, with stout, hollow stems and large, smooth-surfaced dark green leaves. Topping the stems are long, many-flowered clusters. The flowers are often larger than those of *L. nanus* and typically colored a vivid bluish purple. *L. microcarpus* (usually sold as *L. densiflorus*) is best known for its frequent appearance along our highways, often courtesy of human agencies rather than Mother Nature. It is often around a foot high, though sometimes over two feet. It has stout, often hollow stems, leaves with broad leaflets up to two inches long, and long flower clusters usually organized into many distinct whorls. There are three varieties (not of great concern here) and many forms, including commercial seed strains, with a wide variety of flower colors, white, pale yellow to deep gold, pink, and various shades of lavender and blue among them. Finally, I cannot forget the harlequin lupine, *L. stiversii*, of the Sierra foothills and southern mountains. This is a well branched plant of usually eighteen inches or less, with bright green leaves and beautifully bicolored flowers, yellow on the banner and bright pink on the wings.

Having tarried so long with the lupines, I must add that they are indispensable to the native wildflower garden. *L. nanus*, *L. bicolor*, *L. succulentus*, and *L. microcarpus* all thrive in a sunny spot with reasonably well drained soil (or perhaps any soil, in the case of *L. succulentus*). They will hold their own against many of the grasses, though not the tallest, toughest kinds. *L. stiversii* is more difficult but should do well on sandy or gravelly, relatively weed-free banks, or in pots with a well drained mix. Nearly all are relished by animals, from birds and mice to snails and slugs.

Mentzelia. Blazing star. Loasaceae (the loasa family). Your first wild encounter with the blazing stars is likely to leave you puzzled: here is an odd, coarse plant, looking like a weedy daisy, yet adorned by spectacular flowers.

The blazing stars belong to a family that includes many interesting and beautiful plants with viciously stinging hairs. In the case of this genus, the hairs are merely stiff and barbed, making them rough to the touch and hard to detach from clothing. These are plants of exposed, rocky places. They are usually well branched, with stout stems and entire to partially dissected leaves. The flowers are generally large and colorful, borne either singly or in clusters at the shoot tips, and have conspicuous brushes of stamens. Following them are odd tubular seed capsules with flattish end caps.

M. lindleyi is the species you are most likely to grow, since it is at least occasionally available for purchase. This is a plant of rocky places from the coast to the San Joaquin Valley in central and southern California. It grows erect, from four inches to about two feet high. The stems are loosely lined with narrowly lobed leaves, and the flowers are presented singly or in small clusters, each measuring from a little over an inch to three inches across, with broad, pointed golden petals, orange-red at their bases. Occupying much of the same range but extending to Baja California is *M. affinis*, usually a smaller plant with mostly toothed leaves and flowers under an inch broad, though similarly colored.

I cannot resist mentioning the biennial *M. laevicaulis* here, for it is one of the strangest and showiest of our wildflowers, encountered in many of the drier parts of California. This is a stiff, widely branched plant up to four feet high, with nearly white stems, large, narrow, rough-surfaced leaves, and huge (to four inches) brilliant yellow, rather narrow-petaled flowers that appear to be made of silk floss.

The blazing stars are not for beginners. They refuse to negotiate about matters like soil drainage—which must be perfect—and exposure. They also do not respond favorably, like some clarkias and other annuals, to extended irrigation in late spring and summer. Yet they are undeniably beautiful, in a most dramatic way.

Mimulus. Monkey flower. Scrophulariaceae (the figwort family). Some of the perennial monkey flowers, both herbaceous and shrubby, are now widely grown in California; the annuals are largely ignored. Yet they may be seen on any spring trip in the country, from the coast to the deserts, and everywhere they are delightful.

These are plants of highly variable size and habit. Those from rocky and sandy places in the interior may rise barely an inch from the ground, while those from moist places near the coast may grow three feet or more high. The larger ones are well branched; the smallest often consist only of a single, tiny stem. They have paired, mostly pointed-oval leaves, sometimes toothed. Their colorful two-lipped, snapdragon-like flowers are carried mostly at the shoot tips.

M. guttatus, yellow monkey flower, is the species most often grown. This is a plant of wet places, widely distributed in California and the West. It is of highly variable size and has both annual and (short-lived) perennial forms. The plants are clothed with broad bright green, scallop-edged leaves and bear many clusters of glowing yellow flowers, up to an inch long, with red-spotted throats. Another yellow-flowered species, found on open slopes, is *M. brevipes*, also a plant of highly variable size, with furry stems, narrower leaves, and bright yellow flowers one-half to an inch long.

There are many smaller—sometimes tiny—species with rose- to magenta-colored flowers, often beautifully marked in the throats. *M. douglasii* and *M. kelloggii* are found on gravelly slopes in northern California. *M. nanus* occupies similar habitats in northeastern California and the Northwest. And *M. bigelovii* is a common and beautiful sight in the deserts.

Each annual monkey flower needs one of at least three distinct regimes in the garden, according to its origin. *M. guttatus* is a moisture lover, not only easy to grow but often becoming a pest in irrigated portions of the garden, in either sun or part shade. *M. brevipes* may be negotiable about exposure but needs well drained soil, minus the wet. The rest are ideally suited for the rock garden or carefully tended containers, unless you are willing to construct a scree slope and keep it well cleared of weeds. All are clearly worth this extra effort.

Nemophila. Hydrophyllaceae (the waterleaf family). Whether or not you are familiar with them in the wild, you have almost certainly seen *N. menziesii*, baby blue-eyes, one of the standard components of "California wildflower" seed mixes (which are often dominated by exotics like red flax). Nemophilas are low, often mounding plants with mostly toothed or lobed leaves and solitary five-petaled flowers borne along the stems. The flower segments are fused into broad saucers or bells, with flaring tips.

Nemophila menziesii.

N. menziesii is seen in meadows and in light woods over much of California, usually forming a low mound or mat. The leaves are closely paired, deeply lobed, and fresh, bright green in color. The flowers are broadly saucer-shaped, from a little over half an inch to nearly two inches broad. They are bright to sky-blue in color with paler, often black-dotted centers. A somewhat similar plant with much smaller flowers (to one-third of an inch), colored blue to white, is *N. pedunculata*, also widespread in similar sites. *N. maculata*, in contrast, is largely a plant of light woods and forest edges. Of about the same size and habit as *N. menziesii*, it has similarly large but white flowers, with darker veins, conspicuous dots, and purple tips on the free segments.

The nemophilas are among the easiest of our native annuals to grow, in both sun and light shade and many soils. They should be kept moist while in growth and flower. Continued irrigation can prolong their season by several weeks.

Phacelia. Hydrophyllaceae (the waterleaf family). There seems to be a phacelia nearly everywhere one travels in the California outback, though many, including a good number of herbaceous perennials, are too modest to be much noticed. Those that concern us here are truly showy—and for the most part, easily grown—annuals.

These have leafy stems with variously shaped leaves, usually toothed, lobed, or dis-

Phacelia tanacetifolia, **detail of flowers.**

sected. Coiled flower clusters are arrayed at the shoot tips, gradually unrolling as the buds develop. The individual flowers are bell- to saucer-shaped and range in color from deep blue or violet to white, often with contrasting markings in the throats.

P. campanularia, desert bluebells, is familiar to gardeners and desert explorers alike. It occurs widely in the desert mountains, making stunning displays as early as February. Growing six inches to nearly two feet high, it has sturdy stems and broad, dark, lobed leaves. Its bell-shaped blossoms, sometimes over an inch long, are colored a deep blue, with white markings around the throat. A similar species of the southern mountains west of the deserts is *P. minor*, with equally large but purple flowers.

P. tanacetifolia, tansy-leaved phacelia, widespread in both northern and southern mountains and the Mojave Desert, is quite distinct from these. It is a conspicuously hairy plant, from six inches to nearly three feet high, with narrowly parted leaves and long, well branched clusters of small lavender-blue flowers. Also of interest is *P. viscida*, a plant of the central and southern coast. It grows up to two feet high and has toothed leaves, many-flowered clusters, and vivid true-blue flowers up to two-thirds of an inch long, with white to purple throats.

The phacelias are plants of rather harsh environments, though surprisingly adaptable to garden conditions. They need a sunny spot with at least reasonably well drained soil. Moderate watering can prolong their show by a month or more.

Platystemon californicus. Cream cups. Papaveraceae (the poppy family). Though not large plants, cream cups are easy to pick out in a community of annual wildflowers. They occur over much of California, growing in meadows and other open spots and flowering earlier than many of their neighbors. The plants rise four to twelve inches and are usually branched, with slender, hairy stems and narrow leaves. Like those of many poppies, the flowers nod in bud, then turn to face the sky as they bloom. The six-petaled flowers open widely, from one-half to over one inch across. The petals are roughly oval in outline, polished in surface, and cream to pale yellow in color (often beautifully bicolored). They nearly beg for a closer look. The small seed capsules are cylindrical and beaked.

Cream cups thrive in a variety of soils and sunny exposure. They are particularly beautiful in a mixed wildflower meadow.

Salvia. Sage. Lamiaceae (the mint family). The perennial salvias, both shrubby and herbaceous, are introduced elsewhere in this book. California is also host to two beautiful annuals, as different from one another as they are from the perennial species. What they share are the square stems, paired leaves, and irregular, two-lipped flowers typical of the mints.

You may be familiar with *S. columbariae*, chia, by way of its legendary food value. Early natives of the Southwest, so the story goes, traveled for days with only a few handfuls of its seeds for nourishment. Whatever the actual truth, they are high in fats and provide a compact energy source. Chia is also a showy wildflower, brightening otherwise barren slopes and washes from Mendocino County southward in California and throughout much of the Southwest. It varies in size from a few inches to nearly two feet, partly in response to richer or poorer conditions and fire (the most robust plants are often to be seen in recently burned areas). The leaves are up to four inches long, mostly basal, and once- to twice-cut, their tiny hairs often imparting a grayish cast. Dense ball-like flower clusters are carried one to several per stem in spring and early summer. The half-inch flowers are bright blue, contrasting nicely with purplish stems, bracts, and calyces. They open in succession over several weeks, beginning in March and April.

Salvia carduacea **on Carrizo Plain.**

S. carduacea, thistle sage, is an exceedingly showy annual. It inhabits our interior Coast Ranges and desert margins from south-central California to Baja California. At first it forms rosettes of rather narrow, raggedly cut, sharply toothed basal leaves, white-woolly on at least the lower surface. From these rosettes single or branched flowering stems rise from a few inches to nearly two feet, along which are set circles of spiny bracts from which the flowers emerge. Individual blossoms are usually around an inch long, with flaring, conspicuously fringed lobes. Normally they are lavender-blue in color, standing out against a background of white "fluff." The overall impression of even one individual is breathtaking; the sight of an entire colony will force you to stop, sit, and stare in reverence.

Though they inhabit similar settings, the two sages are not equally easy to grow. Chia simply needs a sunny spot and reasonably well drained soil. Thistle sage is much more emphatic about soil drainage and is best on banks and in rock gardens with a gravel-dressed surface. Both perform beautifully in large pots and tubs.

My special thanks to Steve Edwards and Ginny Hunt for their observations and wise comments.

RESOURCES

. . . .

FURTHER READING

Many fine books have been written about California's native plants, though few are specifically addressed to their cultivation. Here are some you should find particularly interesting and helpful. In addition to the works listed below, several regional floras are also in print. Check the California Native Plant Society Web site (www.cnps.org) for references and availability.

FLORAS AND OTHER WORKS OF GENERAL INTEREST

Hickman, James C., ed. *The Jepson Manual: Higher Plants of California*. Berkeley: University of California Press, 1993. A massive and comprehensive work, abundantly illustrated and reflecting taxonomic work through the early 1990s. Its sheer size, weight, and ultra-abbreviated geographical references severely limit its use in the wild.

McMinn, Howard E. *An Illustrated Manual of California Shrubs*. Berkeley: University of California Press, 1970 (first ed. 1939). Part flora, part well detailed descriptive guide, with valuable location information.

Munz, Philip A., and David D. Keck. *A California Flora with Supplement*. Berkeley: University of California Press, 1968. Though many of its plant names are now obsolete, I use this work constantly for its detailed descriptions and location data.

Pavlik, Bruce M., Pamela C. Muick, Sharon Johnson, and Marjorie Popper. *Oaks of California*. Los Olivos: Cachuma Press, 1995. A beautifully illustrated book, covering many topics but especially concerned with oak ecology and conservation.

Van Rensselaer, M., and H. E. McMinn. *Ceanothus*. Santa Barbara: Santa Barbara Botanic Garden, 1942. A treasure if you can find it, including information from botany to culture.

JOURNALS

California Native Plant Society. *Fremontia*. The official journal of the society, it addresses nearly every imaginable issue pertaining to California native plants, including cultivation. Subscriptions are included with your membership; certain back issues are available. Contact www.cnps.org.

Louise Lacey, ed. *Growing Native*. A periodic journal specifically about growing California's native plants. It has been discontinued, but back issues may be available through the Web site at www.growingnative.com.

HORTICULTURAL BOOKS

Emery, Dara. *Seed Propagation of Native California Plants*. Santa Barbara: Santa Barbara Botanic Garden, 1988. A practical, detailed guide, valuable to amateurs and professionals alike.

Keator, Glenn. *Complete Garden Guide to the Native Perennials of California*. San Francisco: Chronicle Books, 1990. An informative book on gardening, with useful lists of plant combinations and special sites.

————. *Complete Garden Guide to the Native Shrubs of California*. San Francisco: Chronicle Books, 1994. The companion to the above work, covering California's shrubs and their culture.

Lenz, Lee W., and John Dourley. *California Native Trees and Shrubs*. Claremont: Rancho Santa Ana Botanic Garden, 1981. An encyclopedic work, written from an authoritative southern California perspective. It is extensively illustrated with photographs and diagrams.

Larner Lowry, Judith. *Gardening with a Wild Heart: Restoring California's Landscapes at Home*. This is the antithesis of the common gardening encyclopedia. powerfully advocating a more constructive engagement with the land and its natural inhabitants.

Mathew, Brian. *The Genus Lewisia*. Portland, OR: Timber Press (for the Royal Botanic Garden, Kew), 1989. A well written and beautifully illustrated treatment of the genus, including both botanical and horticultural information.

Rowntree, Lester. *Flowering Shrubs of California*. Stanford: Stanford University Press, 1947. If you can find it, you will be delighted by this passionate, quirky ode to native shrubs.

———. *Hardy Californians*. New York: Macmillan, 1936; repr. Salt Lake City: Peregrine Smith, 1980. Another treasure of enthusiastic and opinionated writing, in this case on native perennials.

Schmidt, Marjorie G. *Growing California Native Plants*. Berkeley: University of California Press, 1980. A systematic and informative book, capturing a wealth of "hands on" gardening experience.

PLACES TO VISIT

Rancho Santa Ana Botanic Garden, Claremont, www.rsabg.org. My first visit to "Rancho" left me in awe. It is a garden on the grand scale, with a large Cultivars Garden specifically addressed to ornamental natives and their use.

Regional Parks Botanic Garden, Tilden Regional Park, Berkeley, www.nativeplants.org. A beautiful garden, shaped by some of the most colorful characters on the native plant scene. It has many unique design features and a wonderful array of unusual and visually striking natives.

Santa Barbara Botanic Garden, Santa Barbara, www.santabarbarabotanicgarden.org. This is one of the oldest existing botanic gardens in California, set in a beautiful oak-lined canyon with a natural creek. The collection of native plants is extensive, the settings inspirational.

University of California Botanical Garden, Berkeley, botanicalgarden.berkeley.edu. The diverse native section here includes extensive rockeries, a native pond, and several collections organized by both geography and plant community. The bulb collection is magnificent.

University of California Arboretum, Davis, (no dedicated Web site as of this writing). Spring is a grand spectacle here. The California portion of the Arboretum occupies a long, narrow strip along the banks of a duck-lined canal.

University of California Arboretum, Santa Cruz, www2.ucsc.edu/arboretum. Though it has had a precarious existence, "the Arb" reflects the indomitable spirit of a devoted staff. The California section is smaller than that of other gardens described above but contains many plants of interest to gardeners.

PLANT AND SEED SALES

California native plants are now available in retail nurseries throughout the state. There are also several specialty nurseries largely or entirely devoted to native plants and their use. A few are listed below, with apologies to those I have missed. (All are in California.) Finally, each of the botanic gardens and arboreta described above, as well as several local CNPS chapters, have special plant sales at least once a year.

CNPS PLANT SALE, UCSC ARBORETUM.

California Flora Nursery, Fulton, www.calfloranursery.com. A wholesale/retail nursery carrying a wide variety of both native and exotic plants.

Elkhorn Native Plant Nursery, Moss Landing, www.elkhornnursery.com. Another combined wholesale and retail operation, with consulting services, bulk seed sales, and more.

Larner Seeds, Bolinas, www.larnerseeds.com. A nursery and garden you can visit as well as a mail-order seed house, with an informative and entertaining catalog.

J. L. Hudson, Seedsman, La Honda, www.jlhudsonseeds.net. An extremely diverse international seed source, with a good number of natives among its listings.

Las Pilitas Nursery, Santa Margarita, www.laspilitas.com. A large and diverse native plant nursery, with locations in both Santa Margarita and Escondido as well as mail-order sales.

Seedhunt, Watsonville, www.seedhunt.com. Mail-order source for a wide collection of seeds, stressing the unusual; many California natives are among them.

Theodore Payne Foundation, Sun Valley, www.theodorepayne.org. A nonprofit organization with both a native plant nursery and mail-order seed sales.

Tree of Life Nursery, San Juan Capistrano, www.treeoflifenursery.com. California's premier wholesale native plant nursery. Its on-site retail outlet is the Round House Plant Store.

Yerba Buena Nursery, Woodside, www.yerbabuenanursery.com. One of the oldest retail nurseries devoted to native plants, set deep in a scenic canyon.

INTERNET SITES

Internet sites are included above for public gardens and nurseries. Some other sites of interest are maintained by organizations you are unlikely to visit in person, including wholesale nurseries closed to the public.

California Native Plant Society, Sacramento, www.cnps.org. Through this site you will find references to all things native, including CNPS's conservation programs, local chapter addresses, and native plant publications.

Native Sons Wholesale Nursery, Arroyo Grande, www.nativesons.com. A beautiful and informative Web site, including plants from many Mediterranean climate regions.

San Marcos Growers, Santa Barbara, www.sanmarcos.com. The San Marcos Web site has inspired many other nursery folk, including myself. A diverse, well illustrated collection, including many natives.

Society for Pacific Coast Native Iris, www.pacificcoastiris.org. This organization provides invaluable information on native iris, including current sources for both species and hybrids.

Suncrest Nurseries Inc, Watsonville, www.suncrestnurseries.com. This is where I work and play. Plant descriptions include several hundred California natives, with many illustrations.

INDEX

Adaptability, related to
  natural habitat, 22-25
Alum root (See also
  Heuchera)
  Island, 211, 212
Alum roots, 209-213
  common features, 209
  culture, 210
  propagation, 211
  species descriptions,
    211-13
  uses, 209, 210
Annuals
  collecting and pro-
    cessing seeds, 257,
    260
  common features, 255,
    256
  culture, 256-60
  genus and species
    descriptions, 260-71
    Calandrinia ciliata,
      260, 261
    Castilleja
      densiflora, 261
      exserta, 261
    Clarkia
      amoena, 262
      bottae, 262
      concinna, 262
      purpurea, 262
      rubicunda, 262
      unguiculata, 262
    Collinsia
      heterophylla, 262,
        263
      sparsifolia, 263
      tinctoria, 263
    Downingia
      pulchella, 263
    Eschscholzia
      caespitosa, 264
      californica, 263, 264
      lobbii, 264
    Gilia, 264, 265
      capitata, 264
      tricolor, 264
    Lasthenia
      californica, 265
      glabrata, 265
    Layia
      chrysanthemoides,
        265
      gaillardioides, 265,
        266
      platyglossa, **18**, 265
    Limnanthes
      alba, 266
      douglasii, 266
    Linanthus, 266, 267
      androsaceus, 266
      grandiflorus, 266
      parviflorus, 266

Lupinus
  bicolor, 267
  densiflorus, 267
  nanus, 267
  microcarpus, 267
  stiversii, 267, 268
  succulentus, 267
Mentzelia
  affinis, 268
  laevicaulis, 268
  lindleyi, 268
Mimulus, 268, 269
  bigelovii, 269
  brevipes, 269
  douglasii, 269
  guttatus, 269
  kelloggii, 269
  nanus, 269
Nemophila
  maculata, 269
  menziesii, 269
  pedunculata, 269
Phacelia
  campanularia, 270
  minor, 270
  tanacetifolia, 270
  viscida, 270
Platystemon
  californicus, **254**,
    270
Salvia
  carduacea, 271
  columbariae, 270,
    271
Triphysaria eriantha,
    261
in containers, 259, 260
in the garden, 256-60
sowing and planting,
    257-59
  aftercare, 259
site preparation, 257, 258
Arbutus menziesii (See also
  Madrone), 73-75
Arctostaphylos (See also
  Manzanitas)
  andersonii, 101, 102
  bakeri, 102
  canescens, 102
  densiflora, **99**, 102, 103
  elegans, 101
  edmundsii, 106, 107
  'Emerald Carpet', 107
  glandulosa, 103
  glauca, 100
  'Greensphere', 103, 104
  hookeri, 107
  'Indian Hill', 108
  insularis, 100, 101
  'John Dourley', 104
  manzanita, **95**, 101
  nevadensis, 108
  nummularia, 104

'Pacific Mist', 108
pajaroensis, 104, 105
pringlei ssp. *drupacea*, 101
pungens, 105
purissima, 108
rudis, 105
'Sandsprite', 108, 109
stanfordiana, 105, 106
uva-ursi, **97**, 109
viscida, 106
'Winterglow', 110
Arnica cordifolia, **4**
Artemisia californica 'Canyon
  Grey', **15**
Baby blue-eyes, 269
Bearberry (kinnikinnick),
  109
Beard-tongue See
  Penstemon
Berberis (See also Holly
  grapes)
  aquifolium
    var. *aquifolium*, 123,
      125
    var. *dictyota*, **121**, 123,
      124
    var. *repens*, 125, 126
  fremontii, 124
  'Golden Abundance',
    124
  nervosa, 126
  nevinii, 124
  pinnata, 124, 125
Bitter root, 224
Blazing star, 268
Blue blossom, 85, 86, 91, 92
Blue curls (See also
  Trichostema)
  common features, 161
  culture, 161, 162
  mountain, 163
  propagation, 162
  species descriptions, 162,
    163
  uses, 161
  woolly, 162, 163
Blue dicks, 250, 251
Blue-eyed grass (See also
  Sisyrinchiums), **225**, 227
Books and journals on
  native plants
  floras, 272
  horticultural books, 272,
    273
  native plant journals, 272
Borders
  perennial, 13, 14, 16, 17
  shrubby, 16
Botanic gardens and
  arboreta, 273
  Rancho Santa Ana BG,
    viii, 11, 12
  Regional Parks BG at

Tilden, **9**, **10**, **11**
Santa Barbara BG, **7**, **27**,
  29
Strybing Arboretum, **39**,
  127
Brodiaea (See also
  Dichelostemma, *Triteleia*)
  californica, **245**, 249
  coronaria, 249
  elegans, 249, 250
  jolonensis, 250
  terrestris, 250
Brodiaea
  golden, 253
  harvest, 249, 250
  long-rayed, 253
  twining, 252
  white, 252, 253
Brodiaeas
  common features, 245,
    246
  culture, 247, 248
  propagation, 248, 249
  species descriptions,
    249-53
  uses, 246, 247
Buckbrush, 86, 87
Buckwheat
  ashyleaf, 183
  California, 183
  coast, 185
  red, 185
  saffron (Conejo), 184
  Santa Cruz Island, 182,
    183
Buckwheats (See also
  Eriogonum)
  common features, 179,
    180
  culture, 180, 181
  distribution, 179
  propagation, 181, 182
  species descriptions,
    182-88
  uses, 180
Bush anemone, 138, 139
Bush poppy (See also
  Dendromecon)
  culture, 149
  description, 148
  island, 148
  propagation, 149, 150
  uses, 149
Butter-and-eggs, 261
Calandrinia ciliata, 260, 261
California
  climate, 2, 3
  geography, 1, 2
  geology, 3
  soils, 3, 21, 22
  terrain, 1, 2, **3**
  vegetation, 4, 5, **23**, 24
California buckeye, **16**

275

California fuchsias (See also *Epilobium*)
  common features, 215
  culture, 216, 217
  propagation, 217
  species descriptions, 217-19
  uses, **214**, 216
California Native Plant Society, 273, 274
California poppy, **256**, 263, 264
Calochortus uniflorus, **6**
Carex subfusca, **12**
Carmel creeper, 93
Carpenteria californica (See also Mock-oranges), **77**, 138, 139
Castilleja
  densiflora, 261
  exserta, 261
Catalina perfume, 117, 118
Ceanothus (See also Wild lilacs)
  arboreus, 83
  'Blue Buttons', 83
  'Blue Jeans', 86
  'Concha', 86
  cuneatus, **78**, 86, 87
  'Dark Star', 87, 88
  diversifolius, **92**
  foliosus, 88
  'Frosty Blue', 83
  'Gentian Plume', 83, 84
  gloriosus
    var.*exaltatus*, 88
    var. *gloriosus*, 92, 93
  griseus, 88, 89, 93
    var. *horizontalis*, 93
  hearstiorum, 93, 94
  impressus, 89
  integerrimus, 89, 90
  'Joan Mirov', 90
  'Joyce Coulter', 90
  'Julia Phelps', 90
  maritimus, **80**, 94
  megacarpus, 84
  'Mountain Haze', 84
  oliganthus, 84, 85
  papillosus, 90, 91
  prostratus, 94
  purpureus, 91
  ramulosus, 87
  'Ray Hartman', 85
  rigidus, 87
  'Sierra Blue', 85
  thyrsiflorus, 85, 86, 91, 92
  'Wheeler Canyon', 92
Ceanothus
  bigpod, 84
  blue blossom, 85, 86, 91, 92
  Carmel, 88, 89, 93
  Catalina, 83
  Hearst's, 93, 94
  hollyleaf, 91
  Hoover, **80**, 94
  Monterey, 87

Navarro, 88
Point Reyes, 92, 93
Santa Barbara, 89
wartleaf, 90, 91
wavyleaf, 88
Cercis occidentalis (See also Western redbud), **132**, 133-35
Chaparral mallow, 145
Chia, 270, 271
Chinese houses, 262, 263
Chrysothamnus, **26**
Clarkia
  amoena, 262
  bottae, 262
  concinna, 262
  purpurea, 262
  rubicunda, 262
  unguiculata, 262
Collecting in the wild, issues, 41, 42
Collinsia
  heterophylla, 262, 263
  sparsifolia, 263
  tinctoria, 263
Combining natives and exotics, 18
Coyote mint, 233
Coyote mints (See also *Monardella*)
  common features, 229
  culture, 230
  propagation, 231
  species descriptions, 231-33
  uses, 230
Cream cups, 270
Cultural issues
  irrigation, 31, 32
  mulching, 31
  nutrition, 33
  pests and diseases, 34-37
  planting, 29, 30
  post-planting protection, 31
  pruning, 33, 34
  weeds, 37, 38
Currant
  chaparral, 115, 116
  evergreen, 117, 118
  golden, 114, 115
  mountain pink, 116
  pink flowering, 116, 117
  red flowering, 116, 117
  wax, 115
Currants and gooseberries (See also *Ribes*)
  common features, 111, 112
  culture, 112, 113
  distribution, 111
  propagation, 113, 114
  species descriptions
    the currants, 114-118
    the gooseberries, 118-120
  uses, 112
Cuttings (See also

Propagation), 48-51
Deer brush, 89, 90
Dendromecon (See also Bush poppy)
  harfordii, 148
  rigida, 148
Desert bluebells, 270
Dichelostemma (See also Brodiaeas)
  capitatum, 250, 251
  congestum, 251
  ida-maia, 251
  multiflorum, 251, 252
  volubile, 252
Diseases of native plants, 34-37
Divisions (See also Propagation), 51-53
Downingia pulchella, 263
Enjoying your garden, 39
Epilobium (See also California fuchsias)
  canum, **215**, 217-19
    ssp. *canum*, **216**, 217, 218
    ssp. *latifolium*, 219
    septentrionale, 219
Eriogonum (See also Buckwheats)
  arborescens, 182, 183
  cinereum, 183
  compositum, 184
  crocatum, 184
  fasciculatum, 183
  giganteum, 183, 184
  grande, 185
  kennedyi, 185
  latifolium, 185
  lobbii, 185, 186
  nudum, 186
  ovalifolium, 186
  parvifolium, 186
  saxatile, 186, 187
  siskiyouense, 187
  strictum, 187
  umbellatum, **180**, 187, 188
  wrightii, 188
Eriophyllum lanatum, **4**
Eschscholzia
  caespitosa, 264
  californica, 263, 264
  lobbii, 264
Farewell to spring, 261, 262
Fire
  danger and plant choices, 27, 28
  role in natural setting, 3, 4
Flannel bush
  California, **128**, 130
  Mexican, 130, 131
Flannel bushes (See also *Fremontodendron*)
  common features, 127, 128
  culture, 128, 129
  propagation, 129, 130

species and cultivar descriptions, 130, 131
  uses, 128
Floras of California, 272
Fremontodendron (See also Flannel bushes)
  californicum, **128**, 130
  hybrids, **127**, 131
  mexicanum, 130, 131
Garden as human environment, 10, 11
Garden as wildlife habitat, 11
Garden design (see also Planting considerations), 9-18
  arrangements, 16-18
  elements
    display, 11-15
    environment, 10, 11, **27**
    habitat, 11
    utility, 15, 16
  role of
    colors, 12-14
    fragrance, 14
    sound, 14
    structure, 11, 12
    texture, 12
  scenic
    meadows, 17
    rock gardens, 17
    water features, 18
    woods, 17
  styles, 9
Garden setting
  climate, 19-21
  soils, 21, 22
  terrain, **21**
Garden sites
  and plant choices, 25-27
  preparation, 26, 27
Garrya congdonii, **14**
Gilia, 264, 265
  capitata, 264
  tricolor, 264
Gilia
  bird's-eye, 264
  blue, 264
Globe-mallow
  chaparral, 145
  Fremont, 145
  Indian, 146
  San Clemente, 144, 145
  sand, 146
  Santa Lucia, 145, 146
  sweet, 146
  white-coat, 145
Globe-mallows (See also *Malacothamnus*)
  common features, 143
  culture, 144
  distribution, 143
  propagation, 144
  species descriptions, 144-146
  uses, 143, 144
Godetia, 261, 262

Goldfields, 265
Gooseberry
  California, 118
  canyon, 118, 119
  fuchsia-flowered, 119,
    120
  rock, 119
  Sierra, 119
Heteromeles arbutifolia (See
  also Toyon), **164**, 165-68
Heuchera (See also Alum
  roots)
  elegans, 213
  hirsutissima, 213
  hybrids, **208**, **210**, 212,
    213
  maxima, 211, 212
  micrantha, **209**, 212, 213
  parishii, 213
  rubescens, 213
Holly grape, California,
  124, 125
Holly grapes (See also
  Berberis, Mahonia)
  distribution and habitat,
    121
  common features, 121
  culture, 122
  propagation, 122, 123
  species descriptions,
    123-126
  uses, 121, 122
Internet sites, 274
Iris
  douglasiana, **200**, 203, 204
  fernaldii, 204
  hartwegii, 205
  innominata, 204
  longipetala, 205
  macrosiphon, 204
  missouriensis, 205, 206
  munzii, 205
  purdyi, 206
Iris
  common features, 201
  culture, 202
  Douglas, 203, 204
  hybrids, **202**, 206, 207
  propagation, 202, 203
  species descriptions,
    203-206
  uses, 201, 202
Ithuriel's spear, 253
Lasthenia
  californica, 265
  glabrata, 265
Layering (See also
  Propagation), 51
Layia
  chrysanthemoides, 265
  gaillardioides, 265, 266
  platyglossa, **18**, 265
Lewisia
  cotyledon, **221**, 223, 224
    hybrids, **189**, **222**, 224
  leana, **220**, 224
  rediviva, 224
Lewisias

common features, 221
culture, 222
propagation, 222, 223
species descriptions, 223,
  224
uses, 221, 222
Lilies
  common features, 237
  culture, 238
  hybrids, 243
  propagation, 239
  species descriptions,
    239-243
  uses, 238
Lilium
  bolanderi, 241
  columbianum, 241
  humboldtii, 242
  kelleyanum, 239, 240
  kelloggii, 242
  maritimum, 240
  occidentale, 240
  pardalinum, **235**, 240, 241
  pitkinense, **236**, 240, 241
  rubescens, 242
  washingtonianum, 242,
    243
Lily
  Bolander's, 241
  coast, 240
  Columbia, 241
  Humboldt, 242
  Kelley's, 239, 240
  Kellogg's, 242
  leopard, 240, 241
  Pitkin, 240, 241
  redwood, 242
  Washington, 242, 243
  western, 240
Limnanthes
  alba, 266
  douglasii, 266
Linanthus, 266, 267
  androsaceus, 266
  grandiflorus, 266
  parviflorus, 266
Lupine
  coast or yellow bush,
    157, 158
  grape soda, 158, 159
  silver bush, 156, 157
Lupines, shrubby
  common features, 153,
    154
  culture, 154, 155
  distribution and habitat,
    153
  propagation, 155, 156
  species descriptions,
    156-59
  uses, 154
Lupinus, 153-59, 267, 268
  albifrons, **153**, 156, 157
  arboreus, 157, 158
  bicolor, 267
  chamissonis, 158
  densiflorus, 267
  excubitus, 158

littoralis, 159
microcarpus, 267
nanus, 267
propinquus, 157
stiversii, 267, 268
succulentus, 267
variicolor, 159
Madrone, madroño (See
  also *Arbutus menziesii*)
  common features, 73, 74
  culture, 74
  propagation, 74, 75
  uses, 74
Mahonia (See also *Berberis*,
  Holly grapes), 121-126
  creeping, 125, 126
  longleaf, 126
Malacothamnus (See also
  Globe-mallows)
  aboriginum, 146
  clementinus, 144, 145
  davidsonii, 146
  densiflorus, 146
  fasciculatus, **142**, 145
  fremontii, 145
  jonesii, 146
  palmeri, 145, 146
Manzanita
  bearberry, 109
  bigberry, 100
  Eastwood, 103
  hoary, 102
  island, 100, 101
  Little Sur, 106, 107
  Mexican, 105
  Monterey, 107
  Pajaro, 104, 105
  Parry, 101
  pinemat, 108
  pink-bracted, 101
  Santa Cruz, 101, 102
  shagbark, 105
  Stanford, 105, 106
  Vine Hill, 102, 103
  whiteleaf, 106
Manzanitas (See also
  Arctostaphylos)
  common features, 95, 96
  culture, 97-99
  diseases, **37**, 97, 98
  distribution, 95
  propagation, 99
  species and cultivar
    descriptions, 100-110
  uses, 96, 97
Matilija poppy (See also
  Romneya)
  culture, 149
  description, 147, 148
  propagation, 149, 150
  uses, 149
Meadow foam, 266
Meadows, naturalistic, 17
Mentzelia
  affinis, 268
  laevicaulis, 268
  lindleyi, 268
Mimulus, **6**, 268, 269

aurantiacus, **6**
bigelovii, 269
brevipes, 269
douglasii, 269
guttatus, 269
kelloggii, 269
nanus, 269
Mock-orange
  little-leaf, 138
  wild, 137, 138
Mock-oranges (See also
  Philadelphus, Carpenteria)
  common features, 137-
    39
  culture, 140
  propagation, 140, 141
  species descriptions,
    137-39
  uses, 139, 140
Monardella (See also Coyote
  mints)
  macrantha, 231, 232
  nana, 232
  odoratissima, **229**, 232
  purpurea, 232, 233
  villosa, 233
Monardella, scarlet, 231,
  232
Monkey flower, **6**, 268, 269
Mountain pennyroyal, **229**,
  232
Mountain pride, 198, 199
Native plants
  aesthetic features, 5, 6
  culture, 19-39
  diversity, 4, 5, 7
  propagation, 41-53
  sources, 273, 274
  uses in the garden, 5,
    9-18
Nemophila
  maculata, 269
  menziesii, 269
  pedunculata, 269
Oak
  blue, 66, 67
  Brewer, **67**, 68
  California black, **58**, 68
  canyon live, 66
  coast live, **64**, 65, 66
  deer, 72
  huckleberry, 72
  interior live, 70
  island, 69, 70
  leather, 71
  Oregon, 67, 68
  scrub, 70, 71
  valley, 69
Oaks (See also *Quercus*)
  botanical divisions, 58
  common features, 57-60
  culture, 62-64
  diseases, 60, 63, 64
  distribution, 57, 58
  habitat, 57
  living with wild oaks,
    60, 61
  preserving, 61

propagation, 64, 65
species descriptions
  shrubby species, 70-72
  trees, 65-70
uses in the landscape, 61, 62
wildlife and oaks, 60, 62, 63
Ookow, 251
Oregon grape, 123, 125
Owl's clover, 261
Orthocarpus, 261
Penstemon
  anguineus, 196
  azureus, 196
  centranthifolius, 195
  clevelandii, 196
  davidsonii var. *davidsonii*, 198
  grinnellii, 196, 197
  heterophyllus, **193**, 197
  laetus, 197, 198
  newberryi, 198, 199
  palmeri var. palmeri, 195
  parvulus, 199
  procerus, 199
  purpusii, 199
  rostriflorus, 198
  rupicola, **190**, 199
  spectabilis, 195
Penstemons
  common features, 191, 192
  culture, 192-94
  distribution and habitat, 191
  propagation, 194
  species descriptions, 194-99
  uses, 192
Perennial border, 13, 14, 16, 17
Pests of native plants, 34-36
Phacelia
  campanularia, 270
  minor, 270
  tanacetifolia, 270
  viscida, 270
Phacelia, tansy-leaved, 270
Philadelphus (See also Mock-oranges)
  lewisii, **136**, 137, 138
  microphyllus, 138
Pine mat, 92
Plant and seed sources, 273, 274
Planting considerations
  (See also Garden design)
  for containers, 29
  long-term questions, 38, 39
  soil problems, 28
  spacing, 28
Planting process (See also Cultural issues)
  aftercare, 31-38
  planting level, 30

preparation, 30
root care, 30
timing, 30
Platystemon californicus, **254**, 270
Populus tremuloides, **13**
Propagation defined, 41
Propagation techniques
  cuttings
    aftercare, 50, 51
    materials, 49, 50
    preparing and planting, 50
    selecting, 48, 49
    storing, 49
    transplanting, 51
  divisions
    bulbs as special case, 53
  planting, 52
    preparing, 52
    selecting, 51, 52
  layering, 51
  seeds and seeding
    aftercare, 46
    materials, 44
    obtaining, 43
    storage, 44
    treatments, 44, 45
    sowing, 45, 46
    transplanting, 46, 47
  vegetative, 48-53
Pruning native plants, 33, 34
Quercus (See also Oaks)
  agrifolia, 65, 66
  berberidifolia, 70, 71
  chrysolepis, 66
  douglasii, 66, 67
  durata, 71
  garryana, 67, 68
  kelloggii, 68
  lobata, 69
  sadleriana, 72
  tomentella, 69, 70
  vaccinifolia, 72
  wislizenii, 70
Redbud, western (See also *Cercis occidentalis*), **132**, 133-35
Red maids, 260, 261
Red ribbons, 262
Ribes (See also Currants and gooseberries)
  aureum, 114, 115
  californicum, 118
  cereum, **111**, 115
  malvaceum, 115, 116
  menziesii, 118, 119
  nevadense, 116
  quercetorum, 119
  roezlii, **111**, 119
  sanguineum, **113**, 116, 117
  speciosum, **111**, 119, 120
  viburnifolium, 117, 118
Romneya (See also Matilija poppy)

coulteri, 147, 148
trichocalyx, 147
Rubus parviflorus, **4**
Sage
  black, 176
  Cleveland, 174, 175
  gray, **170**, **172**, 175, 176
  pitcher (hummingbird), 178
  purple, 175
  Sonoma, **169**, 177, 178
  thistle, 271
  white, 174
Sages (See also *Salvia*)
  common features, 171, 172
  culture, 173
  propagation, 173, 174
  species and cultivar descriptions
    shrubby species, 174-177
    perennial species, 177, 178
  uses, 172
Salvia
  apiana, 174
  brandegei, 176, 177
  carduacea, 271
  clevelandii, 174, 175
  columbariae, 270, 271
  dorrii, 175
  leucophylla, **170**, **172**, 175, 176
  mellifera, 176
  munzii, 176, 177
  pachyphylla, 176
  sonomensis, **169**, 177, 178
  spathacea, 178
Scarlet bugler, 195
Seaside daisy, **17**
Seed sources, 273, 274
Seeds and seeding (See also Propagation), 42-47
Silene californica, **17**
Sisyrinchium
  bellum, **225**, 227
  californicum, 228
  douglasii, 228
Sisyrinchiums
  common features, 225, 226
  culture, 226
  propagation, 226, 227
  species descriptions, 227, 228
  uses, 226
Snowberry, **14**
Snowdrop bush (See also *Styrax redivivus*)
  common features, 151
  culture, 152
  propagation 152
  uses, 151, 152
Soils
  in the garden, 21, 22
  in the wild, 3, 21
Squaw carpet, 94

St. Catherine's lace, 183, 184
Styrax redivivus (See also Snowdrop bush), 151, 152
Sulfur flower, **180**, 187, 188
Tidy tips, 265, 266
Toyon (See also *Heteromeles arbutifolia*)
  common features, 165, 166
  culture, 166, 167
  propagation, 167, 168
  uses, 166
Trichostema (See also Blue curls)
  lanatum, **160**, 162, 163
  parishii, 163
Triphysaria eriantha, 261
Triteleia (See also Brodiaeas)
  hyacinthina, 252, 253
  ixioides, **244**, 253
  laxa, **247**, 253
  peduncularis, 253
Weeds in the garden, 37, 38
Western blue flag
Western redbud (See also *Cercis occidentalis*)
  common features, 133, 134
  culture, 134
  propagation, 135
  uses, 134
Whipplea modesta, 137
Wild hyacinth, 251, 252
Wild lilacs (See also *Ceanothus*)
  common features, 79, 80
  culture, 80, 81
  propagation, 82
  species descriptions, 82-94
  uses, 80
Wildlife in the garden, 11, 60, 62, 63
Woolly blue curls, **160**, 162, 163
Yellow-eyed grass (See also Sisyrinchiums), 228
Zauschneria See *Epilobium*